After the Prosperous Age

Harvard-Yenching Institute Monograph Series 101

After the Prosperous Age

State and Elites in Early Nineteenth-Century Suzhou

Seunghyun Han

Published by the Harvard University Asia Center
Distributed by Harvard University Press
Cambridge (Massachusetts) and London 2016

Printed in the United States of America

The Harvard-Yenching Institute, founded in 1928, is an independent foundation dedicated to the advancement of higher education in the humanities and social sciences in Asia. Headquartered on the campus of Harvard University, the Institute provides fellowships for advanced research, training, and graduate studies at Harvard by competitively selected faculty and graduate students from Asia. The Institute also supports a range of academic activities at its fifty partner universities and research institutes across Asia. At Harvard, the Institute promotes East Asian studies through annual contributions to the Harvard-Yenching Library and publication of the *Harvard Journal of Asiatic Studies* and the Harvard-Yenching Institute Monograph Series.

Library of Congress Cataloging-in-Publication Data

Han, Seunghyun, 1970– author.
After the prosperous age : state and elites in early nineteenth-century Suzhou / Seunghyun Han.
pages cm — (Harvard-Yenching Institute monograph series ; 101)
Revision of the author's thesis (Ph. D.—Harvard University, 2005).
Includes bibliographical references and index.
ISBN 978-0-674-73717-4 (hardcover : alk. paper) 1. Elite (Social sciences)—Political activity—China—Suzhou (Jiangsu Sheng) 2. Suzhou (Jiangsu Sheng, China)—Intellectual life. 3. Suzhou (Jiangsu Sheng, China)—History—18th century. 4. Suzhou (Jiangsu Sheng, China)—History—19th century. 5. Provincial governments—China—History—18th century. 6. Provincial governments—China—History—19th century. I. Title. II. Series: Harvard-Yenching Institute monograph series ; 101.
DS797.56.S894H36 2016
305.5'20951136—dc23

2015018468

Index by Robert Swanson

♾ Printed on acid-free paper

Last figure below indicates year of this printing
25 24 23 22 21 20 19 18 17 16

To
my parents, Han Youngwoo and Kim Chaejung
and
my wife, Kwon Nayoung

Contents

Maps and Figures

Maps

Figures

Tables

Acknowledgments

This book developed from my doctoral dissertation presented to the Department of History at Harvard University in 2005. Revising the dissertation into the current book form proved to be a long and challenging journey. At various stages of this project, I have benefited tremendously from the insights of many teachers, friends, and colleagues. My foremost thanks go to the formidable members of my dissertation committee: Philip Kuhn, Peter Bol, Peter Perdue, and Mark Elliott. Their warm encouragement allowed this overdue project to eventually bear fruit. Their lofty and rigorous intellectual standards have always been a source of inspiration for me. In China, I benefited from the care and support of many scholars. Professors whom I would like to thank for their hospitality include Cao Shuji, Fan Jinmin, Gao Xiang, Li Bozhong, Wang Sizhi, and Yu Tongyuan.

Several chapters and the ideas they contain have been presented at conferences, and I am grateful for the invaluable comments of all participants at these venues, especially Benjamin Elman, Robert Hymes, Tobie Meyer-Fong, Susan Naquin, and William Rowe. Portions of chapters in this book have been published in the journals noted at the beginning of each relevant chapter. Certain parts will also appear in the chapter "Changing Roles of Local Elites from the 1720s to 1830s" in the forthcoming *Cambridge History of China* (Volume 9, Part 2). I am grateful to the editors of publications for their permission to reuse or reprint the material.

At Berkeley, discussions with the late Frederic Wakeman Jr., and Yeh Wen-hsin in many ways helped me to rethink and sharpen my points. I am greatly indebted to Steven Miles, Willard Peterson, Michael Reeve, and an anonymous reader who offered thoughtful criticisms, which I have incorporated in the current book. Eric Vanden Bussche read the entire manuscript thoroughly and significantly improved it with his suggestions and meticulous proofreading. During the revision process, conversations with Jim Bonk, Kim Kwangmin, Matthew Mosca, and Daniel McMahon broadened and deepened my understanding of early nineteenth-century China. In Taipei, I enjoyed scholarly interactions with my colleagues and friends, in particular Chu Ping-yi, Paul Katz, Lai Hui-min, Lai Yu-chih, Lee Tsong Han, Li Cho-ying, Li Ren-yuan, Lin Man-houng, Lu Miaw-fen, Ma Ya-chen, and Peter Zarrow. I am also grateful to my colleagues and students in the Department of History at Konkuk University for their moral support. Lee Seung-joon, Lee Sukhee, and Eugene Park encouraged me in various ways to complete this project. Many thanks to Hwang Jun Yeong for preparing the maps and Lee Eun-gyong for checking the Japanese titles in the bibliography.

I would also like to express my gratitude to my teachers, especially Professor Oh Keum-sung at Seoul National University, with whom I first trained as a historian. Special thanks are also due to Professor Won Cheong-sik at the Kangwon University, who generously shared his knowledge about Ming-Qing China during my graduate studies in Seoul. Many librarians and archivists endured my constant nagging requests for materials. I would like to express my deepest gratitude to those individuals at the Harvard-Yenching Library, First Historical Archives in Beijing, Nanjing Library, Shanghai Library, Suzhou Library, Taizhou Library, Fu-ssu Nien Library, and Library of the Institute of Modern History in Taipei.

From the dissertation stage to the completion of this book, I have benefited from generous financial assistance. Fellowships from the Harvard-Yenching Institute and Korea Foundation for Advanced Studies supported my graduate studies. My field research in China would not have been possible without travel grants from Harvard University's History Department, Asia Center, Weatherhead Center, and a Sinclair Kennedy Traveling Fellowship by the Graduate School of Arts and Sciences at Harvard University. The Center for Chinese Studies at the University of California, Berkeley, and the National Science Council in Taiwan graciously supported the revision process.

My parents Han Youngwoo and Kim Chaejung will be most pleased to see this book finally come out. I am always in their debt for their unflagging support. My wife Kwon Nayoung helped me numerous times by resolving stylistic issues in this manuscript, besides providing me with her loving care. My newborn son Manseo has enriched my life, and he became a new center of it during the last stage of the revision. This book is dedicated to them.

Abbreviations

Reign period abbreviations

YZ	Yongzheng (雍正): 1723–35
QL	Qianlong (乾隆): 1736–95
JQ	Jiaqing (嘉慶): 1796–1820
DG	Daoguang (道光): 1821–50
XF	Xianfeng (咸豊): 1851–61
TZ	Tongzhi (同治): 1862–74

Abbreviations used in the notes

CJCB	*Congshu jicheng chubian*
LKSS	*Like shishu*
QHDSL	*Qing huidian shili*
QSL	*Qing shilu*
SKQS	*Yingyin Wenyuange Siku quanshu*
SKZMTY	*Siku quanshu zongmu tiyao*
TYGX	*Tianyige cang Mingdai fangzhi xuankan xubian*
XXSKQS	*Xuxiu Siku quanshu*
YMSLBJ	*Yuan Ming shiliao biji congkan*
ZDJAH	*Zhongguo difangzhi jicheng Anhui fuxianzhi ji*

ZDJJS	*Zhongguo difangzhi jicheng Jiangsu fuxianzhi ji*
ZDJJX	*Zhongguo difangzhi jicheng Jiangxi fuxianzhi ji*
ZDJSD	*Zhongguo difangzhi jicheng Shandong fuxianzhi ji*
ZDJSH	*Zhongguo difangzhi jicheng Shanghai fuxianzhi ji*
ZDJZJ	*Zhongguo difangzhi jicheng Zhejiang fuxianzhi ji*
ZHZQS	*Zhongguo huangzheng quanshu*
ZYJXB	*Zhongguo yeshi jicheng xubian*

MAP 1. Map of China in 1820
Adapted from CHGIS, Version: 5. (c) Fairbank Center for Chinese Studies and the Institute for Chinese Historical Geography at Fudan University, December 2010.

INTRODUCTION

In early 1799, the Wu County magistrate's illegal flogging of a licentiate triggered a literati protest in Suzhou. Upon hearing about it that summer, the newly installed Jiaqing Emperor reproached the provincial officials for mishandling the case. The emperor sympathized with the protesters. He critiqued the provincial officials for suggesting a light punishment for the county magistrate while handing out harsh verdicts to the licentiates: banishment for the ringleader, three years of penal servitude for the other two leaders, and the annulment of the degrees of twenty protesters.[1] The emperor's intervention prompted a review of the judicial deliberations, leading to the acquittal of all but three literati. The principal offender was still sentenced to banishment, but he was allowed to remain home to care for his elderly parents. The other two leaders served penal servitude sentences not far from Suzhou and managed to return home less than two months later thanks to a special imperial amnesty. Meanwhile, the provincial-level and county-level officials all received varying degrees of punishments, with the Wu County magistrate being stripped of his post. Later in the nineteenth century, Suzhou literati seized upon this event as a watershed victory over corrupt local officials. They viewed the Jiaqing Emperor as their benefactor, an emperor who had graciously intervened to rescue the Suzhou licentiates while chastising the officials for misconduct.

The Jiaqing Emperor's attitude toward the protest contrasted with the manner in which his father, the Qianlong Emperor, reacted to a similar incident in 1759. Qianlong criticized the governor-general of Sichuan Province for suggesting the impeachment of an assistant brigade commander who had arbitrarily chained a licentiate: "If we impeach an official for such a trivial matter as having fettered a licentiate, an ignorant crowd will take this as a pretext upon hearing the news, and will necessarily initiate a vicious tide."[2] While the Qing legal code prohibited corporal punishments of licentiates, Qianlong asserted that chastising officials guilty of such minor offenses was detrimental to the disciplining of literati behavior.[3] Under Qianlong, death sentences generally awaited those involved in literati protests and, as a result, such occurrences dropped substantially during his reign.

The episode in 1799 marked a significant departure in the state position vis-à-vis local elites in the Jiaqing period as the imperial court began to adopt a less rigorous stance toward the literati. The emperors strengthened the ban on officials' illegal flogging of licentiates, and indeed many were impeached for that offense during the nineteenth century. Literati protests, such as the one in 1799, foreshadowed the state's more tolerant and lenient approach to these incidents in the nineteenth century. Probing into the causes of literati protests during this period, the Qing regime paid more attention to administrative malfeasance than the occurrence of protests. The regime also refrained from Qianlong's practice of single-handedly attributing the faults to the protesters.[4] The leaders of the protests could possibly expect to have their lives spared as courts commuted the punishments to exile. In a related effort to overhaul local administration, Jiaqing also relaxed restrictions on "capital appeals" (*jingkong*), which led to a substantial increase of such appeals throughout the nineteenth century.[5] These imperial initiatives recognized the role of local elites as whistleblowers of local administrative malfeasance, an issue that the emperors considered a serious threat.

This seismic shift in the relations between the state and local elites was not limited to the imperial court's leniency toward literati protests or the recognition of their role as whistleblowers. The abyss separating the distinct approaches between Jiaqing and Qianlong also encompassed their respective attitudes toward elite participation in local administration. Let us consider the following episodes. In a report on the famine relief operations in the Beijing area in 1801, officials brought to the emperor's attention that private relief resources had supplemented state funds and called for the suspension of private donations.[6] Such a practice had been frowned upon during the Qianlong reign since government funds for public projects could be supplemented with private resources only with prior endorsement from the state. The Jiaqing Emperor, however, criticized the officials, underscoring that donations should be praised and rewarded rather than prohibited. Receiving private donations for relief efforts should not be viewed as a problem, rebutted Jiaqing, adding: "If there is a relief activity aided by private donations in addition to government relief, then one more hungry person will get a meal."[7]

While Jiaqing adopted a more tolerant attitude toward local initiatives, Qianlong sought to aggressively assert the supremacy of the state over civilian leadership, reflecting a concern over the possibility that elite donations might encroach on regular state functions. In 1752, when Shanxi suffered from a serious drought, the provincial governor memorialized the throne informing that silver donations from local leaders had been deposited at the Circuit Intendant Treasury for relief purposes.[8] This led to harsh criticism from the Qianlong Emperor. In times of natural calamities, the emperor explained, local elites could directly succor the needy with their own grains or could instead purchase them for distribution to indigent people. Injecting silver from civilian elites into the government treasury, however, was not acceptable. The emperor remarked:

> As for the state relief or temporary remission of taxes, the large instances amount to several millions of taels while even small ones amount to hundreds of thousands of taels. These are all met by mobilizing regular state revenues. I have always been munificent in spending state revenues on these. How much is it anyway that local wealthy people donate? Preserving donations at state treasuries and helping relief with it is not what an appropriate form of government should be. If this practice should once begin, then not only will the poor people in the locality struck by the disaster suffer from lack of food, but also the wealthy households will be ordered to donate money. In relieving the disaster-stricken people, how can the state go as far as doing this?[9]

Although this passage stresses the welfare of the population, its message is far more nuanced. First, the emperor sought to mobilize regular state funds instead of elite donations, in the belief that this would relieve the people's burden. Second, the emperor drew a strict line between civilian and state resources. Local elites could contribute where officials fell short and, in this sense, they were deemed as supplementary revenue. However, as this case shows, if the primary function of imperial administration was itself managed with resources from civilian elites, then it stained the dignity of the state and Qianlong's perceptions of the duties to be carried out by officials. While acknowledging the contributions of elites for local public matters, Qianlong paid careful attention to maintaining state prerogatives in the public realm.

The contrast between the eighteenth and the early nineteenth centuries in relation to elite functions in various areas of local administration can be illustrated further. In 1748, a censor submitted a memorial to the Qianlong Emperor about the relief activities in Shandong Province, requesting that they be managed by the locals' private wealth.[10] The emperor rejected this proposal, first by insisting that an official-led relief activity would be the ideal course of action, and then by listing the negative side effects of elite-led relief efforts: "There is fundamentally no better remedy for famine relief than local officials distributing grains themselves. Hungry people often instigate troubles, relying on their numbers. Rich people, since the needy are either their relatives or neighbors, do not have the power to control them. The violent ones will not be satisfied though they are given much and will seize others' portions by force. This leads to restraining them with government laws."[11] Elite-led relief efforts not supervised by government officials were an invitation to chaos, Qianlong argued, because they would generate local resentment and hostilities. Moreover, the emperor continued, a more accurate accounting of relief resources could be expected only under official supervision. If the local elites took control of the accounting, then they might exaggerate the amounts of donations, or mistakenly underreport the number of lives saved. Therefore, the emperor concluded, "those who say that a relief [operation] by wealthy people is better than a relief [operation] by government officials, are the ones who know one thing but do not know the other."[12]

Qianlong, as the above case illustrates, believed that official initiatives and supervision were necessary elements in the management of a relief operation. The Daoguang Emperor, Jiaqing's successor, however, disagreed with Qianlong. Just as Jiaqing acted on the principle of blurred lines between official and civilian initiatives, the Daoguang Emperor displayed a willingness to accommodate elite initiatives in local welfare projects. When Daoguang received a report of a natural disaster in Zhejiang in 1820, he worried that the official relief operation might be insufficient to cover the vast calamity-stricken area, and held that a relief program organized by wealthy degree-holders and commoners would be more effective.[13] This represented a reversal in the hierarchy of public works management from Qianlong's assertion of the superiority of official relief programs over those led by local elites.

What do these episodes tell us about the transitional period from the eighteenth century to the early nineteenth century? What happened to the state-elite relations during this period? By looking at the early nineteenth century from these perspectives, this book will explore the rise of elite activism during this period, examining the manifestations of this activism in diverse social and cultural dimensions. Nowhere was this activism as pronounced as in Suzhou, a city in Southeast China renowned for the literati's considerable success in imperial examinations, strong elite power, and the pride in their local tradition and accomplishments. After undergoing the devastation inflicted during the late Yuan (1271–1368) and early Ming upheavals, Suzhou managed to restore its former economic glory by the middle of the fifteenth century, and it remained one of the most prosperous economic centers in China throughout the late imperial period.[14] The wealth that circulated among the elite population of the city, together with the region's long tradition of activism, prompted the urban elites to take action swiftly and earnestly as soon as they sensed the symptoms of a policy shift in public works management and the loosening of the state's control over literati's cultural practices in the early nineteenth century.

This book, however, is not simply a local history of Suzhou. Rather, it is a study of the interplay between central government policies and local reactions. This is the reason that a significant portion of this book is devoted to the examination of central policies, making use of a number of untapped or underutilized central government documents such as the *Like shishu* (Summaries of the routine memorial related to the Board of Rites) and the *Like tiben* (Routine memorials related to the Board of Personnel) preserved in the First Historical Archives in Beijing. These sources, among several others, attest to the dimensions of the transformations in elite social and cultural practices of this period.

In the December 2011 issue of the journal *Late Imperial China*, eminent Qing historian William T. Rowe wrote a stimulating article that highlighted the significance of the early nineteenth century, urging scholars in the field to explore this almost uncharted territory.[15] This book is intended to serve as an answer to his call, an excursion into the social and cultural world of early nineteenth-century China.

A Brief Survey of the Previous Scholarship on the Early Nineteenth Century

Rowe is not the only scholar who recognizes this period as a lacuna in Qing history, one that roughly spanned the four decades of the reigns of the Jiaqing and Daoguang Emperors prior to the outbreak of the Opium War in 1839. In fact, almost all scholars working in the field would agree that the early nineteenth century is the least researched period in the entire history of the Qing. The early nineteenth century has failed to draw sufficient and consistent scholarly attention because it was overshadowed by eras of pivotal historical developments that preceded and succeeded these decades. On the earlier end lay the "prosperous age" (*shengshi*) of the Kangxi, Yongzheng, and Qianlong Emperors in the eighteenth century, while on the later, the post–Opium War period characterized by the impact of Western imperialism, massive domestic rebellions, and modernization efforts.

An early generation of Qing historians in the West, spearheaded by John K. Fairbank, highlighted the West's impact on the institutional, cultural, and economic changes in Chinese society following the Qing's forced entry into an international order dominated by European powers in the mid-nineteenth century. Starting in the 1970s, however, Western scholars began to shift the scope of their analysis to domestic matters, which were relatively free from Western influence but that nonetheless carried far-reaching and crucial consequences. As Paul A. Cohen has aptly pointed out, this shift of attention from the topics related to China's contact with the West to those more germane to China proper signified a critical reflection on the implicit connotations upon which the approaches of the "China's response to the West" school were built: that significant and truly meaningful changes took place in China only in modern times and in the midst of interactions with the Western powers.[16] The "China-centered" approaches that emerged in reaction to the earlier so-called Fairbank school framework focused on the significant historical events during the entire span of the Qing history, many predating the Opium War.[17] While this "China-centered" approach greatly expanded our horizon of knowledge by looking at issues far earlier than 1840, it came short of, however, highlighting the themes that shaped the first four decades of the nineteenth century.

The relative dearth of attention in the early nineteenth century is not only found in the Western scholarship on Qing China, but also extends to mainland Chinese historians. From the 1950s to as late as the 1980s, Chinese historians exerted great effort in identifying the "sprouts of capitalism," signs of modern economic developments that supposedly had appeared in the sixteenth to the eighteenth centuries.[18] Apart from these efforts, they also directed their research focus on the period that began in the mid-nineteenth century. During this time, China was drawn into an international order molded by Europe, a process that mainland Chinese historians characterize as the start of China's experiences with capitalism and imperialist aggression. More recently, Chinese historians have steered their attention away from this gloomy period in Qing history to a more glorious one, the "prosperous age," an age of relative peace, economic prosperity, territorial expansion, and population growth ushered in by the three capable emperors in the eighteenth century.[19] This new orientation is perhaps shaped partly by the Chinese pride soaring in tandem with the country's economic leaps at the turn of the twenty-first century. In an effort to draw lessons from the precedents to better understand and inform contemporary society and politics, scholars have tried to look at a past when China enjoyed a similar age of peace, power, and prosperity. As a result, the early nineteenth century has failed to attract persistent and concentrated attention, as Chinese historians, just like their Western counterparts, have largely overlooked its significance.

This does not mean, however, that the period in question has been entirely neglected. A number of important works have laid the foundation for our seminal understanding of the period. As early as 1952, Suzuki Chūsei broke new ground in this field with his book on the White Lotus Rebellion (1796–1804) that plagued the newly enthroned emperor Jiaqing.[20] Susan Naquin has also contributed to our knowledge of popular religion during the Jiaqing reign in bringing to light vivid details of the Eight Trigram Rebellion (1813).[21] Philip Kuhn and Susan Mann Jones's pioneering chapter for the *Cambridge History of China*, published in 1978, describes the signs of political and social crises that beset early nineteenth-century China and the rise of statecraft thinkers who sought to cope with them.[22] Statecraft ideology during this period has also been closely examined in Benjamin Elman's exploration of the intricate relations between kinship networks and scholarly thinking.[23] Apart from statecraft ideology, another strong orientation in philosophical thinking in the early nineteenth century was evidential research scholarship (*kaozheng xue*), and Steven B. Miles's study of the Xuehaitang Academy in Guangzhou examines the social composition of the Guangzhou local elites as well as their efforts to construct a local identity.[24]

On the political side, James Polachek has demonstrated the reascendance of the late-Ming-style Han literati political activism around the turn of the nineteenth century.[25] In this regard, the breakdown of the Grand Canal system in the mid-Qing period constituted a factor that triggered the Jiangnan literati political activism, and Jane Kate Leonard's book emphasizes the emperor's agency in coping with this problem by illustrating the Daoguang Emperor's meticulous management of the Grand Canal crisis in the 1820s.[26] More recently, Wang Wensheng has illuminated the significance of the Jiaqing Emperor's reform policies as a watershed from the aggressive expansionist stance of the Qing Empire to a less interventionist approach to state-building that purposefully downsized imperial power.[27] Chinese scholars have contributed to our understanding of this period primarily by writing on the two early nineteenth-century rulers. Guan Wenfa's study of the Jiaqing Emperor describes the emperor's policies designed to purge the faction led by Hešen (an imperial favorite and notoriously avaricious official in the Qianlong court) and domestic rebellions, among them the White Lotus and the Eight Trigram sects.[28] Similar studies on the Daoguang Emperor discuss various domestic and foreign challenges that confronted the emperor, among them the Muslim Rebellion in the Northwest during the 1820s and the Opium War (1839–42), crises almost identical to the ones that his father had encountered.[29]

Despite the tremendous debt that we owe these scholars, we still lack a systematic and coherent explanation through which we can relate diverse incidents of the time with one another. In other words, we still need to answer what the historical phenomena of the early nineteenth century shared in common and how this period compared and contrasted with the previous century.

Moving Beyond the "Decline" Paradigm

Previous scholarship has portrayed the early nineteenth century as an epochal moment during which the Qing dynasty declined, with the prosperity, stability, and expansion of the previous era giving way to economic crisis and instability. The deepening of the crises fostered a fragile domestic environment that weakened China and invited foreign aggression in the nineteenth century. Since this "decline paradigm" loomed large in studies on the early nineteenth century, they focused largely on identifying signs of such "decline." Various factors have been presented as symptoms of the empire's downfall: population increase, ecological exhaustion, skyrocketing corruption among government officials, serious shortfall in state revenue collection, deterioration of the salt administration and tribute grain transportation, outflow of silver, and millenarian rebellions led by the White Lotus and Eight Trigram sectarians. Consider, for example, the influential Qing history book by the eminent Chinese scholar Xiao Yishan, published in 1986. Xiao identifies the period from the rise of Hešen to the reign of Jiaqing as the time when the Qing Empire turned from prosperity to decline.[30] He traced the origins of the Qing downfall in multiple dimensions, all rooted in the later years of Qianlong's rule. The Jiaqing Emperor sought to resolve some of these problems, Xiao explains, by purging Hešen's cronies, urging frugality upon his officials, and emphasizing bureaucratic discipline. Despite this imperial campaign, Xiao argues, the Qing Empire continued its downward spiral until its final collapse in 1911.

This book, however, questions whether it is appropriate to label the early nineteenth century simply as an era of "decline." The period requires diversified lenses through which to identify and explain a number of important issues, approaches that can go beyond the decline paradigm. The use of the term "decline" covers as much as it uncovers the historical realities of the early nineteenth century. Clearly, signs of crises that might be interpreted as the evidence of the decline of state capacity were unmistakable. State fiscal conditions worsened and malfeasance among officials and clerks was rife. Portraying the period simply as a time of decline, however, ignores the conscious efforts of the early-nineteenth-century rulers to make accommodation for the social realities and design a form of government more conducive to such realities. The more relaxed ruling style adopted by the Jiaqing and Daoguang Emperors was one that entailed distancing itself from the heavy-handed approach of their predecessors Yongzheng and Qianlong. The rulers of the early nineteenth century also lacked the grand visions and the imperial fervor to launch various social, cultural, and military programs to mold society in accordance with the imperial schemes. Jiaqing and Daoguang, however, did not remain indifferent to the challenges of the day, nor were they idle spectators to the empire's decline. They exercised certain degrees of agency in shaping new policies.[31] Wang Wensheng characterizes the reform measures taken by Jiaqing and his officials as efforts of "political retreat," through which Jiaqing "pulled Qing empire-building away from a vicious cycle of excessive ambition that bred resistance back onto a sustainable track of political development."[32] In this respect, it would be unfair to consider what seems to have been the weakening of imperial power as an all-encompassing sign of decline, since changes in the imperial ruling style is a matter that transcends the simple linear model.

If we shift our standpoint from the center to the locality, then the overall social and the cultural environments that surrounded local elites defy the simple characterization of the early nineteenth century as a period of decline. While the worsening fiscal conditions adversely affected regions and administrative institutions across the Qing Empire, at the same time the reformulation of state-elite relations granted local elites greater say over local matters. This could be evidenced in the rising numbers of enshrinement and the flourishing of local literature. Local elites now enjoyed greater freedom to participate in social and cultural realms that had been restricted, if not denied, to them in the previous century. Observing the choices in cultural activities once again made available to the elite population, it would be difficult to label the period simply as a time of "decline."[33] Rather than frame the early nineteenth century in a linear narrative depicting the downward spiral of the Qing dynasty, this book describes this period as a time that witnessed a transformation from one ruling style to another, one that embodied a more localized nature and was marked by the devolution of power to local elites.

From "State Activism" to "Elite Activism"

While the nineteenth century is characterized by the rise of elite activism, the eighteenth century has often been described as a period of "state activism." Much scholarship has been devoted to illuminating the array of policies aimed at increasing the reach of the state deeper into society. Bolstered by increasingly steady streams of revenue to government coffers and imperial visions to engender society in accordance with the state schemes, the Qing regime under Yongzheng and Qianlong expanded and reinforced its hold on various social sectors, such as lineage, benevolent societies, private academies, famine relief activities, and the market brokerage system.[34] As Rowe has shown in his work on Chen Hongmou, despite occasional attempts by officials to enlist the help of local elites or rely on market mechanisms whenever possible, it is nonetheless apparent that a greater degree of state control was exercised in many aspects of the management of public affairs in the eighteenth century.[35]

State activism in the eighteenth century has been studied mainly from a social history perspective. The Qing state under Yongzheng and Qianlong, however, not only aimed at bringing order to the elites' social actions, but also strove to construct a more centralized cultural order.[36] A significant portion of this book is devoted to the analysis of the cultural dimensions of eighteenth-century state activism and how these interventionist policies ceased and then generated new sets of practices in the early nineteenth century.

To forge this centralized cultural order, the Qianlong Emperor implemented a policy of rigorous censorship of literati writings, most notably the literary inquisitions of the 1770s. A travel diary by a Korean envoy to the Qianlong court reveals the degree of state intervention into the literati's cultural world. According to the author, the Qing officials and scholars, both the Manchus and the Hans, exercised extreme caution in written communications, even with the Korean envoys, to the extent of shredding papers and blacking out characters to avoid their words from being misconstrued.[37] The state intervention in the cultural realm had lasting effects. As a compiler of a local gazetteer in Suzhou in the early twentieth century tells us:

> The loss of book collections in the Southeast region all originated from the havoc wreaked on the literati during the three reigns of Kangxi, Yongzheng, and Qianlong. A man surnamed Jiang of our Suzhou prefecture had an extremely good collection of the Song and Yuan editions. The loss [of this collection] was caused by the poetry incident (*shian*) that happened after the death of Mr. Shen Deqian. Jiang was a student of Mr. Shen, and when he heard of the mishap brought on Mr. Shen, he burned all the books he possessed, no matter old or new, and threw [the ashes] into a well. The water in the well is black even now.[38]

This draconian state control even extended to the dead. Shen Deqian (1673–1769), a Suzhou scholar-official who had enjoyed Qianlong's favor in his late years, faced posthumous accusations of writing a preface for a literary collection that contained seditious elements.[39] In 1778, he had all his posthumous honors withdrawn, his tomb inscription demolished, and his tablet removed from the Shrine of Local Worthies.[40]

This literary inquisition was perhaps the most dramatic representation of the cultural interventionist policies of the time. But the policies extended to more than just finding words implicit or explicit of a pro-Ming sentiment. As this book will demonstrate, the Qianlong court strongly discouraged the production of local histories whose descriptions of local people and traditions deviated from the imperial court's views. As the writing of local gazetteers and private histories was intertwined with the interests of influential families, this practice often exaggerated or distorted achievements of the prominent local figures. The government under Qianlong even mandated that local gazetteers undergo a review by provincial officials and obtain their endorsement before publication. The government intervention in this realm surfaced as an attempt to check the exorbitant influence exercised by local families on this cultural genre. The Yongzheng and Qianlong courts seized control of the enshrinement process of local worthies, another practice tied to the reputation and the status of local families, and applied more rigorous criteria in reviewing candidates' qualifications. These state efforts in subordinating elite cultural practices to the dictates of the central government often clashed with the interests of entrenched local elites.

In a similar vein, the Qianlong court launched the *Siku quanshu* project, the ambitious program of book collection and establishment of imperial libraries, in part to shore up the cultural centrality of the emperor, since the paucity of books in the imperial library certainly undermined the court's authority.[41] Private book collectors in the Jiangnan region played an instrumental role in this project, supplying the overwhelming majority of the publications. The collected books were then copied and preserved in imperial libraries in both northern and southern China, which reminds us of a typical pattern of incorporating southern culture by the imperial state. The emperor, however, did not originally plan to erect imperial libraries in Jiangnan, limiting them to the four imperial palaces in northern China.[42] It was only in 1782 that the emperor belatedly authorized the transcription of three additional sets of the *Siku quanshu* to be housed in the three southern libraries.[43]

I have so far outlined various aspects of state interventionist policies during the eighteenth century, manifested in diverse social and cultural arenas. If the eighteenth century is marked by state activism, then what happened to this orientation after the demise of the Qianlong Emperor? As will be explained more fully in the following sections, the nineteenth century witnessed, once again, the ascendance of elite activism in social and cultural spheres. How do we, then, place the Jiaqing and Daoguang era in terms of its position in the larger process of the development of local elite activism? Focusing on the interplay between politics, social practices and cultural production, this study will trace the unfolding of elite activism in these realms from the eighteenth to the early nineteenth centuries.

Origins of Elite Activism in the Nineteenth Century

One of the most striking aspects of the political adjustment observed by the early nineteenth-century rulers consisted in the establishment of new relations with the elites of the empire. These proved enduring, as they formed the fulcrum upon which the Qing regime lasted for another century. The new policies implemented by the early nineteenth-century rulers, directly or indirectly, opened the door for a reinvigorated elite social activism and enlarged the scope of permissible elite cultural practices. While some changes might have been byproducts of the imperial reform initiatives, others were intended results of this conscious policy shift.

Elite activism in the nineteenth century is often considered a defining feature of the post-Taiping society. By elite activism, I mean the increased participation of elites in local public affairs in terms of their monetary contribution and the assumption of managerial roles. This was accompanied by the strong assertion of local identity, which constituted a cultural representation of such activism.

Since the pioneering work by Philip A. Kuhn on social militarization in the mid-nineteenth century, the Taiping Rebellion (1850–64) and the subsequent restoration process came to be considered as the starting point of the ascendant elite activism in the Qing period.[44] Mary Rankin argues that elite public roles expanded during the restoration efforts in Zhejiang after the Taiping Rebellion. She demonstrates that the public actions of reinvigorated elites at this time were not limited to the local managerial areas but reached further into the national political realm.[45] William T. Rowe's study of the city of Hankow shows the extent of the public engagement of the gentry and merchants in the management of urban public affairs, primarily in the latter half of the nineteenth century.[46]

While this book acknowledges the Taiping Rebellion as a pivotal turning point in the expansion of elite public roles, it challenges the idea that its outbreak marked the beginning of elite activism. Instead, this study suggests that the rise of elite activism can be traced earlier to the Jiaqing and Daoguang periods, when the bureaucratic inefficiency rendered the mobilization of local elites a viable option and aggravating financial difficulties made the reliance upon elite economic resources inevitable. This book does not view the Qing state and society before the Taiping Rebellion as a simple continuum of the previous eighteenth century. Rather, it tries to emphasize the similarities that the early nineteenth century shares with the later Qing period in terms of social and cultural aspects of elite activism, and the dissimilarities this period shows with the eighteenth century. This way, the rise of elite activism in the nineteenth century is examined not as originating entirely from the mid-nineteenth century rebellion but as initially resulting from an effort to respond to various economic and social crises that befell China at the beginning of the nineteenth century.

One of these crises stemmed from rapid demographic growth. The eighteenth century witnessed the doubling of the empire's population from 150 million to 300 million. The demographic pressures persisted as the population continued to climb further thereafter, reaching 430 million in the mid-nineteenth century. Recent studies on the population of the Jiangnan region, the focal area of interest in this book, suggest that the rate of the population growth in this region from 1750 to 1850 might not have been as rapid as in other areas, such as the middle Yangzi region or North China.[47] The population in Jiangnan, however, did increase during this period, although at a slower rate, hovering around 20 million by 1620 to 36 million by 1850.[48] The urban population living in or close to county seats within Suzhou prefecture numbered around 500,000 in the late sixteenth century, and then soared to about one million in the Jiaqing reign, marking a twofold increase.[49]

The population growth during the mid-Qing period is often thought to have weakened administrative control, as the number of local official posts remained largely stagnant despite the population upsurge. This rising disparity between population level and administrative control, together with the declining state fiscal conditions, induced an increased degree of official reliance on local elites.[50] But government policies proved crucial in expediting the expansion of elite public roles.

In an article on the origins of a Chinese public sphere, Mary Rankin mentions that, due to the failure of the regular bureaucracy to keep pace with the population, the managerial roles of local elites expanded from the mid-eighteenth century.[51] She draws this conclusion largely from her observation that the list of local public institutions in gazetteers grew lengthier from this period onward. According to Rankin, elite activism in the late nineteenth century was transformative, distinct from the earlier one, as the former carried political and extra-regional dimensions. The intensification of elite public roles from the mid- to late-Qianlong years, Rankin argues, provided the institutional bases for the full-fledged, transformative political activism that occurred in the late nineteenth century.[52]

In a comprehensive study on eighteenth-century China, Susan Naquin and Evelyn Rawski suggest briefly that the initiatives and responsibilities of managing local public enterprises under strong government supervision in the early Qing—such as irrigation, philanthropy, schools, and granaries—came to be delegated to local elites. They consider that this shift to local initiatives had already become visible at the end of the eighteenth century, but that it "gained rapid momentum in the nineteenth."[53]

The findings by these scholars seem to suggest that elite public roles began to multiply in the later Qianlong years. They provide, however, distinct insights on the significance of the early nineteenth century. In Rankin's view, extra-bureaucratic management of local public works in the early nineteenth century served as a continuation of the pattern that had already emerged in the later eighteenth century. Naquin and Rawski, on the other hand, seem to consider that elite public roles intensified in the early nineteenth century albeit their earlier origin. Despite their differences on the timing of the rise of elite activism, they all drew their conclusions from local gazetteers: the lengthened list of public institutions or biographical information of philanthropic men. In contrast, this book will rely on a quantifiable set of evidence to estimate the degree of elite public functions from the Qianlong to Daoguang period. Based upon this evidence, I argue that the Jiaqing, and especially the Daoguang years, marked a watershed in terms of elite financial and managerial participation in local public works, which clearly demarcates this period from the previous century. I do acknowledge that local public institutions, such as benevolent halls, mushroomed during the Qianlong reign, and that local elites managed certain public works in the later eighteenth century. But I do not subscribe to the view that the early nineteenth-century forms of public works management constituted a simple continuation of the late eighteenth-century pattern. Under aggravated fiscal conditions and deep official distrust of subbureaucratic personnel, elites increasingly ran public works as managers and fund providers in the early nineteenth century. Considering this period as an epochal moment in this dimension is justified not only by quantifiable data, but also by government policies and regulations that encouraged such participation. In this respect, this study corroborates the claims of Naquin and Rawski while further elaborating upon their conclusions.

Chapter Overview

In the chapters that follow, I analyze the shifts in state-elite relations reflected in the social and cultural practices of elites in early nineteenth-century Suzhou. This book consists of two parts. Part I, comprising chapters 1 to 3, illustrates the rise of elite activism in the management of local public works. Chapter 1 traces the changes in imperial attitudes toward elite participation in the local public realm as well as the systematization of state rewards for elites' managerial roles and their contributions for local public causes. Based upon quantitative data drawn from untapped Qing documents housed in the First Historical Archives in Beijing, this chapter shows the growth in the number of people awarded for their contributions during the Jiaqing and Daoguang periods, underscoring the agency of local elites in public works. In response to enlarged elite contributions, the state devised regulations to officially recognize the role of elite managers and to offer more favorable rewards to the contributors. Contrary to the scholarship that traces the origins of elite activism in the efforts to subdue or recover from the mid-nineteenth century Taiping Rebellion, this chapter demonstrates that the activism dates back to the Jiaqing period.

Chapters 2 and 3 discuss the expanded public role of Suzhou elites by examining water conservancy works and famine relief operations during the early nineteenth century. During the eighteenth century, large-scale hydraulic works and famine relief operations in Suzhou had been primarily managed and financed by the state. The Qing state during the Qianlong reign played a central role in relief efforts, pursuing a variety of approaches, such as tax exemption and the distribution of subsidies. Elite-led relief activities did occasionally occur, but they did not reach the frequency or scale comparable to those in the early nineteenth century.

Through a close analysis of the hydraulic and famine relief projects in Suzhou from the eighteenth to the early nineteenth centuries, these chapters demonstrate that these projects came to be regularly financed through civilian contributions and much more frequently managed by the elites in the early nineteenth century.

Part II, comprising chapters 4 to 7, is intended to examine the effects of the ascendant elite social activism on the cultural practices of Suzhou's elites. The central government's monopoly over the interpretation of historical events and its severe criticisms of local literature as parochialism rapidly lost ground in the early nineteenth century. In its place, an attitude that tolerated and even embraced more diverse local voices and practices emerged, distinct from the norms prescribed by the state authority. Local elites in Suzhou began to reassert the significance of their localities on the empire's cultural map.

In chapter 4, the state endorsement of local worthies and eminent officials is analyzed, illustrating that the number of enshrined worthies climbed in the early nineteenth century as the state relaxed its centralized decision-making process and rigid standards. Suzhou was no exception to this empire-wide trend, as the city's enshrined worthies rapidly increased in the early nineteenth century. This chapter argues that this reflects a greater accommodation of elite interests by the central government. The total number of enshrinements for each reign outnumbered the previous one, a gradual trend that illustrates the incremental empowerment of local elites and the progressive advancement of elite activism in the nineteenth century.

Chapter 5 discusses the significance of the Suzhou literati's collective efforts to build a shrine in 1828. Known as the General Shrine of Former Worthies of Suzhou Prefecture and devoted to the worship of more than five hundred local ancestors, this shrine was constructed under the closely coordinated leadership of provincial officials and Suzhou literati. They engraved the portraits of the local ancestors on the shrine's walls and published them in a collective biography. Many of those worshipped might not have been included in the government-monitored official shrines of local worthies, as they had been either the Ming-loyalists or actors in the late Ming factional strife that aroused profound hatred among the early Qing rulers. At times, these local worthies had been excluded simply because the state deemed their merits insufficient to deserve recognition.

This chapter argues that the Suzhou literati's efforts in the construction of this shrine represent a creative strategy to bypass state control and reassert local identity and the locality's cultural supremacy. This chapter also sheds light on the significance of the return of the public display of portraits in a Confucian shrine. The use of visual images in the Confucian Temple had been prohibited by the state since the early sixteenth century, the repercussion of which had also impacted lesser Confucian shrines, such as the Shrine of Local Worthies. The return of public circulation of visual images in both engravings and printed forms in the early nineteenth century symbolizes the retreat of state power from the local cultural realm.

Chapters 6 and 7 illustrate the literati efforts to reconstruct Suzhou's cultural tradition during the early nineteenth century. Chapter 6 chronicles the eighteenth-century measures to strengthen imperial control over the cultural practices of the literati and the dissolution of such state efforts in the early nineteenth century. Under the Qianlong Emperor, the central government initiated the pre-publication censorship of local gazetteers, as provincial officials were required not only to review gazetteers, but also endorse their publication. The government viewed local gazetteers as being fraught with parochialism, criticizing them for their exaggeration, distortion, and omission of information related to historical events and figures. These fraudulent practices, according to the government, functioned to elevate the centrality of a local place and led the narratives in gazetteers to deviate from the state's orthodox positions. Similar criticisms were also leveled against private local histories. This interventionist policy under Qianlong prompted a decline in the number of gazetteers and local literature. By the early nineteenth century, however, private local histories once again flourished. This environment also witnessed the gradual disappearance of provincial pre-publication reviewers from local gazetteers, another sign that testifies to the retraction of the state in the local cultural realm.

In chapter 7, I turn to analysis of the discourse centering on a local hero of Suzhou, Zhang Shicheng. Zhang, who built a kingdom with Suzhou as its capital in the fourteenth century, received favorable appraisals among locals, but he was subsequently vilified in official histories due to his defeat by archrival Zhu Yuanzhang, the founder of the Ming Empire. This hegemonic historical perception was undermined by the collective memory shared by locals in the Suzhou and Taizhou areas, respectively the capital and the hometown of Zhang Shicheng. The collective counter-memory, however, did not always make its presence felt. Its emergence and disappearance paralleled changes in state-elite relationships. It first surfaced in the mid-Ming period and continued to exert some influence into the early Qing period. Under the Yongzheng Emperor and the Qianlong Emperor, the local counter-memory once again became dormant. Then, in the early nineteenth century, it reemerged among the members of the Suzhou and Taizhou elite circles. The early nineteenth-century counter-memory was radical, for it challenged, subverted, and replaced the dominant hegemonic discourse that had survived the initial Ming challenge.

The conclusion places the ascendant elite activism of the early nineteenth century in a comparative perspective with the elite activism that characterized the later part of the century. In the early 1800s, elite managerial roles were generally restricted to public works for social welfare and infrastructure. Elite roles expanded into the realm of military activities for community defense, an area deemed more sensitive from the perspective of the central government, only in the mid-1800s. The public actions of elite managers in the early nineteenth century were largely confined within the boundaries of their localities, lacking the extraregional dimension of networks and activities of elite managers in the late nineteenth century. Around 1900, this activism acquired a decisively political character, as local elites raised their voices against the government to demand broader participation in national politics.

The social and cultural world of the early nineteenth century molded by elite activism should be viewed as distinct from the one in the previous century. But several of the features of that world foreshadowed social and cultural environments that would pervade the empire on a grander scale decades later. In this regard, the early nineteenth century constituted a transitional period from state control to elite activism and from a centralized cultural order to a multicentered one that incorporated stronger assertions of local identities.

PART I

From State Activism to Elite Activism

CHAPTER I

The Ascendant Elite Activism in Local Public Works

In the early nineteenth century, the role of local elites in the public realm expanded.[1] The state's participation in the funding and supervision of public works receded, shifting the burden to the local elites. This chapter will include study of the changes in the general patterns of elite participation in local public works. Imperial court records are examined and the adjustments in government policies analyzed that reflected the elite's increasingly visible public roles throughout the empire in the early nineteenth century. In chapters 2 and 3, this study will examine how elite activism unfolded in the Suzhou region. The purpose of this chapter is, therefore, to provide a context in which this trend in Suzhou can be better understood in relation to the changes in other regions.

The Intensification of the Public Role of Elites

In many ways, the participation of local elites served as an integral adjunct to local government since at least late Ming times. The gentry's financial contributions proved crucial to the success of local officials' administration, not just in aiding poverty-stricken people in times of famine or flood, but especially in implementing local infrastructure projects such as water conservancy works, bridges, roads, schools, and examination halls. Even during the relatively prosperous eighteenth century, elite financial assistance proved indispensable to channeling resources for various local public works. In return, the Qing state recognized those who donated significant amounts, basing its decisions on reports the central government received from provincial authorities. Contributors could be rewarded with permission and funds for memorial arches (*jingbiao*) or with an official rank and title (*yixu*), substantive or honorific. While the Board of Rites handled the process for memorial arches, the Board of Personnel decided on *yixu* cases. Decisions regarding rewards for contributions not deemed significant were left in the hands of provincial and local officials. In these cases, donors usually received plaques for public display. This suggests that one way to gauge the degree of participation by elites in local affairs is to examine the frequency of the bureaucracy's reports and the state's handling of rewards.

Although the norm for local elites consisted in assuming partial or sometimes complete financial responsibility for local public works, it does not mean such degree and the frequency of involvement remained constant throughout the entire late imperial period. As the state's fiscal conditions gradually declined during the early nineteenth century, elite donations for the maintenance of local public works multiplied. Government records on elite contributions, spanning the Qianlong and the Daoguang periods, substantiate this trend. It must be noted that these records are not comprehensive, as they cover only the contributions whose amounts were significant enough to be reported to the central government. The purpose of this study, however, is not to figure out the exact numbers and amounts of contributions, but to measure the extent of elite financial responsibility in public works over an extended stretch of time. An increased number of contribution reports in government sources would imply that the local administration came to rely more heavily on private donations for the management of local public works.

Such references to contributions increased dramatically during the Jiaqing and Daoguang periods, which can be understood as a sign of an expanded public role for elites. In this sense, nineteenth-century elite public activism, often considered to have its origins in the Taiping Rebellion, should be regarded as a second catalyst for the intensification of such elite public roles rather than marking its beginning. Moreover, if we acknowledge the earlier origins of elite activism, then the factors that unleashed it cannot be ascribed entirely to wartime or restoration efforts exerted by local elites during and after the rebellion. Several other factors need to be considered, such as the shortage of revenue, the currency crisis, the escalating administrative expenses, the growth of wealth among elites, and the awareness of the limits and ineffectiveness of state intervention in local public works. Amid this environment, the early nineteenth century should be regarded as a period in which the state was compelled to reconsider its relationship with local elites.

The Increase of Contribution Incidents

In the early nineteenth century, the Qing Empire faced a number of problems on multiple fronts that aggravated the state's fiscal pressures and that can be traced to the eighteenth century. In addition to the soaring population growth during the previous century, the outbreak of the White Lotus Rebellion marked the downward spiral of imperial finances.[2] Aggravating this situation, tax collection had become difficult by the early nineteenth century, a period marked by the accumulation of arrears.[3] The increase of silver outflow in exchange for opium at this time, coupled with the contraction of foreign purchasing power for Chinese commodities that resulted in the reduction of silver flowing back into the empire, also dealt a serious blow to the already poor fiscal condition.[4]

Silver reserves in the imperial treasury had experienced a remarkable improvement during the reigns of the Yongzheng and the Qianlong Emperors, reaching its peak of 80 million taels by the end of the 1770s.[5] This fiscal surplus formed the financial basis that made possible the numerous and costly imperial southern tours by Qianlong.[6] However, the surpluses in the imperial treasury began to deteriorate rapidly during the early nineteenth century. In 1795, the last year of the Qianlong reign, the silver reserves in the treasury amounted to about 69.3 million taels, but the outbreak of the White Lotus Rebellion during the next year relegated the level of silver reserves to about 56.5 million taels in 1796.[7] During the Jiaqing and Daoguang years, the amount of silver reserves continued to decline with some fluctuations and reserves never recovered the levels recorded during the Qianlong period. In 1797, 1801, and 1804, the silver reserves in the imperial treasury dropped to about 27.9 million, 16.9 million, and 21.6 million taels, respectively. When the Jiaqing reign ended in 1820, the amount in the treasury stood at 31.2 million taels. During the Daoguang period, the silver reserves largely remained within the range of 20 to 30 million taels before the outbreak of the Opium War, a conflict that further depleted the state treasury. In 1842, the reserves dropped to 13 million, further declining to 9.9 million the next year and ultimately shrinking to as low as 8 million taels by 1850.[8]

To alleviate fiscal problems, officials often resorted to the sale of academic degrees and government positions (*juanna*). The three Qing emperors preceding Jiaqing had also relied on selling degrees and offices to secure means for military expeditions, granary stocking, land reclamation, famine relief, or water conservancy works.[9] This practice, however, expanded during the Jiaqing government, reaching a level unprecedented in Qing history.[10] As Elizabeth Kaske explains, a "moderate and controlled level of office selling" shifted to a "situation where official honors were in oversupply" around 1800.[11] The three successive office sale campaigns in response to the White Lotus Rebellion and two river works at the beginning of his reign alone brought in 30 million, 7.95 million, and 21 million taels, respectively.[12] The revenue collected through provincial sales of *jiansheng* academic degrees during the first two decades of the nineteenth century amounted to more than 40 million taels.[13]

The amount of contributions from local elites during the early nineteenth century also reflected the deteriorating situation of the state finances.[14] The *Qing shilu* (Veritable records of the Qing) scarcely mentions *jingbiao* cases during the Qianlong to Daoguang periods, but it does contain much information about the *yixu* cases. Only significant amounts were reported to the throne through memorials, based upon which the compilers of the *Qing shilu* made entries in the volume. This alerts us to the fact that recording was capricious: the compilers of the *Qing shilu* might have left out a certain number of contribution entries. Given that the *Qing shilu* does not cover every single major contribution reported to the central government, the extreme disparity of the numbers recorded between the Qianlong reign and the Jiaqing and Daoguang reigns allows us to draw a valid conclusion that elite contribution cases increased substantially in the early nineteenth century. Moreover, this conclusion is further corroborated by the evidence from other sources discussed below.

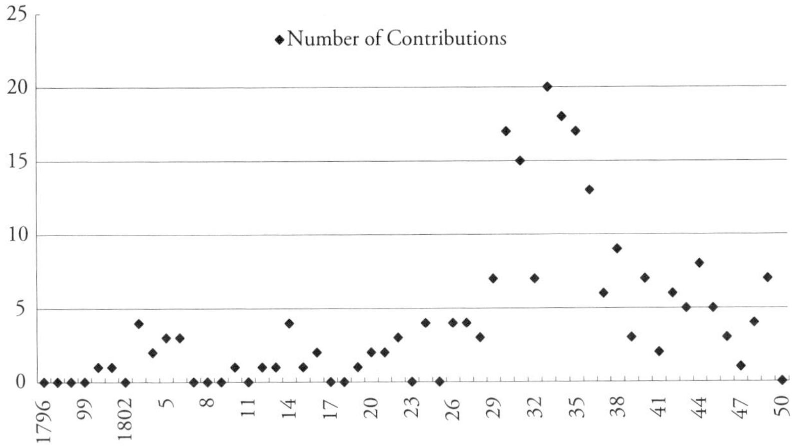

FIGURE 1. Number of contributions recorded in the *Qing shilu* for the Jiaqing (1796–1820) and Daoguang years (1821–50)

During the sixty years of the Qianlong reign, *Qing shilu* recorded only six cases of contributions.[15] This extreme paucity of reported local contributions during the Qianlong reign, however, dramatically increased in the subsequent Jiaqing and Daoguang periods. Figure 1 illustrates the number of contributions during these reigns as recorded in the *Qing shilu.*

The range of public projects benefiting from these contributions included a wide variety of local institutions and works: gruel houses, famine relief, city walls, Confucian Temples, examination halls, private academies, charitable schools, bridges, water conservancy efforts, and so forth. While the *Qing shilu* at times records both local officials and elites as donors, it generally lists only the names of local officials while lumping the rest under the ambiguous terms meaning "others" (*deng* or *yu*). However, the usual brief accounts in the *Qing shilu* can be compared with the detailed records of the same cases in the *Like tiben,* routine memorials related to the administrative concerns of the Board of Personnel, including those requesting the grant of official honors as a reward for the contributors. In this way, we can conclude that the majority of the contributors belonged to the local elites.[16] Therefore, even for the cases of abbreviated lists of contributors, we should assume that the major contributors were those locals who were affluent rather than local officials.

The *Qing shilu* reports only six cases of contributions during Qianlong's sixty-year reign. Figure 1 shows that the number jumped to as high as twenty-seven within a shorter twenty-five-year time period during the Jiaqing period, climbing to 200 during the thirty years of the Daoguang reign. As state finances went from bad to worse in the early years of the nineteenth century, the government mobilized increasing amounts of private resources to maintain local order and welfare. Although not included in the numbers in figure 1, the *Qing shilu* also reveals a far greater frequency of elite contributions for military purposes after the Opium War broke out in the 1840s, another indication of the pivotal role played by private financial support in the first half of the nineteenth century.

In nearly all the cases documented in the *Qing shilu*, donors received honorary ranks and titles from the state for their contributions. The Board of Rites processed compensations involving memorial arches. These cases can be found in the *Like shishu*, a summary of routine memorials involving matters of the Board of Rites, including a number of documents requesting memorial arches for the donors who contributed at least 1,000 taels for the welfare of local communities. Before proceeding with an analysis of the totals recorded in the *Like shishu*, some caveats need to be mentioned. The memorials relating to the *jingbiao* cases in the *Like shishu* usually consist of two types: in the first, provincial officials reported the donations and suggested rewards; and in the second, the Board of Rites requested the emperor's approval of its decisions. In cases involving memorial arches, these two memorials make up the majority. But some, particularly from the early nineteenth century, have only one type of request, either from provincial officials or from the Board of Rites. The widespread practice of secret memorials was probably responsible for these lacunae. The weight of the source, however, should not be downplayed by these caveats, since only a few requests for memorial arches were presented through secret memorials under Qianlong.[17] Figure 2 illustrates the pattern of reported donations in *Like shishu*; these include those with either one or both types of memorials.

The number of the memorial arch cases multiplied rapidly in the Jiaqing period, and this trend persisted throughout the Daoguang reign. In my sampling of nineteen years in Qianlong's six-decade-long reign, as many as twelve contained no reference to memorial arches; three years recorded two each; and another three only one each. In only one of the

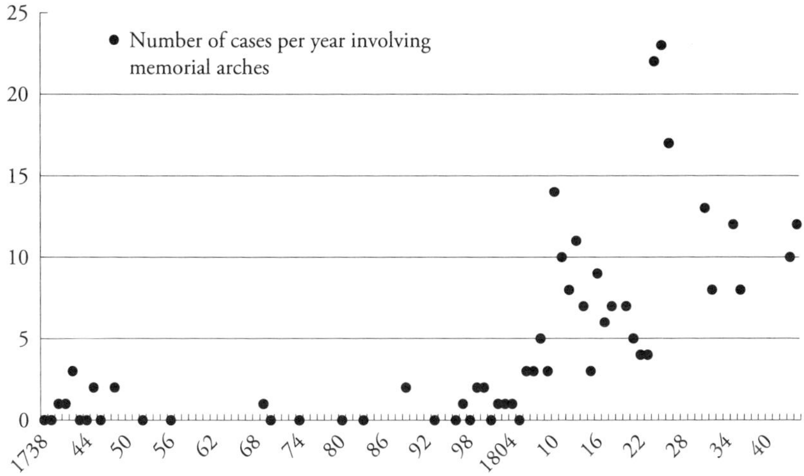

FIGURE 2. Memorial arch cases for selected years between 1736 and 1850 (Source: *LKSS*)

years were three memorial arch cases recorded. By contrast, my survey of Jiaqing's entire twenty-five-year rule—excluding 1819 for which no data are available—reveals fourteen years with three or more memorial arch cases each. Following 1805 there were at least three cases per year. During the span of fourteen years from 1806 to 1820 (excluding 1819), the annual average reached 6.8 cases, a leap from the annual average of 0.6 for the nineteen selected years of Qianlong. Furthermore, this annual average jumped to 11.5 for twelve selected years under Daoguang: 1821–26, 1831–32, 1835–36, and 1843–44. This incremental pattern from the Qianlong to Daoguang reign is consistent with that observed in the *Qing shilu*.

A third source, the *Like tiben*, presents information on the official rank and title cases. Unlike the *jingbiao* cases in which donors were rewarded for contributions amounting to more than 1,000 taels, the *yixu* cases conferred various official honors for contributions ranging from several hundred taels to an amount well over 1,000 taels. The related documents of the *Like tiben* have been categorized as the "Evaluation of Achievements and Encouragement and Appointment" (*kaoji jiangxu*) by the First Historical Archives in Beijing and they feature only the cases processed through routine memorials. It contains a large number of official rank and title cases absent from the *Qing shilu*. Due to the volume

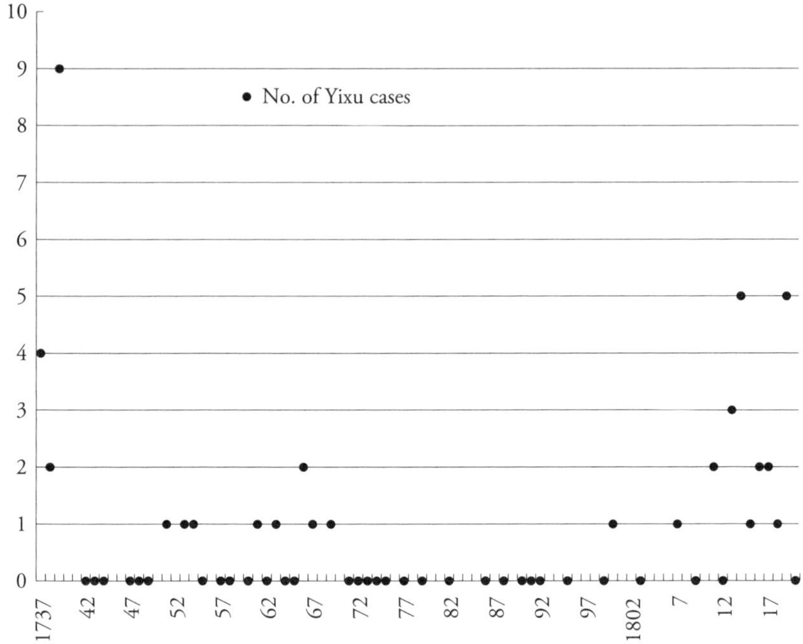

FIGURE 3. Honorary or substantive official rank and title (*yixu*) cases for selected years in the Qianlong and Jiaqing reigns in the *Like tiben*

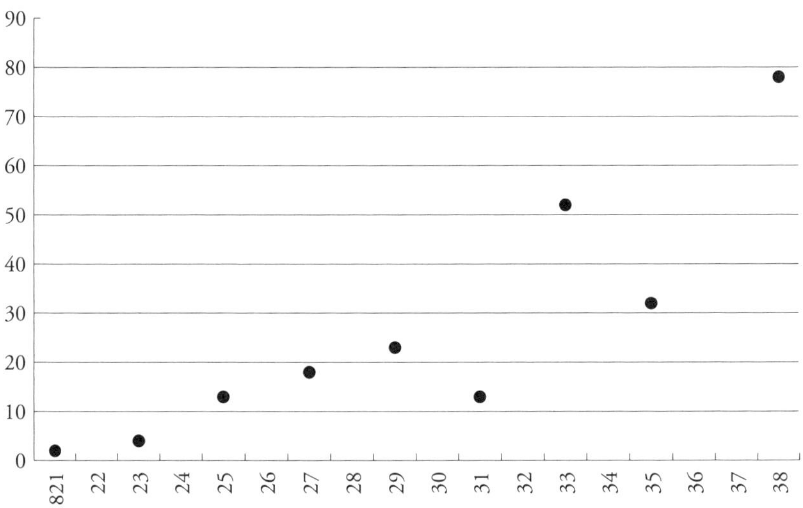

FIGURE 4. Honorary official rank and title cases for selected years in the Daoguang reign (notice change of scale)

of cases, I have chosen thirty-eight years from the Qianlong reign, fifteen from the Jiaqing, and nine from the Daoguang. The number of official rank and title cases for these sample years are indicated in figures 3 and 4.

In figure 3, the number of contribution cases referenced in the *Like tiben* substantiates my argument that the Jiaqing period marked the initial stage of growing public financial and management roles for local elites. The donations climbed during the Daoguang reign as the trend gained momentum (figure 4). It should be noted that the frequency and scale of donations recorded in the *Like tiben* during the early nineteenth century differed from those in the previous period, as they included costlier public projects that demanded greater involvement from the elites and larger sums. In the relief operation set in motion in 1823 following floods in Jiangsu, for example, the donations by local degree-holders, rich commoners, and merchants amounted to no less than 1.95 million taels of silver (detailed in chapter 3), and those rewarded under the jurisdiction of the Suzhou provincial administrative commissioner alone numbered more than 1,000, not factoring in those under the jurisdiction of another commissioner stationed in Nanjing.[18]

Elite contributions gained momentum throughout the empire (see table 1). Donations varied by region, with some—such as Jiangsu, Zhejiang, and Anhui in the Jiangnan area—figuring more prominently due to the concentration of wealth in these areas. In contrast, provinces such as Gansu had fewer contributions, which suggests less wealthy elites in the peripheral provinces of China proper. A variation in preferences of rewards can also be observed. While Jiangxi ranked near the bottom for official ranks and titles, it topped the list for memorial arches. On the other hand, elites in the northern provinces of Zhili, Shaanxi, and Shanxi preferred to be rewarded with official ranks and titles.

Changes in Regulations for Contribution Rewards

The multifold increase in contributions during the early nineteenth century led to more specific regulations on how to recognize and reward them. The Qianlong and the Jiaqing editions of the *Da Qing huidian* (Collected statutes of the Great Qing) show that the categories of public

Table 1
Geographic distribution of recorded contributions during the Jiaqing and Daoguang reigns

Recorded in *Shilu*		Recorded in *Like shishu*	
Province	Number	Province	Number
Zhili	30	Jiangxi	80
Jiangsu	29	Jiangsu	53
Shaanxi	22	Zhejiang	28
Anhui	19	Anhui	24
Zhejiang	15	Hunan	23
Sichuan	13	Sichuan	12
Hubei	12	Hubei	9
Shanxi	11	Shanxi	3
Shandong	10	Fujian	3
Fujian	9	Henan	2
Henan	8	Yunnan	2
Guangdong	8	Shaanxi	1
Xinjiang	8	Guangdong	1
Hunan	7	Gansu	1
Guizhou	7		
Guangxi	6		
Jiangxi	5		
Gansu	4		
Xizang	2		
Hainan	1		
Fengtian	1		
Total	227	Total	242

activities for which contributions could be made had become more detailed and expansive. First let us examine the regulations in the Qianlong edition of the *Da Qing huidian*.

> (a) The ritual that rewards the righteous actions (*yixing*) by constructing memorial arches (*jingbiao*). . . . If there are people who relieve lineage members, neighbors, or other indigent people by contributing grain, or people who repair bridges or roads by donating money, all these people should be rewarded through local officials by constructing memorial arches. If the amounts of donations are large, then the donors should be memorialized and request should be made for official appointment (*xulu*).[19]

> (b) The ritual regarding the interment of bones and corpses. If these [bones and corpses] belong to the members of the Eight Banners or company commanders in the Imperial Household Department, burial grounds should be provided. In departments and counties of every province, charitable graveyards should be created. If there are corpses which cannot be properly buried due to poverty, or unclaimed bones, all these should be collected and buried. If there are among people those who diligently collect and bury the corpses over many years, these people should be given the reward of memorial arch.[20]

By comparison, the regulations in the Jiaqing edition of the *Da Qing huidian* read as follows:[21]

> (c) If, among the *shi* and commoners, there are those who render benefits to local society by fostering orphans, succoring the poor, relieving lineage members by donating money, helping the relief efforts during years of bad harvest, repairing public buildings, bridges, or roads with their money, collecting and burying corpses and bones, they should be memorialized by the Commander-in-Chief if they belong to the Eight Banners, and by governors-general and governors if in provinces. These officials should prepare a document and send it to the Board [of Rites]. If the amount of donation or the value of grain is more than a thousand taels, then the officials should request an imperial decree to erect a *leshan haoshi* memorial arch, and local officials should award thirty taels of silver. If the amount of the donation does not reach one thousand taels, officials should request an imperial decree to award the "leshan haoshi" plaque and deliver the decree to local officials. If there are people whose qualifications merit the *jingbiao* reward but want the *yixu* reward instead, the Board of Personnel should make the decision and bestow official hat buttons.[22]

From this comparison, we can draw the following conclusions. First, the Qianlong edition does not specify the amount of contributions to be rewarded by the central government, but the Jiaqing edition explicitly fixes it at 1,000 taels (c). Although the more specific regulations in the Jiaqing edition had functioned as guiding principles in the Boards of Rites and Personnel in the earlier reign, their inclusion in the statutes in the Jiaqing period suggests the growing weight of contributions.

Also, the list of public or philanthropic actions for which the state promised rewards grew in detail in the Jiaqing period. While the Qianlong edition simply says "relieve lineage members, neighbors, or other indigent people" (a), the Jiaqing edition makes a more specific statement as to the kinds of philanthropic gestures that would be rewarded: "fostering orphans, succoring the poor, relieving lineage members by donating money, helping the relief efforts during years of bad harvest" (c). The Qianlong edition designates only the repair of bridges or roads as public actions to be rewarded, but the Jiaqing edition expands to include the repair of "public buildings" (*gongsuo*) in the list of actions to be rewarded (c). Regarding the collection and burial of corpses and bones, the Qianlong edition placed it in the category to be rewarded with a memorial arch, separate from other "righteous" actions to be compensated with either the *jingbiao* or the *yixu* rewards. In the Jiaqing edition, the collection and interment of bones and corpses is treated the same as other public or philanthropic actions such as famine relief and the repair of bridges and roads, entitled not only to *jingbiao*, but also to *yixu* rewards, signifying the elevated importance of the activity now placed on a par with other "righteous" actions.

The clauses in the Jiaqing edition stipulating that the Board of Personnel would bestow official hat buttons in the event that donors preferred the *yixu* to *jingbiao* reward are also noteworthy. According to the Qianlong edition, donors with large amounts of contributions could receive official appointments. In the Jiaqing edition, however, official appointments were replaced by the bestowal of official hat buttons. The *yixu* cases during the Jiaqing period frequently included honorific official titles and promotion in degrees and merits as well as official hat buttons. Therefore, we should assume that the mention of official hat buttons in the Jiaqing edition also carried the bestowal of honorific official titles and promotion in merits and degrees.

In the early Qianlong years, the central government frequently rewarded donors with substantive (*shizhi*) and not merely honorific official ranks.[23] With the flood of expectant officials awaiting appointment by the late eighteenth century, however, the government found it increasingly difficult to honor the contributors in this way. By the late Qianlong years, contributors were generally no longer compensated with substantive ranks; rather they were remunerated with brevet ranks, official hat buttons, or promotions in degrees or merits.[24] These policies, inherited by the Jiaqing and Daoguang administrations, continued to guide the reward process until the implementation of a new reward program in 1827.[25]

As financial contributions became more crucial for local governments and the reward process more complicated, the state was faced with the need to devise regulations that would render the task of offering rewards more efficient as well as encourage further donations. This led to the enactment of regulations in 1827 for the Board of Personnel. Prior to these regulations, officials at the Board of Personnel determined recommendations for awards based on precedents to assess the social status of the contributors and the amount of their donations. This practice, however, grew cumbersome as the number of cases rose. With the new regulations in 1827, officials were no longer obliged to locate and cite a precedent; rather, they could decide the appropriate reward by referring to the prescribed regulations that matched various ranges of amounts of contribution to the corresponding reward form.[26] Below I have reconstructed the specific details of the 1827 regulations based upon the Board of Personnel memorials submitted after that year by quoting certain clauses.

1. If the lower degree-holders (*shi*) and commoners (*min*) donate two hundred taels, then they will be given the official hat button (*dingdai*) of rank nine. If three or four hundred taels, then the official hat button of rank eight will be given. If one thousand taels, the title (*zhixian*) of the administrative clerk of a salt control station (*yanzhi shi*, 8b). If more than two thousand taels, the title of assistant county magistrate (*xiancheng*, 8a). If more than three thousand taels, the title of assistant department magistrate (*zhoupan*, 7b). If more than four thousand taels, then the title of registrar in the office of judicial commissioner (*anchasi jingli*, 7a). If more than five thousand taels, then the title of registrar in the office of financial commissioner (*buzhengsi jingli*, 6b). If more than six thousand taels, then the title of subprefectural magistrate (*tongpan*, 6a). If more than eight thousand taels, then the title of salt distribution supervisor (*yantiju*, 5b). If more than ten thousand taels, then the title of assistant prefect (*tongzhi*, 5a). If more than thirty thousand taels, then the title of circuit intendant (*daoyuan*, 4a).

2. If someone currently holding an official title or a hat button makes a donation, then he will have added to the amount of his own contribution half of the amount that the lower degree-holders and commoners without either official title or hat button need to contribute in order to be assigned the official title or hat button that he currently holds. He will be awarded according to this aggregate amount.[27] The category of the person who holds an official title or hat button does not include those who possess the hat button of rank 8 or those who have the hat button or official title of rank 9 or below. These people will be considered the same as regular *shi* and commoners (without official hat button or title) and awarded accordingly.
3. Tribute students by virtue of imperial favor (*engongsheng*) or by virtue of special selection (*bagongsheng*), and tribute students who were successful candidates on a supplementary list (*fugongsheng*), these tribute students who have not yet advanced to official ranks should be considered as having the rank of 8b and awarded accordingly. Provincial graduates (*juren*) who have not yet been selected to official positions should be considered as having the rank of 8a, and should be awarded accordingly.
4. Donors entitled to official hat buttons or official titles, if the imperial decree is issued to reward them more favorably than usual (*congyou yixu*), will receive the hat button or official title of the level one degree higher. If the reward is degrees (*ji*) or merit-recording (*jilu*), not official titles or hat buttons, then the donors should receive the reward of having their merits recorded three times.
5. Those who exerted efforts in encouraging donations from people, or who worked as managers (*dongshi*), will receive the additional reward of having their merits recorded twice, in addition to the regular reward that will be offered to them according to the amount of their donations. Those gentry (*shenshi*) or local officials who performed managerial roles or otherwise actively participated in public works, if there is a special imperial decree to reward them more favorably, will receive the reward of having their merits recorded three times.
6. If officials currently holding positions donate more than two hundred taels, they will have their merits recorded once. If more than five hundred taels, then twice. If more than one thousand taels, then they will have one degree added. If more than one thousand taels, then the reward will be calculated in the same way.
7. Officials-awaiting-appointment (*houxuan renyuan*) and those who currently possess official titles or hat buttons, if the amounts of their

donations do not meet the criteria for bestowing an official title, will receive the reward of having their degrees added or merits recorded. If their donations are more than two hundred taels, then they will have their merits recorded once. If more than five hundred taels, twice. If their donations are one thousand taels, they will have one degree added. If more than one thousand, the reward will be calculated in the same way.

8. If a person donates money and dies due to illness before receiving the *yixu* reward, then he will receive a plaque or have a memorial arch erected for him. The matter will be transferred to the Board of Rites and discussed there.

These 1827 regulations prescribed rewards ranging from official titles and hat buttons to promotions in degrees and merits. One of their major features was the Board of Personnel's decision to adjust the practice of differential treatment according to the status of contributors. In the earlier system, lower degree-holders (*shi*) and commoners (*min*) were rewarded differently for the same contribution. Lower degree-holders referred specifically to holders of *shengyuan* and *jiansheng* degrees, official hat buttons of rank eight and nine, and titles of rank nine. Commoners consisted of men, however wealthy, who did not possess any degree, rank, or title. Under this old system, even though commoners made large-scale contributions, the state normally did not reward them with official titles but only with official hat buttons, which were considered one level lower than the reward given to degree-holders, who could receive an official title for contributing the same amount. For example, in the 1815 famine relief project in Liuan department of Anhui Province, *shengyuan*, *jiansheng*, and *gongsheng* who donated from 1,000 to 2,000 taels were awarded the official title of jail warden (9b), but commoners such as an apprentice candidate (*tongsheng*) and a salt merchant received the official hat button of rank 9.[28] In 1827, just before the introduction of the new regulations, the central government rewarded those for contributions in the aftermath of the great flood in Jiangsu in 1823. Degree-holders such as *gongsheng*, *jiansheng*, and *shengyuan* who had donated between 1,000 and 2,000 taels all received the official title of jail warden, but the commoners were granted only the hat button of rank 9. Likewise, *gongsheng*, *jiansheng*, and *shengyuan* received the official title of assistant county magistrate (8a) after donating between 2,000 and 3,000 taels, but for the commoners, only the hat button of rank 8.[29]

The 1827 regulations abolished this distinction and extended the bestowal of official titles to commoners if their contribution amounts met certain criteria. For example, the aforementioned *tongsheng* and salt merchants in Anhui who had donated 1,000 to 2,000 taels in 1815 and received the official hat button of rank 9 would, after 1827, be granted the official title of rank 8b. Similarly, a commoner rewarded with the official hat button of rank 8 after contributing 2,000 taels in the aforementioned Jiangsu relief project in early 1827 would receive, after the introduction of the 1827 regulations, the title of an assistant county magistrate (8a). These changes sought to encourage more generous contributions from commoners by promising them more attractive rewards.

The *shi* contributors benefited from the new regulation as well, as the Board of Personnel now bestowed higher-rank official titles than the previous regulation for the same donation. The *shi* donors, before the 1827 regulations, received the title of a subprefectural magistrate (6a) for donating 4,000 taels. After the 1827 regulations, they needed to give only 3,000 taels to be rewarded with the same official title. In the Jiangsu famine relief operation in early 1827 mentioned earlier, the *shi* whose contributions ranged from 2,000 to more than 3,000 taels received the title of assistant county magistrate (8a). Yet, after the introduction of the 1827 regulations, this title was awarded for amounts between 2,000 and less than 3,000 taels, while 3,000 taels would have earned a *shi* donor the more coveted title of assistant department magistrate (7b). In the Anhui famine relief case in 1815, *shengyuan*, *jiansheng*, and *gongsheng* degree-holders who contributed within the range of 1,000 to 2,000 taels received the title of registrar (9a), but after 1827, the title of administrative clerk of a salt control station (8b).

Another important addition in the 1827 regulations consisted in the special treatment offered to managers of public works projects who showed initiative in promoting contributions or managing the activity. These managers, apart from the regular rewards bestowed on them according to the amounts of their contribution, received additional rewards by having their merits recorded twice, in normal cases, and three times if there had been an imperial decree that ordered a special reward. Local officials sometimes performed managerial roles, but more often they were undertaken by the local gentry. Elite managers who contributed were given not only an official title or hat button, but also promotion in their merits. Even without donating money, they could still be rewarded in recognition of their services in the managerial role.[30]

The special treatment of managers in public works preceded 1827. By 1814, local elite managers in public work projects who donated less than the minimum amount to qualify for state rewards were nonetheless honored by the state in recognition of their service.[31] The Qing employed a similar policy in early 1827 before the new regulations came into existence in the aforementioned famine relief operation in Jiangsu, as a means of actively promoting elite managerial roles in public works.[32] This fact illustrates the growing importance and expansion of managerial service performed by local elites, in addition to the financial contributions of these individuals. As civilian resources increasingly funded public works, it was expected that the local donors would be increasingly willing to take charge of the projects they financed. The state also considered the expansion of elite managerial roles as a necessary condition to counteract malfeasance by local officials and subbureaucratic personnel.

Five years later in 1832, the Board of Personnel added another set of reward regulations, this time targeting officials-awaiting-appointment (*houxuan renyuan*). If the 1827 measures intended to appeal to lower degree-holders and commoners, the 1832 regulations were aimed at officials residing in their home districts while waiting for an appointment to a post. These regulations were designed to offer a faster track to appointment for those who contributed certain amounts prescribed by the Board of Personnel for public works projects.[33] Previously, officials-awaiting-appointment had been granted advancement in degrees and merits for their donations. The new regulations in 1832 allowed them to move one step closer to receiving substantive posts.[34] With the 1832 regulations, the state further broadened the pool of contributors in an effort to mobilize more private wealth for public projects. These regulations underwent some minor changes in 1838.[35] A comprehensive reward program, announced in 1843, reflected a series of changes enacted since the Qianlong period.[36] The primary reason behind such frequent emendations of reward measures was to process the increasing number of contributions more efficiently and systematically and to provide attractive incentives to encourage further contributions.[37]

During the Daoguang reign in 1841, an additional donation category was created to mobilize more civilian resources. This new category, the "Prioritizing the Public and Delighting in Righteousness" (*jigong haoyi*), was set up primarily to reward contributions for military expenses. With the outbreak of the Opium War, the state was forced to spend more on defense, further increasing the government's reliance on elite contributions.[38]

The state's decisions to actively promote donations by elites and accommodate their managerial roles in public works are closely related to the shifts in the Qing's perception of the ideal model of public works management, namely, how best to apportion roles to local elites and officials in coordinating these projects.

Yongzheng and Qianlong's Policies Regarding the Role of Local Elites in the Local Public Realm

A more statist government marked the Yongzheng and early Qianlong years. Throughout this period, the Qing state employed financial resources to intervene in the operations of many local educational and philanthropic institutions, such as private academies and benevolent halls, as well as in the management of public works, such as water conservancy and famine relief projects. The healthy state fiscal conditions buttressed this statist policy and the emperors often ordered the replacement of civilian financial obligations for local public works with government funds. In 1726, for example, after severe floods hit the Jiangnan region, the Yongzheng Emperor launched a water control project in the Suzhou and Songjiang areas. He underscored that the project should be carried out with government funds, thereby saving people from hardships. A provincial official had originally suggested to the emperor that, in accordance with the precedent and to preserve state finances, local landlords and tenants should fund and provide labor for the project, a request adamantly dismissed by Yongzheng.[39] The emperor's confidence in the state's relatively stable finances and his determination to bolster paternalistic rulership found expression in another occasion. In 1733, he ordered the officials in charge of a sea dike project in Zhejiang not to refrain from spending even 10 million silver taels from government coffers.[40]

In 1736, shortly after his enthronement, the Qianlong Emperor proclaimed that the customary civilian contributions for water control projects related to the Grand Canal would be replaced by state funds. He emphasized that donations from individuals increased hardships for those with little actual benefit to state finances.[41] In the same year, Qianlong discontinued a practice in five counties in Zhejiang that assessed surcharges on local land to finance hydraulic projects. For the emperor, the collection methods led to the harassment of locals by yamen runners and local ruffians.[42] Instead, he ordered that provincial officials draw the expenses from provincial coffers and dispatch their own subordinate officials to assume control of the works. The emperor also brought to the attention of his officials the current practice that held local residents liable for the costs of registering households that had sustained damages from drought or flood. He mandated that local authorities should provide the required funds instead.[43] Also in 1736, the emperor forbade delegating financial responsibilities to merchants for a dredging project in the Yangzhou area. He required salt administration officials to furnish the necessary expenses from the treasury of the salt controller and to send government personnel to manage the project.[44] The 1739 regulations that encouraged provincial authorities to request government funds for various water control works if local people could not afford them indicate the continued presence of such imperial vision to promote statist rule.[45]

As shown above, during the early years of the Qianlong reign the emperor sought to transform some of the public works previously carried out through elite initiatives into government-run projects. This policy, however, was later modified as officials and the emperor corrected inefficiencies to again allow the participation of local elites.[46] Nonetheless, the emperor did not altogether abandon his statist approach toward local public works. Even when he compromised by granting a greater degree of involvement by local elites, the hybrid system still necessitated a degree of government control in providing funds and management.[47]

The following case illustrates Qianlong's vision of the proper balance between initiatives by the state and local elites in large-scale local projects. In 1750, the governor of Jiangxi memorialized the throne in requesting that local residents carry out repair works of city walls and embankments in Jiangxi. He suggested that the state should recognize their donations and efforts with rewards.[48] The emperor, however, dismissed it outright, stating that the recommendation was not an appropriate way to handle a large-scale public project. Qianlong explained that elite contributions could be accepted only for small-size public works that could easily be financed by locals or other works originally prescribed to be the responsibility of the civilian population. Works of sizable expenditures, however, were beyond the capacity of local residents. Therefore, even though the government had created the system of encouraging and rewarding local elites' contributions, the emperor considered civilian donations in large-scale works as inappropriate.

The case above illustrates that the emperor envisioned elite contributions for local public works as playing a secondary role, complementing, but never replacing, regular state funds. The Qianlong Emperor's policy delegated to the state the primary responsibility for funding and managing public works. Officials who violated this norm could be punished. In 1752, the governor of Shanxi memorialized that some areas in the province suffered from drought and local elites had made contributions to the government treasury for future relief efforts.[49] The emperor severely reproached the governor. According to Qianlong, contributions of grain and money from affluent inhabitants could be deemed acceptable following a natural disaster. But he did not embrace the idea of amassing civilian donations in the state treasury for remote future purposes. Qianlong insisted that his government had always been generous in alleviating the suffering of his subjects, either by canceling and remitting taxes or through direct state relief projects worth hundreds of thousands or even millions of taels of silver. Compared to such massive use of state funds, the emperor emphasized, elite donations proved insignificant. Qianlong vetoed the governor's decision to store civilian contributions in the state treasury for a need which was not even urgent. He viewed the governor's actions as inappropriate and detrimental to the disaster-stricken local population. Based on this conviction, the emperor decided that the governor should go before the Board of Personnel for punishment.

When the short-term mobilization of government funds proved challenging, the emperor at times permitted civilians to shoulder the expenses of public works whose maintenance had been the responsibility of officials.[50] But in most cases he berated officials who entertained this idea. In a 1764 edict, Qianlong reproached Zhuang Yougong (1713–67), the governor of Jiangsu, for the way he planned to administer pivotal hydraulic projects in Songjiang and Suzhou prefectures.[51] Provincial coffers were supposed to provide more than 180,000 taels for these projects, but the governor needed additional funds to complete them. To make up the shortfall, he proposed to enlist financial support from local elites. He also requested imperial permission to mobilize local gentry to perform managerial functions. This reliance on local elites displeased the emperor. Since these projects were financed largely by state funds, Qianlong said, the proper way to manage them was to dispatch commissioned officials, not to rely upon local gentry. Qianlong did not flatly reject Zhuang's idea of drawing on civilian donations, but he insisted that Zhuang should find a way to avoid resorting to elite funds.

As the edict above illustrates, Qianlong's emphasis on the primary role of the state in large-scale public works manifested itself with respect not only to the provision of funds, but also to the management of public works. The emperor conveyed a similar stance in his reply to Wang Xianxu (1717–85), a censor who in 1748 suggested that the state allow the elite to manage famine relief operations in Shandong and later recompense them.[52] Qianlong maintained that an officially led famine relief program outweighed one led by local elites. If the local gentry took the reins of famine relief activities, Qianlong explained, it could trigger chaos, since the elites, unlike officials, lacked the authority to impose order and were entangled in local kinship networks. The prospect of disorder would further aggravate the already miserable condition of the famine victims. Moreover, government-led famine relief had another merit. Officials could provide more precise records of the relief amounts in grain and silver than local elites. If left to the discretion of local elites, the emperor feared that the accounts of the contributions would be inflated to secure more favorable rewards from the government. Qianlong concluded that famine relief programs managed by officials had unquestionable advantages over ones directed by local elites.

In 1742, the Board of Works reported to Qianlong that officials overseeing famine relief projects often entrusted local degree-holders with the task of assessing damages, frequently leading to questionable management of the charitable efforts.[53] To curb this practice, the minister suggested that provincial officials, along with the regional imperial commissioner, order officials in charge of the relief projects to keep a close eye on fraudulent practices. Accusations should be leveled against any degree-holders attempting to obstruct official operations. The Board of Works also underscored that the officials should personally assess the damages rather than delegating this responsibility to degree-holders. The emperor endorsed all these suggestions.

In 1788, the emperor issued an edict on a water control project in Hubei that had been conducted by locals. Although severe flooding led the government to ensure its funding and management temporarily, eventually the responsibility for this project would once again shift to local residents.[54] Yet, even after its return to the hands of the local elites, the project still demanded official supervision. The emperor deemed unattainable the ancient agrarian ideal of the Well Field system—one in which local peasants pursued the public good—in expressing doubts that locals would donate money for the repairs unless officials intervened. He further required official supervision of future hydraulic works financed by locals.

An edict the emperor issued in 1789 underscored the need for official intervention in a water project in Hubei.[55] The governor-general requested permission to trust local elite individuals with the management of the state funds for the project. In response, Qianlong notified him that it was imperative to investigate and supervise the work, warning him that fraudulent acts by officials or local elites would be difficult to conceal.

In 1793, the governor-general of Liang-Jiang submitted a report on an elite-led hydraulic project in Anhui. Qianlong commented that the risk of embezzlement in elite-financed projects exceeded that in state-funded ones.[56] Although he expected the involvement of local officials in public works, he urged higher officials to strengthen control of their subordinates to prevent malfeasance. For this project, he directed the prefect and the department magistrate to oversee construction of the hydraulic system and required the governor of Anhui to monitor the activities of his subordinate officials on the site.[57]

The relatively healthy state finances buttressed the centralized, statist character of Qianlong's approach toward local public works, especially in the early years of his rule. The emperor also trusted his officials, in particular those in higher positions, to pursue the public interest. As fiscal conditions deteriorated in the early nineteenth century, the state could no longer afford such costly management.

Changing Attitudes under the Jiaqing and Daoguang Emperors

The early nineteenth century witnessed a shift in imperial attitudes toward public works management: both the Jiaqing and the Daoguang Emperors distanced themselves from Qianlong's statist policies. These emperors encouraged public works financed and directed by nonofficials (*minjuan minban*), and they often emphasized that these projects should be shielded against undue interference from officials and their underlings. This indicated that the emperors became increasingly aware of fiscal shortages and understood the dangers of overextending bureaucratic intervention and the possible breakdown of official discipline.[58] The emperors thus sought, whenever possible, involvement by elites.

The imperial edicts on public works dating from the early nineteenth century reflected the government's keen awareness of the state's growing financial pressures, frequently noting that "state revenue is limited" (*guojia jingfei youchang*). In the last years of his rule, the Qianlong Emperor had indicated the fragile state of the empire's finances.[59] But its severity was felt more acutely under Jiaqing and Daoguang. In 1803, Jiaqing urged officials to stop carrying out repairs on low-priority construction projects in the provinces. Government coffers, he added, should not fund annual routine repair works, which by definition were not urgent. Given that "state revenue was limited," the emperor also temporarily forbade any requests for nonurgent public works around Beijing.[60]

By the time Daoguang assumed the throne, the grave worries about the deterioration of state finances were thoroughly rooted in the imperial mind, practically turning into an obsession. Throughout his reign, Daoguang reminded officials that the empire's revenues were limited, urging them to save state funds.[61] Sharing the emperor's concerns, provincial officials often attempted to delegate the responsibility to fund certain public projects to local elites. Faced with growing obstacles in securing sufficient funds, they either proposed their postponement or stressed that the works would be undertaken by mobilizing elite donations or imposing surcharges on local land.[62]

In 1833, a censor proposed that funding of hydraulic projects in Zhili should shift to local elites due to the dearth of state resources.[63] In the same year, the governor-general of Hunan and Hubei reprimanded local officials and civilians for failing to raise resources and deliberately sabotaging a water conservancy work in hopes of borrowing state funds.[64]

Daoguang's reply to a proposed project to dredge three rivers in Suzhou and Songjiang in Jiangsu in 1827 conveyed the transformation in the court's attitudes toward elite involvement in public works. The emperor instructed provincial officials to survey possible ways to mobilize financial and managerial cooperation from local elites for small-scale waterworks.[65] The sea dike repairs in Zhejiang in 1833 also revealed the emperor's concerns about the depleted state coffers. Daoguang underscored the necessity of the repairs to ensuring the security of the residents and the prosperity of seven prefectures in Jiangsu and Zhejiang, the empire's economic heartland. Recognizing the difficulty in securing funds, the emperor required the governor of Zhejiang to report on possible means of financing the project as well as the feasibility of eliciting donations from local elites and merchants.[66]

Aside from fiscal constraints, the Qing court's mounting awareness of the problems in excessive control over public works by officials played a role in the central government's diminishing presence in these endeavors. In his study of the Qing state's granary management, Bin Wong argues that effective government coordination of grain storage that had marked the thriving eighteenth century was no longer as visible in the post-1799 period. He points out that grain storage policies after that period prioritized small-scale granaries run by local elites.[67] The reason behind this shift, Wong explains, was that its proactive efforts during the eighteenth century did not generate the desired results. This fact is exemplified in a 1799 edict from the Jiaqing Emperor concerning the mismanagement of community granaries, corruption, and misuse of funds. To fix this problem, the emperor suggested placing management back in the hands of local wealthy men.[68]

The promotion of leadership by local elites and the restriction on official intervention in public works were not confined solely to the granary system, reaching various public projects, as can be evidenced in the Jiaqing and Daoguang portion of the *Qing shilu*. As for famine relief operations around Beijing in 1801, Jiaqing stipulated that the local elites take the initiative in relief activities rather than wait for directives from officials. Moreover, private donors no longer had to report their intention of contributing, freeing them from cumbersome official supervision. Furthermore, the state assured donors that their virtuous actions would not go unnoticed and would be rewarded.[69] In 1810, upon hearing that degree-holders and commoners in a city in Fujian Province would fund the repair of the city wall, the Jiaqing Emperor warned the governor-general of Fujian and Zhejiang that the contributions and the expenses should be managed exclusively by local elites with no interference from government clerks.[70] Similarly, in the case of a local landowner-financed water control work in Jiangsu in 1816, Jiaqing demanded that local managers take complete charge of the project, prohibiting area officials from intervening. Since it was funded and managed by locals, they were exempt from submitting burdensome financial reports to the central government.[71]

In 1817, a censor informed Jiaqing of an agreement among the local gentry of Changzhou prefecture in Jiangsu for managing future relief activities in the area. Local degree-holders, merchants, and rich commoners were to accumulate a fixed amount of funds on a daily basis. These savings would then be deposited monthly at a local pawnshop to earn interest and, at the end of the year, the local leaders would submit a fiscal report to the magistrate. In case a famine struck the region, the local leaders would withdraw money from the pawnshop for relief efforts upon the magistrate's approval. According to the censor, this initiative gained wide popularity in adjacent areas, such as Suzhou, Taicang, and elsewhere.[72] This standardized relief agreement marked an effort to regularize elite-led relief operations. Its rapid diffusion to adjoining areas reflected the popularity of relief actions administered by local elites rather than officials in the early nineteenth century. The Jiaqing Emperor conveyed his favorable view of this initiative. Comparing this initiative to a community granary, he commented that helping those through local funds served as the appropriate means for famine relief. He praised the measures taken by local elites as virtuous. This was a case in which there existed no impending, urgent need of elite contributions.

The transformations set in motion during the Jiaqing reign continued unabated under his successor. In 1820, upon receiving word of a natural disaster in Zhejiang, the Daoguang Emperor underscored that a relief operation run by wealthy degree-holders and commoners rather than officials would prove more successful.[73] This constitutes a reversal in the hierarchy of public works management from the view prevalent in the Qianlong era that official relief programs were superior to those led by local elites.

With the proliferation of public works projects financed by local elites, Daoguang promoted agreements that regularized the local population's engagement in public works and forbade official intervention. In Henan, for example, degree-holders and wealthy commoners set up charitable schools, funded with interest monies from their deposits in pawnshops. In 1829, a censor requested that the practice of managing deposited funds be transferred from the officials to the donors. In response, Daoguang proclaimed that local residents should draft proper regulations that could prevent misappropriation of these funds by local officials.[74]

The expansion of public works funded and managed by local elites often manifested itself in the form of clashes between the gentry and local government underlings. Clerks and runners understood that the growing role of elites in the public realm led to a decrease in their income, as local elites increasingly took over the collection of administrative fees from them. In the early nineteenth century, tensions between these two groups surfaced, escalating into violent clashes. According to a memorial presented by a censor to the Daoguang Emperor in 1830, two types of convoy soldiers (*bangding*) in Jiangsu Province had been in charge of the transportation of tribute grain. One type transported the grain (*yunding*) and the other navigated the boat (*kuaiding*). The collection of fees was consistently the target of extortion by clerks and runners. To expedite grain transportation, degree-holders and other local leaders of the counties of Jiangning and Shangyuan established a public fund in 1822 and deposited it at a pawnshop. The accrued interest paid for the transportation fee for the convoy soldiers. Clerks and runners were aware that, unlike those soldiers, the local elites could not be easily preyed upon. Having been deprived of a source of extra earnings, the clerks and runners later forced the pawnshop manager to refuse the deposits with the excuse that the interest was more than he could afford. The censor asked for the emperor's intervention to foil the clerks' plot and secure the project's control in the hands of local leaders.[75]

A similar case occurred during a waterwork project in Jianli County in Hubei Province in 1836. This project had been jointly conducted by officials, who raised the required funds, and by locals, who undertook the repairs. After the collection of the annual funds, the county magistrate selected local managers and provided them with the donations collected by the local government. During this process, however, clerks often embezzled donations, leading to a shortage of funds that prevented the completion of the work. To end this practice, the governor-general of Hubei and Hunan dispatched officials, who, in conjunction with local elites, set up a bureau for the collection of funds. Meanwhile, locals selected eight managers and dozens of subordinate managers to supervise the resources. In this regard, locals carried out the entire process—from the levying of fees and receipt of expenses to the project's supervision. The clerks, who were bypassed, retaliated by successfully pressuring the locals to end payments to the elite-sponsored bureau. Despite protests from managers, pressure by the clerks continued, causing the bureau-collected funds to repeatedly fall short of the necessary amount. In 1836, the animosity between the clerks and the literati erupted into a brawl at the bureau. When news of the incident reached the emperor in 1836, he applauded the efforts by the local elites to create and manage the bureau. He also reprimanded the local officials for their failure to lend a hand to this initiative. The emperor reproached the clerks for obstructing the bureau and assaulting the literati, warning the magistrate against sheltering them. His staunch support of the literati bolstered the role of elites in public works management.[76]

While the central government encouraged local elites to play a more prominent role, it did not delegate full responsibility of administering public works to them. During the Jiaqing and Daoguang reigns, the government still undertook famine relief and hydraulic works whenever funds were available and civilian contributions were not an option. However, it is beyond doubt that managerial and financial functions of local elites broadened in the early nineteenth century, especially in the Jiangnan area. In comparison to the Qianlong reign, the Jiaqing and Daoguang periods witnessed growing support for initiatives by local elites. In chapters 2 and 3, the manner in which elite activism unfolded in local public works in the Suzhou area in the early nineteenth century will be more closely examined.

CHAPTER 2

"Civilians Donate and They Manage"

Elite Activism in Hydraulic Works in Suzhou

Chapters 2 and 3 entail examination of the ascendant elite activism in light of their expanded roles in two representative areas of local public works in the early nineteenth century: water conservancy and famine relief. These two chapters will demonstrate that the involvement of local elites in Suzhou in the funding and management of local public works grew exponentially during this period, propelling them to more formal and pivotal positions in the community. As these elites embraced a higher public profile, they also enjoyed greater freedom in their pursuit of cultural practices, paving the way for the dissolution of the highly centralized cultural order once dominant under Qianlong. The elite activism in waterworks and famine relief projects foreshadowed the rise of a cultural order buttressed by more diverse local voices in the early nineteenth century.

In this chapter, a closer look is taken at waterworks enterprises in Suzhou prefecture during the Qing dynasty, with a focus on changes in the procurement of funds and in work leadership. Previous works on the water conservancy system during the late imperial period have delineated the general trajectory of changes in this system. In the early Ming, waterworks were largely performed by means of local inhabitants' corvée labor through the *lijia* system, although the state financed some large-scale projects on major waterways. Water conservancy in rural areas, however, gradually deteriorated as state revenues dwindled and a growing number of absentee landlords residing in towns—many of them local gentry—often evaded the burdensome corvée labor. To redress these problems, a new approach to waterworks projects was introduced and gained prevalence in the late Ming. Based upon the idea of more equitable distribution of duties for local waterworks, it required landlords to undertake the responsibility for providing labor in accordance with their landholdings. Functioning under the principle "Landlords supply food, and tenants supply labor" (*yeshi dianli*), landlords were no longer exempt from duties. In the event of conscription, landlords were required to compensate with either food or fees the losses in income that their tenants would incur from not being able to work in the handicraft industry during the agricultural off-season.[1]

As the state experienced a fiscal recovery and expanded its administrative reach in the early Qing period—in particular during the Kangxi, Yongzheng, and Qianlong reigns—local waterworks enterprises, especially large-scale ones, came under closer bureaucratic supervision and were often generously funded by the state.[2] Waterworks for which the state was unable to provide financial aid were carried out on state loans later reimbursed by local inhabitants, while small-scale works on tributaries or inner-city creeks were financed through the *yeshi dianli* strategy.

However, as Japanese scholars Ōtani Toshio and Morita Akira have pointed out, the depletion of the state treasury led to a significant transformation in the maintenance of waterworks in the early nineteenth century, especially during the reign of Daoguang. The most visible feature of these changes was the multiplication of waterworks financed by private resources from local gentry and merchants and the increased presence of the local elites in the management of such endeavors.[3] After the Taiping Rebellion in the mid-nineteenth century, the *lijin*, a transit tax levied on commodities, emerged as a key source of revenue for these projects along with elite donations, with elites continuing to exercise managerial roles, sometimes through public bureaus or benevolent halls.[4]

This chapter will examine the hydraulic projects in Suzhou during the Qing period so as to demonstrate that the region experienced the transformation described above in the early nineteenth century. Drawing on sources from various county and prefectural gazetteers of Suzhou, it is argued that, compared to the previous century, local elites in Suzhou carved out more prominent roles in waterworks projects as financiers and managers.[5]

The Suzhou gazetteers contain 129 waterworks projects conducted within the prefecture during the entire Qing period, among them four under the Shunzhi reign, thirteen under Kangxi, fourteen under Yongzheng, and thirty-three under Qianlong. During the nineteenth century, the hydraulic projects during the Jiaqing period numbered eleven, followed by nineteen under Daoguang, while the remaining ones were undertaken after 1850.

The ways in which these hydraulic projects were financed in Suzhou can be roughly divided into four types: (1) Direct mobilization of state funds; (2) State loans later reimbursed in multiple-year installments by the community through levying surcharges on the land (*jietang xinggong, fennian tanzheng*); (3) Local donations (*juanshu*); (4) "Landlords supply food, tenants supply labor."

With the increased stability of the Qing Empire under the Kangxi Emperor, the government financed the repair of major waterways in Jiangnan with regular state funds.[6] Certain small-scale waterworks projects during this period relied on labor and funds provided by the local people rather than the state.[7] Large-scale works requiring large sums, however, were carried out with the funds generously provided from the state coffers. For the repair works in 1671 on two of the three major rivers in Jiangnan, the Liu and the Wusong, the state generously expended 140 thousand taels of silver.[8] Despite the request by local officials that state funds be reimbursed by locals who would benefit from these projects, the Kangxi Emperor dismissed this proposal. Baimaogang, a major river running through Changshu County, was dredged ten years later in 1681, again with state funds totaling 56,000 taels.[9] Similarly, drainage works performed in the counties of Wujiang in 1708 and Changshu the following year relied on state funds totaling 3,200 taels and 34,997 taels, respectively.[10] Map 2 shows the counties of Suzhou prefecture.

During the Yongzheng reign, out of the fourteen conservancy projects, the state treasury financed as many as eleven. For the dredging works on Liuhe, Baimaogang, and Fushantang in Suzhou prefecture, the state coffers disbursed 62,577 taels in 1727, although some surcharges were levied on the land of local inhabitants.[11] In 1728, waterworks on the Grand Canal in Wujiang and Zhenze Counties were financed with 19,523 taels provided by the state.[12] Locally financed hydraulic works in the Yongzheng reign were limited to three small-scale works maintained either

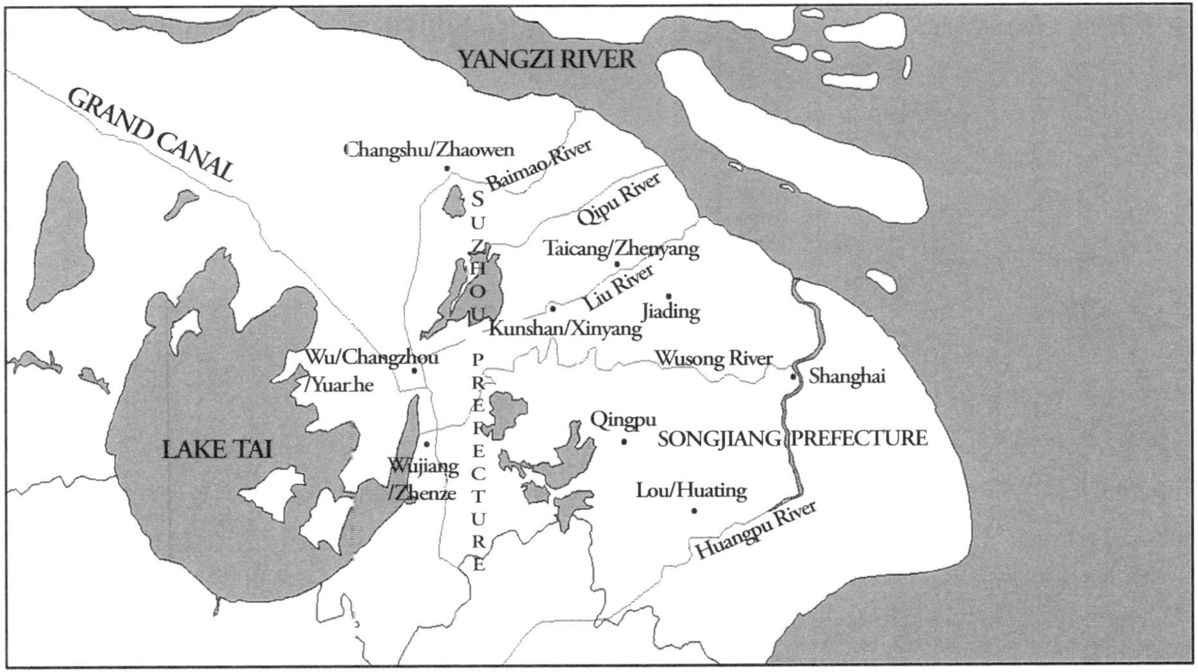

MAP 2. Map of the counties in Suzhou prefecture
Adapted from CHGIS, Version: 5. (c) Fairbank Center for Chinese Studies and the Institute for Chinese Historical Geography at Fudan University, December 2010.

through the "landlords supply food, tenants supply labor" strategy or through the levying of surcharges on local inhabitants' lands.[13]

The Yongzheng Emperor's endeavors to relieve local people from bearing the fiscal burden of local public works were closely related to imperial efforts to promote the idea of paternalistic rule. During the reign of Qianlong, Yongzheng's successor, repair and dredging waterworks projects in Suzhou totaled thirty-three. By breaking down these projects according to the year they were undertaken, we can observe that thirty took place during the first forty-three years of the Qianlong reign, while the remaining seventeen years witnessed only three. The state promoted hydraulic projects in the Suzhou area more actively during the first four decades of the Qianlong reign. The decline that ensued following the first four decades would reflect the decline of state fiscal conditions and the deterioration of administrative efficiency on the occasion of Hešen's ascendance to power.

During the first fifteen years of the Qianlong reign, the government mobilized state funds for water control in Suzhou and attempted to spare local people from assuming any financial responsibility, reflecting a continuation of the policy adopted under Yongzheng. The Qing state, however, gradually began to transfer the financial burden for the maintenance of local waterworks to the local community. As several Qing historians have shown, in the first fifteen years or so of Qianlong's rule, the vigor of highly aggressive state activism that characterized the reign of Yongzheng diminished in some areas of state policies, represented by the government's decision to cut back the storage targets of ever-normal granaries in 1748–49.[14] By 1752, this shift in policy orientation was already apparent with respect to hydraulic works as well, as large-scale waterworks projects in Suzhou came to be increasingly funded through the "state loans later reimbursed" (*jietang xinggong, fennian tanzheng*) strategy until the end of the Qianlong reign. Unlike the direct provision of state funds, this method consisted of a loan to be repaid by locals. Several projects of this nature were undertaken throughout the region. In 1755, for instance, the state treasury provided 21,382 taels to dredge the Baimao River in Zhaowen County, a sum that the community had to return through yearly installments.[15] Similarly, drainage works on the Fushantang in Changshu County were carried out in 1761 thanks to a loan from the provincial treasury totaling about 8,900 taels, an amount defrayed by local inhabitants in two years through the payment of surcharges levied on their lands.[16] In 1764, works on Wusong, Lou (also known as Liu) and Huangpu Rivers required state loans of 221,619 taels, which was eventually paid off by the people of Suzhou, Taicang, and Songjiang.[17]

This reorientation in fundraising represented a setback for the imperial ideal of paternalism since it eventually relieved the state of its obligations and placed financial responsibility in the hands of the local population.[18] The surcharges were collected together with the regular land tax, magnifying the financial burden for local communities. In this respect, surcharges were different in nature from contributions by locals, which, at least theoretically, were voluntary and rewarded by the state.

With the state in the last two decades of the Qianlong reign less prone to initiate large-scale hydraulic projects and increasingly feeling the weight of fiscal pressures, Suzhou confronted the task of mounting small-scale waterworks with its own local resources. For these kinds of small-scale projects, local officials mostly chose to rely upon the method of "landlords supply money and tenants labor" (*yezi dianli*).[19]

The Directors of Waterworks during the Eighteenth Century

For the Kangxi period, Suzhou gazetteers depict local water control as orchestrated mainly by provincial and local officials.[20] They seldom indicate the presence of the gentry in managerial roles in local water conservancy, the only exception being a *juren* actively engaged in drainage works in Changshu.[21] As such, no evidence in the Suzhou gazetteers suggests that local gentry assumed the roles of directors in hydraulic works during the Yongzheng reign. These sources suggest, instead, that local officials, such as prefects, magistrates, and submagistrate officials, usually supervised works.[22] During the repair work on Zhihe Creek in Xinyang County performed in 1731, for example, the local gazetteer singled out the county magistrate as the one responsible for the completion of this project. It is important to note that the same gazetteer mentions that the local community took the initiative in undertaking two projects on the same waterway in 1812 and thereafter (year not specified), indicating the transfer of leadership from officials to local people.[23]

Sources suggest that local officials sometimes enlisted the assistance of local residents. These individuals were not, however, members of the local gentry, but people who occupied positions at the lowest rung of the local administration or water conservancy system. In the conservancy works on Liuhe, Baimaogang, and Fushantang in 1727, local constables (*baozheng*) from each ward (*tu*) were assigned supervisory roles in Kunshan and Xinyang Counties.[24] On the occasion of the dredging works on the Grand Canal in Wujiang and Zhenze Counties in 1728, the magistrate of Wujiang County selected a prominent landowner in each polder (*yu*) and temporarily appointed these individuals as polder captains (*yuzheng*), distributing work expenses to these captains and entitling them to hire laborers for the work.[25] In nearby Zhenze, a similar process of selecting polder captains was employed for the county's portion of this project.[26]

Hydraulic maintenance carried out in Suzhou in the first fifteen years of Qianlong's rule remained in the hands of local officials, with no evidence suggesting elite participation. Instead, one case reports that local constables worked as supervisors of dredging works in Kunshan and Xinyang Counties in 1743.[27]

Developments in the latter period of the Qianlong reign, however, depict the Suzhou gentry undertaking managerial functions on limited occasions. Throughout the Qianlong reign, gentry managers for waterworks appear in only four instances. The first two refer to projects in 1752 and 1764, both undertaken by Governor Zhuang Yougong. While the Suzhou prefect and the Changshu County magistrate led the project on the Fushantang in Changshu County in 1752, conscientious and able members of the gentry class were among those in charge of receiving and dispensing funds.[28] In 1764, Governor Zhuang Yougong launched a second water control project on the Wusong, Liu, and Baimao Rivers that demanded more than 220 thousand taels. Zhuang decided to borrow the necessary expenses from the state treasury, a loan local people would defray in multiple years.[29] For this work, the governor entrusted "gentrymen and elders" (*shenqi*) with supervisory roles, although further information about these managers is unknown.[30] In 1767, the government coffers supplied 20,000 taels for dredging works in Wu County. The governor selected five affluent local residents as managers, with each in charge of a section.[31] Qian Dixiang, one of the five managers, was a *juren* degree-holder who happened to be in his hometown on leave from the post of county magistrate in Shanxi.[32] While all the other four managers simply relied on government funds, the sources tell us that Qian donated voluntarily more than 4,000 taels from his own pocket. In 1785, the magistrate of Changshu obtained approval from his superiors to dredge six creeks within the county. The local gazetteer notes that the managers reached an agreement on the proper ways to carry out the project, although it was undertaken only on a smaller scale after being postponed until 1796.[33]

Apart from these four instances, two other examples from the Qianlong period indicate that local gentry assumed some form of supervisory role in hydraulic maintenance without bearing the formal title of managers. In the case of the Yantie dike project in Zhaowen County in 1766, the magistrate in charge mentioned that landlords supplied the funding and tenants the labor. He also praised the "virtuous gentrymen" (*shanshi*) of adjoining villages and market towns who assisted him with functions beyond his means.[34] In a letter that the Wujiang County magistrate wrote to the Suzhou prefect on the dredging works of waterways within the county capital in 1785, the official demanded the participation of each household in dredging an acreage of waterways in front of their houses. At the same time, these works required the mobilization of local gentry; some of their members were to be selected to oversee the participation of local people in these efforts and to assist less affluent neighbors by dredging the allotted waterways of several adjoining poor families.[35] Nevertheless, those selected gentrymen would not hold any official title as managers. The absence of such titles, the magistrate claimed, would serve to curb corruption. On the other hand, he acknowledged that gentry leaders could exercise some degree of supervision so as to prevent the embezzlement of funds by clerks and runners.

Through the examples above, certain conclusions can be drawn on the nature of the leadership positions assumed by local elites in water control during the eighteenth century. Out of a total of forty-seven hydraulic projects gathered from the local gazetteers for Suzhou from the Yongzheng to Qianlong periods, the projects with any degree of elite participating in the management are relatively few, only six. The establishment of gentry-led waterworks projects does not seem to have appealed to the state during these periods. This stands in sharp contrast to the prevalence of elite managers in the early nineteenth century.

It is difficult to pinpoint with certainty why the local elites were continuously sidelined in public works under Qianlong. One factor might be that state coffers provided the funding for conservancy works, regardless of whether or not they had to be reimbursed. We have already seen in chapter 1 that, in 1764, the emperor reprimanded the Jiangsu governor for his plan to rely upon gentry managers for hydraulic projects largely financed by state funds, ordering instead that commissioned officials should be dispatched for managerial functions.

Additionally, we have reason to believe that imperial suspicions about the efficiency of elite managers further contributed to forestalling its spread. Water conservancy works carried out in Hubei in 1767 illustrate the state's uneasiness with the prospect of an expanded role of elites. Although the responsibility for raising funds for the project in Hubei originally lay in the hands of the local community, provincial officials requested the emperor to provide a government loan in light of the natural disasters that had devastated the region.[36] At the same time, they suggested that wealthy and reliable degree-holders and commoners, under the direction of deputy officials (*weiyuan*) and regular local officials, be selected to supervise the works. In a gesture that epitomizes Qianlong's paternalistic nature, the emperor ordered that the state funds need not be returned, expressing his belief that obliging the disaster-stricken community to repay the loan would only exacerbate their financial woes.[37] In addition, the emperor also rejected the proposal of entrusting local elites with managerial roles, arguing that handing all the responsibilities to managers from the gentry would be detrimental to the project, as had been the case earlier that year when a *juren* degree-holder serving as a waterworks manager embezzled funds.[38] Fearing corruption, the emperor ordered that local officials manage the projects. It is difficult to gauge the degree to which this edict influenced the managerial patterns of waterworks throughout China during the remaining years of Qianlong's rule. It is nonetheless clear that, in comparison to the rulers of the early nineteenth century, Qianlong displayed far less enthusiasm in encouraging installing members of the gentry in managerial positions of hydraulic projects.

The Emerging New Patterns in Water Control in Suzhou

As mentioned earlier, during the period spanning the Yongzheng reign and the first two decades under Qianlong, the state demonstrated a heightened sense of activism by funding local hydraulic works in Suzhou. After its activist stance somewhat diminished, the state resorted to an alternative pattern in financing sizable hydraulic projects, mainly through the method of "state loans later reimbursed." But even this less paternalistic strategy all but disappeared in the last two decades of the reign, giving way to a few sporadic small-scale works carried out with local people's money and labor.[39]

This section will demonstrate that the management and financing of water conservancy works underwent a seismic shift in the early nineteenth century, a transformation characterized by an increase in the number of hydraulic projects carried out on the initiative of local elites. One of the key factors that prompted the changes in this direction was the deterioration of state revenue, as mentioned in the previous chapter. Under these circumstances, the allocation of state funds for water control projects without requiring local inhabitants to return the loan, a practice once prevalent during the Yongzheng and early Qianlong reigns, virtually disappeared in Suzhou in the early nineteenth century. Providing state funds under the condition that the local community reimburse the government treasury, a practice often employed after the first two decades of the Qianlong reign, continued to be an important channel of securing money for large-scale hydraulic works during the Jiaqing period. The Liu River, for example, was dredged twice, first in 1797 and then in 1813, by means of state loans later defrayed through surcharges levied on local people's lands.[40]

At the same time, evidence indicates the growing importance of civilian resources in the maintenance of water conservancy during the Jiaqing reign. The dredging project on the Wusong River carried out in 1818 illustrates this point.[41] This project was planned in 1816 but its start delayed until 1818, as the state treasury was not able to loan the required sum of 283,060 taels. Officials were obliged to wait until they collected the necessary amount through surcharges levied on local land properties.

As Jiangsu governor Hu Kejia mentioned in his memorial, this was "a work based on donations" (*juanban*).[42] For Suzhou at least, this fundraising strategy is not evidenced in the previous century, and it reflects the state's fiscal fragility that resulted in the unavailability of loans from the government coffers.

A number of water conservancy works in this period were also maintained on local elite contributions. In 1807, a resident of Changshu donated money to dredge a creek near the south gate of the Changshu County seat.[43] In 1814, locals dredged a section of a waterway in Kunshan County.[44] Over two years from 1819 to 1821, local gentry and commoners of Kunshan County collectively funded another project in the Zhihe Creek.[45] Also in 1819, a local man in Wu County drew on local donations for a waterway project in the market town of Zhouzhuang.[46]

The growing indispensability of elite contributions in water control was accompanied by signs that indicated the expanded role of local elites as managers of hydraulic projects. These new patterns in waterworks management are best illustrated by two cases during the first years of the Jiaqing reign. The dredging of a creek in the Suzhou prefectural capital in 1796 was initiated by provincial and local officials' donations from their "honesty-nourishing money" (*yanglian yin*), an extra allowance paid to those officials.[47] Following their example, gentry, merchants, and rich commoners in the town also contributed money. The governor of Jiangsu Province, Fei Chun (1739–1811), described the situation: "Money came from voluntary donations and state funds were thus not expended. Labor force came from those hired for money and the corvée labor was thus absent. Gentry in the prefecture managed the work and thus we were able to keep it out of the hands of clerks and runners."[48] Fei also engraved the names of gentry managers and donors on the stele erected to commemorate this occasion. We should underscore that no mention is made of funding requests from the government treasury or levying surcharges on local lands. This project was made possible by donations from officials, local gentry, and merchants.

Although the exact sum of the donations amassed during that time is unknown, it exceeded the expenditures of 21,596 taels for the aforementioned inner-town creek work, as funds left over still covered the repair of dikes and the building of bridges the following year, public works that exceeded 34,900 taels.[49] Encouraged by the Suzhou prefect, the local gentry "willingly" accepted managerial roles in these projects.[50]

These waterworks in 1796 and 1797 foreshadowed the emergence of a new pattern of fundraising strategies for such public works in Suzhou that would endure into the nineteenth century. Local officials usually took the initiative in fundraising by donating their *yanglian* allowance, which served as a call to urge local people to follow suit. This pattern was distinct from the earlier forms of financial responsibilities shouldered by locals. The previous measures included two types: "landlords supply food (or money), tenants supply labor" and surcharges levied on lands in proportion to their acreage. Under this new method, however, the collection of fees was not uniformly imposed. Donors had to be persuaded, and only those who had enough economic resources could contribute. As such, this type of fundraising obviously relied on affluent local elites capable of responding to the call of officials. Albeit they were pressured by persuasive efforts of officials and by the demands of the community, their donations were not tantamount to taxes or surcharges. Unlike paying taxes, they were providing a favor to the officialdom for the upkeep of the local administration and they were rewarded by the state.

The hydraulic projects in 1796 and 1797 also signaled the beginning of the emergence of a gentry managerial system in this area. The establishment of this system received support from the Jiaqing Emperor. Responding to Jiangsu governor Hu Kejia's memorial on his plan to dredge the Wusong River in 1816, the emperor ordered that "upright and affluent managers" (*gongzheng yinshi dongshi*) should be selected. Magistrates should provide them with seals and record books for the collection of surcharges and their transfer to the state treasury.[51]

During this period, a native scholar of Suzhou advocated the installation of elite managers in conservancy works. *Wumen bucheng*, a private local record of Suzhou compiled by Qian Siyuan, contains "A Treatise on the Water Conservancy of Cailian Creek" (Cailianjing shuili lun) penned by his son Qian Shiqi around 1817. Qian Shiqi lamented that no dredging works of the Cailian Creek in Wu County had been undertaken since 1767. Although the waterworks of this creek had been completed with state funds in 1767, Qian argued that it was now inevitable that its funding should consist of local donations from landowners and merchants.[52] He also favored the selection of three to four talented wealthy inhabitants as managers, following the precedent set in 1767. From local scholars all the way up the political ladder to the emperor, the gentry managerial system gradually widened its support base throughout Jiaqing's rule, foreshadowing its blossoming in the Daoguang period.

Elites' Role in Waterworks Management in the Daoguang Period

The managerial system often revealed complexity and sophistication, and elites performed directorial roles at different tiers of that hierarchy. Elite managers worked in close collaboration with the local government, receiving directions from and reporting to the magistrate. Empowered through their new role in local public works, albeit not completely autonomous from the influence of local officials, they performed quasi-bureaucratic functions, replacing some previously undertaken by local officials, clerks, and runners. This managerial system reflected the co-optation of local elites in certain areas of local administration. In this sense, the consolidation of the elite managerial system in local public works can be considered symptomatic of an embrace of civilian participation in local administration in a context marked by a bureaucratic retreat. A similar trend was apparent in the transportation of tribute grain north in commercial ships in the 1820s and in monetary policy.[53]

Local sources indicate that a number of small-scale conservancy works in Suzhou were funded by local inhabitants in the early Daoguang period.[54] For example, the magistrates of Changshu and Zhaowen Counties actively encouraged local donations for the drainage works on the Fushantang in 1826, but they encountered obstacles in soliciting sufficient subscriptions. However, a local named Huang Tai donated sufficient funds and managed the project.[55]

What is most striking for our purposes, however, is that during the reign of Daoguang even some of the large-scale works on major rivers around the Suzhou area were funded with donations from local elite circles, and, at times, their members assumed managerial roles, a trend encouraged by the emperor and provincial officials alike.

THE WUSONG RIVER (1827)

In 1827, the emperor engaged in a discussion with provincial officials on waterworks on the Wusong River. These officials had been well aware of the dire need to maintain waterworks on Liu, Wusong, and Baimao, the main rivers in Jiangsu. An agreement had been reached between officials and the emperor in 1824 to accelerate the works, but the lack of funds forced them to limit the scope of the work to the Huangpu River, which was completed in 1825.[56]

Shortages of funds still plagued provincial officials in 1827. In a memorial submitted in September, the Liang-Jiang governor-general Jiang Youxian (1766–1830) and Jiangsu governor Tao Zhu (1779–1839) recognized the necessity to either end or postpone public works amid the state's fiscal woes.[57] Nor was it possible to employ the method of "state loans later reimbursed," since the disaster-stricken locals were still recovering from the flooding in 1823.[58] Jiang and Tao, therefore, requested that the revenue to be saved by the introduction of sea transport of tribute grain the following year should be directed toward the completion of this project. Emphasizing this argument, they persuaded the emperor that it would neither adversely affect the state finances nor impose economic hardships upon the local people. In an edict issued in the same month responding to a report by Li Peng, the investigating censor of Jiangsu who had requested waterworks in Jiangnan, Daoguang ordered officials to deliberate on ways to collect funds for hydraulic works on main rivers. He also wanted to know whether local gentry and elders could be mobilized to perform managerial roles for branch waterways and creeks.[59] In another edict, the emperor ordered that some portions of the tribute grain collected from Suzhou, Songjiang, and other adjoining areas be exempt from being sent to Beijing, a surplus that would be forthcoming with the experiment of sea transport of tribute grain the following year. Instead, the emperor noted, those portions of tribute grain should be commuted to silver and be used to fund water control in Jiangsu.[60] The works were first launched by borrowing about 260,000 taels from the government treasury, which was to be recovered by the savings expected from the sea transport of tribute grain. Unlike 1826, however, the experiment of sea transport never materialized, leaving the government with no means to procure the expenses required for the works.[61] The central government had no other choice but to agree that the expenses for the Wusong work need not be recompensated. The shortage of about 33,000 taels was filled by donations from local officials.[62] At this time, no gentry members were among the donors. Moreover, the officials in charge of this project preferred local magistrates to elites in management positions.[63] Even though the Jiangsu financial commissioner Liang Zhangju (1775–1849) was aware of the imperial directive encouraging the presence of local elites for managerial roles in smaller-scale hydraulic projects, he argued that the emperor's promotion of elite roles in management was limited to branch waterways, not main rivers such as the Wusong.[64] His objection to gentry managers stemmed largely from concerns that local government clerks and runners would extort money from the local elites.[65]

WATERWAYS IN SONGJIANG PREFECTURE (1827–1828)

Sources indicate that Liang did not oppose installing elite managers in works on smaller branch rivers. In a report Liang submitted to his superiors in 1827, he even praised elite managers who had participated in the various waterworks in Songjiang prefecture in the spring of that year, stressing the collection of individual donations or the method of "landlords supply money and tenants labor."[66] In the case of dredging works carried out on the Puhuaitang in Songjiang in 1828, Liang ordered the magistrate of Qingpu County to deliberate with officials from adjoining counties concerning the selection process of elite managers and the division of responsibilities.[67] Following the Songjiang prefect's meeting with the magistrates of Huating, Lou, and Shanghai Counties and the calculation of the expenses of dredging silted-up Puhuaitang, gentry managers of urban and surrounding rural areas were advised to carry out the dredging works through the strategy of "landlords provide money and tenants labor."[68]

THE DIAO'E RIVER IN WU COUNTY (1830)

In 1830, the Diao'e River in Wu County underwent dredging works following a commonplace pattern of elites' collecting funds and managing the project. The magistrate of Taihu subprefecture in Suzhou initiated the effort by donating his "honesty-nourishing money" and the region's gentry following suit, reaching sums that totaled 15,111 taels.[69] In his memorial to the emperor, the Jiangsu governor Tao Zhu proudly announced: "The gentry managers and others performed the work by making donations, and state funds were not expensed at all."[70]

After the completion of these works, Liang Zhangju, still in his post of financial commissioner of Jiangsu, requested that the central government reward those officials and gentrymen who had either managed this endeavor or provided funds. Apart from those whose donation amounts were less than 300 taels, a number of local gentry in Suzhou contributed between 300 and 4,049 taels.[71] The donors who also worked as managers were awarded additional honors in recognition of their service, such as Xu Xuexun, an expectant assistant controller of the salt distribution commission who had donated 4,049 taels and held a managerial role. Originally he received a promotion in degrees, and his service as manager earned him the privilege of having his official merits recorded three times.[72] Besides Xu, other gentry managers included a *juren* degree-holder, an expectant appointee, and official titleholders by purchase. These managers worked in tandem with the magistrate in measuring the yards and calculating its expenses.[73]

XINGFUTANG IN WU COUNTY (1830)

In the account of a water conservancy works on the Xingfutang River carried out in Wu County in 1830, the local gazetteer describes how a member of the local gentry decided to fund this project after realizing the deplorable state of water conservancy. Pan Zengyi (1792–1852), a *juren* of Wu County and the first son of Pan Shi'en (1770–1854) who would become a grand secretary in 1833, made it his own duty to start the repair work. He first attempted to procure funding by allotting certain sums according to the acreage held by local landholders. However, after witnessing the strenuous working conditions of the peasants, he predicted that the sum to be collected in this manner would be meager and decided to actively lead the repair work by donating funds himself.[74]

In 1833, Pan, in collaboration with other gentry members of the county, led another waterway project in Wu County.[75] In addition to Pan's high-profile role in the management of the operation, his biography in the local gazetteer portrays him as a philanthropic man, who established a charitable estate to assist his indigent lineage members; provided food, clothing, and medicine to those victims from natural disasters; and was involved in virtuous deeds, such as nourishing foundlings or building a charitable school. For his efforts in relief activities, he received the honorary official title of acting director of the Banqueting Court.[76]

LIU RIVER IN KUNSHAN AND XINYANG COUNTIES (1834)

In the summer of 1833, Governor-General Tao Zhu and Jiangsu governor Lin Zexu submitted a joint memorial to the throne requesting dredging works on the Liu River that cut through Kunshan and Xinyang Counties in Suzhou. A similar proposal had already been submitted to the central government in early 1829, but vetoed on the grounds that the fragile economic environment would temporarily hinder the procurement of the resources.[77] In the memorial Tao and Lin submitted in 1833, they emphasized the necessity of works on the silted Liu and Baimao Rivers, estimating that these projects required about 165,320 taels. They proposed that the financial resources would be borrowed from the state treasury and reimbursed within eight years by levying surcharges on lands in sixteen counties and departments in Suzhou, Taicang, and Songjiang.[78]

For the work on the Liu River, the Suzhou prefect and county magistrates led the deputy officials and gentry-managers, allowing them to divide the work areas and take charge of each work unit.[79] They later requested state rewards for those officials and gentry-managers whose outstanding efforts merited special state recognition.[80] These gentry-managers included a *juren* degree-holder named Qian Baoying of Taicang independent department and Li Zenghou of Kunshan County, who was an expectant assistant commander at the Warden's Office. Qian was publicly selected (*gongju*) as the general manager (*zongdong*) by the residents of Taicang and Zhenyang, while Li assumed the responsibilities of the general manager for Kunshan and Xinyang, working alongside another manager, Zhu Dasong (1776–1842), who was also representing these two counties.[81] A senior licentiate by purchase (*ligongsheng*), Zhu earned an entry in the "Delighting in Righteousness" (*haoyi*) biographical section in the local gazetteer for his activism in local public works during the early nineteenth century.[82] This included the leading role he played in collecting donations to repair the city wall in 1814 and his efforts to provide food and clothing to the disaster-stricken after the severe flooding in 1823. That year, he also donated a large sum of rice to alleviate hunger among the inhabitants in neighboring Zhaowen County. Like many philanthropists of his time, he established a charitable estate to assist his less-affluent lineage members, funded the compilation of the county gazetteer by subscribing 5,000 to 6,000 taels, repaired bridges and roads, and contributed money for charitable institutions. The central government rewarded him with the honorary title of assistant magistrate for his meritorious deeds.[83]

The plans designed by Jiangsu financial commissioner Chen Luan in 1834, for the works on the Liu, illustrate the degree of sophistication of the gentry managerial system. At the top tier of the hierarchy, six "general managers" (*zongdong*) in the headquarter bureaus would be responsible for the supervision of all the procedures. Below them twenty "dispersed managers" (*sandong*) scattered throughout branch bureaus would be placed in charge of the apportioned work unit. Underneath "dispersed managers," Chen proposed installing a "rural manager" (*xiangdong*) at each level of canton (*xiang*), township (*du*), and ward (*tu*), who would shoulder the responsibility of supervising the heads of workers (*futou*) of each ward.[84] "General managers" were to receive from officials the wages to be paid to those workers, and then distribute the money to "dispersed managers," who, in turn, would hand it over to "rural managers." The rural managers would distribute wages to the workers and collect receipts, which would then be handed over to the general managers and sent to officials for inspection. Chen envisioned that this system would bypass the usual suspects of corruption: government clerks, runners, and local constables.[85] These elite managers would thus supervise workers and cooperate with deputy officials as well as regular local officials.

THE BAIMAO RIVER IN CHANGSHU AND ZHAOWEN COUNTIES (1834)

In 1833, the Suzhou area suffered from a famine. The dredging project launched on the Baimao River in Changshu and Zhaowen Counties the next year would serve a twofold purpose: improve water conservancy conditions and relieve the poor, as the works would provide local indigents with the opportunity to earn wages. For this dredging project, Tao

Zhu and Lin Zexu proposed raising funds through donations from officials and local elites. They rationalized their mobilization of civilian resources in this manner: "Since state funds are limited, we cannot uniformly request the borrowing of state funds."[86]

Eliciting such donations, however, proved no easy task. Tao and Lin acknowledged in their memorial that successive bad harvests had impoverished even wealthy households.[87] For these works on the Baimao, an expectant circuit-intendant revealed to Tao Zhu his intention to donate 20,000 taels.[88] The man, a native of Anhui Province, had heard while traveling in Jiangsu on his way to Beijing to await his official appointment that the waterworks and famine relief in Jiangsu required a large sum of money. Tao and Lin reported to the emperor that they intended to use 10,000 taels from his donation for the works on the Baimao, while saving the rest for famine relief projects. Aware that the current regulations guiding state rewards could not be applied in this case because of the donor's high official rank, they nonetheless persuaded the emperor that this man should be rewarded given his exceptionally large donation. They explained: "Currently it is relatively difficult to encourage donations. It is imperative that [officials] bestow extraordinary rewards to donors, thereby expecting that this would encourage [future] donors."[89]

To encourage donations from local residents, Tao and Lin contributed one thousand taels each. Subordinate officials followed suit. Financial commissioner Chen Luan visited Changshu and Zhaowen Counties and asked the magistrates to persuade local elites to contribute funds. His pleas resonated among the gentry, merchants, and rich households in these two counties. Apart from 20,000 taels donated by officials and 10,000 taels by the aforementioned expectant circuit-intendant, local elites provided the remaining 80,000 taels.[90] One person donated 4,000 taels while six others contributed between 2,000 and 3,000 taels. Thirteen provided between 1,000 and 2,000 taels, while as many as ninety-five people made contributions ranging between 300 and 1,000 taels.[91]

Similar to the works on the Liu River, the project on the Baimao witnessed the installment of elite managers who cooperated with local and deputy officials.[92] Local elite donors who served in managerial roles accumulated additional honors on top of the rewards bestowed in exchange for their donations. Those managers who did not concurrently make any contributions were still rewarded in recognition of their services.[93]

WATERWAYS IN THE SUZHOU PREFECTURAL CAPITAL (1835)

The water conservancy works inside the city of Suzhou in 1835 illustrate the prominent role of elite activism in the area. In the aftermath of the poor harvest that devastated the region in 1833, provincial officials staged a campaign to raise donations for famine relief. They set up a public bureau and summoned elite managers to solicit subscriptions, an initiative that resonated with wealthy households in both town and countryside.[94] The contributions collected for this "voluntary relief" (*yizhen*) in 1833 exceeded the amount required for relief. After spending more than 130,000 Western silver dollars to alleviate the distressed victims, the government still had 9,000 dollars left in the provincial treasury.[95]

Two private sources added donations: 300 Western silver dollars from the Dongting merchant guild and 1,000 dollars from previously promised but unpaid donations, raising the total to 10,300 Western silver dollars.[96] The gentry leaders in Suzhou's urban center agreed that this money should be channeled into the dredging works on silted waterways inside the city. They found additional financial resources from a private source and recommended to the financial commissioner, Chen Luan, that this amount be used for the work on inner-city creeks. At their request, Chen Luan released from the provincial treasury a sum of 9,000 Western silver dollars to the gentry-managers in 1835.[97] These managers cooperated with the Suzhou prefect and the magistrates of Changzhou, Yuanhe, and Wu Counties. At the urging of the gentry managers, the Suzhou prefect dispatched deputy officials to the worksite to enforce the order. According to the magistrates' reports, however, the role of officials was limited to prohibiting disturbances, while the gentry managed the project, including the supervision of workers.

ZHANGJIATANG IN WU COUNTY (1836)

In 1836, a series of hydraulic works on a number of streams in Suzhou, Songjiang, and Taicang were completed. With the exception of the works on the Yanglin River in Taicang and the Guajing Creek in Wujiang County that were financed with the savings from the dredging work on the Liu River, all others relied upon official and elite donations or the method of "landlords provide food and tenants labor."[98] For those on the six waterways in Wujiang County, for example, the required amount of 8,967 taels was met by channeling 5,204 taels left from the previous works on the Liu and the magistrate's donation to fill the gap.[99]

For the works on the Zhangjiatang and other streams in Wu County, the magistrate of the county considered it difficult to employ the method of "landlords supply food and tenants labor" because the expenses of 2,257,660 cash of copper coins were deemed too high, not to mention that successive bad harvests had exacerbated the tenants' living conditions.[100] Instead, the magistrate set up a public bureau through which elite managers discussed strategies to amass donations from merchants and wealthy households.[101] Several degree-holders, including *jiansheng* and *shengyuan*, took up managerial roles in the bureau. Despite their visits to surrounding rural areas to encourage contributions, these degree-holders ended up raising only about 1.2 million *cash*, falling far short of their expectations. At that time, You Songzhen, a degree-holder in Wu County, managed to persuade the governor to donate 200,000 *cash*.[102] To fill their coffers, elite managers also decided that relatively affluent landlords and tenants should, by the ratio of seven to three, pay together 200 *cash* per *mu*.[103]

The functions of the manager varied depending on the progress of the works. The managers not only encouraged donations, but also drew up maps of the work area and calculated the expected expenses for each stream. When the work was completed, the magistrate recommended these elite managers and other donors for state rewards.[104]

FUSHANTANG IN CHANGSHU AND ZHAOWEN COUNTIES (1836)

Next we will look at the management of waterworks on the Fushantang and two other creeks in Changshu and Zhaowen Counties. The works on the Fushantang in 1836 occurred simultaneously with the repair work on the city wall in Changshu County. The magistrates of Changshu and Zhaowen Counties, along with the gentry managers, calculated that the works on the Fushantang and other related waterworks demanded 37,157 taels, with an additional 21,068 taels for the rebuilding of the city wall.[105] To procure the sum of about 58,200 taels for these two works, the prefect and magistrates launched a campaign aimed at the local gentry and wealthy commoners. The donors included expectant officials, *juren*, *jiansheng*, *shengyuan*, *tongsheng*, and commoners, who either worked as managers or made significant contributions or both and received rewards from the central government.[106]

This water conservancy work on the Fushantang had been carried out twice during the Qianlong period, first in 1761 and then in 1767, through "borrowing state funds and then reimbursing" (*jietang xinggong fennian tanzheng*).[107] The transition from this method to "elite donations" revealed the gradual crumbling of the state revenue system. In such an environment, loans were temporarily unavailable and the dismal economic conditions would have strained local communities, making it difficult to reimburse the state treasury.

PATTERNS OF WATERWORKS MAINTENANCE IN OTHER AREAS OF JIANGNAN

The new patterns observed in waterworks in Suzhou during the Jiaqing and Daoguang reigns were not limited to that region. These newly dominant patterns also characterized hydraulic projects in neighboring counties in the early nineteenth century. The dredging works on various waterways in and outside of Jiangning city carried out in 1830 highlight this trend. A memorial submitted by Governor-General Jiang Youxian and Governor Tao Zhu in 1830 reported the completion of waterworks outside the city of Jiangning at the cost of several tens of thousands taels.[108] Given the troubling situation of state finances, they noted that funds from the central government could not be requested, leaving them with civilian contributions as the only source of revenue for this project. In an attempt to promote such contributions, provincial financial commissioner He Changling (1785–1848) donated his *yanglian* allowance. With the engagement of the gentry and merchants of Shangyuan and Jiangning Counties, the amount of their donations collected within several months reached 40,000 taels.[109] He Changling then ordered the prefect of Jiangning to commission appropriate officials to measure the work areas and calculate the amount of expenses, while selecting competent and experienced members of the local gentry to work as managers responsible for collecting and expending fees.[110] Twenty individuals provided donations amounting to more than three hundred taels, with the largest individual donation reaching 4,500 taels.[111] After the completion of this work, donors and managers received their rewards from the state.[112]

In the winter of 1830, Governor-General Tao Zhu and Governor Liang Zhangju submitted a joint memorial to the throne asking for permission to embark on water control projects on the Mengdu, Desheng, and Zaogang Rivers in Wujin County. They estimated that the works would require a total of about 206,700 taels, out of which 134,570 taels would be destined for the Mengdu River.[113] They intended to finance these works through the method of "state loans later reimbursed," and the loaned state funds would be returned by levying surcharges on local lands in six counties over the course of ten years.[114] Despite acknowledging that the Board of Revenue had halted the undertaking of public works, they emphasized the urgency of such a project. They also guaranteed the throne the repayment of the borrowed funds and persuasively explained that this method was distinct from the expenditure of state funds not requiring local communities to reimburse the central government.[115] Following the completion of these works in 1833, local officials and elites who had offered particularly meritorious services received rewards from the throne. Under the category "managers at the worksite" (*zaigong dongshi*), Tao Zhu and Liang Zhangju listed several gentry-managers, including a retired magistrate, a *juren*, and an expectant official.[116] Many more lower-level elites had also contributed, performing managerial services at various stages. According to a report submitted by the Jiangsu financial commissioner Chen Luan, these managers included a number of *jiansheng* and *shengyuan*, and even those not bearing any degree-titles (which strongly indicates their commoner origin), who took various titles such as "rural manager" (*xiangdong*), "ward manager" (*tudong*), or "manager" (*dongshi*).[117]

In 1834, the water conservancy works on Lian Lake in Danyang County of Zhenjiang prefecture featured two fundraising strategies: the "landlords supply food and tenants labor" for the upper lake, while the lower lake received donations calculated in proportion to the size of taxable lands.[118] The managerial role for the upper lake was assumed by a *jiansheng* while that for the lower lake by a *shengyuan* degree-holder.[119]

The hydraulic works on the Qipu River in Taicang in 1835 showed the state's reliance on the gentry managerial system. Although the project had originally drawn on the "landlords supply food and tenants labor" strategy, the large-scale devastation since the floods in 1823 forced officials to resort to loans from the state treasury to be repaid by local inhabitants over eight years.[120] The acting prefect of Suzhou and the magistrate of Taicang established a set of regulations that mirrored the managerial hierarchy drawn up for the works on the Liu River.[121] As the roles assumed by managers at each level suggest, elite managers forged close working relationships with local officials, and they took on the roles of clerks and runners.

The Significance of the Early Nineteenth-Century Changes in Waterworks

While the 1820s and 1830s can be characterized as a period marked by constant attempts of provincial administrators to promote various water control projects, these efforts in the subsequent decades nearly reached a standstill. Gazetteers record only two waterworks projects in the 1840s after the outbreak of the Opium War. In 1842, an effort was launched to dredge the Wusong River in which a *gongsheng* of Wujiang County performed the managerial role.[122] After heavy flooding in 1849, a water conservancy project was implemented on the Baimao and the Fushantang Rivers in Changshu County the following year, undertaken by funds borrowed from the provincial treasury. These costs were later defrayed by local inhabitants in the counties that benefited from it.[123]

Together with the method of "state loans later reimbursed," elite donations continued to be a major source of financing water control projects in Suzhou throughout the nineteenth century. The installation of elite managers, a trend that intensified during the Jiaqing reign and, in a more vigorous manner, under Daoguang, continued to be adopted in water conservancy works carried out in the second half of the nineteenth century. In addition to water conservancy, the public roles assumed by elite managers expanded to include functions related to policing and tax collection by the mid-nineteenth century. In the early Tongzhi period, the Changzhou County magistrate assigned to elite managers the task of registering population for the *baojia* public security system and investigating the land tax burden, which were in disarray since the Taiping

Rebellion.[124] Elite managers in the Suzhou area controlled various public bureaus and benevolent halls, and they actively sought to expand the scope of their political action and participation in self-governing movements during the late Qing and early Republican periods.[125] Here lies the historical significance of the early nineteenth century in marking the formative stage of elite activism, a period that left an enduring legacy to the historical development of the later nineteenth century. Elite activism manifested itself not only in water conservancy works, but also in another representative area of elite public action undertaken for the common good of their local community: famine relief operations.

CHAPTER 3

Fighting Famine

The Rise of "Civilian-Led Famine Relief"

This chapter compares the patterns of elite participation in local famine relief efforts in Suzhou during the eighteenth and the early nineteenth centuries. The manner in which relief funds were raised and who directed these operations are examined. This chapter will argue that the first half of the nineteenth century in Suzhou witnessed an expansion of a locally based relief system, as elites gradually undertook more prominent roles in the funding and management of such efforts. This pattern stands in stark contrast to the limitations and less ambitious scope of elite-led operations during the Yongzheng and Qianlong periods in the eighteenth century. By the early nineteenth century, elite-led relief operations increasingly came to supplement, or even replace, government relief efforts during famines. This dimension of ascendant elite activism, coupled with the analogous changes observed in water conservancy examined in the previous chapter, strengthened the claims of local elites to formal positions of power in the local administration.

Famine Relief in Suzhou during the Eighteenth Century

As Pierre-Étienne Will and others have pointed out, during the Qianlong period the state-run famine relief programs achieved an unprecedented scale and sophistication, as revenue surpluses provided the state with the means to energetically implement these operations.[1] The efficiency of the state relief system also required a certain degree of local elite participation. Nonetheless, Will still characterizes the eighteenth century as distinct from the late Ming and the nineteenth century, when locally led initiatives gradually replaced the state's deteriorating relief system.[2]

The trajectory of the changes in famine relief operations in Suzhou from the eighteenth century to the nineteenth century substantiates Will's observations. Local gazetteers convey some sporadic episodes of elite involvement in famine relief during the Yongzheng and Qianlong periods, usually recorded in biographical sections or sections on natural disasters. When their home areas suffered from floods or droughts, Suzhou elites donated money or grain to succor the poor or set up relief kitchens to distribute gruel.[3] Wang Nan, for example, a resident of Shengze market town in Wujiang County, designed a set of regulations for relief operations and submitted it to the county magistrate when the county experienced a serious famine in 1755. The magistrate then entrusted him with the responsibility of supervising the relief work for the county.[4] In comparison to the Jiaqing and Daoguang periods, however, famine relief led by local elites was less common under Yongzheng and Qianlong. Elite participation in famine relief during the eighteenth century did not reach the frequency or scale comparable to that in the early nineteenth century.

In the section on "calamities and good omens" (*zaixiang*) in the Guangxu edition of the Wujiang County gazetteer in Suzhou, Xiong Qiying (1837–79), a famous philanthropist of the late Qing, remarked:

> The reign of Qianlong was not a time of extreme prosperity as is referred to by the elders. However, although great disasters such as floods and droughts caused by the disharmony of *yin* and *yang* sometimes took place, history books endlessly record numerous imperial edicts ordering universal tax remissions, tax exemptions, and state reliefs. Notwithstanding, the imperial edict issued in the 42nd year [of Qianlong] reveals that the government [silver] reserves in the treasury of the Board [of Revenue] were still more than seventy million taels. How can this not be a way of accumulating wealth in people and making them live in plenty while still leaving the ruler affluent?[5]

Xiong envisaged the Qing state during the Qianlong reign as the protagonist in relief efforts, pursuing a variety of approaches such as tax exemption and the distribution of subsidies. He also underscored that sufficient state revenues were the key to the state's central role in relief operations. Xiong's characterization of the state as an active agent during the Qianlong period contrasts sharply with the diminished role of government in the early nineteenth-century relief programs. During the latter period, relief operations directed and financed by locals appeared in greater frequency and relevance.

The elite activism during the famine that plagued the county of Yuyao, Zhejiang, in 1795, the final year of Qianlong's rule, anticipated the changes in the general patterns of famine relief system in Jiangnan in the early decades of the nineteenth century. In response to the severe famine that spread throughout Yuyao after the county suffered massive floods in the fall of 1794, the local gentry requested that the magistrate endorse a relief plan financed through local donations. The prefect and the magistrate then led the relief efforts by donating their honesty-nourishing money, which was followed by elite contributions.[6] Cooperation between the local government and elites also extended to the institutions leading the relief efforts. The gentry took charge of the general bureau (*zongju*), with managerial positions being occupied by a former magistrate, an expectant official, and degree-holders.[7] Nine relief kitchens under the gentry's management were established in all four sections of the rural areas surrounding the county capital.[8] These managers encouraged donations and supervised their collection and expenditures, reportedly with no official intervention. The gentry managers, however, were never completely immune from official intervention and cooperated closely with the local government. When managers went about promoting donations, the magistrate saw to it that clerks would not interfere.[9] Despite the presence of the state, the emphasis that contemporary local sources place on the elite's autonomy in these relief efforts suggests the existence of a certain degree of gentry initiative.[10]

Other famine-stricken regions adopted similar strategies. In 1795, relief kitchens mushroomed throughout Baoshan County, Jiangsu. To provide relief for the distressed rural population, a kitchen was established in every market town in the county. This policy was not a novelty in the region. In 1670–71, the county witnessed the implementation of market town-based kitchens, albeit on a smaller scope and limited to certain places. By encompassing every market town, the 1795 operation was more massive in scale and, for the first time, regulations determined where residents of a particular rural region could receive relief.[11] Although various types of locally led relief programs certainly existed during the reign of Qianlong, it was not until the subsequent Jiaqing and Daoguang reigns that relief operations of this style became widely prevalent.

Incipient Changes in Famine Relief

The state granary system that had developed vigorously and expanded under Yongzheng and Qianlong began to deteriorate beginning in the 1780s. Granaries became increasingly less effective in fighting famines in the first half of the nineteenth century, as their capacities gradually dwindled due to the growing problems encountered by the local administration in collecting revenue and the slackening of the discipline of those officials who presided over famine administration.[12] From 1799, the Qing state discontinued official monitoring and coordination of granary activities, signaling a shift from the state activism of the eighteenth century to the expansion of the gentry-led management of granaries that would take place in the following decades.[13]

Suzhou was no exception to this empire-wide trend. By the late eighteenth and early nineteenth centuries, ever-normal granaries and community granaries were already in decline.[14] To supplement the depleting state granary reserves, local officials in Suzhou and Songjiang areas promoted the building of new charity granaries (*yicang*) and elicited contributions from the gentry.[15]

The problems that plagued the state granary system also stimulated the proliferation of small-scale famine relief programs in Suzhou directed and financed by local people during the Jiaqing and, more prominently, Daoguang reigns.[16] The government still continued to offer tax deferrals to disaster victims, but the frequency in the distribution of relief subsidies, a more direct form of state intervention, decreased substantially.[17] Instead, provincial and local officials had no choice but to encourage civilian donations for famine relief, as they did for waterworks. These relief programs, known as *yizhen* (voluntary relief operation), *xiangzhen* (relief operation by the locals), or *tuzhen* (local relief), provided assistance to those in distress through operations funded and led by members of the community.

In the summer of 1804, heavy rains caused serious flooding in most areas of Jiangsu. Starvation among the population fueled a riot in Suzhou. Famine-stricken victims launched a concerted attack on the storehouses of affluent households. To restore order and stability, the central government implemented various measures, including tax exemption and deferral, distribution of subsidies, and reduced-price sales of grain (*pingtiao*).[18] Local officials simultaneously encouraged elite donations for the distribution of gruel or sales of grain at reduced prices, which eventually pacified the area.[19] In the market town of Pingwang in Zhenze County, a *juren* named Wu Shijian actively sought donations in 1804 for reduced-price sales of grain.[20] Changshu County also resorted to the *pingtiao* strategy after a flood in 1804. A resident of the county donated 500 *shi* of grain for famine relief and received as reward a tablet bestowed by a provincial official.[21]

When a drought struck Jiangnan in 1814, the governor-general of Liang-Jiang encouraged *xiangzhen*, or relief operation funded and directed by residents. Elites in various localities responded to his call for action. In the counties under the jurisdiction of the Suzhou administrative commissioner alone, the amount of donations reached 600,000 taels of silver.[22] In Wujiang County, which also suffered from the drought in 1814, a certain Jin Zhiyuan generously contributed to the relief efforts through the cut-price sales of grain.[23]

As the state's role in relief operations receded, local governments devised new strategies during the 1814 drought. With the prefect's encouragement, counties in the Changzhou prefecture introduced the *tuzhenfa* (the method of relief action based on a ward), a locally based relief program implemented in rural areas, with *tu* being a subcounty administrative unit roughly equivalent to 110 households.[24] The *tuzhen* method was particularly directed toward those in extreme poverty who could not easily make trips to towns nor afford to purchase grains even at reduced prices.

In Wujin and Yanghu Counties, the general bureau (*zongju*) pooled together local subscriptions and then handed them over to elite managers for distribution to the disaster victims in each ward.[25] The magistrates of neighboring Jingui and Wuxi Counties adopted a slightly different measure. Unlike Wujin and Yanghu, donations from wealthy inhabitants of each ward in these counties were not pooled together at the bureau. Instead, these funds remained in the hands of that ward, to be used for their victims. Each ward selected a coordinator for the relief work, while the funds were stored in the houses of donors. Officials and bureau managers only kept fiscal records and supervised the transfer of donations to another ward, as distressed residents of poorer wards benefited from the surpluses in more affluent areas. Each ward publicly posted the number of people in need of relief, the donations raised, and the transfer of funds from one ward to another.

One contemporary portrayed *tuzhen* as an unprecedented strategy that garnered success in Changzhou prefecture.[26] The donations collected in Wujin and Yanghu amounted to 134 million *cash* in copper coinage while those from Wuxi and Jingui reached 130 million and 124 million *cash*, respectively. Qi Yanhuai, the magistrate of Jingui who presided over the *tuzhen* efforts in his county, argued that this method motivated donors to contribute because they sympathized with those benefiting from these relief efforts. The limited spatial boundaries and transparency of the operations left little room for official or managerial malfeasance.[27] Besides participating in the *tuzhen* method, wealthy households in Jingui County also set up more than ten relief kitchens in and outside of the city and distributed gruel to the poor, an initiative that further demanded well over 10 million *cash* in donations.[28]

In the case of a relief project carried out in Haining department, Zhejiang, in 1815, the magistrate Yi Fengting appealed to the literary sentiment of local elites by penning poems encouraging donations. Several hundred literati, from Haining and regions far beyond the department boundaries, responded to them with their own poems and donations. Within ten days, the amount of contributions reached tens of thousands of taels.[29] Local elites in Haining department also assumed managerial roles in the relief program. Chosen based on the standards of "uprightness and impartiality," these members of the local elite undertook the management of relief kitchens.[30]

In Jiading County, Jiangsu, thirty-one relief kitchens were set up in market towns for relief operations financed by civilian resources in 1806. Several years later in 1814, donations enabled the establishment of a kitchen in each market town as well as in the county seat. This structure continued to serve as the basis for other similar efforts throughout the nineteenth century. As in the neighboring county of Baoshan, the purview of relief operations centering on a market town and including a particular surrounding rural area became formalized in the nineteenth century, ultimately forming the basis of self-governing administrative units introduced in the late Qing.[31]

Evidence indicates that locally led relief efforts gained ground not only in Jiangnan, but also in North China throughout the early nineteenth century. When famine struck Gansu Province after a severe drought in 1810, the central government generously granted a tax deferral and relief subsidies.[32] Aware of the limited coverage of the state-sponsored relief, Na-yan-cheng, the governor-general of Shaan-Gan, simultaneously promoted a program directed and funded by local elites. Na-yan-cheng also officially allowed local elites to survey the hardships experienced by each household, thereby bypassing government clerks and local constables who had routinely performed these roles.[33] Na-yan-cheng grounded his decision on the justification that local elites possessed a thorough understanding of local conditions and could also act to prevent malfeasance by clerks and local constables.

A massive operation mounted in response to a drought in Henan Province in 1813 further exemplifies the growing weight of local elites in famine administration in North China. To provide relief, the central government deferred tax collection and also mobilized state funds for the distribution of subsidies.[34] At the same time, officials at the provincial and county levels contributed donations and actively encouraged local elites to follow suit. Magistrate reports from various counties and departments depict a similar pattern of local relief operations in Henan. Officials aroused interest in the relief projects among the local community by being the first to contribute; degree holders, merchants, and other wealthy households followed the lead, and the donations served to open relief kitchens in towns and in the countryside.[35] These kitchens remained under the management of local elites, with interference from government clerks and runners strictly prohibited. Luoyang County, for example, boasted about eighty kitchens, known as "gentry kitchens" (*shencang*).[36] The relief operations carried out in Henan in 1813 testify to the fact that in North China too, local elites had emerged as an indispensable partner in famine administration, both as sources of funds and as managers of the operations.[37]

Proliferation of Elite-Led Relief Operations

THE ROLE OF PROVINCIAL OFFICIALS IN ENCOURAGING GENTRY DONATIONS: THE CASE OF LIN ZEXU

During the Daoguang reign, local relief programs directed and financed by the local elites fully blossomed in Suzhou and other parts of the Jiangnan area. Faced with the constraints of the state's deteriorating fiscal conditions, provincial and county officials endeavored to enlist the aid of local elites in famine administration, as they did with hydraulic projects. The ability of these officials to solicit subscriptions from local elites without causing their explicit discontent constituted a pivotal issue for the state.

These points are well illustrated by Lin Zexu, who held provincial posts in Jiangsu during the first decades of the Daoguang reign. In response to the great flood that swept the province in the summer of 1823, the central government decided to mobilize about 1.1 million taels to feed the disaster-stricken people during the winter.[38] Lin Zexu predicted, however, that the state revenues would only be sufficient to maintain the relief efforts for a limited time. Additional funding was in dire need to sustain the relief efforts. Hence, provincial and local officials desperately sought to mobilize the help of local elites. Through a concerted effort, the magistrates amassed donations from local elites in Jiangsu Province totaling more than 1.95 million taels, surpassing the amount of state relief funds granted on this occasion.[39]

As the Jiangsu judicial commissioner, Lin Zexu issued a proclamation in 1824 that emphasized the prominent role of officials in soliciting civilian funds.[40] From the governor-general down to the county magistrates, Lin stated, officials should first donate their *yanglian* allowance and establish bureaus (*ju*) to elicit civilian donations. To underscore the socioeconomic benefits of the contributions to donors, Lin insisted that relieving the poor was none other than a means to secure the wealth of the affluent. At the same time, doing so elevated one's social reputation and prestige, since donors would be praised by the locals and be rewarded by the government. On other occasions, he argued his case from a religious standpoint, noting that donors would be posthumously rewarded by heaven through the accumulation of "virtuous merits" (*yingong*). He warned the local elites: If the gentry and the affluent hesitated to donate even when their superiors, the local officials, had done so, how would the former have the courage to face the latter? If all counties had contributed with donations, with the exception of one, he continued, how would the people in that county face the others? He then raised the example of the elites in Jiading and Baoshan Counties, praising them for funding famine relief operations originally planned to be carried out with government resources, thereby aiding the government to save revenue.[41] Lin commended their actions as truly righteous deeds prioritizing public interest. At the same time, Lin criticized those who often hesitated in responding to the magistrates' call for donations, out of suspicion that "donations" were in fact tantamount to "extortion." Lin Zexu's carefully crafted arguments in his 1824 proclamation reflect the difficulties officials encountered in soliciting subscriptions from the local population, while at the same time highlighting the indispensability of the local elites in financing and administering the famine relief system.

THE 1823 FAMINE RELIEF OPERATIONS IN SUZHOU

The deluge that hit the Suzhou area in 1823 triggered a calamity that necessitated relief operations organized by local elites. Changzhou County native Peng Yunzhang (1791–1862) documented these efforts in his "Record of the Famine Relief by the Locals in 1823" (*Jiwei xiangzhen ji*).[42] Poor families in Suzhou benefited from the relief funds graciously distributed by the Qing court, noted Peng. Locals eventually supplemented state relief efforts, with county officials first initiating the project through their own donations, prompting contributions from the local gentry and rich commoners that Peng estimated at tens of thousands of taels.[43] Peng proudly stressed that no less than several hundred thousand lives had been saved through this "relief operation by the locals." Enumerating the advantages of this initiative, he explained that the local relief program not only benefited the poor households, but also saved the affluent from worries about riots among the poor. He thus labeled these local relief efforts as "the way of making all peaceful" (*jun'an zhi dao*).[44] On these grounds, he blamed the rich households who attempted to hide their wealth in hopes to avoid making contributions. Peng criticized these "foolish people," noting that they were guided by the desire to pursue immediate interests without being able to foresee the impending harm of their actions. He then eulogized the local officials and the members of the local gentry class who had contributed their wealth for the famine relief efforts, and he described various honors and benefits showered upon the donors, including memorial arches, exemption from corvée labor, and records of their names in history books. Peng was explicit about the nature of the transaction between contributions and state rewards. Honor (*rong*) is something that all the rich desire, Peng insisted, and benefit (*li*) is something that the poor needed. Exchanging honor with benefit, he concluded, would satisfy both parties.

In another record on the relief efforts in 1823, Peng specifically described his own role in the 1823 famine relief program. He detailed the manner of his participation in the sale of grain, by which he purchased, transported, and sold grain at reduced prices.[45] This method actually bore a particular family brand, having been inherited from Peng Shaosheng (1740–96), his granduncle.

Peng Shaosheng, a renowned philanthropist, had frequently employed reduced-price sales of grain in a ward. Peng distributed tickets to the hungry masses. To prevent duplicate sales to the same person, Peng printed the date of sale on the tickets, thus broadening the pool that would benefit from his efforts.[46] In a similar vein, he also capped the amount of grain sold to three *sheng*. Peng Shaosheng's particular brand of *pingtiao* was replicated by Peng Yunzhang's uncle in 1804 and in 1805. When Suzhou suffered from natural disasters—droughts in 1814 and 1819 and a devastating flood in 1823—another uncle of Peng resorted to his family's *pingtiao* strategy to contribute to the relief efforts. He generally limited the scope of his operations to one ward, although at times he expanded it to three.[47] Acting independently from his uncle, Peng Yunzhang also launched a *pingtiao* sale outside Suzhou city's Feng gate in 1823. The money for this project was channeled through the donations of over a thousand taels from his own pocket as well as from other contributors. When he heard that the residents of the lowlands in the eastern suburb were subsisting on the bark of elm trees, he redirected his efforts to that area and sold grain at reduced prices. He also purchased dried potatoes in Zhapu,

Zhejiang, and transported them to the eastern suburb to sell them at lower prices. Peng noted that other like-minded people led similar relief efforts elsewhere.

Local gazetteers for Suzhou contain far more entries of local philanthropy during the early decades of the 1800s than in the previous century. This biographical information particularly abounds in various episodes describing local philanthropic actions undertaken in the wake of the famine in 1823.

The gazetteer for Kunshan and Xinyang Counties records that the flooding in 1823 sparked disturbances among the victims, who targeted the storehouses of the affluent. This unrest prompted the wealthy households to donate funds to alleviate the distress among the famine victims and appease the rioters.[48] The gazetteer features numerous personal biographies of those who embraced philanthropy in the aftermath of the flood, among them Zhu Dasong, a native of Kunshan County. In addition to providing food and clothing to the victims, he also funded programs to repair the city wall and for relief efforts in adjoining Zhaowen County.[49] Another Kunshan native, Jin Dayong, assumed the managerial role in the relief operations at the request of the county magistrate.[50] Lu Xuejian, a *jiansheng* and a resident of Chenmu market town in Kunshan County, sold grain at reduced prices and participated in other relief measures.[51] A local native of Kunshan named Jin Chenglie empathized with the famine-stricken population, contributing money and land to build a charitable institution.[52] Another man from Kunshan contributed to the effort by distributing gruel, selling grain at reduced prices, and providing medicine and clothing.[53]

Wujiang County also witnessed local elite-led relief operations during this period after flood waters retreated in 1823. The county magistrate resorted to gentry managers, expecting that they would solicit donations from wealthy households.[54] Tao Rong, for example, donated grain for relief, and he was compensated by the state with a reward.[55] Likewise, the contributions of Cai Weichuan, a *juren* and a resident of Lili market town in Wujiang, earned him a government reward. His efforts in succoring the poor and his weak neighbors were featured in the local gazetteer.[56] Wang Kun, a holder of official-title by purchase and a resident of Shengze market town in Wujiang, was asked by the county magistrate in 1823 to take control of the relief expenses for the entire county, an offer he persistently declined. Wang, however, mapped out a set of regulations to guide the relief program and submitted it to the provincial authorities. He set up kitchens and distributed grain on a daily basis to the hungry masses for three months.[57]

THE ROLE OF MANAGERS IN THE FAMINE RELIEF OPERATION IN 1823: THE CASE OF FEI LANCHI

Fei Lanchi, a native of Zhenze County and a former junior compiler in the Hanlin academy (*js* 1802), personified the changes in the management of famine relief in the early nineteenth century. After a brief career as an official in Beijing, he returned to his hometown and never again held a government post. When the flood waters hit the area in 1823, he had long been ensconced in the local social circle, lecturing at a private academy and interacting with renowned local figures.[58] Fei was also actively engaged in various charitable activities in his hometown, which attracted the attention of local gazetteers. In 1823, he set up the Public Bureau of Benevolence and Virtue, a charitable institution based in his residence within the county seat.[59] He built another one, presumably in the same year, in the neighboring market town of Tongli.[60] These two institutions specialized in burying unclaimed corpses and providing shelter to abandoned children. Fei collected subscriptions from local residents and launched an operation to save the coffins that had been swept away by floodwaters. In the absence of land to bury the bodies in his hometown, he would send the coffins to the Suzhou prefectural seat. As a growing number of poverty-stricken households abandoned their children in an attempt to subsist during the famine, his organizations led the work of taking in the children and sending them to a higher charitable institution in the Suzhou prefectural capital.[61]

Fei also assumed the directorial role as a manager in the 1823 relief operation in his hometown, and he left a record of this operation, which illuminates its modus operandi. The rains in the spring and summer of 1823 in Wujiang and Zhenze Counties caused rivers to overflow, leading to the inundation of many areas and incurring serious damages to crops.[62] Locals braced for the looming threat of starvation. At this point, Fei wrote a letter to Cheng Bangxian (1767–1832, *js* 1802), who was serving as provincial censor of the Jiangxi Circuit. Cheng also hailed from Zhenze County and had passed the *jinshi* exam together with Fei in 1802.[63] In the letter, Fei expressed his concerns about the impending famine and emphasized that the key to the success of relief efforts lay in the hands of eligible and qualified local officials. But Fei raised doubts about the competence of the local officials in Suzhou to conduct relief efforts in earnest that would bring concrete benefits to the starving population. Reminding Cheng of the strategic importance of Jiangsu and Zhejiang, he pointed out that the region was the source of a substantial portion of state revenue and home to a large population.[64] Since Cheng was a censor who had the obligation and the privilege to report on regional matters, Fei urged him to inform the throne directly on the severity of the disaster and the problems encountered in the past relief efforts. Through these efforts Fei hoped that the Qing court in Beijing would order provincial officials to appoint the most competent officials to carry out the relief operation.

Predicting that state relief would be insufficient to alleviate the hungry masses, Fei reminded Cheng that these efforts would be supplemented by the locally managed relief (*tuzhen*). He underscored the high expectations among the local population of the benefits they would reap from this program.[65] Fei also attempted to persuade Cheng that the current state reward system for donors was insufficient to promote donations and proposed that an extraordinary reward package should be designed. If Cheng shared these views, Fei added, he should memorialize the throne on his behalf for imperial endorsement.

In Fei's other writings on this operation in 1823, he details the emergence of *xiangzhen* efforts in his hometown to emphasize the pivotal role of elite activism. Despite the generous state subsidies allocated to Wujiang and Zhenze Counties in the wake of the 1823 floods, they proved insufficient to alleviate the victims. The provincial officials thus pushed local magistrates to urge affluent households to donate grain and money for an operation managed by local inhabitants.[66] Fei recorded that this *xiangzhen* relief effort was launched in other adjoining areas in Suzhou, Songjiang, and Changzhou prefectures and Taicang independent department as well as in Wujiang and Zhenze Counties. Elite-led operations, noted Fei, expanded throughout Jiangnan, acting as a crucial component of a changing relief system.

Local gazetteers credited Fei with leading the first locally led relief operation (*xiangzhen)* in the history of Wujiang and Zhenze Counties, praising him for launching the efforts by donating funds and taking control of the distribution of relief money.[67] Another gazetteer also pointed out the unprecedented nature of the 1823 *xiangzhen* in its hometown history, while praising Fei for successfully eliciting donations and not relying on local officials for the distribution of relief money.[68]

Fei himself also noted the unprecedented nature of these *xiangzhen* efforts. While not excluding the possibility that this might not have been the first time Jiangnan elites resorted to a *xiangzhen* relief operation, he nonetheless underscored the extraordinary nature of the one that required broader participation of local residents in 1823. For Wujiang and Zhenze Counties, Fei indicated, such an operation was unprecedented: "There has previously been no *xiangzhen* in Wujiang and Zhenze Counties."[69] These counties had never implemented *xiangzhen* relief, continued Fei, not even when natural calamities struck the region in 1769, 1785, and 1804. Amid the crisis that swept through Jiangnan during a drought in 1814, the governor-general of Liang-Jiang actively encouraged *xiangzhen*. Despite the soaring prices of grain in Wujiang and Zhenze, Fei lamented, no attempt had been made in these counties to mount a relief project based upon local donations. He noted that the only instance that involved some degree of local participation had occurred during the distribution of gruel in 1755. However, the distribution of gruel, Fei explained, was a relief operation sustained on a limited supply of funds, a strategy usually employed amid few donations and numerous victims. The distribution of gruel certainly differed in scale from that of relief money to victim households.[70]

Fei then examines the emergence of the *xiangzhen* operation, portraying it as a turning point in the transformation of the relief system.[71] After witnessing the extent of the disaster, the provincial government ordered that subscriptions should be solicited from the local elites. Then a provincial financial commissioner or judicial commissioner, along with the Suzhou prefect, initiated the *xiangzhen* project in Wujiang County during an official trip to the area. When bureaus (*ju*) were first established to collect donations, local people, perhaps not accustomed to donating funds for such purposes, grew suspicious and criticized such efforts, leading some magistrates to consider abandoning it. Fei credited provincial officials for their relentless efforts to rescue and support the project, eventually pushing this operation forward successfully. According to his calculations, the total contributions from the two counties of Wujiang and Zhenze exceeded 100,000 taels. Despite candidly admitting that not all the donations had been voluntary, he nonetheless appreciated the impact of these efforts on the famine victims: "*Xiangzhen* has brought great benefits to the people of Suzhou."[72]

Fei characterized this endeavor as a path-breaking change in relief institutions. Funds were collected from local sources and managed by the local wealthy households. Bureaus were established for the distribution of grain, for example, in the market towns of Shengze and Zhenze, in Wujiang and Zhenze Counties, respectively. In other urban and rural areas, funds were distributed to each household enrolled in the Registrar of Relief, originally used for regular state relief. This method, Fei argued, resembled state relief (*lizhen*), although in this case the funds originated from civilians. He estimated that the project benefited well over 300,000 people. He articulated his optimism in regard to elite activism nicely: "The benefit provided through *xiangzhen* to Wujiang and Zhenze Counties is tremendous."[73]

Fei's explanations capture the significance of the 1823 *xiangzhen* operation, the first such endeavor in the history of his hometown. As Fei proudly noted, civilian donations reached unprecedented levels, and the relief funds were distributed to each distressed household under the supervision of elite managers. Unlike handing out gruel, the distribution of relief funds demanded larger sums and constituted a more complex administrative process, a procedure that resembled one undertaken with government support and funds.

The 1823 relief operations in Wujiang and Zhenze Counties included a certain degree of involvement of provincial and local officials. They first introduced these operations to the localities and actively encouraged the participation of local elites. Close cooperation with officials, however, did not mean that local elite managers functioned as mere executors of the magistrates' directives. In fact, these managers staked out a space in which they exercised considerable decision-making power and discussed problems with a certain degree of autonomy from local magistrates. The functions regarding the distribution of relief money serves as an example that testifies to their initiative. The bureau managers in urban and rural centers formed a network through which they communicated and cooperated in tandem with one another, as attested in Fei's correspondence with Zhao Zhihe, a *juren* degree-holder apparently working as a bureau manager in the county seat.[74] Local managers from the elites worked through bureaus, which were established throughout the county, including its seat and the scattered market towns located at the nodes of vast rural areas.[75] The managerial network linking urban and rural centers functioned as a channel for discussions and decision making among the managers themselves, as suggested below.

In the wake of the relief efforts in 1823, managers had to decide how to dispose of donations left over from the relief efforts. Portions of the donations stored in the bureaus in market towns (*xiangju*) were transferred to the central bureau in the county seat. The managers in the central bureau decided that the funds still available in market town bureaus should be handed over to the central bureau to cover the expenses for the rebuilding of the Confucian Temple as well as future repair works on the Guandi Temple and the Shrine for Three Loyalists (*Sanzhong ci*), all located within the county seat.

A manager of the relief operations in his county, Fei commented in a letter to Zhao that the central bureau's decision to spend the money on the repair of the Confucian Temple would encounter little opposition from the managers in market town bureaus, possibly because of its cultural significance. He also praised various terms agreed upon by the central bureau managers, such as the selection of work managers from both the towns and the countryside and the printing of expense receipts. Fei, however, gently took issue with their decision to mobilize the remaining donations for future repair of other shrines in the city. He pointed out the possibility that the decision might encounter resistance, bringing to Zhao's attention the case involving the managers at the Luxu town bureau. They had filed numerous petitions with the local authorities to reclaim funds that had been transferred from their market town to the central bureau during the relief operations. The Luxu bureau planned to reclaim its money to cover expenses of the town's charitable institutions. Although the central bureau eventually prevailed over the managers at Luxu, Fei pointed out that this case illustrated the kinds of obstacles it would encounter from the localities in such matters. Likewise, to finance the town's charity granary, a manager in Lili, a town southeast of the Wujiang County seat, had also attempted to safeguard funds from transfer to the central bureau. Amid this environment, Fei predicted that the central bureau's decision to channel the remaining donations in market towns into its coffers for future works in the city would certainly invite opposition from rural managers.

To assuage the discontent of rural managers, Fei proposed that the central bureau should first try to minimize the expenses required for the repair of the Confucian Temple. He suggested inviting managers from the market town bureaus to the county seat for face-to-face meetings to ascertain the amount of donations not yet submitted to the central bureau and the total funds originally stored in the rural bureaus. The managers of both city and market towns should reach a consensus on spending the remaining donations and then report the plan to the county magistrate.

Fei was concerned that the possible tensions between the central and town bureaus over this issue would jeopardize future famine relief efforts. He stressed to Zhao that such a consensus between urban and rural managers over the remaining funds was pivotal for the system. Sidelining rural elites from the management of donations, Fei argued, would provide them with a pretext to adopt a passive stance in future famine relief operations. If this occurred, Fei feared that rural elites would dismiss a call for donations in the aftermath of natural disasters by arguing that "rural people made contributions and the city people filled their stomachs with them."[76] Fei warned Zhao about the danger of alienating rural managers and monopolizing the power of decision making in the hands of the central bureau.[77]

Paralleling the changes in hydraulic control, managers from elite circles emerged as key players in relief operations in the early nineteenth century, undertaking the role of soliciting subscriptions and directing the efforts. These managers, as in waterworks projects, forged and operated in a system of networks that spanned urban and rural areas. Collaboration was pivotal, not only with local officials, but also among themselves.

1823 FAMINE RELIEF OPERATIONS IN OTHER AREAS OF JIANGNAN

The spread of elite-led relief operations in this period was not a phenomenon unique to Suzhou, but one that gained traction throughout other areas in Jiangnan.

1823 relief efforts in Taicang and Zhenyang As in Suzhou, the adjoining independent department of Taicang and Zhenyang County were also submerged by heavy rains in 1823. Apart from the distribution of relief subsidies and the exemption or deferral of tax collections granted by the state, the local gentry and wealthy households of the area mounted a relief operation based on their donations.

In Taicang, the sum of donations amounted to 4,117,620 *cash*, while in Zhenyang it reached 12,110,400 *cash*.[78] To supervise the relief efforts in Zhenyang, a general bureau was established, with managerial positions staffed by four members of the local gentry and eight "ward-managers" (*tudong*) from rural areas.[79] In addition to the distribution of relief aid to the victims, the *pingtiao* measure was introduced and a number of elite-managed kitchens established. To purchase grain for cut-price sales, the Taicang magistrate borrowed 40,000 taels from the provincial treasury.[80] The grain was then distributed to managers who received it in the department capital and sold it in rural areas below the market prices. Elite managers also procured grain elsewhere for similar sales in their home areas. The gentry shouldered the difference between the actual sales prices and market prices.[81]

Water conservancy works also functioned as a measure designed to fight the famine in 1823. Besides enhancing commercial and transportation networks, these dredging works also served as an opportunity to feed many among the starving population, who were hired as laborers for the works. After the 1823 flood, waterworks projects commenced on three rivers that cut through the Taicang and Zhenyang areas: the Liu, Qipu, and Zhujing. Costing about 7,800 taels, the work on the Liu River was supervised by a specially commissioned official—originally a police chief—and a number of gentry managers.[82] Many of them actively contributed to famine-related relief operations through donations.

While the management of the Liu River project counted with a heavy presence of the local gentry, the work on the Qipu was largely overseen by a commissioned official and subbureaucratic personnel.[83] Both projects benefited from local gentry donations. With the work on the Qipu estimated at slightly less than 3,000 taels, the total expenses for the two projects reached about 10,800 taels.[84] To finance the project, the local gentry provided 868,600 *cash* to supplement the 8,814 taels drawn from the government treasury.[85]

The work on the Zhujing, completed in the fall of 1823, engaged massive local elite involvement, both as sources of funds and as managers. Apart from a police chief specially commissioned to expedite the work, the managerial board was composed of twelve members of the local elite.[86] The project expenses were fully financed by these elites.[87]

Besides the distribution of relief money, cut-price sales of grain, or the initiation of waterworks, the local elites of Taicang and Zhenyang also participated in various other philanthropic activities: establishing and managing foundling homes, infirmaries, and poorhouses as well as providing clothes, medicine, and coffins.[88]

In response to the flood disaster that struck Taicang and Zhenyang in 1823, the state spent a total of 54,887 taels for official state relief efforts in addition to the usual tax deferrals and exemptions granted to the victims.[89] The amount was equivalent to roughly 65,864,400 *cash*.[90] Apart from these funds, an additional sum of 74,546,761 *cash* was mobilized for various other relief measures described above.[91] Of this amount, individuals among the local elites provided 44,068,950 *cash*, while donations from officials paled in comparison, reaching only 15,652,781 *cash*. The provincial government treasury covered the remaining expenses of approximately 14,825,000 *cash*. While the funds mobilized for official state relief amounted to about 65,864,400 *cash*, elite donations played a critical role in supplementing state funds with 44,068,950 *cash*, approximately 67 percent of the sum for state relief.

1823 relief operations in Zhejiang Elites in Zhejiang Province similarly emerged as active players in famine administration in the aftermath of heavy rains in 1823. In Huzhou, Hangzhou, and Jiaxing prefectures, local gentry and merchants were encouraged to provide donations for a three-month "civilian relief" (*minzhen*).[92] The local gentry drove this initiative, establishing and staffing bureaus in towns. According to the regulations that guided this "civilian relief" in Huzhou prefecture, elite managers in rural areas were expected to perform various roles. They were to greet deputy officials in villages and accompany them in surveying the damages.[93] To receive relief money or grain, rural managers had to travel to the county seat. Upon their return, they had to announce to the disaster victims the date and venue of the distribution of relief, of which they were expected to be in charge.

In the summer of 1823, the relief operations carried out after flooding in Chun'an County, Zhejiang, relied primarily upon the financial and managerial assistance of local elites. Soon after the disaster, officials commissioned by the Zhejiang governor released 7,000 taels for emergency relief in Chun'an and adjoining Jiande Counties.[94] For a more effective recovery, however, elite donations were essential. Although the gentry and merchants in the city had already contributed for relief purposes three years earlier, they were obliged to do so again.[95] Efforts were first undertaken to encourage donations from the gentry and merchants in cities, with the elites in rural areas asked to follow. The Yanzhou prefect had originally ordered the dispatch of local educational and subcounty officials to encourage donations, but the one in charge of the Chun'an County relief operation opted instead to install members of the gentry and the elderly as managers on the grounds that they were better informed of local conditions and less likely to squeeze contributions out of the local population.[96] More than 3,300 taels were collected in the county seat alone, with the total amount of contributions from both the city and the countryside surpassing 17,000 taels. The elite managers then held cut-price grain sales to feed the victims, with supplies acquired from the government granary as well as purchased with civilian donations.

FAMINE RELIEF OPERATIONS IN JIANGSU IN 1831 AND 1833

After the natural disasters in 1823, local elites in Suzhou and other parts of Jiangsu continued to play a pivotal role in famine administration during the Daoguang reign. For the relief of the flood victims in Jiangsu in 1831, a hefty sum of 1,420,000 taels was procured through donations elicited from local people in the entire province.[97] While the amount of donation did not reach the 1823 sum of 1,950,000 taels, it was still substantial. When heavy flooding once again hit the province in 1833, the Qing court provided funds for grain rations to the victims and offered tax exemption. Fully aware of the court's concerns for the state's deteriorating fiscal conditions, Governor Lin Zexu encouraged donations from officials and local elites.[98] He then reported that the full mobilization of state funds, as had been originally planned, was unnecessary. He explained that he had carried out the famine relief operation with state funds only in those counties where the damages had been serious and the collection of donations challenging: Shangyuan, Jiangning, Jurong, Jiangpu, and Yizheng. Wherever he could somehow find a way to save government revenue, he explained to the emperor, he had not dared to expend it lightly. Lin thus proudly reported that he had already returned to the provincial treasury the state funds originally allocated for this relief operation.

Lin Zexu actively publicized his efforts in collecting donations to the Daoguang Emperor, while at the same time underscoring the obstacles he encountered. Local gentry and affluent households were reluctant to make contributions, Lin confessed, as in recent years the government had frequently turned to them in times of crisis. He detailed the dwindling amounts of elite contributions over recent years, from 1,950,000 taels in the aftermath of the floods in 1823 to 1,420,000 taels in 1831, even though the floods that year triggered a crisis of similar magnitude. He associated this decline to the deteriorating economic conditions.[99]

His pleas for donations did not fall on deaf ears among local elites in Jiangsu Province. In fact, contributions from these elites fueled the relief efforts undertaken in various counties in the wake of the famine in 1833.[100] Many counties in Jiangsu successfully collected sufficient donations through this "voluntary relief" (*yizhen*) project, with some counties boasting particularly large amounts. Suzhou had amassed roughly 143 million *cash* while Baoshan, Shanghai, and Jiading Counties in the neighboring Taicang independent department and Songjiang prefecture had elicited about 92 million, 78 million, and 55 million *cash*, respectively. Dantu County in Zhenjiang prefecture and Jiangyin County in Changzhou prefecture recorded about 80 million *cash* and 50 million *cash*, respectively.[101] The subscriptions collected in other counties ranged between 10 million and 40 million *cash*.[102]

In the spring of 1835, the Liang-Jiang governor-general Tao Zhu and the Jiangsu governor Lin Zexu summarized the operation's achievements and requested to the emperor the bestowal of government rewards to the officials and local elites who had performed managerial roles or donated money. Tao and Lin calculated the contributions collected from local elites in the entire Jiangsu Province at roughly 1.39 million taels, lower than the 1.95 million taels in 1823 or the 1.42 million taels in 1831.[103] Out of this amount of 1.39 million taels, 241,700 taels came from the counties under the jurisdiction of the Jiangning financial commissioner while the remaining 1,148,300 taels from the counties under the Suzhou financial commissioner.[104] In the counties under the Jiangning financial commissioner, twenty-one donors contributed between 1,000 and 10,000 taels, while 114 donated between 300 and 1,000. As for the area under the Suzhou financial commissioner, the number of donors whose contribution totaled between 1,000 and 10,000 taels was 116, while as many as 791 provided between 300 and 1,000 taels.[105] In Dantu and Baoshan Counties, officials collected 110,000 taels and 101,000 taels, respectively.[106]

Lin also brought to the emperor's attention small-scale famine relief efforts undertaken by Suzhou elites in 1833. During the previous winter, a relief kitchen had been established within the Suzhou city walls. Feeding gruel to the poor through these kitchens, however, posed challenges. The starving crowd from far and near gathered together and stirred disorder, with the strong taking advantage and shoving the old and the weak aside. To redress these problems, Lin explained, the method of "gruel by porter" (*danzhou*) was introduced. As Pierre-Étienne Will has explained, this system had "porters make rounds through the streets and the countryside bearing a yoke with two buckets of porridge, which was reserved for the old and the sick who were unable to move about."[107] Lin Zexu informed the emperor that he had advised the families of local gentry and commoners in Suzhou to employ this method of distribution in their ward or somewhere nearby, proudly boasting of its effectiveness.[108]

Two members of the local gentry assumed the leadership roles in the famine relief operation in Suzhou in 1833: Han Feng (1758–1834), a Suzhou native and a former minister of punishments, and Wu Tingchen (1773–1844, *js* 1802) who was in his hometown awaiting his official appointment in Beijing. In addition to their financial contributions, these two supervised the building of a public bureau to raise donations and distribute relief money.[109]

Apart from these two gentry leaders, the local gazetteers indicate that a number of Suzhou elite members were active in relief operations in the 1830s and 1840s. After witnessing numerous children abandoned on the streets in the wake of the famines in 1830 and 1831, a degree-holder from Changshu County established an institution to raise them. The same man also donated 600 taels in 1840 for another relief project when flooding struck the area once again.[110] Another individual from Changshu frequently donated money for relief purposes when the county suffered devastation from floods and droughts, and he served as a manager in the dredging work on the Baimao River in 1834.[111] His father had also donated 1,000 taels and set up a relief kitchen following the 1823 flood. Xu Degui, a *jiansheng* in Changshu County who worked as a manager in the hydraulic work on the Baimao in 1834, also raised funds to build various charitable institutions.[112] The gazetteer for Wujiang County records that a local relief project directed and funded by local people (*xiangzhen*) was launched for the second time in 1834 after its first appearance in 1823.[113] Elite-led and financed relief operations continued to proliferate in the 1830s as in the 1820s.

1849 RELIEF OPERATION IN SUZHOU

Heavy rainfall in the summer of 1849 once again inundated the Suzhou area. Depicted by local sources as causing devastation on a larger scale than the floods in 1823, this natural disaster not only brought starvation to local residents, but also incurred massive damage to their houses and land. The price of grain soared and countless people died of hunger, many of whom had no proper burial because of the insufficient supply of coffins.[114] The state offered relief subsidies and tax exemption, but the elites of Suzhou once again supplemented state relief by opening their wallets.

The wealthy households in the urban and rural areas of Kunshan and Xinyang Counties sold grain at reduced prices, fed the hungry masses through relief kitchens, and funneled contributions for charitable institutions.[115] A *jiansheng* degree-holder, for example, took control of the relief of a ward by collecting donations and staging a cut-price sale of grain. He followed the example of his father, whose name had been recorded in the local gazetteer for his charitable efforts in the wake of the 1823 floods.[116]

In Changshu and Zhaowen Counties, local elites displayed a similar degree of activism. The gazetteer of these two counties contain many episodes of local residents who performed philanthropic actions for neighbors, raised donations, or worked as managers for waterworks and famine relief operations throughout the nineteenth century.[117]

For example, a stipend student (*linsheng*) donated his funds for relief actions following the floods of 1849 and the severe drought of 1856, in addition to working as a manager in the water conservancy project on the Baimao River in 1850.[118] A *jiansheng* of Zhaowen County participated in both the famine relief project in 1849 and the water control work on the Baimao in 1850. His enthusiasm for local public works derived from his father, also a *jiansheng*, who had assumed the managerial role in the efforts to repair the city wall in 1833 and the waterworks project on the Baimao in 1834.[119]

In the county of Wujiang, the grain stored in the local government granary was first dispensed to feed the hungry during the famine of 1849, being followed by relief efforts directed and funded by local elites.[120] The bureau they established distributed ten *cash* of relief subsidy to adults and five to children.[121] Efforts were also made to alleviate starvation by having the porters make rounds in the streets with buckets of porridge.[122] Local philanthropists took in abandoned infants and collected the corpses from the streets.[123] When a flood struck northern Jiangsu in 1848 and prompted several hundred refugees to move south to find temporary shelter in Wujiang, Ren You, a *shengyuan* of Tongli town, distributed gruel and food and provided coffins for the dead.[124] Amid the flooding that hit the Jiangnan area the following year, Ren sold grain at reduced prices and buried more than three thousand coffins floating on the river. The scope of action among Suzhou elites at this time surpassed the boundaries of their hometown. When the province of Henan suffered from an extended drought in 1848, Wang Yuanxiang, a resident of Shengze town in Wujiang, collected more than 10,000 taels for the victims.[125]

Benevolent Halls and Charitable Estates

The growing participation of local elites in famine administration was paralleled by similar changes in philanthropy, which also necessitated financial and managerial assistance from their members. As local elites enthusiastically embraced philanthropy, the establishment of charitable estates and benevolent halls—both representative local charitable institutions—also accelerated in Suzhou in the early nineteenth century.

According to Liu Zhengyun's study, charitable estates in Suzhou witnessed a significant increase in number in the first fifty years of the nineteenth century, as demonstrated by table 2. The upward trend began

Table 2
The number of charitable estates in Suzhou established during the Qing period

Kangxi (1662–1722)	4
Yongzheng (1723–35)	0
Qianlong (1736–95)	11
Jiaqing (1796–1820)	7
Daoguang (1821–50)	31
Xianfeng (1851–61)	14
Tongzhi (1862–74)	20
Guangxu (1875–1908)	71
Xuantong (1909–11)	5
Not Clear	4

SOURCE: Liu Zhengyun, "Yizhuang yu chengzhen," 639.

during the Qianlong reign, but its incremental pattern intensified during the Jiaqing and Daoguang periods. While eleven charitable estates were erected during Qianlong's sixty-year reign, their number reached as many as thirty-eight during the next fifty-five years under the Jiaqing and Daoguang Emperors. The Taiping Rebellion in the mid-nineteenth century seems to have fueled this trend, as the postbellum restoration efforts brought a substantial increase of charitable estates in the late nineteenth century.[126]

The purpose of charitable estates was to help lineage members in need as well as to provide expenses for ancestral worship. It seems reasonable to believe that the deterioration of state relief capacities and the general decline of the state granary system after 1780 lay behind the expansion of charitable estates. Such an expansion in Suzhou signified that local residents increasingly sought relief functions at family and community-based levels. According to Liu Zhengyun, among those 167 people who established charitable estates in Qing Suzhou could be counted thirty-six officials, thirty-three degree-holders, twenty-nine office-purchasers, and fourteen merchants and commoners, while the social status of fifty-five remained unclear.[127] This analysis leads to the conclusion that the local elites of Suzhou were the ones who actively performed relief functions for their poor lineage members during this period.

While the charitable estate was an institution especially geared toward providing lineage members with relief, various benevolent halls functioned to succor a wider range of local inhabitants within the community. Similar to charitable estates, benevolent halls operated by local elites exhibited a remarkable growth in the early nineteenth century. As Fuma Susumu and Liang Qizi have shown, benevolent societies and halls that flourished in the late Ming came under tighter government control during the reigns of Yongzheng and Qianlong.[128] The financial pillars that sustained their activities were often provided by land endowed by local officials, who at times took control of these organizations. During the eighteenth century many in local elite circles perceived benevolent halls as a financial burden, as those who accepted management positions in these organizations were often forced to utilize their private assets to cover their expenses. This led many to avoid assuming any leadership roles. Nonetheless, as Liang Qizi argues, in the early nineteenth century Jiangnan experienced an increase in the number of benevolent halls whose financial patronage and managerial roles were largely performed by local elites with less government intervention.[129] Thus the Daoguang edition of the Suzhou prefectural gazetteer, after listing the benevolent halls, added: "Aforementioned various benevolent halls established by people (*minjian*) perform the roles such as caring for the old and the sick, providing coffins and medicine, and burying corpses. These activities are funded by the people and managed by the people (*minjuan minban*). Officials do not interfere."[130]

As table 3 shows, only six benevolent halls were set up in Suzhou during Kangxi's sixty-one-year reign. During the subsequent seventy-three years under Yongzheng and Qianlong, the number soared to thirty-five. The momentum increased under Jiaqing, as his twenty-five-year reign witnessed the construction of thirty-two new halls. While only thirty-five halls were erected over a seventy-three-year period in the eighteenth century, it took almost one-third of the time to see a similar number of the halls emerge in the Jiaqing period. During the subsequent thirty years of Daoguang's reign the number of halls increased by eighteen, raising the total of halls built in the fifty-five years under Jiaqing and Daoguang to fifty, far exceeding the thirty-one recorded during an even longer period under Qianlong. One characteristic of the progressive increase in the early nineteenth century was the dissemination of these organizations into market towns.[131]

Table 3
The number of newly established benevolent halls in Suzhou prefecture, 1662–1850

Kangxi (1662–1722)	6
Yongzheng (1723–35)	4
Qianlong (1736–95)	31
Jiaqing (1796–1820)	32
Daoguang (1821–50)	18

SOURCES: *Wujiang xianzhi*, 1747, *juan* 8; *Changzhou xianzhi*, 1753, *juan* 4; Qian Siyuan, *Wumen bucheng*, *juan* 2; *Suzhou fuzhi*, 1824, *juan* 23; *Kun Xin liangxian zhi*, 1826, *juan* 3; *Wujiangxian xuzhi*, 1879, *juan* 2; *Kun Xin liangxian xuxiu hezhi*, 1880, *juan* 3; *Suzhou fuzhi*, 1882, *juan* 24; *Chang Zhao hezhigao*, 1904, *juan* 17; *Wu xianzhi*, 1933, *juan* 30.

NOTE: There are sixteen benevolent halls whose founding years are unclear. Most of these benevolent halls first appear in the late Qing and Republican period local gazetteers. Only three are first mentioned in the Suzhou prefectural gazetteer compiled in 1824, but the founding years are not noted. All others are recorded for the first time in the gazetteers compiled in the period after 1850. Therefore, it is safe to assume that these halls were probably erected during the nineteenth century.

Numerous benevolent halls in Suzhou faced destruction during the civil war between the Qing army and the Taiping rebels in the mid-nineteenth century. Many, however, were restored during the Tongzhi and Guangxu periods, while new ones were also built. Although an accurate total of newly built benevolent halls from 1851 to 1911 is difficult to calculate due to the unavailability of complete data, at least eighty-three newly erected or restored benevolent halls can be counted during this period.[132] While the dramatic increase in benevolent halls from 1851 to 1911 should be duly noted, the significant incremental pattern observed during the first five decades of the nineteenth century should also be evaluated.[133]

How should we understand the expansion of benevolent halls in the early nineteenth century? In his case study of Sichuan Province, Japanese scholar Yamada Masaru identifies a substantial rise in elite-led "public bureaus" (*gongju*) in the province from the Jiaqing to the Daoguang periods.[134] Yamada argues that they were established to fill the deficit in government personnel caused by massive migrations into Sichuan, as the expansion of state administrative institutions did not keep pace with the population growth. This required more administrative fees and services, encouraging cooperation between officials and the local elites. Yamada underscores the complementary character of the public bureaus to the official local administration. Focusing on the gentry's protection of their class interests, Japanese scholar Yamamoto Susumu offers another perspective. He argues that the expansion of benevolent halls in Jiangnan and public bureaus in Sichuan in the early nineteenth century represented the gentry's efforts to curb the exorbitant extortion by clerks and runners, themselves compelled to find other sources of revenue amid the government's worsening fiscal conditions.[135] Their disparities notwithstanding, both scholars recognize the dynamism of elite activism, whether driven by the urge for self-protection or by public-minded aspirations. They also share the perception that the Qing government's fiscal predicament at this time served as the major catalyst for elite activism.

The social changes in Suzhou during the early nineteenth century discussed above, from the increase in water conservancy and famine relief projects led by elites to the growing number of benevolent halls and charitable estates, testify to the reinvigoration of local elite public activities. The Jiaqing and Daoguang Emperors and their officials, when compared to the Qianlong Emperor and his subordinates, were more tolerant of, even encouraging, local elite participation in the public realm. While the Qianlong period is characterized by state concerns in strengthening bureaucratic supervision of the various local public sectors, during the Jiaqing and Daoguang periods the state attempted to manage such sectors by encouraging further participation of the elites. In this regard, how did these social changes shape the cultural environment in the early nineteenth century? How was the literati culture of the period different from that of the eighteenth century? The cultural scene is considered in the next four chapters.

PART II

Cultural Manifestations of Elite Activism

CHAPTER 4

The Shrine of Local Worthies and the Changing Patterns of the Enshrinement

Beginning in the mid-Ming period, two types of shrines spread throughout the empire: the shrines for eminent officials (*minghuan ci*) built to commemorate former local officials known for their distinguished administrative achievements, and the shrines for local worthies (*xiangxian ci*) erected in honor of deceased local natives, mostly from influential families, whose virtuous deeds or accomplishments deserved recognition.[1] While the former served to elevate officials as paragons for subsequent local administrators, the latter celebrated some local ancestors as role models in the community.

The enshrinement of one's ancestor as either an eminent official or a local worthy brought fame to the family, enhancing its prestige in local societies. Enshrinement was especially important in the case of local worthies, since their relatives and descendants, unlike those of eminent officials, usually remained in the same locality where their ancestors were worshipped. Commemorating one's ancestor through enshrinement by a consensus of the local gentry confirmed public recognition of his family's elite status. The benefits, especially in the case of local worthies, stimulated fierce competition among elite groups for this honor.

As families sought to secure a seat for their ancestors in the local shrine, the phenomenon of "excessive enshrinement" (*lansi*) gained momentum, that is, the enshrinement of unqualified or underqualified figures. Distorting its original purpose, enshrinement increasingly became a cultural channel through which powerful families reinforced their status and reputation. Faced with this dilemma, the central government during the Ming and Qing periods imposed more rigorous standards on the enshrinement process. Such measures, however, did not always generate the desired effects. It was only during the Yongzheng and Qianlong periods in the Qing that the state managed to effectively curb the rising trend of enshrinement numbers. The state's efforts, however, did not last through the remaining years of the Qing period, as the enshrinement numbers once again soared during the Jiaqing Emperor's reign, signaling the relaxation of state control and a greater accommodation of elite interests by the imperial court. An analysis of the policies concerning enshrinement during the Yongzheng and Qianlong reigns and its subsequent changes convey another facet of the shifting relations between the state and local elites during the Qing dynasty. Before discussing these transformations, a brief introduction as to how this practice unfolded under the Ming and the early Qing is in order.

The Enshrinement of Local Worthies in the Ming and Early Qing Periods

Prior to the fifteenth century, the veneration of eminent officials and local worthies occurred by and large in the same shrine, commonly known as the Shrines for Former Worthies (*Xianxian ci*). The worship of eminent officials and local worthies in separate shrines, a practice established by either active local officials wishing to promote a Confucian agenda or local elites, began in the fifteenth century.[2] The imperial government encouraged the proliferation of these shrines, as the court recognized their role in the moral edification of the people.[3] An imperial order for the construction of these types of shrines was issued during the Hongzhi reign (1488–1505), followed by at least two similar ones during the Jiajing period (1522–66).[4]

Besides promoting Confucian values, these shrines served another purpose for the Ming court: rewarding deserving men. The enshrinement in a local worthy shrine was usually accompanied by other rewards, such as a posthumous title or rank.[5] While these examples show that the state promoted the spread of enshrinement, the Ming court was normally not involved in the decision making for enshrinement. Direct state involvement would occur only under the Yongzheng Emperor during the Qing, when the imperial court established a centralized decision-making process for matters concerning enshrinement.

During the Ming, enshrinement decisions were made at the local or regional level. The 1642 gazetteer for Wu County in Suzhou prefecture notes that in 1525, decisions on the enshrinement of eminent officials lay in the hands of the county magistrate.[6] The same gazetteer explains that thirteen years later the regional inspector selected the local worthies. According to this gazetteer, sometime after 1525, an imperial statute granted to the provincial education intendant censor the authority to decide both categories of enshrinement.[7] This practice continued until the Yongzheng reform in 1725, when the decision-making process shifted into the hands of the central government. As part of the enshrinement process, a recommended candidate had his qualifications ascertained by local government school officials and students before the local magistrate or prefect submitted his name to the education intendant censor. A number of local gazetteers in the late sixteenth, seventeenth, and early eighteenth centuries mention that the enshrined figures received the approval of the education intendant censors or commissioners.

This reform, however, fell short of meeting the expectations of the central government, as locals voiced numerous complaints about unqualified candidates.[8] Already by 1534, officials raised doubts about the enshrinement of figures with questionable morals or qualifications. The issue of improper candidates intensified by the late sixteenth century.[9] In 1574, the Ming court directed provincial officials to investigate the lists in the shrines for eminent officials and local worthies and purge the tablets of those whom they deemed unworthy.[10] In his memorial to the Wanli Emperor (r. 1573–1619), the minister of rites Shen Li (1531–1615) blamed local elites for abusing their influence in the enshrinement process to serve their own interests. In addition, he proposed that, at the end of each year, education intendant censors present reports to the court highlighting evidence of each person's eligibility.[11] The persistence of similar requests and orders during the late Ming dynasty indicates that these measures failed to deal effectively with excesses in enshrinements.[12]

In the early Qing period, the dynamics of "excessive enshrinement" remained largely unaltered. The provincial education commissioner (*xuezheng*), a Qing title corresponding to the Ming-era education intendant censor, was responsible for enshrinements, but the influence peddling by local families persisted. In the absence of the central government's intervention in the process, provincial education officials seem to have been incapable of imposing any strict standards that clashed with the interests of local elites. Such initiatives only served to strain the relations between provincial officials and the gentry.

During the Kangxi years, enshrinements climbed, contributing to the Qing state's popularity among local elites as the new dynasty consolidated its power over the empire. Although the total number of worthies during the Kangxi period is unavailable due to the lack of a centralized decision-making system, scattered evidence strongly supports the assertion that the enshrinements rose steadily. In 1686, for example, the governor of Jiangsu Tang Bin (1627–87) selected thirty-one eminent officials from ancient times to the Ming for enshrinement at the Suzhou prefectural school, and subsequently added twelve more names.[13] Among the thirty eminent Qing officials enshrined at the same school prior to 1745, no less than twenty-eight received the honor during the Kangxi years. In 1717, the Jiangsu administrative commissioner Yang Chaolin enacted measures that resembled those adopted by Tang Bin. Yang selected forty-six local worthies from the Tang to Ming and had their tablets featured in the shrine for local worthies of Kunshan County.[14] In these two cases, a striking contrast can be observed between the soaring numbers of enshrinements during the Kangxi reign and their precipitous drop in the ensuing two reigns.

A similar pattern can be observed in some counties in Zhejiang. In Jinhua prefecture's Tangxi County, the enshrinement of six out of eight eminent Qing officials whose time of enshrinement is known occurred during the Kangxi reign.[15] Likewise, in the neighboring Pujiang County, six out of the seven eminent Qing officials enshrined before the late nineteenth century and whose time of enshrinement is recorded dated from the Kangxi period.[16] As for the local worthies of the same county, five out of seven entered the shrine for local worthies in the same period. An episode during the Kangxi reign is symptomatic of this overflow of the enshrined figures. During his reign, an official provoked the ire of the emperor by approving as many as 658 local worthies over a mere three-year period and awarding official hat buttons to more than 1,100 descendants of the worthies.[17]

The State Control of Enshrinement in the Eighteenth Century

The lax enshrinement policy, however, was reversed during the Yongzheng period. In 1724, the Board of Rites declared:

> As for eminent officials and local worthies who have already been enshrined, governor-generals, governors, and provincial education commissioners of every province should investigate them closely with fair mind. If their meritorious achievements do not betray the titles of famous officials, and if their scholarship and virtues truly accord with local opinion, then they should make a book that contains their names and facts, and submit it, together with stamped certificate, to the Board [of Rites] for investigation and endorsement. [Only then] should they allow [the worthies] to remain in the shrine. If they do not have actual achievements, then [provincial officials should] report them to the Board in order to expel them [from the shrines]. From now on, if there is someone who presents a petition to the superiors to request enshrinement, then governor-generals, governors, and provincial education commissioners should follow precedent and report it to the Board for a transparent investigation. If they privately endorse enshrinement, if it is found, then both petitioner and the one who accepted the petition will be punished. The local officials who gave the written guarantee and who submitted the report will all be considered for punishment.[18]

The Yongzheng Emperor endorsed this empire-wide reappraisal of the qualifications of already enshrined eminent officials and local worthies and the removal of names.[19] To establish those who qualified as worthies, their merits had to be presented to the Board of Rites for examination.[20] The same applied for new candidates for enshrinement. Beginning in 1724, provincial officials no longer had the power of decision over enshrinements. They had to submit such requests along with evidence of the candidates' qualifications to the Board of Rites for investigation and endorsement, reducing the role of provincial officials from decision makers to recommenders.[21]

This centralizing trend advanced a step further the following year. In 1725, the Shandong education commissioner suggested that provincial officials submit memorials with candidates for enshrinement directly to the emperor for his endorsement, in addition to the evidence that they were already required to submit to the Board of Rites.[22] The rationale behind this request was that the examination by the Board of Rites proved insufficient in curbing abuses. With the inclusion of the emperor in the process, it was expected that provincial and local officials would demonstrate greater rigor in selecting candidates. This proposal constituted the basis of a new policy suggested by the Board of Rites, promptly endorsed by the Yongzheng Emperor.[23] From this time onward, the three highest provincial officials had to convene to discuss the petitions for enshrinement and memorialize their evaluation before the eighth month of each year. This meant that their memorials were directly submitted to the emperor, while the fact books were delivered to the Board of Rites for investigation. At the end of each year, the minister of rites had to submit their evaluation and decision to the emperor, who would decide whether to endorse it.[24] The emperor expected memorials from the provincial officials to gain an understanding of those recommended. The policy changes in 1724–25 strengthened the centralization of the decision-making process concerning enshrinements, with the emperor now standing at its top. This shift should be understood as an effort to save the worship of local officials and worthies from appropriation by influential local families and officials in league with them.

In 1728, to further ensure the qualifications of the worthies, the minister of rites proposed that board officials who shared the same provincial origins with the candidates should meet with the Nine Chief Ministers (*jiujing*) to deliberate on the merits of the recommended candidates.[25] The Yongzheng Emperor dismissed this suggestion, mainly out of concern that provincial ties shared by the candidates and the court officials would hamper unprejudiced evaluations. Instead, the emperor commanded a reassessment of the suitability of the worthies recommended since 1726, and he was informed of the results in 1731.[26] The reappraisal deemed ineligible no less than ten out of forty-three candidates.[27] This follow-up action, coupled with Yongzheng's earlier measures, illustrated the extent to which he was determined to ensure tighter government control over enshrinement, an effort tied to a larger imperial initiative to dilute the power of local elites.[28]

In the first decade of Qianlong's reign, the number of enshrined worthies climbed in comparison to those during his father's rule. This short-lived increase, however, was soon reversed and the numbers remained at a low level throughout the remainder of the Qianlong reign. Confronted with the rise in numbers during the first decade of his reign, the emperor manifested his concern over enshrinements by reprimanding provincial officials who recommended too many candidates. He insisted that their actions represented no more than "reputation seeking" (*guming yaoyu*), referring to winning the good graces of the local elites by satisfying their wishes to enshrine their forebears.[29] He became annoyed with a governor's recommendation to anoint his own uncle as an eminent official. Qianlong refused this request by condemning it as based on a "private motive" (*sixin*) rather than the public interest.[30] The critical turn occurred in the thirteenth year of his reign (1748). In that year, the emperor called into question the eligibility of a candidate whom he regarded as ordinary, at most, in declaring that the candidate's recommendation was based solely on the fact that he had been a high minister at the court.[31] In an edict issued the following year, the emperor blamed provincial officials and local elites for misjudging the qualifications of the candidate. Qianlong added sarcastically that behind such a lax evaluation lay the desire by officials and local elites to oppose strengthening the criteria so that their own tablets might enter the shrines more easily.[32] The emperor conveyed his rising distrust of the candidates' eligibility through a regulation in 1748, which prescribed that the Board of Rites should reject enshrinement requests if the qualifications of the candidate were concocted and those officials responsible for them were to be penalized.[33]

Enshrinement numbers began a downward trajectory after the first decade of the Qianlong reign, a product of the emperor's stern measures from 1748 to 1749. This marked the beginning of his campaign to enact a rigorous evaluation system of enshrinement. In 1755, the emperor discovered that two local worthy candidates endorsed by the Board of Rites had sons serving as high ministers, while another candidate with no such connections had been dismissed. This aroused the fury of the emperor. Qianlong suspected that the high ministers at court and provincial officials shared a bond and an affinity that derived from their sense of belonging to the highest echelon of the bureaucracy, which he believed spawned an unreasonably generous support of each other.[34] If the shrines were filled with the ancestors of high ministers, then, the emperor asked, how could the system fulfill its original goal of raising the true worthies detached from politics and power? For Qianlong, bureaucratic favoritism was superseding official duty.

The emperor's analysis dealt with one of the crucial problems inherent in the enshrinement process. Even if the forebears of high ministers were recommended under the guise of public opinion (*gonglun*), those shaping "public opinion" were the local elites who were either lineage members or affines of high ministers. Thus, concluded the emperor, this did not represent the views of a broad range of the public. Qianlong demonstrated skepticism toward "public opinion," which he believed sometimes amounted to little more than the representation of the private interests of a small number of powerful families. The emperor perceived the discord between the noble ideals of enshrinement and the appropriation of the system by ministers and local elites for their own private gains. His harsh words about this selective "public opinion" were repeated almost verbatim in the campaign against the fraudulent practices regarding gazetteer compilation.

Qianlong was not only vigilant about the complicity between ministers and local elites. Ancestors of high ministers breezing through the selection process presided over by provincial officials and the Board of Rites conveyed the existence of a bureaucratic alliance that operated during the enshrinement process. Qianlong's remarks made at the end of his accusation demonstrated this concern: "The distortion or illicit protection generated by private emotions is none other than opening the door to factionalism." The emperor demanded the removal of the two undeserving worthies from the shrines and punishment of the governors-general, governors, and the Board of Rites officials implicated in this scandal. Soon a regulation forbade recommending the grandfathers and fathers of the Nine Chief Ministers.[35] The total enshrinements after 1750 remained consistently low throughout the Qianlong period, a phenomenon stemming from these imperial initiatives.

Although the emperor had the final say over enshrinement decisions, the Board of Rites also exercised the right of veto or deferral before submitting its suggestions to the emperors.[36] Deferrals affected candidates with insufficient evidence to substantiate their claimed virtues and merits, and rejections occurred when the examining officials found serious flaws in the candidates' careers or were left unimpressed by their qualifications. At times, the board officials found merits greatly exaggerated. On other occasions the board denied candidates because their merits were not deemed significant. In 1749, for example, the board rejected the enshrinement of a local worthy candidate from Fujian and an eminent official candidate in Zhejiang on the grounds that they were simply wealthy philanthropists, a qualification the board considered insufficient to satisfy the criteria of "performing deeds of merit and accumulating virtue" (*ligong shude*).[37] The board declared that merely wealthy candidates (*sufeng*) who lacked outstanding achievements or virtue should not be enshrined. Six years later, another local worthy candidate encountered a similar fate. The board acknowledged that the man had been engaged in a number of praiseworthy public actions—establishing a charitable estate, community school, and private academy—but it downgraded the significance of these deeds as mere "philanthropic actions" (*haoshan leshi*). According to the board, the candidate failed to meet the board's expectation of studying Neo-Confucian teachings and offering his contribution to it (*qianxin lixue, yougong wenjiao*).[38] This is not to say that the board dismissed candidates' philanthropic actions in its evaluation. The extant records of eminent officials (*minghuan lu*) and local worthies (*xiangxian lu*), which were compiled after the enshrinement of a worthy and which usually included the official documents and memorials pertaining to the matter, show that philanthropic actions were frequently mentioned as part of the evidence to substantiate the candidate's overall qualifications: administrative achievements, evidence of Confucian scholarship, and attitudes that exemplified moral virtues.[39] The rejection of philanthropists shows that the board expected a certain degree of scholarship, often exemplified by the candidates' written works, in addition to their virtuous actions.

The efforts by Yongzheng and Qianlong to impose tighter government controls on enshrinement proved effective, as indicated by the significant reduction in its numbers, especially in the last four decades of

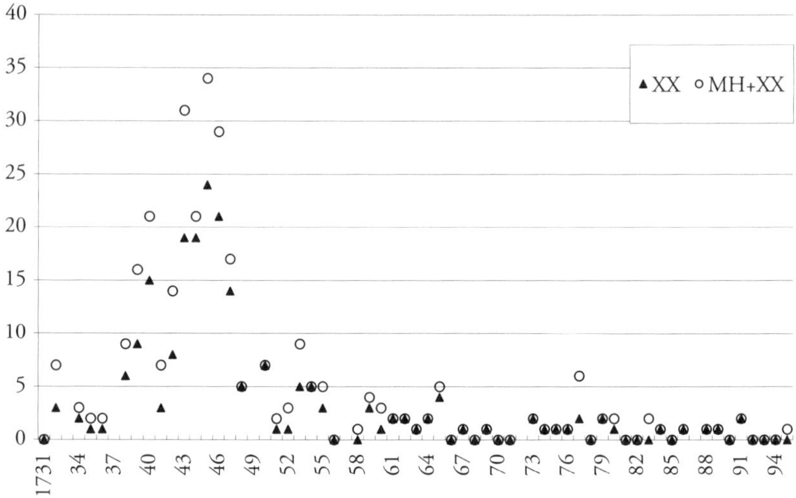

FIGURE 5. Number of eminent officials (MH) and local worthies (XX), 1731–95

the Qianlong years (see figure 5). These efforts stand in contrast to the unwillingness of nineteenth-century emperors to resort to such strict measures to prevent abuses. While the Jiaqing Emperor issued edicts complaining about "excessive enshrinement," his officials often turned a blind eye to the issue, as suggested by its remarkable increase during his reign. Jiaqing's successors did not even share a limited interest in controlling "excessive enshrinement." In the nineteenth century, the state no longer pursued a vigorous agenda of curbing elite power. The near disappearance after Jiaqing of any related entries in the eminent officials and local worthies sections in the Guangxu edition of the *Qing huidian shili* is emblematic of this change.[40]

The Increased Number of Local Worthies in the Nineteenth Century

This section examines the number and the provincial distribution of eminent officials and local worthies from 1726 to 1874. Its purpose is to use the fluctuations in enshrinement numbers as an indicator of the shifting state-elite relationship, particularly in the early nineteenth century. The data is from the *Qing shilu* and the *Like shishu*, except for the three years (1750, 1751, 1786) for which I draw on the routine memorials of the Board of Rites.

ENSHRINEMENTS FROM 1726 TO 1795

From 1726 to 1795, with the exception of the six years for which the data are unavailable, ninety-eight eminent officials and 231 local worthies were enshrined (see appendix), forty-nine in Jiangsu Province alone. Compared to the eighty-two names enshrined as eminent officials and local worthies just in the Suzhou prefectural school from 1644 to 1724, the rate of enshrinement experienced a remarkable drop under Yongzheng and Qianlong.[41] The period covered by the Suzhou case is eleven years longer than the one in Jiangsu, but the conclusion still holds because the Suzhou numbers refer to only one prefecture, while the latter is the aggregate total of an entire province. These numbers underscore the tangible effect of the centralization of decision making and the imposition of rigorous standards under Yongzheng and Qianlong.

From 1726 to 1795, Jiangsu Province produced the most worthies. But the second, third, and fourth places were occupied by the provinces in the North; Zhili, Henan, and Shandong. It is rather surprising to see northern provinces outnumber southern ones, such as Zhejiang, Anhui, and Jiangxi, that were traditionally considered centers of elite power and culture. Although the reasons behind this phenomenon are not entirely clear, it is not far fetched to assume that the high numbers in the North stemmed from the conscious promotion of elite traditions by state officials during the eighteenth century rather than a flourishing elite culture and power. As will be discussed later, during the Jiaqing period, the higher enshrinement numbers in the North were superseded by higher numbers in the South.

During Yongzheng's reign between 1726 and 1735, the total of enshrined figures reached about forty-five. Due to the adoption of more rigorous criteria, the annual numbers of enshrinements stayed in the single digits during the Yongzheng period. They climbed in the first twelve years of Qianlong's rule, triggering a series of imperial interventions and initiatives from 1748 to 1755. As mentioned above, officials involved in a complex recommendation scandal ended up being punished, particularly in 1755. The decline in the annual numbers from 1748 and its further drop after 1755 stemmed from these imperial interventions. During Qianlong's last thirty years of rule, only about twenty-six enshrinement candidates were endorsed for either of the two shrines. Excluding the two years for which the data are missing, the annual average of enshrinement comes to 0.9 per year. If we narrow our focus to one particular locality, Suzhou prefecture, no more than ten local worthies made it into the shrine between 1726 and 1795, among them Shen Deqian, a renowned poet and high official at the Qianlong's court.[42] Posthumously enshrined as a local worthy in 1769, Shen's tablet was removed from the shrine following Qianlong's discovery that he had penned a biography of a writer whose collection included seditious poems.[43] Moreover, of these ten worthies, nine were enshrined in the first thirty-four years of the Qianlong reign. Even Suzhou, a center of elite power and thriving elite culture under the Ming, failed to escape from the new imperial disposition.[44]

ENSHRINEMENTS FROM 1796 TO 1820

During the Jiaqing reign, particularly after the emperor seized power following his father's demise in 1799, enshrinement policies underwent changes. While enshrinement patterns were well documented during the Qianlong period in the *Like shishu*, one of the two primary sources with information on this issue, some related documents for the Jiaqing period are missing. These gaps perhaps resulted from the fact that the ministers of rites occasionally chose to write secret memorials instead of routine ones for enshrinement requests made at the end of the year. While the *Like shishu* provides the names of selected candidates and the provincial officials who recommended them, it does not necessarily tell us which candidates received imperial approval. Fortunately, the *Qing shilu* from this period contains thorough information about enshrinement for every year until the end of the Tongzhi period in 1874, with the exception of two years in the Xianfeng reign. Even for those two years, the gaps in data are likely attributable to the absence of recommendations rather than the carelessness of compilers. For the Guangxu period, however, the *Qing shilu* has glaring gaps and provides only vague data, limiting its value for this research. Therefore, the temporal scope of the analysis for this section ends in 1874, the final year of the Tongzhi reign. See figure 6.

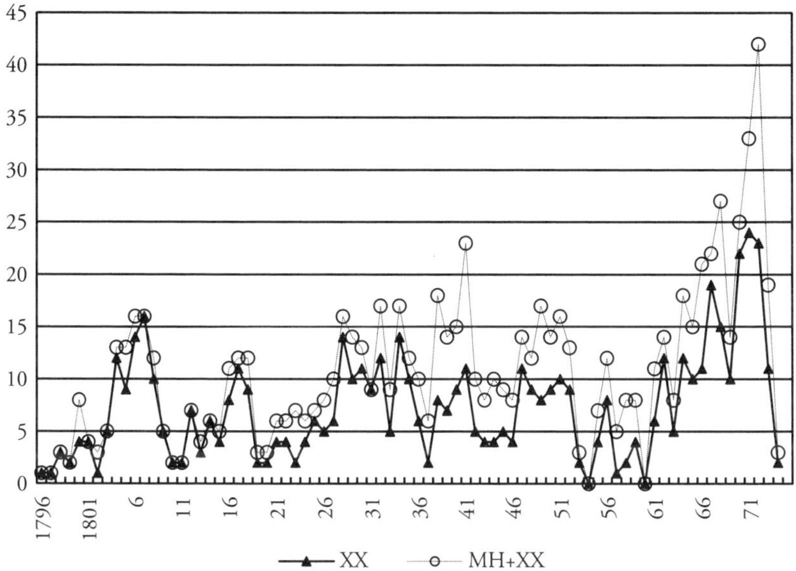

FIGURE 6. Number of eminent officials (MH) and local worthies (XX), 1796–1874

Between 1726 and 1795, approximately 329 eminent officials and local worthies were enshrined. If we exclude the six years for which no data are available, then the annual average of enshrinement reached 5.1 persons per year. But if we narrow our focus to the last thirty years of the Qianlong period (1766–95), then this average drops to only 0.9 (excluding two years for which no data are available). On the other hand, Jiaqing's twenty-five year reign witnessed a rapid rise in the number of enshrinement to 169, with the annual average of the enshrined worthies jumping to 6.7 (see figure 7) and surpassing the 5.1 annual average from 1726 to 1795. It also marks more than a seven-fold increase from the 0.9 annual average recorded during the immediately preceding thirty years. This tendency during the Jiaqing period is even more remarkable if we consider only the local worthies. Their annual average during the span of sixty-four years in the eighteenth century was 3.5, dropping to 0.6 during a period of twenty-eight years in the latter half of the Qianlong reign. This number then soared to 5.7 in the subsequent twenty-five years of the Jiaqing reign, marking more than a ninefold increase from the preceding thirty years. While the number of both eminent officials

FIGURE 7. Annual average of the total enshrinement (MH+XX) and of local worthies (XX), 1766–1874

and local worthies augmented dramatically in the Jiaqing years, the incremental curve proved even steeper for local worthies. The ratio of eminent officials to local worthies widened from 1:2.3 in the eighteenth century to 1:5.5 in the Jiaqing period. As mentioned earlier, the worship of local worthies was more intimately associated with the interests of local families than that of eminent officials, and it is not surprising to see that elite families responded more agilely to enshrining their ancestors when they noticed the window opening wider for this opportunity. The active enshrinement efforts by local elites in this period were closely related to the relaxation of the government's enshrinement criteria. The parties involved in the enshrinement process—families and decision-making officials at various administrative levels—seem to have shared an optimism in regard to prospects that their requests for enshrinement would be granted by the emperor and that responsible officials would not be penalized.

In addition to the overall rise in enshrinements, changes can also be observed in the regional distribution of the enshrined worthies. During the eighteenth century, the provinces in the North ranked second, third, and fourth on the table of provinces featuring the most worthies. Between 1796 and 1820, however, Jiangsu, Zhejiang, and Jiangxi, all three in the

Lower Yangzi region, occupied the top spots. Their combined percentage in empire-wide enshrinements jumped from 25 percent in the eighteenth century to 48 percent during the Jiaqing reign. In the same period, the combined percentage of the top three northern provinces dropped from 32 percent to 15 percent. This abrupt reversal of the north-south balance cannot be accounted for by fluctuations in the elite population or shifts in regional cultural achievements, but should be understood in the context of policy changes. This transformation implies that the Qing government in the eighteenth century sought to foster the cultural identity and pride of local elites in the North while limiting the overall number of enshrinements, a policy reversed during the reign of the Jiaqing Emperor. Moreover, this north-south shift in enshrinements was accompanied by a similar one in the number of local gazetteers, as will be discussed in chapter 6.

The rise in enshrinements during the Jiaqing reign likely stems from the government's heavier dependence on the financial and managerial support of local elites for the preservation of order and infrastructure. With the healthy fiscal condition of the eighteenth century now a memory and deeper gentry involvement in local community projects now evident, state policies could no longer be directed at curbing their power, in particular in Jiangnan. In this regard, the changes concerning enshrinements in Suzhou are quite revealing. Suzhou boasted a mere ten local worthies from 1726 to 1795, nine of them in the first thirty-four years of the Qianlong reign. In the early years of Jiaqing, however, Suzhou elites stepped up their efforts to enshrine local worthies. During Jiaqing's twenty-five-year reign, eleven Suzhou men received such honor, in contrast to only ten in the previous seventy years. Ten of these eleven names were enshrined in the first thirteen years of the reign, more accurately, during the eleven years from 1798 to 1808. The phenomenon has a simple explanation. For several decades under Qianlong, only a few Suzhou men had been fortunate enough to be honored with enshrinement. The yearnings by local elites to secure a spot in a shrine for their ancestors, which built up during the eighteenth century, materialized only in the early years of Jiaqing's reign.[45] Not only did enshrinement in Suzhou soar, but also so did those for Jiangsu Province. During the seventy years between 1726 and 1795, the enshrinement numbers in the province hovered around forty-seven, but after 1795 it took only twenty-five years to nearly reach this mark. As a result, Jiangsu's share in the overall enshrinements in the empire almost doubled from 14 percent in the eighteenth century to 27 percent in the Jiaqing period. The existing balance in the numbers of enshrinement between northern and southern provinces in the eighteenth century ceased to exist in the Jiaqing reign.

ENSHRINEMENTS FROM 1821 TO 1850

The thirty years under the Daoguang Emperor from 1821 to 1850 witnessed the continuation of the incremental Jiaqing pattern. The total number of enshrinements from 1821 to 1850 peaked at 345, boasting an annual average of 11.5, far higher than the 6.7 in the previous reign. The rise that had begun under Jiaqing not only persisted, but also actually accelerated under Daoguang. Suzhou produced seven worthies during this period, including Wu County with the enshrinement of two local worthies for the first time since 1747.[46]

Concerning the percentages of northern and southern provinces, the pattern in enshrinements during the Daoguang reign distinguished itself from the preceding reign. From 1821 to 1850, the enshrinements in the four Lower Yangzi provinces—Jiangsu, Zhejiang, Anhui, and Jiangxi—reached eighty-one, constituting 23.4 percent of the empire-wide total. During the same time span, the total of enshrinements from the four northern provinces of Henan, Shaanxi, Zhili, and Shandong reached 103, about 29.8 percent of the empire-wide total. Narrowing our focus to the number of local worthies alone, however, we find that the northern provinces outnumbered the southern ones by only one worthy. This suggests that while the northern provinces fared better in the Daoguang period, the margin they enjoyed over the southern ones was not as significant in comparison to the eighteenth century. The pattern of eighteenth-century enshrinement is characterized by two particular features: the rapid decline of enshrinement numbers and the northern dominance. These two features can be considered a direct consequence of the state interventionist polices designed to actively curb the entrenched power of local elites, especially in Jiangnan. In the early nineteenth century when the state relinquished this stance, these two features of the government's enshrinement policy were either largely renounced or seriously compromised.

ENSHRINEMENTS FROM 1851 TO 1874

The increase in enshrinements that began in the Jiaqing period experienced a brief setback with the outbreak of the Taiping Rebellion. The total number of enshrined names from 1851 to 1861 reached eighty-three, equivalent to an annual average of 7.5 persons, lower than the Daoguang one of 11.5 but still higher than the 6.7 of the Jiaqing reign. With the suppression of the rebellion in 1864, the annual average skyrocketed to 20 (figure 7). During the eighteenth century, approximately 231 local worthies were enshrined, with the combined total reaching 329 in a seventy-year period. From 1796 to 1874, a time span only nine years longer, as many as 583 local worthies were enshrined, boasting a combined total of 858. If we consider only the local worthies directly related to the interests of local elites, then the annual average changes from 5.7 in the Jiaqing to 7.2 in the Daoguang, 4.1 in the Xianfeng, and ultimately 13.5 in the Tongzhi period.

This increase in the number of enshrined worthies during the nineteenth century can to some extent be attributed to the acceptance of unqualified candidates. In the nineteenth century portion of the *Qing shilu*, several references are made to local disturbances triggered by the discontent among the populace over local worthy candidates whose enshrinement did not have their support.[47] To understand this trend solely as a result of lax state control, however, would explain only part of the story. Financial or managerial participation of local elites in various public works constituted an important element in assessing the overall qualification of the worthy candidates, though this merit alone did not guarantee a spot in the shrine. Elite roles in the management of public works became increasingly prominent from the Jiaqing period, as examined in the previous chapters. To promote participation of the elites in local public works, the central state furnished fund contributors and managers of these projects with more favorable reward programs. Local worthies consisted of members of the elites who often assumed these public roles. It is reasonable to link the expansion and greater importance of their public roles to the enhancement of their qualifications. Moreover, the public functions performed by the descendants of the worthies also increased their chances of enshrinement. As they were also likely to be members of the local elite, their participation in public works created symbolic capital, which officials could not easily dismiss. This merging of the past with the present is exemplified by a case involving Zeng Guofan (1811–72), a prominent nineteenth-century official who organized the Hunan army to suppress the Taiping rebels. In 1854, Zeng led a militia to protect his home province. That year, he submitted a memorial to the Xianfeng Emperor requesting the enshrinement of Yang Jian, a fellow Hunan native, as a local worthy.[48] The person in question had been the governor of Hubei and already been denied entrance into the shrine during the earlier Daoguang period. His rejection stemmed from problems in his administrative career and questionable personal morality. Despite these issues, Zeng resubmitted the request on the ground that the grandson of this former official had donated 20,000 taels of silver for military use. Zeng's attempt failed and evoked the ire of the emperor because his memorial constituted an explicit violation of many regulations.[49] The case, however, provides a glimpse into the relationship that existed between contributors and officials, and it indicates clearly that the monetary contribution by a descendant of a worthy candidate could strengthen the qualifications of his ancestor. During the nineteenth century, as elite public roles became increasingly vital to local administration, officials found themselves under mounting pressure to provide rewards. A direct correlation between elite financial contributions and the number of enshrinements can be observed; both increased during the Jiaqing period and skyrocketed in the subsequent Daoguang reign. Although I do not have the data for elite contributions after Daoguang, we know from existing scholarship that the Tongzhi years are distinguished by the significant expansion of elite public roles, which corresponds to the steep rise in the enshrinement numbers.[50] The correlated numbers indicate that the growing prominence of elite public roles was closely linked to the state's necessary embrace of elite interests. In this respect, the numbers can be considered barometers of changing state-elite relations. These transformations challenge the assumption that the Taiping Rebellion marks the origin of nineteenth-century elite activism.[51] Instead, the emergence of elite activism should be characterized as a gradual process originating in the Jiaqing period and gaining momentum under Daoguang. The Taiping Rebellion and the post-Taiping restoration efforts intensified a trend already set in motion two generations earlier.

CHAPTER 5

Shrine, Images, and Power

The Worship of Former Worthies in Early Nineteenth-Century Suzhou

In 1824, Suzhou scholar Gu Yuan began collecting the portraits of 570 worthies from his city.[1] His maternal uncle Han Feng, a former minister of punishments (see chapter 3), showed the portraits to Tao Zhu, the governor of Jiangsu. Tao's colleagues—notably provincial administration commissioner Liang Zhangju—asked that the portraits be engraved on stone to preserve the memory of the worthies. Coincidently, Liang had just finished rebuilding the Pavilion of Green Waves (Canglang ting), a historical monument that dated back to Su Shunqin (1008–48) in the Song period. Tao decided to build a shrine near the pavilion and have the portraits engraved on the inner walls (figure 8). Completed in 1828, it became known as the General Shrine of Former Worthies of Suzhou Prefecture (*Wujun xianxian zongci*). Twice a year, rites for worshipping the worthies were performed to invoke their memories and virtues. To encourage contemporary literati to emulate them, the shrine's second story featured their writings.

Liang Zhangju then discussed publishing the portraits with Gu Yuan. At his request, Gu proceeded to add short biographies and poetic eulogies for each of the worthies.[2] Although only a minor scholar, he mobilized several high officials to write prefaces to his work. These included not only Tao Zhu, Liang Zhangju, and Han Feng, but also Shi Yunyu (1756–1837), a native of Wu County and former compiler of the Hanlin Academy, and Tang Jinzhao (1772–1856), minister of rites at the time.

In 1834, Shi Yunyu and others selected another 596 worthies. The names of these individuals had not been included in the General Shrine

FIGURE 8. Engraved portraits of the Suzhou worthies in the Pavilion of Green Waves (Photograph by the author)

either because their portraits did not survive or their biographies had not been collected on time to be included.[3] Shi wrote their names on tablets, placing them in the Pavilion for Respecting the Wise (Jingxian ge) to be worshipped together with the worthies in the General Shrine. Furthermore, Gu Yuan and several other Suzhou scholars proceeded to compile a volume with their biographies. A group of Suzhou scholars also identified in various histories and literary collections the names of more than 980 ministers, martyrs, hermits, and soldiers, all of Suzhou origin, who embodied the virtue of loyalty, and they compiled the *Wumen gongci chongsi xingming lu* (A record of the names worshipped in public shrines of Suzhou).[4]

This collective engagement in asserting local traditions among the Suzhou literati during the first half of the Daoguang reign raises a number of questions on the changing political and cultural environment of early nineteenth-century China. Why did locals strive to reassert local traditions on such a massive scale? What was the significance of the Suzhou literati's cultural practices in the shrine-building process? As discussed in the previous chapter, from the mid-Ming period, the paired shrines of eminent officials and local worthies had become a regular presence in all the counties and prefectures of China. Suzhou was one of the first places where the shrines made their appearance during the Ming period. If the people of Suzhou already had sacred places to worship their former worthies, why were new ones erected?

This chapter will explore the extent to which the early nineteenth century departed from the previous century in terms of the cultural practices available to the literati in the construction of their local identity. The changes in these practices contributed to the shifting state-elite relations in the early nineteenth century. This chapter will further illuminate the significance of that period as the starting point for the reassertion of local identity in the Suzhou area. To grasp the specific meanings surrounding shrine-building and publications, this chapter will focus on two features that exemplify most clearly the transformations in the early nineteenth-century cultural milieu—building a shrine devoted to local worthies and resorting to visual images both in the shrine and in the imprint.

The Use of Visual Images in the "Xiangxian ci" and "Minghuan ci" in the Ming

The reappearance of portraits in the form of wall engravings and book imprints in the early nineteenth century departed from the entrenched cultural practices inherited from the previous century. Confucian tradition considered the use of portraits as a dubious practice susceptible to criticism. Thus, the emperor discouraged the display of portraits in public Confucian shrines, such as the *minghuan ci* or *xiangxian ci*. For this reason, during the eighteenth century, the literati seldom resorted to them. Their reappearance reflected a more liberal interpretation of the dominant cultural norm sustained and imposed by the central government.

Let us start with a brief description of how the use of such visual representations as portraits or statues in Confucian shrines changed over time from the Ming period onward. Shrines for former local worthies first appeared in the Chinese cultural landscape during the Song.[5] Whereas the Shrine for Former Worthies devoted to native worthies and model local officials was a more common institution, in the Shrines for Local Worthies (*xiangxian tang* or *xiangxian ci*) only the native worthies were worshipped.[6] Portraits, statues, or wooden tablets adorned the interior of these shrines. As was the case with the Confucian Temples, portraits or statues seemed to have been the favored medium of worship in Song and Yuan times.

The Ming, however, challenged the practice of placing visual images for worship, and the sculpted or pictorial images in the former worthies' shrines encountered a fate similar to those in the Confucian Temples. To be sure, venerating Confucian sages in front of their portraits or statues could effectively serve didactic purposes by allowing the worshippers to contemplate the concrete form of model worthies and inspiring them to follow their path. But this iconic tradition was viewed with suspicion by Song Neo-Confucian scholars such as Cheng Yi (1033–1107) and Zhu Xi (1130–1200), and it received even stronger criticism from early Ming Confucians such as Song Lian (1310–81) or Song Na (1311–90).[7] As Deborah Sommer has explained, the practice of placing concrete images for worship ran the risk of profaning the numinous realm of the deceased, which should remain unfathomable and mysterious.[8] The risk also existed that the images failed to represent the likeness of the deceased, which would amount to worshipping another person. Moreover, critics argued, this practice had no precedent in the much idealized ancient history of China.[9]

The rise of voices hostile to images among early Ming Confucian scholars during the reign of the Hongwu Emperor led to their abolition. The first target, however, was not the Confucian Temple but the shrines for the gods of walls and moats (*chenghuang miao*), as the emperor adopted a policy of de-anthropomorphizing them by placing spirit tablets.[10] He then did the same at the Confucian Temple. In the new Imperial Academy in Nanjing, he placed a tablet, rather than a statue, of Confucius.[11]

This measure, however, was limited in scope to Nanjing because Hongwu allowed the statues from the Yuan period to remain in government schools all over China.[12] It was also short-lived. By 1462, the new Imperial Academy of Beijing restored the practice of placing a statue of Confucius.[13] Generally speaking, during the early Ming the worship of Confucius and other Confucian worthies in the Confucian Temples continued to be performed in front of actual statues or portraits, as it had been in the Song and Yuan, despite the continued effort of critics to end this practice.[14] In Suzhou, gazetteers frequently mentioned the decoration of statues or portraits of Confucius and other sages in the Confucian Temple during the Song, Yuan, and early Ming periods.[15]

The use of visual images in the worship of Confucius and other Confucian worthies was again challenged by the mid-Ming politician Qiu Jun (1421–95). Qiu argued that the tradition of erecting a statue of Confucius in the Confucian Temple originated from Buddhist practices in the Tang period and did not conform to the orthodox ritual preached by the former sages.[16] Echoing similar concerns and taking advantage of the rebuilding of the Confucian Temple, the prefect of Suzhou replaced the statues of the Confucian sages with wooden tablets in 1460, as he believed that statues did not conform to "ancient customs."[17] He then disposed of all the statues in the Eastern and Western Chambers of the Confucian Temple in nearby Lake Tai.[18] But he dared not touch the statues of major Confucian figures on the altar in the main building.[19]

Such drastic measures could not be maintained for long without stronger support from higher authorities. Fifty years later, in 1510, a prefect found his predecessor's measure "inappropriate," and, along with more than 300 licentiates, he donated private money to remold the statues of 110 Confucian worthies to be placed in the Eastern and Western Chambers of the Confucian Temple. The cult of these worthies apparently regained its older form.

Historical evidence suggests that, in many instances, not only Confucius and his disciples, but also local worthies and eminent officials had their portraits or statues placed in shrines prior to the mid-Ming period. A source on Anping County in Hebei states that in the Dade reign (1297–1307) during the Yuan dynasty a local official built a pavilion for the local worthies and installed their portraits inside.[20] Likewise, sources recount that following the death of a prominent local figure in Yiyang County, Jiangxi, in 1457, the county magistrate visited the shrine for local worthies and copied the man's portrait there to offer him sacrifices.[21] The most striking example, however, concerns Wujiang County, Suzhou prefecture, in the mid-Ming period: as can be seen, the Wujiang County gazetteer, published around 1488, contains a group portrait of the fifteen people worshipped in the shrine for local worthies, as well as a group portrait of eminent officials (figure 9).[22]

In 1530, however, there was a drastic reversal in the display of visual representations in the temples related to Confucianism following the Jiajing Emperor's edict ordering the replacement of all the portraits and statues in the Confucian Temple with tablets.[23] While the reformers of

FIGURE 9. Group portrait of the local worthies in the 1488 edition of the Wujiang County gazetteer (Source: *Wujiang zhi*, 1.16b-17a)

ritual practice in 1530 could support the legitimacy of their measures by relying on prior advocates of the aniconic tradition within Confucianism, the reform immediately stirred up the Confucian literati, who perceived it as an insult from an autocratic ruler.[24] Despite their protests, however, the statues of Confucius and other Confucian worthies in the Confucian Temple were destroyed by imperial fiat. In the late Ming and early Qing, many Confucian scholars, such as Shen Defu (1578–1642) or Gu Yanwu (1613–82), endorsed Jiajing's iconoclastic measure.[25]

Though the Jiajing Emperor's policy of de-anthromorphization targeted primarily Confucius and his disciples, it had repercussions for all the lesser worthies worshipped within the boundaries of the government schools. Eminent officials and local worthies faced a fate similar to that of the greater Confucian sages.[26] Following Jiajing's reforms, local gazetteers or literary collections barely mentioned portraits or statues in the government school shrines.[27] Throughout the Ming and the Qing, many sources note the existence of only tablets in the *minghuan ci* or *xiangxian ci*.[28] The Wujiang County gazetteer, which featured the portraits of both local worthies and eminent officials in its edition published around 1488, no longer mentioned them in the 1588 edition. The 1642 Wu County gazetteer lists the names of eminent officials and local worthies under the titles *minghuan ci chongsi zhuwei* and *xiangxian ci chongsi zhuwei*, respectively: in this case, *chongsi zhuwei* meant tablets for worship. During the Qing period, the 1731 Zhaowen County gazetteer (Suzhou prefecture) discussed the 1530 reform to replace the portraits or statues with tablets, noting: "The order of the wooden tablets of the former worthies and former Confucians has long been in disorder, and the tablets . . . have been missing. After the second year of Yongzheng . . . the order [of the tablets] has been arranged according to the time sequence."[29] The gazetteer also indicates that tablets were the only acceptable and legitimate object of worship. The author of the same gazetteer even lists the names of the eminent officials and local worthies under the rubrics of *minghuan ci muzhu* and *xiangxian ci muzhu*, making clear that wooden tablets rather than statues or portraits were the objects of worship. In the case of the gazetteer of Yuanhe County, published during the Qianlong period, only the existence of wooden tablets is confirmed.[30]

Local resistance to the 1530 ritual reform policy arose sporadically, as people found ways to bypass directions imposed from the top. After a long absence in the Confucian Temple in Changzhou County, Suzhou, the local gentry there reinstalled the sage's statue sometime after 1705 and, in addition, molded the statues of lesser Confucian worthies about twelve years later.[31] The relevant section in the county gazetteer for Changzhou printed in 1753, however, does not mention the existence of these statues.[32] As Gu Yanwu lamented, some local officials hid the statue of Confucius by building a wall in front of it rather than blasphemously removing it.[33] Kunshan, Gu Yanwu's home county in Suzhou prefecture, is a case in point. During the Chongzhen period (1628–44), the Kunshan literati had renewed and reorganized the wooden tablets in the Eastern and Western Chambers of the Confucian Temple. In 1670, responding to the Kangxi Emperor's endorsement of a memorial by the Shuntian director of education, the county magistrate of Kunshan tore down the wall and brought the statues back to their original places. The Shuntian director had asked for permission to bring back the statues of Confucius and his disciples, which had been stored behind the walls of the temple during the Ming. In 1672, the magistrate and other local residents donated money to renovate the Great Hall of Accomplishment and embellish the statues of Confucius and other sages. Yet there is no indication during the Yongzheng and Qianlong reigns of the existence of statues in the Confucian Temple of Kunshan. Instead, local gazetteers mention that the wooden tablets were reinstalled in the Confucian Temple in 1735. Only in 1807 did another instance of redecorating the statues occur.[34]

It is difficult at this moment to assess exactly why Kangxi allowed a more liberal interpretation of Confucian ritual practices. In 1670, when Kangxi accepted the proposal of the Shuntian director of education, the Qing Empire still stood on shaky foundations, forced to deal with active Ming loyalist forces along the eastern coast and semi-autonomous powerful satraps in the southern territories. In this historical context, Kangxi's generous gesture seems to have been a way to appeal to the large masses of Confucian elites. Huang Chin-shing has argued that the 1530 ritual reform that initially removed the portraits and statues from the Confucian Temple was primarily motivated by an imperial concern to suppress the power of the literati. If this is the case, then the Kangxi Emperor manipulated the images to enlist the support of literati elites in a time of crisis.

After the Qing Empire found itself subjected to a more authoritarian style of rule under Yongzheng and Qianlong, however, we seldom find traces of official or literati efforts to restore the pre-1530 style of worship, as suggested by the examples above. Even allowing that the images remained in the temples, they were not officially patronized by local officials and local elites.

It seems clear that the shrines contained only tablets of eminent officials and local worthies in Suzhou as late as the early nineteenth century. A local source states that while various shrines located within the county schools of Changzhou and Yuanhe were being rebuilt in the early Daoguang reign, a local man donated money to engrave the names of the worthies on stone tablets in the Shrine for Eminent Officials.[35] Gu Yuan provides another important piece of evidence that corroborates the absence of visual images in the shrines. When Gu embarked on his project to collect the portraits of former worthies, he copied them from collections compiled by an early Qing figure and a local antiquarian. He also visited the descendants of the worthies and copied the images from the statues inside the family shrines devoted to their ancestors.[36] Had the shrines in government schools housed portraits of former worthies, Gu Yuan would have mentioned his visits to the shrines.

Another case in the adjoining Taicang independent department runs parallel to the Suzhou case. The *Lianchuan mingren huaxiang* (The portraits of the famous men in Lianchuan), first published in 1850, is a collection of brief biographies and portraits of local worthies from Jiading County as well as eminent officials and sojourners. To obtain the biographical information and the portraits, the compiler of the volume visited Buddhist temples, the homes of the worthies' descendants, and private book collectors rather than the *minghuan ci* or *xiangxian ci*.[37] This suggests that the worship of the local worthies in Jiading was practiced before their tablets, not their portraits, in the nineteenth century.

These examples attest to the absence of visual images in the shrines of eminent officials and local worthies within the government schools. Portraits or statues of many worthies did exist, but they were housed either by antiquarians, individual families, or in family shrines. They were not displayed in public Confucian shrines, indicating that the 1530 ritual reform seems to have been effective, at least in shrines of eminent officials and local worthies.

In addition to the ideological authority of the aniconic tradition within Confucianism itself, which could justify the 1530 reform, the Qing imperial attitude in support of that reform can be considered another important factor that largely discouraged the return of portraits during the eighteenth century. The Qianlong Emperor remarked:

> I regard placing images as a wiser act than having an impersonator of an ancestor (*gongshi*). Why is it so? Images can be made from iron, wood, and earth. Iron, wood, and earth are without knowledge (*wuzhizhe*). An impersonator of an ancestor is drawn from among men. Therefore he has knowledge (*youzhizhe*). If you imitate a thing that has knowledge with another that also has knowledge, then this is one thing that has knowledge, and that is also another thing that has knowledge. Like water and fire, can they mix together? If you imitate a thing that has knowledge with another

> that has no knowledge, the worshipped spirit that has knowledge may cling to the image that has no knowledge and enjoy the sacrifice. . . . *However, ultimately [the images] are less desirable than written spirit tablets. . . . The written spirit tablet of Confucius in the Imperial Academy conforms to the orthodox way of the sages. The statue in the Queli* (i.e. Qufu) *is something that can be left undisturbed because it is already there.*[38]

Qianlong's statement shows that the emperor considered spirit tablets as the most orthodox object of worship, after which came the images, and then the impersonators of ancestors. His statement also indicated that at that time the Imperial Academy of Beijing had no statue or portrait of Confucius, only his spirit tablet. The imperial court considered the absence of visual images in Confucian shrines as the proper way of worship.[39] The return of the public display of portraits in early nineteenth-century Suzhou, therefore, should be considered as a challenge not only to the entrenched ideological norm, but also to the political power that created and enforced it. The challenge was "indirect" because the portraits could not be found in the regular shrines of the worthies located inside the government school, only in the General Shrine, a less official place. This should be viewed as a creative attempt to avoid having to alter the existing cultural norm while promoting new changes. It conveyed the relaxation of state power in the cultural realm and the greater freedom of the literati's cultural activities in the early nineteenth century.

Biographies with Portraits

Gu Yuan, one of the key figures in the establishment of the General Shrine and collection of the portraits, organized a volume with brief biographies and poetic encomiums attached to the portrait of each figure. Published around 1829, the book was entitled *Wujun wubai mingxian tuzhuanzan* (Portraits, biographies, and poetic eulogies of five hundred famous worthies of Suzhou prefecture) (see figure 10). As one of the writers of the preface aptly pointed out, the printed volume would disseminate the images and the contributions of the worthies to a broader public outside the walls of the shrine. Like the installation of portraits in the

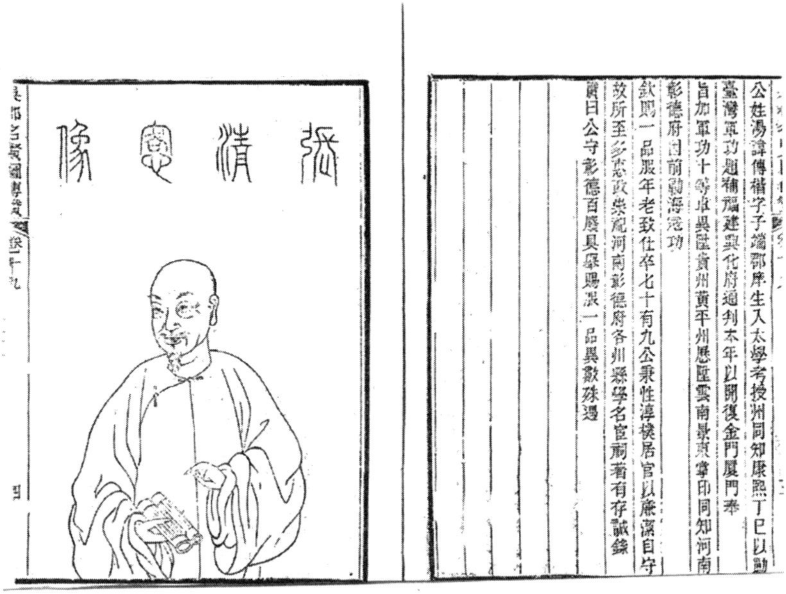

湯清惠像

公姓湯諱傳楷字子端郡庠生入太學考授州同知康熙丁巳以勦
臺灣軍功題補福建興化府通判本年以開復金門廈門奉
旨加軍功十等卓異陞貴州黃平州歷陞雲南景東掌印同知河南
彰德府因前勦海寇功
欽賜一品服年老致仕卒七十有九公秉性淳樸居官以廉潔自守
故所至多惠政祟祀河南彰德府各州縣學名宦祠著有存誠錄
贊曰公守彰德百廢具舉賜服一品異數殊遇

FIGURE 10. Sample pages from *Portraits, Biographies, and Poetic Eulogies of Five Hundred Famous Worthies of Suzhou Prefecture* (Source: Gu Yuan, *Wujun wubai mingxian tuzhuanzan*, 19.3b-4a)

shrine, the publication represented a return to an earlier practice. In this section, the development of biographies of worthies with portraits as a genre since the Ming period is examined, and it is argued that pictorial biographies of worthies show patterns in their emergence and disappearance over time similar to those of statues, portraits, and tablets.

Gu Yuan's style note in the *Portraits* states clearly that the genre experienced a long hiatus during the eighteenth century. According to him, the tradition of publishing portraits of Suzhou local worthies began with a pre-Tang text, *Kuaiji xianxian xiangzan* (Portraits and eulogies of former worthies of Kuaiji), which had been long lost by his time but whose title could be found in the *Sui shu* (Sui history). Gu also noted that the tradition of drawing portraits of eminent local officials (*minghuan*) in Suzhou began during the Shaoxing reign (1131–62) of the Southern Song, when they were displayed in the Zhanyi Pavilion (Zhanyitang tuxiang). During the Ming, Wang Shizhen (1526–90) revived this practice with his *Wuzhong wangzhe xiangzan* (Portraits and eulogies of past savants of

Suzhou), a collection of portraits of Suzhou worthies from the first half of the dynasty. This volume was supplemented in the late Ming by a scholar named Qian Gu, but the added portion was not significant. After the founding of the Qing, another Suzhou native, Zhang Chan, added the portraits of worthies from the Longqing, Wanli, Tianqi, and Chongzhen periods. Zhang Chan's portraits were later handed over to two Suzhou families, the Shen and the Jiang, with the portraits housed by the Shen family being later passed on to the Peng family. Gu Yuan visited the houses of these two families and copied around two hundred portraits for his own work, the first to cover the Qing period and to include ancient figures dating back to the Zhou and Han periods.

From Gu's description of the genealogy of pictorial biographies in Suzhou, it is evident that the eighteenth century represents a lacuna in the tradition of the genre. This is also confirmed in the *Taicang xiangxianxian huaxiang* (Portraits of Taicang local former worthies), another collection of pictorial biographies of the Suzhou area, published in 1947. In the preface it states:

> The beginning of the portraits of our famous Suzhou worthies was the five-volume *Kuaiji xianxian xiangzan*. This can be seen in the bibliographic treatise of the *Sui shu*. This was the oldest form of a book with portraits. During the Shaoxing period of the Song there were portraits in the Zhanyi Pavilion, but they were only portraits and did not form a book. With the passage of time it has become impossible to get an idea of what they were like. Then Mr. Wang Shizhen of our Taicang compiled a book called *Wuzhong wangzhe xiang*. Afterward, Qian Gu and Zhang Chan took turns in supplementing it. During the Daoguang period of the Qing, Gu Yuan of Suzhou collected and combined the portraits that had been preserved in his home and made them into a book.[40]

Here the author repeats almost verbatim the genealogy of the pictorial biographies in Suzhou traced by Gu Yuan. The preface suggests that the tradition of the genre revived by Wang Shizhen in the middle of the Ming was inherited by late Ming and early Qing figures, but underwent a long hiatus before Gu Yuan restored it in the early nineteenth century.

How representative was Suzhou in this pattern empire-wide? To anticipate the conclusion, it can be said that these other examples largely confirm that the genre experienced a flourishing period in the late Ming and then almost disappeared from public circulation during the Yongzheng and Qianlong periods, only to reemerge in greater numbers in the nineteenth century. Yet, in order to answer this question, other works belonging to the same genre must be examined.

The *Runzhou xianxianlu* (Record of the former worthies of Runzhou) was compiled in 1463 by Yao Tang while he was prefect of Zhenjiang (Runzhou being an old name) in Jiangsu. Yao had been prefect of Suzhou before coming to Zhenjiang. When he arrived at his new post, he was dissatisfied that Zhenjiang did not have a shrine for its local worthies. A shrine called the *Qingfeng dajie ci* existed in the government school, but the shrine featured only three former worthies. Yao decided to peruse local gazetteers and, from them, he selected twenty Zhenjiang worthies, reporting his findings to the grand coordinator. With his permission, he erected a shrine for them and placed their tablets inside.[41] As the prefectural gazetteer proved inadequate in providing concrete information about these worthies, Yao collected additional biographical data on them from a variety of books; by visiting village elders and the worthies' descendants he was able to have their portraits drawn.[42] When all of this was done, he published the results. Although Yao had portraits of the local worthies prepared and published in his collection of pictorial biographies, there is no indication that he actually installed them in the shrine. Instead, he placed wooden tablets there, suggesting that the portraits and tablets of the Zhenjiang worthies coexisted before the 1530 reform: the tablets in the shrine and the portraits outside in printed books.

The *Shengxian xiangzan* (Portraits and eulogies of sages and worthies), a book with prefaces dating back to 1632 and reprinted in 1878, contains the portraits and poetic encomiums of Confucius and other Confucian sages worshipped in the Confucian Temple. It is noteworthy that it was written in the late Ming, long after the 1530 reform. During this period, apparently, presenting images in book form emerged as an acceptable alternative as long as they could perform their didactic function of edifying the people with the sages' moral virtues and encouraging them to emulate their deeds.[43] The sentiment that the images of Confucian sages should be readily accessible to the public may have been heightened as a reaction to the prevailing practices of Buddhism, Daoism, and

Christianity, all of which employed visual images for worship. As the preface to the *Shengxian xiangzan* notes:

> [Thanks to the author's effort to include portraits of Confucian sages in this book] those minds that flowed [toward Buddhism and Daoism] will return, those that were diverse will come to unity, and those that moved away will come back. Truly, the law of heaven and earth and the foundation of fortune and misfortune rest on this. [If one] criticizes these [portraits] as too intimate and too ostentatious, is it then acceptable to allow the Buddhists, Daoists and Christians, who are busy [having statues or portraits] nowadays, [do the same]?[44]

A final example illustrating the popularity of the genre in the late Ming is the *Yue sanbuxiu tuzan* (Portraits and encomia of Zhejiang worthies whose three things do not perish). This book was originally compiled by the famous late Ming/early Qing scholar Zhang Dai (1597–1679) and printed later in the Qing. According to Cai Yuanpei's preface for a 1918 reprint, Zhang Dai lamented the disappearance of the traces of the former worthies. He visited the homes of their descendants to obtain their portraits and ultimately published them in this book.[45] The preface dated 1888 provides a more detailed description of how the book acquired its current form. Before his death, it says, Zhang Dai had asked Cai Erda in Ningbo to publish twenty-some portraits. Forty years later, Zhang's son gave the unpublished fifty portraits to his nephew to put them in print. Only twenty years later, however, did Cai Erda's son combine in a book the twenty-some portraits that his father had printed with those fifty portraits. The entire process of producing a volume lasted sixty years. Its first edition dates from the early Qianlong period (1739), long after Zhang Dai's death in 1679. After fifty years, however, the original printing blocks had become dilapidated. Aware of this problem, a person surnamed Yu supplemented the decrepit printing blocks in 1795. Later, in 1820, they were given to yet another person, who reprinted the book.[46]

While the examples discussed so far can all be considered products of the late Ming or early Qing, the following cases reveal that the genre was revitalized only after the end of the eighteenth century. Apart from the *Wujun wubai mingxian tuzhuanzan*, Gu Yuan compiled two other pictorial biographies. The first, entitled *Shengmiao sidian tukao* (An illustrated investigation of the sacrificial rites at the temple of the sage), contains two prefaces by Suzhou literati and another by the famous statecraft official He Changling. In his preface dated 1826, Changzhou gentryman Peng Xizheng claimed the book's merit lay in the fact that its collated content concerned not only Confucius and Mencius, but also the worthies closest to Confucius in the Confucian Temple. Before this, Peng explained, the dates of birth and enshrinement of the worthies, as well as the details of their moral virtues, had been scattered throughout various sources.[47] Like Gu Yuan, Peng first retraced the history of the worthies' portraits, beginning in the Han dynasty with Wenweng, who drew the portraits of the Confucian worthies in a stone chamber in Chengdu, Sichuan. In the Southern Song, portraits of the worthies were engraved on a stone stele in the Imperial University. Later, the *Shengxian jitu* (Pictures of the traces of the sages and worthies), compiled by Hu Wenhuan, carried this tradition into the late Ming. Yet the figures included in these three collections were limited to the direct disciples of Confucius and did not cover the Confucians of the Han and Tang dynasties. In the late Ming, Peng continued, the *Shengxian xiangzan* appeared, but with many flaws: first, it contained a number of interpretations regarding the names, official titles, and places of origin of the worthies that were either forced or far-fetched. In addition, the portraits were unauthentic and untrustworthy. There was also a book entitled *Wenmiao jilüe*, whose author was only identified by his surname, Hong. It contained no more than explanations on the figures and had no portraits; in addition, its coverage did not extend beyond 1714, ignoring the many individuals whose tablets were added later. The virtue of Gu Yuan's compilation lay in the inclusion of the worthies whose tablets had been officially added during the eighteenth and early nineteenth centuries. Gu was also commended for the accurate information on his subjects, which he acquired based on consulting a number of historical sources. Moreover, he had searched for the genuine portraits of the worthies from the Han and Tang period onward and included them in this compilation; when one could not be found, he left the space empty in the book in hopes that someone would be able to supply it someday.[48]

A few years later in 1830, Gu Yuan printed another pictorial biography, entitled *Gu shengxian xiang zhuanlüe* (Portraits and abridged biographies of the ancient sages and worthies), which supplemented his earlier

Shengmiao sidian tukao. While the *Shengmiao sidian tukao* focused on Confucius and other Confucian sages, the *Gu shengxian xiang zhuanlüe* featured a collection of portraits and short biographies of 425 renowned ministers from the ancient Three Dynasties to the Ming.[49]

The compilation of these works shows that Gu Yuan devoted his energies to collecting the portraits not just of Suzhou local worthies and eminent officials, but also of reputable Confucian sages and exemplary ministers from other areas throughout the empire. In short, he did much to revive the tradition of publishing biographies with portraits, after the practice had been discontinued under the Qing. A number of pictorial biographies followed his three publications during the nineteenth and twentieth centuries that collectively bear witness to the genre's revitalization. The list includes the previously mentioned *Lianchuan mingren huaxiang*, a collection of brief biographies and portraits of local worthies from Jiading in 1850, and the *Yuyue xianxian xiangzhuanzan*, first printed in 1856 and reprinted in 1877. This genre persisted in the twentieth century. The *Qingdai xuezhe xiangzhuan*, a collection of pictorial biographies of representative scholars from the Qing, appeared in 1930, followed by the *Taicang xiangxianxian huaxiang* and the *Chaozhou xianxian xiangzhuan*, both in 1947.

The dates of publication or reissue of the pictorial biographies discussed above illustrate the genre's pattern in late imperial China: it emerged quite prominently in the seventeenth century, only to become inactive during most of the period from Shunzhi to Qianlong until its revival in the early nineteenth century. If we compare it with the portraits and statues kept in the worthies' shrines, we can see that, in both cases, forms of visual representation that had largely vanished by the Qianlong period reemerged in the early nineteenth century.[50] The late Ming is an exception, however, as it can be surmised that installing images in Confucian shrines reflected a more direct breach of the Confucian norm than circulating them in print. While an audacious gesture, the reinstallation of portraits by Gu Yuan and others in the General Shrine in the early nineteenth century occurred only in a shrine without the same official stature as those devoted to eminent officials or local worthies.

What, then, was the rationale behind the early nineteenth-century revival of pictorial biographies? The logic is suggested in Gu Yuan's *Gu shengxian xiang zhuanlüe,* in which the author of one of the two prefaces,

Wu Tingchen (who appeared in chapter 3) from Yuanhe, explained why people needed to visualize the actual images of the former worthies:

> [If the people] live in the same period as the worthies and share the same place, they will necessarily feel fortunate to have a chance to see them. If the places are far away and mountains and rivers block the roads, then they will hear of their reputation and become reverent, feeling remorseful that they have not been given a chance to see them [in person]. After the generations have passed, the worthies will be a thing of the past. Those who want to go and become the friends of the former worthies will recite their poems and read their books, thereby hoping to understand their personalities; but in the end they will not be able to see them. Therefore, they will remember the worthies' appearance and bearing and draw their shapes to record the timelessness of their admiration.[51]

The former worthies played a pivotal role in edification. They were expected to provide moral examples for posterity. The portraits could, it was believed, create an awe-inspiring environment in which people would feel a sense of intimacy with the worthies and revere them. As Patricia Ebrey has explained, visual images could more powerfully "move people emotionally" than written words.[52]

As explained earlier, however, a number of major concerns emerged surrounding iconic practices, leading a group of Confucian scholars to preach against them. One such concern was the fear that images might not resemble the individual worshipped; this served as the rationale for the promoters of the 1530 ritual reform that banned the use of visual images for worship in Confucian Temples. Wu Tingchen noted: "There might be someone to cast doubt on [the images] and say that the transmitted portraits may not represent [correctly] even [close] ancestors. How can they represent those who are farther away in time?" Wu, echoing the words of the then junior compiler Xu Jie (1503–83), who had criticized the iconoclast policies in a debate with Grand Secretary Zhang Fujing (1475–1539) during the 1530 ritual reform, immediately refuted this aniconic stance: "If the trust and fondness are sincere," he said, "then one can recall [the former worthies] even in the soup one is drinking or on the wall one is looking at, as if one were seeing them directly, still more so when one actually has authentic portraits."[53] Wu Tingchen emphasizes in his preface the practical advantages of installing images rather than the problem of whether or not the portraits represent the real likeness of the former worthies. In his mind, these practical effects outweighed the problem of verisimilitude. The author of the second preface, dated 1827, adopted a similar position:

> In ancient times, both images (*tu*) and history (*shi*) were cherished. Before characters came into being, there existed images first. . . . In the Ming, Zhang Fujing established [new] ritual practices and ordered the school instructors in the whole realm to replace statues with wooden tablets. He said, "The images cannot necessarily represent reality. If there is the slightest difference in [the images of] ancestors, then we should not consider them as our ancestors and worship them." But someone criticized him saying, "If there is [even] the slightest resemblance with the ancestors, then can we disregard them as not being our ancestors and destroy the images?" Zhang Fujing was unable to give an answer to this.[54]

Here the author is referencing the debate between Xu Jie and Zhang Fujing during the 1530 ritual reform that led to the destruction of many statues in the Confucian shrines, even though he is actually prefacing a book belonging to the genre of pictorial biography. In his remarks, statues and portraits are both included in the category of *tu*. They are both images representing real figures and, in this sense, they both confront the issue of authenticity. It is therefore natural to expect that the portraits and statues should experience similar vicissitudes following the contours of power across dynasties. In this regard, the author is legitimating the reintroduction of images by invoking Xu Jie's voice. Xu's opinion, which represented the view popular among the literati at the time, lost ground in the assertion of autocratic control by the Jiajing Emperor; but it was rescued by early nineteenth-century scholars who favored the use of visual images.

As the authors of the prefaces quoted above argued, the visual images of Confucian sages and worthies were expected to be more effective in performing an edifying function. Thus, provincial officials and Suzhou literati proffered a more liberal interpretation of Confucian ritual practices to take advantage of the practical effects attributed to images. One can probably account for the strong demand for such edifying functions in the early nineteenth century by considering the social context of the time and the rise of statecraft scholarship. As is well known, a sense of impending crisis characterized the thought of many officials and scholars, which reflected the difficulties arising from internal and external factors, such as population pressure, rebellions, or the outflow of silver. The spread of this crisis consciousness is generally regarded by modern scholars as having spawned the rise of statecraft thinking. A concern for practical political and social problems and a pragmatic approach to solving them, distinct from the scholastic philology of *kaozheng* scholarship or the empty speculation of Song *lixue*, lay at the core of this thinking.[55] This growing awareness of crisis-ridden social conditions and the pursuit of practical solutions prompted officials and scholars in early nineteenth-century Suzhou to encourage the return of images.

Reinstalling images, as explained earlier, could be controversial when considered in the context of a more orthodox interpretation of Confucian ritual practices. In the minds of those who engaged in this practice, however, the edifying role and practical benefits outweighed the ideological ambiguity. In this respect, we should note that Tao Zhu, Liang Zhangju, He Changling, Shi Yunyu, and Zhu Jian (1769–1850, *js* 1802), who had the portraits of the worthies engraved in the General Shrine or wrote prefaces to pictorial biographies of them, were all statecraft-oriented officials and scholars. As Jiangsu provincial officials, Tao Zhu and He Changling (both alumni of the Yuelu academy in Hunan, which produced a number of eminent statecraft reformers in the nineteenth century) were actively engaged in renovating the water conservancy system and exhorting the court to implement the maritime transport of tribute grain in the 1820s.[56] In 1825, He Changling, along with fellow Hunanese Wei Yuan (1794–1857), began the compilation of the *Huangchao jingshi wenbian* (Collected writings on statecraft of the reigning dynasty), which would become a canonical statecraft collection. Along with Tao Zhu, both Liang Zhangju, another Jiangsu provincial official who supported Governor Tao Zhu's reforms in the 1820s, and Zhu Jian, who lectured at academies in Suzhou, had been members of the Xuannan Poetry Club (Xuannan shishe), an association of reform-minded officials and literati.[57] Shi Yunyu, who had passed the young Tao Zhu first in the county licensing examination while serving as the educational commissioner of

Hunan, became closely associated with him afterward and influenced his statecraft policies.[58]

The return of portraits also challenged the central government's authority in controlling ritual practices. As Qianlong's statement on the presence of images in the shrines showed, the use of tablets instead of images was supported by a supreme political power that publicly identified itself as the guardian of orthodox Confucian norms. The reintroduction of portraits in shrines and print during the early nineteenth century suggested that provincial officials and literati sensed a relaxation of the state's grip on culture, and it is illustrative of the greater choices in cultural practices enjoyed by the literati. Provincial officials and Suzhou elites were quick to appropriate this freedom in the cultural construction of their local tradition. Yet portraits were not the only symbols of the changing relations between central government and local elites. This trend could also be observed in the nature of the shrine and the choice of those to be worshipped.

The Building of the General Shrine of Suzhou Former Worthies

This chapter began by asking why the Suzhou literati needed to build another shrine for their former worthies in a less official setting, the Canglang ting, if shrines for eminent officials and worthies already existed. Following the steep reduction of the enshrinement numbers under Yongzheng and Qianlong, no place existed in the regular shrines of government schools for many of the eminent officials or local worthies deemed as candidates for enshrinement. With the Jiaqing Emperor in power, the number of enshrined worthies endorsed by the state climbed rapidly. In Suzhou, eleven local men were enshrined as local worthies during the twenty-five years of the Jiaqing reign as opposed to only ten during the preceding seventy years. Yet this increase was apparently not enough to satisfy Suzhou's residents, whose expectations had already been raised.

The General Shrine for the Former Worthies of Suzhou was built to meet this local demand. The selection of the worthies to be enshrined was entirely left to the discretion of local people, unlike the shrines for regular worthies, whose qualifications had to be examined by the central government.[59] At the General Shrine for the Former Worthies, no limit was placed on the number of worthies that the Suzhou literati could worship without alarming the central court—there were to be 570 of them. The enshrined worthies now included a number of Suzhou late Ming martyrs and loyalists officially rehabilitated by an imperial edict in 1776 (QL 41) as well as minor individuals who had not received attention from the imperial court—a combined total of over sixty. Not until 1776 could these figures be officially mentioned, and, for this reason, they are seldom found in official and private writings. They were a forgotten part of the local history of Suzhou until legitimate attention was duly paid to them in the early nineteenth century. The relaxation of the state's sensitivity to anti-Qing sentiment was apparent in the sphere of enshrinement and was also felt in the realm of publication. Some Jiangnan book publishers in the early nineteenth century began to reprint previously banned volumes that had been destroyed by Qianlong for their anti-Qing contents.

It was not only the Ming loyalists who managed to find a home in the General Shrine: the Suzhou figures involved in the late Ming and early Qing factional strife who were much hated by the Qing emperors also made it into the shrine. Now the Donglin faction members—Gu Xiancheng (1550–1612) and Gao Panlong (1562–1626)—as well as the Fushe members—Zhang Pu (1602–41), Gu Yanwu, Yang Tingshu (1595–1647), Yang Yi, and Wang Chun—all claimed their seats on the altar. Most of these figures had not been included in the official martyr list promulgated by Qianlong. Once again, their resurrection as prominent local figures in the public shrine represented a prompt response by the Suzhou elite to the relaxed politico-cultural environment of the early nineteenth century.[60]

The 570 worthies enshrined in the General Shrine included a large number of minor figures whose qualifications would not have merited a place in the regular *minghuan ci* and *xiangxian ci*. The evaluation process of the worthies by the central government placed emphasis on scholarly or administrative contributions with empire-wide significance. In contrast, selection by locals enshrined minor scholars and officials whose qualifications did not merit imperial attention and who would never have qualified for shrines devoted to eminent officials or local worthies.

The centralized cultural order that held sway during the eighteenth century, in which the imperial court monopolized the power and authority to evaluate historical events and figures, lost ground rapidly in the early nineteenth century. The trend shifted toward allowing more diverse local voices, distinct from the central government. The construction of the General Shrine made up part of a larger local agenda during the early nineteenth century to reassert the importance of Suzhou's local tradition, an effort that engaged its literati.

The retreat of state power from the local cultural realm constituted a key factor in the return of the portraits in the General Shrine. Exhibiting them in public spaces such as the Canglang ting, let alone in the regular shrines in government schools, would have been unlikely in the eighteenth century. Even in the early nineteenth century, it was an audacious initiative to be introduced to the official *minghuan ci* and *xiangxian ci*. For those who failed to do so, as an alternative, another shrine for these portraits was built in a less official place.

CHAPTER 6

State Control of Local Gazetteers and Private Local Literature

During the Kangxi, Yongzheng, and Qianlong periods, the emperorship came to embody the traditions of the Dao (*daotong*) and the governance (*zhitong*) that until then had belonged separately to the literati and the emperors.[1] Now the emperors were eulogized as sages, a role that no contemporary scholars could claim.[2] The Yongzheng and Qianlong Emperors drew a distinction between official history (*guanshi*) and private miscellaneous histories (*baiguan yeshi*). The court denied the authenticity and value of private histories and established official histories as the sole reliable sources for future generations.[3] The elevation of the official histories solidified the emperors' authoritative position in judging the value of historical works, especially during the Qianlong period. The emperor himself claimed and was claimed by his subordinates to surpass even Zhu Xi in the authority of historical comments, and the works by the emperor were espoused as equaling to, if not superseding, the value and authority of those by Confucius. Qianlong exemplified a "model of imperial rulership," and he was dedicated to the idea that the sovereign should be master of everything and impose order upon the world under his rule.[4]

Such an elevation of the emperor's cultural authority during the Qianlong reign was paralleled by state interventionist policies concerning the realm of literati writings. As Kent Guy's study has shown, during the last three decades of the Qianlong reign the court launched a campaign to review the contents of published books and it systematized the state censorship program.[5] In 1778, the governor of Zhejiang proposed that the literati across the empire should, prior to publication, submit two copies of the draft of their work to be examined by their hometown's local education officials and the provincial education commissioner.[6] Only those works free of any fallacies and deemed beneficial to scholarship should be allowed to be published, the governor argued. Worried about tarnishing his self-image as a patron of scholars, Qianlong viewed this proposal as too radical.[7] Had it been endorsed, it would have meant an extensive prepublication censorship of all genres of literary production. The extreme nature of his proposal, however, provides a glimpse into how far some officials wished to venture in order to streamline the thoughts of local elites and strengthen the state's presence in an area that scholars considered a secure domain.

While the prepublication censorship of all literati writings did not materialize, the central government under Qianlong did extend control to particular genres of literati writings that were closely intertwined with the interests of local elites: local gazetteers and privately written local literature. Following the classification of the *Siku quanshu*, this local literature—writings on local history, customs, and worthies—belonged to the categories of biography (*zhuanji*), miscellaneous history (*zashi*), or geography (*dili*) in the historical section (*shibu*), or to the category of individual collections (*bieji*) in the section of literary collections (*jibu*). Powerful local families viewed private local literature as a medium for enhancing their prestige, as these books recorded the names, virtues, and accomplishments of their members. At the same time, it served as a vehicle through which local people could acclaim the cultural traditions of their local community and highlight the importance of their hometown.

The production of local gazetteers and local literature underwent dramatic changes from the Qianlong to the Jiaqing and Daoguang reigns, reflecting another aspect of the changing relations between the state and local elites. Just as the shrine of local worthies was one activity in which the shifting weight of power between the state and local elites could be observed, so too was the realm of local literary production.

Local gazetteers and local literature faced the danger of clashing with state interests on two fronts during the eighteenth century. First, the appropriation of these genres by local elite families was incompatible with the state agenda to rescue public cultural media from the private control of powerful families. Through personal connections, kinship, local ties, and occasionally pressure or bribery, those families coerced compilers of local gazetteers to include the names of unworthy forebears or provide them with undeserved accolades in the biographical chapters. For privately written local literature, the selection of recorded figures was largely left to the discretion of the author. In this regard, controlling local writings corresponded to the government's measures concerning the enshrinement of local worthies. Both checked the arbitrary exercise of power by local elite families. Second, Qing officials during the Qianlong period realized the unreliable and destabilizing nature of local writings, as these were riddled with distortions, exaggerations, omissions, and other fraudulent practices that were frequently used to unduly enhance the reputation of certain families and localities.

Under Qianlong, ongoing state efforts sought to replace deviant local ideas with ones dictated by the court. The emperor and his officials strove to build a cultural order in which supreme authority was vested in the emperor and, by extension, the central government, an order that tried to suppress diverse local voices. Under this centralized order, the state viewed with suspicion any claims of cultural autonomy at the local level. In the early nineteenth century, as it became apparent that the court no longer displayed the eagerness to impose rigorous control on the local cultural realm, local writings rapidly gained popularity.

State-Imposed Control over Local Gazetteer Compilation

In 1766, the governor of Zhejiang Province, Xiong Xuepeng (d. 1779), requested to the Qianlong Emperor the adoption of more stringent controls over the compilation of local gazetteers.[8] Unlike provincial gazetteers submitted to the court for investigation, Xiong maintained, prefectural and county gazetteers were usually produced at the discretion of local officials, who collaborated with local elites. The governor named this practice "private" (*sizi*) compilation. The local gazetteers published under the initiative of prefects and magistrates could certainly have been regarded as "official" (*guan*). In Xiong's eyes, however, the absence of provincial or central government review of these gazetteers characterized them as "private."

More fundamentally, however, he labeled these publications as "private" due to problems pervading the existing compilation practices. Xiong charged that local officials frequently drew on the local elite for financial assistance during the compilation of their gazetteers. In return, the elites expected these gazetteers to reflect their personal interests. As a result, Xiong insisted, local gazetteers had been relegated to untrustworthy reservoirs of local knowledge, as they habitually heaped praise on unworthy local figures while ignoring their faults.

Based on a report presented by Qian Weicheng (d. 1772), a former educational commissioner of Zhejiang, Xiong cited three specific pieces of evidence to validate his allegations. The first concerned Mao Yilu (*js* 1604), a late Ming figure from Suian County in Zhejiang known for his association with the infamous eunuch faction of Wei Zhongxian (1568–1627). Mao was held partly accountable for the death of Zhou Shunchang (1584–1626), a Donglin faction member whose arrest by order of the eunuch leader provoked a mass riot in Suzhou.[9] Regardless of this disreputable connection, Xiong noted critically, the county gazetteer of Mao's hometown featured an embellished biography trumpeting his political career and alleged achievements. Xiong's second piece of evidence concerned a member of the eunuch faction from Jiaxing in the late Ming who had launched attacks on righteous men. Nevertheless, the prefectural gazetteer of Jiaxing, rather than mention that he had conspired with the eunuchs, actually highlighted his resistance against them.

Xiong drew his third piece of evidence from the Xiaoshan County gazetteer, which featured an unflattering portrait of Ming official Chen Dashou (*js* 1595) as an avaricious and cruel figure during the Jiajing period. Highlighting Chen's antagonism toward literati, the gazetteer claimed that he always blamed and humiliated literati involved in lawsuits with commoners. The gazetteer also claimed that Chen could not swallow food if he failed to cashier several licentiates in a month. Challenging these assertions, Qian Weicheng pointed out that Chen Dashou was an education intendant censor of Zhejiang during the Wanli period, not Jiajing, known for his fidelity and benevolence. Therefore, the gazetteer's inaccurate description of Chen had, in the eyes of Qian, entirely inverted right and wrong. On these grounds, Qian requested that Governor Xiong order these parts to be erased from the local gazetteers. Xiong Xuepeng agreed with Qian's report, underscoring that the first two accused figures had been unequivocally listed in the imperially sanctioned *Ming History* (*Ming shi*) as followers of Wei Zhongxian and members of the "treacherous faction" (*nidang*). By showering them with praise, the gazetteer compilers had undoubtedly distorted the truth. Xiong informed the emperor that he had already instructed local officials to expunge the offensive passages. As for Chen Dashou, Governor Xiong preferred a more cautious stance, requesting permission to investigate this matter further to obtain more information.

Convinced that this problem was not limited to a particular gazetteer, Xiong proposed specific remedies. Common practice, Xiong explained, dictated that local gazetteers be presented to newly arrived provincial officials to aid in governance. Given that gazetteers were too voluminous to have their details verified by these officials, Xiong proposed that the provincial education commissioners, who shouldered relatively lighter administrative burdens, be responsible for inspecting them. These commissioners should be tasked with identifying and eliminating offensive sections and provide annual lists of expunged parts to the governor-general and the governor, who, in turn, would report them to the emperor. Xiong also suggested that local officials must inform their superiors prior to revising an existing gazetteer or compiling a new one. Upon completion of the draft gazetteer, the provincial education commissioner should review it for the emperor, who would decide whether to grant permission for its publication. Xiong also insisted that local officials bear the expenses for the compilation themselves, banning them from collecting money for this purpose. By freeing them from their financial dependence on local elites, Xiong believed that the compilers would no longer be susceptible to pressure from local elites, ensuring the accuracy of the information recorded in gazetteers.

Following a discussion of Xiong's memorial among high court officials, the Grand Secretary Fuheng (d. 1770) confirmed Xiong's assessment of the gazetteers' unreliable evaluations of two of the late Ming figures.[10] Similar to Xiong, Fuheng substantiated his claim in the imperially endorsed *Ming shi* that had included these two in the category of the "eunuch faction" (*yandang*). In the minds of Xiong and Fuheng, this judgment outweighed any claims espoused by the gazetteers.

Fuheng also discussed the Chen Dashou case. After examining the stele with the list of metropolitan graduates at the Imperial University, Fuheng ascertained that Chen had been a *jinshi* of the Wanli reign, corroborating Xiong's claims. Fuheng approved the governor's removal of these grossly imprecise passages from the gazetteers.

Fuheng accepted Xiong's overall suggestions, but he revised them. He expressed certain hesitations about Xiong's insistence that provincial education commissioners review local gazetteers while on their regular tours of prefectures. Fuheng noted that various circumstances would not always allow them time to verify gazetteers. Instead, he provided commissioners with greater flexibility to work on revisions by not fixing deadlines. If problematic sections surfaced, the commissioners were expected to direct local officials to remove or revise them and report the changes to the provincial officials. With respect to local gazetteers being compiled at the time, he concurred with Xiong that printing should occur only after the provincial education commissioners reviewed and approved the draft gazetteer.

Fuheng did not embrace Xiong's more radical proposals. He expressed doubts on the feasibility of having the emperor review the drafts of all gazetteers before publication. The massive volumes of the gazetteers, he explained, would raise the workload of an already tired emperor. Fuheng's decision to refuse this extensive censorship plan stems from the compilation process of a new *Gazetteer of the Unification* (*yitong zhi*) that was under way.[11] Unlike local gazetteers, the *Gazetteer of the Unification* and the provincial gazetteers had been sanctioned by the emperor. Believing that reliable local information had already been secured in this way, Fuheng did not sense the urgency in establishing an extensive prepublication official review of all future gazetteers. Fuheng also rejected Xiong's request to ban private donations for gazetteer compilation. Unlike Xiong, who worried about interference by local elites, Fuheng insisted that the practice of gazetteer compilation had belonged to the domain of local public affairs, and that the state should not forbid donations from elites.

Although Qianlong embraced Fuheng's report, subsequent developments suggested that the Qing government moved toward Xiong's more restrictive approach of compulsory prepublication censorship of all new gazetteers. The *Qinding Xuezheng quanshu* (The imperially authorized compendium of records of the education commissioner), printed sometime after 1773, included Fuheng's memorial presented in 1766. Although this entry listed Fuheng's main points, his dismissal of Xiong's request for prepublication censorship was not included. In his original memorial, Fuheng had categorized gazetteers into three types: published gazetteers, gazetteers being compiled at the time, and future gazetteers. While he supported the review of the first two, he dismissed it for the third. With the omission of the phrase "future gazetteers" in the *Qinding Xuezheng quanshu*, the term "currently compiled gazetteers" encompassed all new gazetteer projects. This suggests that Fuheng's original recommendation was reversed to include the future ones as well.[12]

More direct evidence of prepublication censorship can be gathered from local gazetteers compiled after 1766. Following that year, the practice of featuring the names of education commissioners as authors of a preface or under the category "appraisal" (*jianding*) in local gazetteers became the norm until the end of the eighteenth century. The 1768 Wangjiang County gazetteer of Anhui contains a preface by the Anhui education commissioner. He stated that a recent imperial decree required that past and new gazetteers undergo a thorough examination by education commissioners to redress errors. Local officials were also required to submit drafts to the commissioner prior to publication.[13] The 1770 edition of the Lu'an prefectural gazetteer in Shanxi included the names of the governor and the education commissioner under the category of "appraisal" (*jianding*) and the names of administrative and judicial commissioners under a similar one.[14] Likewise, the 1779 Chizhou prefectural gazetteer (Anhui) featured a preface highlighting this practice and the 1792 Shaoxing prefectural gazetteer (Zhejiang) included the names of the governor-general and the education commissioner under the category of "appraisal."[15] The *Chang Zhao hezhi* (Combined gazetteer of Changshu and Zhaowen Counties) of Suzhou prefecture, published in 1805, even contained a document from the county officials of Changshu and Zhaowen submitted to the Jiangsu education commissioner in 1793 requesting the commissioner's permission to publish the draft of *Chang Zhao hezhi*.[16]

These cases demonstrate the institutionalized practice of prepublication censorship of local gazetteers by provincial officials across the Qing Empire after Xiong Xuepeng's memorial in 1766. Table 4 illustrates this

Table 4
The number of county and prefectural gazetteers in Jiangnan and North China produced between 1644 and 1850, by reigns

	Jiangnan Provinces					North China Provinces				
	Jiangsu	Zhejiang	Jiangxi	Anhui	Total	Shandong	Zhili	Shanxi	Henan	Total
Shunzhi	10	10	7	24	**51**	14	13	18	59	**104**
Kangxi	64	107	106	68	**345**	115	151	82	105	**453**
Yongzheng	12	12	4	9	**37**	5	18	24	5	**52**
Qianlong	53	49*	85	47	**234**	60	82	74	101	**317**
1–30	44	28	57	32	**161**	42	63	37	77	**219**
31–60	9	19	28	15	**71**	18	19	37	24	**98**
Jiaqing	23	23	12	22	**80**	15	10	7	20	**52**
Daoguang	18	21	74	26	**139**	35	15	13	18	**81**

SOURCE: Zhongguo kexueyuan Beijing tianwentai, ed., *Zhongguo difangzhi lianhe mulu.*

*Here I included the two gazetteers compiled during the Qianlong reign but whose exact compilation dates are unknown.

trend, listing the numbers of local gazetteers compiled in four provinces in the Jiangnan area and another four in the North from the beginning of the Qing era through the Daoguang reign.

During the early years of Qing rule, provincial officials in the North enthusiastically organized the production of provincial gazetteers. This project encouraged the publication of many county and prefectural gazetteers to supply materials for the provincial gazetteers. In 1661, the governor of Henan Jia Hanfu (1606–77) compiled the *Henan tongzhi* (Provincial gazetteer of Henan Province), and he encouraged the publication of local gazetteers under his jurisdiction.[17] Satisfied with the favorable reception, upon assuming the post of governor, Jia replicated such efforts in Shaanxi in 1662.

In 1672, the Qing court decided to organize the *Gazetteer of the Great Qing Unification*. To facilitate this endeavor, imperial orders for the compilation of provincial and local gazetteers were issued in 1672, 1683, and 1728.[18] As a result, more than one thousand local gazetteers were printed across the empire from the start of the project until its completion in 1743.[19] The response to these government initiatives differed depending on the region. The northern provinces demonstrated greater enthusiasm than the Lower Yangzi region, producing more local gazetteers from the beginning of the Qing until the end of the Qianlong period (see table 4). This discrepancy reflected, to some extent, a more active response of officials in the North to imperial initiatives on the compilation of gazetteers.[20]

The number of local gazetteers in the North and in Jiangnan experienced a substantial decrease during the latter half of Qianlong's rule, a time that coincided with the duration of prepublication censorship. The scrutiny appears to have inhibited local officials and elites from producing gazetteers for fear of mistakenly including unauthorized passages that could put them in trouble with the state. Jiangsu witnessed an astounding fall from forty-four gazetteers in the first half of the Qianlong reign to only nine in the second half. In addition to more stringent regulations, the fallout from the Qian Qianyi case might have discouraged compilation projects in the province.

Qian Qianyi (1582–1664), a renowned and widely respected literary leader of the Jiangnan elite community, was a late Ming high official from Suzhou. Although Qian served the Qing dynasty after the fall of the

Ming, the Qianlong Emperor viewed with disdain his disloyalty to the Ming. Moreover, after finding a number of anti-Qing phrases in Qian's poetry collections in 1769, the emperor promptly ordered officials in Jiangnan to confiscate Qian's books and their printing blocks.[21] A decade later in 1779, Min Eyuan (1720–97), the governor of Anhui, requested the removal of the titles of prohibited works by blacklisted authors from all the county and prefectural gazetteers.[22] In response, Qianlong explained:

> This memorial is correct. For a long time the poems and prose of Qian Qianyi, Qu Dajun (1630–96), Jin Bao (1614–80), and others have been prohibited, in order to help teach the people and to rectify the people's minds. Current county and prefectural gazetteers of the provinces frequently include their poems and prose under the heading of famous scenic sites or historical remains. They also include their lives, stories, and the titles of their books under the headings of persons and literature. These should be eliminated one by one.[23]

Following this edict, a campaign was undertaken to investigate local gazetteers for the titles of forbidden books and the names of banned authors. This measure was executed with rigor, as evidenced in the document in the *Chang Zhao hezhi*. This document reveals that in 1779 an order mandated that any texts written by, or facts relevant to, Qian Qianyi and others be erased from the gazetteers.[24] Before long, existing gazetteers of Changshu and Zhaowen Counties were brought to the local Confucian school for examination and the offending sections removed.[25]

Table 4, however, shows significant changes in the production of gazetteers in the North and in Jiangnan in the early nineteenth century. The numbers compiled in the four northern provinces declined from ninety-eight in the latter half of the Qianlong period to fifty-two under the Jiaqing, while the numbers in the four Jiangnan provinces conversely climbed from seventy-one to eighty. Subsequently, during the Daoguang reign, the southern provinces repeatedly outnumbered their northern counterparts in gazetteers, widening the margin from twenty-eight in the previous reign to fifty-eight. In the early nineteenth century, the production of gazetteers in Jiangnan surpassed that in the North for the first time in Qing history. This reversal seems to be closely related to the loosening of government control over gazetteer compilation.

The "Siku Quanshu Zongmu Tiyao" and Criticisms against Local Literature

The Qing state's determination to tame the localism that it felt had permeated many genres of local writing can also be detected in the *Siku quanshu zongmu tiyao* (Compendium of the Complete Library of the Four Treasuries). The compilation of the Compendium began in 1773 and its first draft was completed in 1781.[26] After revisions, the final version appeared in print during the last years of the Qianlong reign.[27] The Compendium contains bibliographical explanations of the works included in the *Siku quanshu* as well as an even greater number of books noted only by their titles. The Compendium includes a discussion by the compilers of a sizable number of works on local writing, including local gazetteers and private local literature. Their comments also reflected, to a considerable extent, the view of the Qianlong Emperor. During the compilation of the *Siku quanshu*, the emperor had reviewed the books and commented on historical events and figures through edicts and his own writing. This influenced the selection and evaluation of books by officials and evidential research scholars.[28] By comparing the comments on the included and excluded books, we can reconstruct the criteria employed by the court officials in selecting desirable local writings.

Let us first look at the *Qiantang xianxian zhuanzan* (Biography and encomium of the former worthies of Qiantang) organized by a Song author and included in the *Siku quanshu*. The compilers noted:

> Although [this book] recorded only the elders of one locality, more than ten people including Lang Jian (968–1056), Xie Jiang (995–1039), and others are also found in the official history (*zheng shi*). . . . This book is very detailed and rich, as much has been gathered from the inherited knowledge of the elders. Therefore, those who compiled the official history collected information [from this book] and inserted it in the biographies. Therefore [this book] coincides with the *Song History* (*Song shi*) to

> a considerable degree. The biography and the encomium are also archaic and elegant, and therefore can be recited. Truly, this [book] cannot be compared with the practices of exaggeration, embellishment, and the far-fetched interpretations of later local literature compilers.[29]

The Compendium compilers valued this book because many local worthies discussed in it were prominent enough to be recorded in the *Song History*. The local claim that the virtues and merits of these men were worthy of recording was corroborated by their inclusion in a history written on a far larger geographic scale. Moreover, that history was not a private but an official one, compiled by an earlier government and endorsed by the current emperor, the authority and the authenticity of which was unquestionable.[30] The official histories, to borrow the words of the compilers, constituted the most authoritative historical works, and their supreme authority stemmed from their recognition by the Qianlong Emperor. These works, the compilers argued, stood on a par with the ancient classics (*jing*), and they were not something private individuals could arbitrarily add to or subtract from, a characteristic that differentiated official histories from the miscellaneous and unofficial stories.[31] On these grounds, the *Qiantang xianxian zhuanzan* stood in stark contrast to other local literature that was often faulted for exaggeration and distortion. Here we find that the official history was held in high regard by the compilers, to the extent that it served as a standard against which to evaluate private literature.

On the other hand, local works such as the *Jinhua xianda zhuan* (The biography of the Jinhua wise) had only their titles included in the *Siku quanshu*. Compendium compilers viewed local literature as permeated with "exaggerations" and "distortions." In the case of the *Jinhua xianda zhuan*, compilers had found the inclusion of two local Southern Song figures problematic; one man had catered to a pro-peace treaty faction with the Jin, and the other had been a protégé of Qin Kui (1090–1155), a prime minister at the Southern Song court and the infamous leader of the peace negotiation faction.

The *Jinhua xianda zhuan* was excluded because it was perceived as providing a "distorted account" of history that challenged Qianlong's view. Qin Kui has been notoriously known as an "evil minister," responsible for the death of Yue Fei (1103–41), a military general highly regarded for leading a series of heroic wars against the invading Jin forces, on the false charge of treason.[32] Qianlong held Qin Kui in extremely low regard and disapproved the legitimacy of the peace negotiation faction led by Qin. In his commentary on the incident in the *Yupi lidai tongjian jilan* (Imperially approved and edited mirror of successive dynasties), the emperor wrote that since Qin "was vicious and misled the state, everyone ground their teeth" (*jianxie wuguo hainei qiechi*).[33] For Qianlong, Qin Kui advocated peace negotiations to strengthen his power by currying favor with the reigning emperor Gaozong (r. 1127–61), who feared that his authority might be compromised if the two last emperors of the fallen Northern Song held as hostages by the Jin were released should Yue Fei recapture Kaifeng.[34] Qianlong claimed that Gaozong's efforts to secure a peace treaty had been rightfully resented by everyone in the Southern Song state.[35] Qianlong explicitly disapproved of Qin Kui and his followers who favored peace negotiations, describing such efforts as "wrong" (*heyi zhi fei*).[36] Gaozong might have known that the treaty might not bring lasting peace, Qianlong surmised, but his fear of the return of the two previous emperors propelled him to move in that direction rather than confronting the Jin with military might.[37]

On the other hand, Qianlong admired Yue Fei. During his six southern tours, Qianlong regularly sent officials to the Temple of Yue Fei in Hangzhou to offer sacrifices, reflecting the imperial espousal of this historical figure.[38] On one of those trips, he brought to the temple a plaque bearing the four-character phrase "extraordinary achievement and genuinely loyal" (*weilie chunzhong*).[39]

The inclusion of the two local men closely associated with Qin Kui as the "wise" men of their hometown in the *Jinhua xianda zhuan* ran counter to the prescribed historical interpretation of the Qing state. The Compendium compilers thus concluded that the book could not avoid the charge of "parochialism" (*xiangqu zhi si*), which implied exaggeration and distortion in the pursuit of local fame.[40] These negative comments exemplified the Qing official position to castigate the pro-peace faction of the early Southern Song court. The word "*si*," often translated as "private-mindedness" or "self-interest," was used in contrast to "*gong*," translated as "public-mindedness," "fair," or "legitimate."[41] The compilers considered the Qing official perception of the Southern Song pro-peace faction to be *gong* and the local interpretation to be *si*.

Similar cases in the Compendium abound. The *Wuzhong wangzhe ji* (The biography of the past wise of Suzhou) by mid-Ming Suzhou author Yang Xunji (1456–1544) featured a biographical section for a fellow Suzhou compatriot Xu Youzhen (1407–72) that Compendium compilers viewed as problematic. In tandem with the official portrayal of Xu in the imperially endorsed *Ming shi*, the compilers commented that Xu lost power only because he invited other people's wrath through libeling. On the other hand, Yang Xunji described Xu as a "respected figure of the whole realm," leading the compilers to label this work as another example of "parochialism."[42] The attacks on parochialism, reminiscent of similar state efforts to control local gazetteers, served as an attempt to streamline divergent local voices and make them conform to prescribed state interpretations.

The word "parochialism" was also employed to downgrade the value of local literary works when the compilers believed that the authors had magnified the merits and achievements of ordinary local figures. In these cases, the works were criticized less for deviating from the state's prescribed historical interpretations than for showering praise on unworthy men. The *Jiahe zhengxian lu* (Records of collected works from Jiaxing), which dealt with local worthies of Jiaxing, Zhejiang, was faulted for overstating a local figure's achievements in repelling Japanese pirates, a fault compilers labeled as parochialism.[43] They employed the same term to criticize the *Jinhua zhengxian lüe* (Summaries of collected works from Jinhua) for including accounts of men whose extraordinary distinction was limited to the high official posts they occupied.[44] The compilers also paid attention to the role of kinship in parochialism. In the *Sucai xiaozuan* (A short collection of the Suzhou talents), written by mid-Ming Suzhou scholar Zhu Yunming (1460–1526), the compilers identified the author's attempts to hide or embellish the life of his maternal grandfather Xu Youzhen.[45] Here parochialism could be considered highly powerful, because these individuals were kinsmen as well as Suzhou compatriots. The efforts of the compilers in unmasking these practices reflected the government's aim to impose more rigorous standards on the evaluation of figures in local literature. Their comments paralleled the contemporaneous policy to control the shrines of local worthies. They aimed at limiting the access of powerful but underqualified families to local cultural mechanisms through which they could perpetuate and enhance their statuses.

Historiographical criticism of local literature also extended to the practice of treating eminent figures as local men despite their tenuous relationship with the locality. A case in point is *Xin'an xuexi lu* (The Xin'an record of scholarly lineage), a text by a Ming author from Xiuning, a county in Huizhou prefecture (previously named Xin'an). Compilers accused the author of creating a Neo-Confucian lineage in Huizhou with Zhu Xi and the Cheng brothers as the founders of a local intellectual tradition. In their view, the author had been motivated by the fact that Zhu Xi originated from Xin'an, even tracing the distant ancestral branch of the Cheng brothers, namely, Cheng Hao (1032–85) and Cheng Yi (both renowned Neo-Confucian philosophers of the Northern Song period), to the region.[46] Based on this understanding, the author included all the former Neo-Confucian scholars from Xin'an who supposedly belonged to these two scholarly lineages. Compilers criticized the book for narrowly focusing on a locality and on scholarly branches. Despite the universal nature of the sages' teachings, the compilers continued, the author offered a parochial construction of a localized intellectual faction, an act interpreted as motivated by private interest (*sili*). This effort constituted nothing more than "self-interest of a scholarly faction" (*menhu zhi si*).

Moreover, the compilers were cynical about the author's basic premise that both Zhu Xi and the Cheng brothers originated from Xin'an. The Cheng brothers had never mentioned Xin'an or identified Huizhou as their hometown, they argued. Even though their remote ancestors had come from Huizhou, the brothers considered Luoyang, Henan, as their hometown. Compilers concluded that the author refashioned the Cheng brothers as hometown heroes to assert the superior cultural tradition of his particular locality.

Compilers' criticisms also extended to official types of local writing, such as gazetteers. Their opinion of these works was hardly more favorable than their view of private local literature. In their minds, local gazetteers usually embellished the positive aspects of local people and places while downplaying or even ignoring their drawbacks.[47] Compilers also complained that these works often contained information not appropriate for county or prefectural gazetteers, a practice they referred to as "forced implication" (*qianyin zhi xi*). They pointed out that the 1529 *Wuyi zhi* (Wu County gazetteer) featured a section on the history of the state of Wu from the Spring and Autumn Period (722–481 BCE), even though covering the history of a state was beyond the scope of a local gazetteer.[48] Moreover, the gazetteer contained another section entitled "Reflections on the Classics" (*jingkao*) that discussed the affairs of the ancient Wu state based on the materials from the classic *Spring and Autumn Annals*, a topic that Compendium compilers regarded as not within the bounds of local affairs. Another gazetteer, the *Jiangdu xianzhi* (Jiangdu County gazetteer) of the Wanli period, drew criticism for its section on *ji* (annals): "A history contains a *ji* for an emperor. It is presumptuous to use the term for a county."[49]

The Compendium compilers also paid close attention to place names used in local gazetteers. To enhance the elegance of the volume and to convey a sense of moral edification by pretentiously emulating antiquity, gazetteers occasionally employed the old names of localities rather than the current administrative ones. In the case of the *Gusu zhi* (Gazetteer of Suzhou), compiled by Wang Ao (1450–1524) during the Ming, the Compendium compilers drew on an episode that allegedly had taken place upon the gazetteer's completion. When Wang Ao's fellow Suzhou compatriot Yang Xunji saw this gazetteer, he commented that "Gusu" referred to a platform erected for the king of Wu during the Spring and Autumn period and for this reason was totally inappropriate as the name of a prefectural gazetteer.[50] The Qing Compendium compilers cited this episode in arguing that the practice of using such archaic names for gazetteers had been viewed as inaccurate even in Ming times.[51]

The compilers also believed that local gazetteers shared the same problems that they had identified in private local literature: the practice of including local figures whose achievements or virtues were not particularly significant or who could only claim ambiguous or tenuous relationships to the localities.[52]

The criticisms by the compilers of the Compendium against local writing, together with the imposition of prepublication censorship of local gazetteers, suggest that during Qianlong's reign the government staged an extensive overhaul of local writing practices to make local knowledge more normative. Viewing localism as detrimental to the unity of the empire and the authority of the state, the Qing court launched a campaign to create a more centralized cultural order. The local gazetteers published during the latter half of the Qianlong period underwent changes dictated by this new policy. The 1767 Tangshan County gazetteer of Anhui, for example, denounced earlier gazetteers for offering historical narratives of the locality that differed from the official dynastic history. It criticized the earlier practice of using inappropriate section headings not pertinent to the history of the county, such as "Imperial Genealogy" (*dixi*).[53] Likewise, in the 1788 Lou County gazetteer in Jiangsu, the compilers criticized the recent gazetteers for their exaggerations in praising of local traditions and for their inaccurate personal information.[54] To redress these problems, the compilers claimed, they placed emphasis on organizing a concise gazetteer with succinct contents and precise information.

In the preface of the 1792 gazetteer of Shaoxing prefecture, Zhejiang, the prefect addressed an earlier edition's use of the prefecture's archaic name of Kuaiji. He acknowledged that this practice had invited criticism from others, and, for this reason, the current edition employed the prefecture's official administrative name, Shaoxing, as required by "current regulations" (*jinxian*).[55]

In the 1779 Chizhou prefectural gazetteer of Anhui, the compilers dropped the section entitled "Learning of Principle" (*lixue*) which had been a part of the earlier edition of the Kangxi gazetteer.[56] They explained that, while the *Song shi* contained the section "*daoxue*" (Learning of the Way), it had been removed from the *Ming shi*, the official history of the Ming compiled during the Qing dynasty. Therefore, maintaining the "*lixue*" section raised concerns that their gazetteer would depart from the *Ming shi* model. The compilers believed that local gazetteers should not compete with the official dynastic history by adopting section titles that had been discarded, and they decided to use the title "Confucians" (*rulin*) instead.

These examples illustrate that many local gazetteer compilers of the time shared the critical views espoused by government officials. This uniformity strongly suggests that not only the censorship policy, but also the compilation of the Compendium had an impact on the guiding principles adopted by the gazetteer compilers during the last decades of the eighteenth century.

The Resurgence of Local Gazetteers and Private Local Literature in the South

Although the official prepublication review of local gazetteers persisted during the Jiaqing and Daoguang periods, the policy's rigor waned, particularly in the latter period. A growing number of gazetteers had neither prefaces written by provincial education commissioners nor names of provincial officials as reviewers.[57] The compilation of these gazetteers was once again an increasingly local matter, engaging primarily local officials and elites.

This more relaxed government control did not have a uniform effect across the empire. As discussed above, the Jiangnan provinces recorded a fast recovery in gazetteer numbers during the Jiaqing period from the decline in numbers in the previous thirty years of the Qianlong reign. Meanwhile, the Jiaqing period marked the beginning of a downward spiral in the number of gazetteers for the northern provinces. These differences can be explained in regard to the central government policies. The government overhaul of local writings in the eighteenth century had primarily targeted Jiangnan, a region that boasted strong elite power and intense cultural pride. This explains the correlation between the number of gazetteers of the region and the rise and fall of state control. At the same time, the active promotion of gazetteer compilation by provincial and central government officials in the North accounted for the rise in numbers there until the end of the eighteenth century. For reasons that require further research, the eighteenth-century Qing state seemed to hold an interest in fostering cultural heritage in the North.

The loosening of state control in local gazetteer compilation changed the publication landscape. By the early nineteenth century, as the state's firm grip over local cultural matters receded, local gazetteer compilers no longer benefited from government initiatives. This development brought about a transition to a pattern in which the South surpassed the North in gazetteer production. Previously propelled by the northern-based imperial court, gazetteer compilation was transformed into a southern-based initiative, driven by elites whose wealth was largely derived from the highly commercialized economy located here.

Private local literature experienced a virtually identical pattern of changes from the eighteenth century to the early nineteenth century. Until the Kangxi period in the Qing, the Suzhou literati had occasionally produced private local literature, such as the *Baicheng yanshui* (Mist and waters of 100 cities) and the *Caifeng leiji* (Categorized records of gathered customs). During the Yongzheng and Qianlong periods, however, private local literature disappeared from Suzhou, only to make a dramatic return in the early nineteenth century.[58]

Beginning in the Jiaqing period, Suzhou saw the gradual flourishing of private local literature, which focused on local themes and reasserted the cultural splendor of the locality. Qian Siyuan, a licentiate of Wu County, began writing a local history of Suzhou in 1771. Completed in 1803, his *Wumen bucheng* (Supplement to the gazetteer of Suzhou) featured the history and tradition of three counties, Wu, Changzhou, and Yuanhe in Suzhou prefecture.[59] Qian Siyuan died in 1803 without seeing the publication of his book, but it was supplemented by his son, Qian Shiqi, up to 1820 and was published afterward.

Qian Siyuan's *Wumen bucheng* is just one of many local histories of Suzhou that appeared in the early nineteenth century. *Wujun wenbian* (Collection of literature of Suzhou prefecture), compiled by Changzhou County scholar Gu Yuan (see chapter 5) in 1827, is a colossal volume containing 246 chapters.[60] In this volume, Gu collected writings on Suzhou penned by the region's natives and the occasional sojourners and local officials from the Han dynasty to his own time. As one preface writer aptly noted, this was the "compilation of Suzhou writings by a Suzhou native."[61] Materials in the collection varied widely and were drawn from previous collections of Suzhou writings, among them Zheng Huchen from the Song dynasty, Qian Gu from the Ming, and Wu Weiye (1609–72) from the late Ming and early Qing periods.[62] Gu Yuan's work built on this existing literature, and his own contribution lay primarily in collecting writings of the Qing period. As the genealogy of Suzhou local literature traced by Gu Yuan illustrated, few collections of Suzhou writings had been published since Wu Weiye's. One of the merits of Gu's work was that it could "supplement what the local gazetteers have left out."[63] In that sense, it was similar to Qian Siyuan's *Wumen bucheng*. This popular rhetoric acted as a means of justifying the production of private local literature. Authors claimed that their works were supplementing, not supplanting, the official local gazetteers.

Despite the length of the time period covered by the volume, the geographic boundary still encompassed only one single prefecture, no matter how much pride Suzhou natives placed in their cultural tradition. This was especially true in the eyes of non-Suzhou natives. Thus a preface writer from Anhui noted:

> Those works that are entirely devoted to the discussion of one dynasty are Yao Xuan's (968–1020) *Wencui*, Lü Zuqian's (1137–81) *Wenjian*, and Zhen Dexiu's (1178–1235) *Wenzhang zhengzong*, and so forth. Recently, *Jiangxi wenzheng* and *Diannan wenlüe* are about a whole province. Isn't that which is just about an out-of-the-way place too narrow? However, the *Book of Odes* said one should always venerate one's own native place. When recording past events, gentlemen should begin with what they have personally experienced. It is generally because what they have seen and heard is relatively complete and the collection is relatively convenient. If they can really preserve what their localities have, when those are combined, it will eventually cover the whole realm.[64]

Here the writer is contrasting the literary collection of Suzhou, an "out-of-the-way place," with the collections of an entire dynasty and of the provinces. If the boundaries of collection were broader, it signified that the works would better represent a worthy, respectable, and qualified selection. On the other hand, collections limited to a narrow unit such as a prefecture might apply criteria too generous in their selection. Eighteenth-century Compendium compilers were conscious of that fact when they charged local literature with being inseparably intertwined with "parochialism." Perhaps aware of such criticism, the writer provided his own justification for the work. He began by quoting a passage from the classic the *Book of Odes,* stating that local men should revere their own localities, and he notes the comprehensiveness and ease of collection of materials assembled by locals because they are familiar with the place. But ultimately, he had to attach a higher significance to the work by regarding it not just as isolated local material, but also as a component of the empire-wide collection that such writings would eventually form.

Further evidence of a departure from eighteenth-century practices comes from the inclusion of materials related to Taicang independent department in Gu Yuan's *Wujun wenbian*, in which it is considered a part of Suzhou prefecture.[65] Taicang remained a subunit of the Suzhou prefecture until 1725, after which it became a separate department directly affiliated to the province of Jiangsu by order of the Yongzheng Emperor. Reflecting the state concerns for "matching names with realities," Suzhou local gazetteers during the Yongzheng and Qianlong periods had excluded Taicang from the compilation. The inclusion of Taicang challenged the eighteenth-century norms and reasserted the long-standing convention of local elites, who regarded Taicang as a part of Suzhou prefecture.

Interest in compiling a local history of Suzhou was shared by Gu Yuan's nephew, Gu Zhentao (1750–?), who published *Wumen biaoyin* (Manifestation of the unknown in Suzhou) in 1834.[66] A later edition published in the late Daoguang years contains poems written to commemorate this work by as many as 581 people.[67] As Gu Zhentao pointed out in the author's note, the book represents the collective efforts of Suzhou literati. Visits to historical sites, collection of information, and proofreading were all aided by fellow Suzhou literati.[68] The style note stated that the work covered only the three counties surrounding the prefectural seat—Wu, Changzhou, and Yuanhe—and aimed to include information not mentioned or superficially described in local gazetteers. As the title of the book suggested, the work was indeed a collection of minor details regarding the temples, shrines, bridges, offices, and people of the locality often not recorded in local gazetteers. As many of the preface writers emphasized, the work was indeed sufficient to "complement local gazetteers," a gesture intended to carve out a legitimate niche for these works.

The efforts to legitimate local writings abound in this volume. One preface writer remarked, "Somebody said: 'These are just minor details. Why is there a need to write about this?' [However, this man is someone who] does not know that recording big things and small things originally share a single principle."[69] Another preface writer voiced a similar view.

> Historians write a mirror of governance and disorder during a thousand-year period. They put in what is major and leave out what is minor. They excise what is confused and omit what is dubious. Therefore, provincial gazetteers are relatively more detailed than the *Gazetteer of the Great Qing*

> *Unification*, and prefectural gazetteers are even more detailed than provincial gazetteers. Going down the scale to the small unit of a county or an [subcounty] area, one should collect even more, without exception. Minor details must be recorded. Not only is it proper that the form [of history] be that way, but also in doing so, big things and small things will be recorded and not be lost. . . . How great, how excellent, is the recording of small things![70]

These remarks display the eighteenth-century emphasis in cultural politics turned upside down. When measured against the standards delineated in the Compendium, a local history overflowing with minor local details would have been disparaged. In the nineteenth century, these writers developed the counter-logic that private local literature constituted a legitimate means to record minor details of the locality. In this way, they launched a renewed effort to once again glorify local tradition, assert local particularism, and present a claim that the locality was a noteworthy place on the dynasty's cultural map.

Gu Lu, another native of Wu County and an uncle of Gu Zhentao, also wrote three local histories of Suzhou during this period. The first, entitled *Qingjia lu* (Record of Suzhou) and first published in 1830, recorded the customs, tourist sites, and seasonal festivals of Suzhou. As its preface indicated, books about seasonal divisions and festivals in general had been published, but none specifically focused on one locality.[71] As one preface writer remarked: "Climate is different every thousand *li*, and customs are different every hundred *li*. Though seasons are the same throughout the realm, one locality has its own climate and human emotions. Therefore, [universal customs and festivals] cannot be forcibly imposed on it."[72] As Gu Lu himself put it, this work was "speaking about native place in one's own native place."[73] He argued that the records of customs should be specific and included not only what had already been included in local gazetteers, but also what had been ignored and deemed as too trivial. He enlivened his depiction of Suzhou customs with street talk (*jietan xiangyi*), village proverbs, and mountain songs, sources that might invite questioning of their authenticity. Aware of possible criticisms for using these sources, he explained that his writing was also based on numerous written works, and that he remained very cautious in his conclusions.[74]

Another work by Gu Lu was even more limited in geographic terms. His *Tongqiao yizhuo lu* (Record of Paulownia Bridge written while recumbent on a table), featured the landscape, temples, mansions, historical sites, markets, and handicrafts of the Tiger Hill area in Suzhou. In this subcounty record, the author drew a clear line between his work and local gazetteers. The latter ignored the aspects of daily life in the local area: mountain dikes, stores in the market, occupations, boats, and vegetable and fruit gardens. His work, he argued, differed from gazetteers in that it recorded minor but unique features of a small local area, Tiger Hill.[75]

In a similar vein, Yao Chengxu, a native of Jiading County, Taicang independent department, emphasized the detailed livelihood of a locality by including more poems than prose in his *Wuqu fanggu lu* (Record of visiting the past in Suzhou). Published in 1839, the book began with the names of historical sites followed by an explanation of their location, history, and related events, along with 546 poems about those sites, all composed by Yao.[76]

Yao's decision to use the place-name "Wuqu" in the title violated one of the principles emphasized under Qianlong. Originally the name of the local songs of Suzhou, Wuqu later came to signify Suzhou itself, just as the term *Qingjia* (literally meaning "pure and good") in the title of the book *Qingjia lu* was an old name used for Suzhou. This popular practice of employing old names in local literature had been criticized by the Compendium compilers on the grounds that they did not "match the reality," and they did not constitute the basis of good governance. Besides discouraging local writers from engaging in this practice during the eighteenth century, the government also emphasized that works on regions had to match the current administrative boundaries. Just as Gu Yuan's *Wujun wenbian* had ignored this directive by featuring Taicang, *Wuqu fanggu lu* also included discussions on this area.[77] The reemergence of practices that had been attacked during Qianlong's reign reflected the retrenchment of the state interventionist policy in the production of local literature.[78]

The genre of private local literature experienced a dramatic efflorescence in early nineteenth-century Suzhou. If the focus on local themes in literary endeavors and the assertion of local cultural pride can be called a "localist" orientation, it was not confined to Suzhou. Recent studies suggest that particularistic literati efforts to emphasize the tradition of their localities and elevate the cultural importance of their hometowns resurfaced across the Qing Empire in the early nineteenth century in areas such as Yangzhou, Canton, and Hunan, a phenomenon largely absent during the eighteenth century.[79] The reinvigoration of private local literature during this period represented the dissolution of the centralized cultural order of the eighteenth century, triggering important changes in publication patterns and scholarly discussions.[80] In the early nineteenth century, with no strong authority to denounce them as "parochial," the literati in cultural centers across the empire began to voice competing claims for recognition of their glorious cultural past and of noteworthy items peculiar to their locality. Centralized cultural order was rapidly giving way to local particularism.

Private Book Collectors and Republication of Local Literature and Forbidden Books

In the early nineteenth century, not only new local historical works were produced, but also previous works that had been preserved in private libraries were now often republished, a phenomenon that continued into the late nineteenth and early twentieth centuries. In Suzhou, Changshu County private book collector Zhang Haipeng (1755–1816) published and republished numerous books relevant to Suzhou history or written by local authors during the Jiaqing period.[81] During the nineteenth century, preservation, publication, and republication of local materials by private book collectors could be observed throughout the Jiangnan region. The publication of local materials increasingly flourished in the latter part of the nineteenth century.[82] The reemergence of the genre called "local collectanea" (*difang congshu*) is also significant. Ye Dehui (1863–1927), a private book collector, devoted a section on this genre in his *Shulin qinghua* (Pure talks in the forest of books).[83] Ye traced the beginnings of collecting books on one's own locality and publishing them in a single collection to the Ming with the *Zaiwu*, followed by Fan Weicheng's (*js* 1619) *Yanyi zhilin*. Ye points out that the reemergence of this genre in the Qing happened during the Jiaqing period, after a hiatus of a century and half. During the Jiaqing and Daoguang periods, Ye continued, a series of local collectanea appeared, such as *Taizhou congshu*, *Pucheng yishu*, *Jingchuan congshu*, *Loudong zazhu*, and *Lingnan yishu*. As this trend gained momentum in the early nineteenth century, an increasing number of localities across the empire engaged in similar publication projects.

These efforts were accompanied by the republication of those books forbidden or destroyed by the state during the *Siku quanshu* project, a development that marked the beginning of the "emancipation of writings." Huang Chengliang, a licentiate and book collector who lived through the Qianlong and Jiaqing periods, built a private library in a market town in Yuyao County, Zhejiang, in 1807. He published some of his collections, one of which featured ninety-seven Ming literary works. Entitled *Jinwen leiti* (Categorized collection of contemporary writing), it contained as many as thirty books that had been forbidden since the Qianlong period.[84] While the Qianlong emperor decided in 1776 to elevate the Ming loyalists and downgrade the "twice-serving ministers" (those who had served both the Ming and the Qing regimes), any private publication effort on the fallen Ming still consisted a very risky matter during his reign. We have so far no clear evidence that the Jiaqing government officially approved the individual publication projects regarding the forbidden books related to the Ming, and the attempts to republish them in the early nineteenth century seem to have been made in unofficial individual capacities.

The entries in the index of the *Siku jinhuishu congkan* (Collected publication of the forbidden and burned books while compiling the Emperor's Four Treasuries) show that as many as twelve were republished in the Daoguang period, in addition to three in the Jiaqing period.[85] Collections of unofficial histories concerning the Ming-Qing transition, such as *Nanjiang yishi kanben* (Seeking out the history of the southern territory, collated edition) and *Jingtuo yishi* (Lost history of Jing Tuo) also surfaced during the early nineteenth century.[86] In Hunan, the publication of works by Wang Fuzhi (1619–92), known for his fierce hatred of the Manchus, during the late Daoguang years further illustrated this relaxed atmosphere.[87] The retreat of state power from the local cultural realm brought about emancipation of local literature and triggered a revival of books related to the Ming-Qing transition.

CHAPTER 7

Bandit or Hero?

Memories of Zhang Shicheng in Late Imperial and Republican Suzhou

The founding of the Ming dynasty by Zhu Yuanzhang in 1368 was built on the defeats of a number of rival contenders for power in the late Yuan period.[1] Among those ill-fated contenders was Zhang Shicheng, who built his short-lived kingdom in the Lower Yangzi region with Suzhou as its capital.[2] This chapter explores the transformation of the discourse on Zhang Shicheng, a local hero in Suzhou, with a particular emphasis on the changes taking place in the early nineteenth century.[3]

In Suzhou, politically sensitive ideas permeated the discourse on Zhang Shicheng. During the late Yuan, the residents of Suzhou had rallied around a rival of the Ming Taizu, and from this experience local historical memories emerged that were often in tension with the Ming orthodox view on that period of history. This historical memory of Zhang Shicheng thus became a site of contestation between court historians and local Suzhou literati throughout the late imperial period. The episodic emergence and disappearance of a narrative based on local loyalties, which I shall hereafter call a "localist discourse," and the extent to which it deviated from the official historiography, could be regarded as indicators of the changing power balance between the state and local elites. By examining the Zhu-Zhang rivalry amid mutations of central-local power relations at various historical periods in this chapter, the friction between the creation and dissemination of the official memory and the local one that persistently resisted the orthodoxy imposed by the state will be revealed. Through this lens, this study will place the early nineteenth century in a larger historical perspective in terms of the shifting state-elite power balance.

Representations of Zhang Shicheng in Ming Official Historiography

The Ming government's orthodox view of the late Yuan period, in particular the rivalry between Zhu Yuanzhang and Zhang Shicheng, first surfaced in the *Yuan shi* (Yuan history) and *Ming shilu* (Veritable records of the Ming). This view was then inherited, though in a somewhat altered form, by the Qing dynasty and proved decisive in shaping the literati's understanding of late Yuan history. The orthodox view approached late Yuan history from Zhu Yuanzhang's perspective, portraying him as the legitimate ruler with the mandate of heaven to establish a new dynasty and viewing all other contenders as mere villains. Political partisanship permeated the officially sponsored *Ming shilu*. The compilers blatantly expressed support for Ming Taizu by employing the epithet "our" (*wo*) to describe his army and the localities under his control.[4]

It is not surprising, then, that early Ming official historiography depicted Zhu Yuanzhang's arch rival Zhang Shicheng with intense hostility. The compilers of *Yuan shi* deliberately chose words that would deprive Zhang of any degree of legitimacy. They labeled Zhang and his followers as "bandits" (*zei*) and described their military actions as "pillages" (*kou*).[5] In general, they denied any legitimacy to the dynasty he founded and the royal title he assumed.

Although the *Yuan shi* offers scattered references to Zhang Shicheng, the *Ming shilu* provides a more coherent biographical account that paints an unflattering portrait. It describes Zhang as a "ruffian" (*wulai*), a person lacking firm roots in local society or a regular occupation, although it mentions that he earned his living by selling salt.[6] Often humiliated by others, Zhang was alleged to have burned the houses of many innocent people while retaliating against his personal enemies; and, according to the compilers of his biography, his primary motivation for engaging in open rebellion was the fear of punishment. In short, the compilers deprived his rebellion of any socially righteous cause, depicting the movement as nothing more than an unlawful escape from criminal justice and a personal vendetta.

The *Ming shilu* also accused Zhang of breaching Confucian norms. Although the Yuan conferred on him an official title, they argued, Zhang betrayed the court by ignoring its orders and illegitimately adopted the royal title for himself. Moreover, he surreptitiously murdered a Yuan provincial official and arbitrarily established state institutions. By emphasizing that Zhang once had served the Yuan, the compilers attempted to draw the readers' attention to his disloyalty and underscore the illegitimate nature of his regime. The *Ming shilu* further asserted Zhang's lack of the basic qualifications expected from a ruler, claiming he and his brothers were arrogant, extravagant, and lascivious, and that they were lazy in governance and clumsy in political resolution and control. Such incompetence prompted Zhang's subordinates to wrest power from him.

Zhang's oft-acclaimed virtue of benevolence toward scholars and officials is also described in *Ming shilu* with an explicit mix of cynicism and antagonism. According to the compilers, Zhang "sought the reputation that he treated scholars well" and lavishly showered them with gifts without considering their personal qualifications and integrity. Ultimately, those who joined his regime were no more than "literati who coveted profit," motivated not by the conviction of Zhang's worthiness as a ruler but by the prospect of personal aggrandizement. The compilers thus portrayed Zhang's virtue of generosity as mere hypocrisy. That a number of scholars joined Zhang's regime was undeniable, yet the compilers chose to ignore all grounds for a more favorable view of his regime.[7] For them, Zhang's seemingly generous attitude was a sign of incompetence. They maintained that Zhang's generals often ignored his commands to proceed to the battlefield and could be mobilized only through the bestowal of rewards. Zhang did not punish his generals even when they lost battles but instead foolishly reappointed them. This negative appraisal of Zhang and his state came to mold the Ming orthodox view that would shape the general literati perspectives for generations.

While, on the one hand, the Ming compilers vigorously debunked the myth of Zhang's virtues, on the other, they underscored the magnanimity and humaneness of their dynastic founder. The *Ming shilu* claims that following Zhang's capture, Ming Taizu wanted to spare his life.

When Zhang instead committed suicide, Zhu Yuanzhang offered a coffin and even gave him a proper burial.[8] Furthermore, before launching the final attack on Suzhou, Zhu declared that soldiers who pillaged the properties of innocent citizens would face the death penalty.[9] Consequently, Suzhou inhabitants managed to remain "undisturbed."[10] Similarly, Zhu prohibited his armies from desecrating the tomb of Zhang's mother on the outskirts of Suzhou. In response, the "men of Suzhou thanked the emperor for his generosity and there was no one who did not feel happy."[11]

Diverging Portrayals of Zhang Shicheng in Private Literature

Representations of Zhang Shicheng can also be found in private literature produced by witnesses to the late Yuan political upheaval. While each author's political stance depended on whether he had served Zhang or Zhu Yuanzhang, the extant literature tilted heavily in favor of the victor, Zhu. The preponderance of the pro-Zhu private literature also reflected the state-elite relations of the early Ming, a period marked by the reorganization of political institutions to strengthen imperial power and extend the state's reach into the locality. Fearing government persecution, scholars dared not write positively about Zhang Shicheng.

The portrayals of Zhang Shicheng in pro-Zhu private writings generally resembled those in the official records. Accordingly, the early Ming minor official Ye Ziqi called Zhang a "thief," and other sources emphasized his extravagance.[12] But disparities do surface in the descriptions. Whereas the *Ming shilu* ascribed Zhang's rebellion entirely to his fear of criminal punishment and thus undermined the possibility of seeing him as a "social bandit," Ye Ziqi elaborates on Zhang's background to explain his rise as a rebel leader through another lens: "Such was [Zhang's] personality that he made light of material wealth and liked to share it with others, and very much won the hearts of his subordinates. At that time, the salt laborers were suffering from the corvée labor, and ultimately they chose him as their leader and initiated the rebellion."[13] Perhaps the most extreme deviation from the mainstream account was the *Bao Yue lu*

(Record of preserving the Yue region), written in the late Yuan by Xu Mianzhi, a native of Poyang, Jiangxi, who later resided in Zhejiang. The *Bao Yue lu* narrated the conquest of Zhejiang by Zhu's army, at a time Zhang's commander Lü Zhen ruled the region. Here Xu addressed Lü as Mr. Lü, employing the honorific title *gong*, and referred to Lü's army as "our army," while dismissing Zhu's as "the enemy's army."

The private literature of the early Ming period has far fewer references to Zhang Shicheng than mid-Ming writings due to the literary inquisitions of that period. Indeed, government persecution often targeted Suzhou in the early Ming.[14] The government inflicted a heavy tax burden on the local population and forcibly removed certain wealthy families from their hometowns.[15] Moreover, the government imposed a quota for the civil service examination in Jiangnan, explicitly to prevent the region's literati from monopolizing the bureaucracy. Under these adverse circumstances, Suzhou literati understandably did not risk writing about Zhang Shicheng.

After having long vanished from the arena of public discourse, the memory of Zhang Shicheng revived during the mid-Ming period, reflecting the rise of the gentry's power and concomitant changes in state-elite relations. The heavily publicized view of Zhang Shicheng as an illegitimate ruler in the official histories implicitly meant that the people of Suzhou had made a wrong political decision by supporting a ruler other than the Ming founder. This official verdict obviously could not sit comfortably in the minds of the local population of Suzhou. The literati therefore felt pressed to create their own narrative of late Yuan events to rationalize their political choice and satisfy the desire of Suzhou residents for a more glorious local past. The literati's political stance on Zhang illuminated how they juggled two conflicting demands: to be loyal to the Ming dynasty and to revitalize the memory of local events that emanated from their own experiences of the Yuan-Ming transition.

Compared to their counterparts in the early Ming period, fifteenth-century Suzhou writers frequently discussed Zhang Shicheng in their miscellaneous writings. Wu Kuan (1435–1504), Shen Zhou (1427–1509), Wen Zhengming (1470–1559), Tang Yin (1470–1524), and Zhu Yunming (1460–1526), to name a few, were distinguished figures who associated closely with one another and wrote about Zhang, particularly his reception in Suzhou.

In the *Ping Wu lu* (Record of pacifying the Wu region), Wu Kuan, who rose to a prominent position in the Ming central bureaucracy, strictly adhered to the narrative of the *Ming shilu* and reiterated the view that Zhang rebelled to escape his criminal past. Wu ignored the heavy corvée labor that might have aroused in Zhang feelings of compassion or social righteousness.[16] However, Wu Kuan's student Wen Zhengming departed from his teacher on this issue. In his discussion of the Zhang Shicheng's Guest House for the Wise, Wen opened the paragraph by placing the prefix "illegitimate" in front of the dynasty's name; nonetheless, his description actually praises the hospitality its leaders showed scholars.[17] In Wen's various colophons in poems or paintings, he does not hesitate to mention the past connections those writers or painters had enjoyed with Zhang's regime. In the same laudatory context, he listed the official titles bestowed on them by both Zhang and the Ming court.[18] Wen apparently was not bothered that those scholars and artists had served Zhang's regime rather than the Ming. It was as though Wen considered them all as members of Suzhou's scholarly or artistic community, creators or transmitters of its cultural tradition.

Wen's open attitude toward Zhang was not unique. Yang Xunji, another mid-Ming Suzhou scholar renowned for archaist writing (see chapter 6), depicted Zhang Shicheng as a humane and generous person who treated guests with such courtesy that they regarded visiting his kingdom as a homecoming.[19] In his account of Suzhou's fall to the Ming forces, Yang claimed that Xu Da, one of Ming Taizu's trusted generals who had marched into the city through the Chang gate, restrained his army from committing random killings. On the other hand, another one of Zhu's generals, Chang Yuchun, felt so exasperated by the die-hard resistance of the locals that, after storming into the city through the Feng gate, he had his army "put every man and woman they met to the military law."[20] Chang's atrocities ended only after Xu Da dispatched a messenger with an order to stop. Contrary to the *Ming shilu*'s assertion that Zhu's prior warning had guaranteed that local people remained "undisturbed," Suzhou native Yang told a nuanced and perhaps more accurate account. He judged Zhang as "a person of great righteousness" because he did not use his power to cease the supplies of tribute grain to the Yuan government. Thanks to such virtue, declared Yang, "even now Suzhou people still call him King Zhang."[21]

Zhu Yunming recounted several episodes that conveyed favorable local sentiment toward Zhang. In one episode, Ming Taizu, disguised as an ordinary citizen on a street in Nanjing, approached an old woman from Suzhou. He asked her how Zhang Shicheng had treated the people of Suzhou. The woman replied that when the "emperor of the Great Ming," namely, Zhu Yuanzhang, began his attack, "King Zhang" realized that he did not possess the true mandate of heaven. Thereafter, she continued, Zhang surrendered, sparing Suzhou from the suffering of war. Suzhou residents were "still grateful to him for his virtue."[22]

An almost identical account was featured in a piece by another Suzhou native, Lu Rong (1436–94).[23] In both cases, the old woman's story on the fall of Suzhou stood in sharp contrast to the official account in the *Ming shilu*. The old woman's version refashioned the material to involve Zhang Shicheng's voluntary surrender and to emphasize the humaneness of his heroic self-sacrifice: Zhang surrendered to protect the people of Suzhou.[24] The official history, on the other hand, described that Zhang was defeated by Ming forces after exhausting his abilities. Rather than noting Zhang's intention to surrender, the orthodox view emphasized Ming Taizu's humaneness, as exemplified by his orders that the army protect the people of Suzhou.

In the minds of mid-Ming Suzhou literati, memories of Zhang Shicheng joined memories of the afflictions that were the price of such a partisanship. According to Zhu Yunming, Ming Taizu was irritated that Suzhou had taken such a long time to fall and abhorred the locals' support for Zhang. This, Zhu Yunming explained, led Ming Taizu to punish Suzhou with heavy land taxes.[25] Many other Suzhou literati associated this tax burden with the city's past relationship to Zhang.

Ming Taizu not only felt anger toward the people of Suzhou, but also harbored fear and suspicion, even after the city's fall. Worried about the Suzhou residents' hostility to his regime, he carefully selected a local official for the city. But when he subsequently discovered that this official had rebuilt the prefectural administrative office on the former site of Zhang's palace, he was so infuriated that he punished him with death.[26]

Evidently, not all mid-Ming writings by Suzhou literati displayed favorable sentiments toward Zhang. A short piece by Lang Ying (1487–ca.1566) on Zhang's rise and fall showed no sympathy for him.[27] Huang Xingzeng (1490–1540) and Hou Dian offered unflattering evaluations of

Zhang's regime. These authors derided, in particular, the marginal social groups that played leadership roles in Zhang's regime and the few inept scholars who monopolized power.[28] The 1506 edition of the Suzhou prefectural gazetteer compiled by Wang Ao presented Zhang's vicissitudes from the Ming perspective, noting that he "set fire [to the properties], ransacked the villages, and drove the people to become bandits." According to Wang, Zhang was "cunning and deceptive in hundreds of ways" and, upon occupying Suzhou, his "plundering, raping, and killing were unbearably inhumane."[29]

The rise of a discourse centering on Zhang Shicheng—one that challenged the official orthodox view—can be understood both in terms of a power shift from the center to the locality and a revival of Neo-Confucianism, a movement that entailed a heightened sense of localism and whose leaders were highly critical of the central government.[30] Through this discourse, Suzhou natives disseminated their own perspectives of late Yuan history that competed with the prevalent official narratives.[31]

In the late Ming, localist understanding of late Yuan history became more neutral politically than it had been in the previous period. The decisive shift in the balance of power, away from the center toward local elites, provided Suzhou literati with an environment congenial to a localist historiography. The local histories that surfaced expressed sentiments amicable toward Zhang Shicheng and were less burdened by the Confucian moral demand to be loyal to the reigning dynasty; they could therefore foreground local experience and memory.

The late Ming literati of Suzhou believed that writers from the dynasty's early period had sacrificed the historical reality of the late Yuan in the interest of consolidating the Ming regime's legitimacy. The accurate local history had, they believed, long been suppressed by the fiat of the reigning dynasty. They wished to rescue the local memory of the late Yuan from oblivion and systematize it through literary endeavors. The rescued local memory served as a counter-memory, a corrective to the Ming orthodoxy, which had stigmatized Suzhou as having served a politically illegitimate ruler who lacked moral qualifications. The late Ming pro-Zhang historiography reinterpreted past events in a manner that would be more palatable to the locals, preserving their pride in their region's glorious past. Late Ming Suzhou scholars did not dare to endow Zhang's regime with full legitimacy—that status would have to wait until the Qing and Republican periods, but they came close in their discussions of Zhang's vicissitudes.

The efflorescence in the writing of private histories during the late Ming and early Qing periods provided opportunities for authors to reexamine Zhang Shicheng. Whereas the mid-Ming sources that dealt with Zhang (generally in the form of miscellanies) had been the product of Suzhou natives, late Ming and early Qing writings on him had been penned by men of diverse geographic origins who treated the theme as part of a larger narrative on Ming history.

As the geographic provenance of the authors dealing with Suzhou expanded, it became only natural that the majority of the works reflected the standpoint of the Ming court. To show their alignment with the dynasty, many commentators often placed the word "our" (*wo*) before any references to Zhu Yuanzhang's generals, army, and the territories under his control.[32] While they addressed Zhu by such honorary titles as Ming Taizu, Taizu, or Wu wang, they cited Zhang by name and his army as "bandits."[33]

Since private Ming histories of the late Ming and Qing periods were primarily written for didactic purposes, they usually contained evaluations of specific historical events that sought to identify the causes of the dynasty's fall. These works generally shed a negative light on Zhang, often criticizing his alleged mistakes: the lack of a grand strategy to advance beyond his own power base, the devolution of power to a small group of incompetent officials, the leaders' indulgence in sexual and leisurely pleasures, and the absence of transparent regulations in promoting or demoting subordinates.[34]

As in the mid-Ming, however, some late Ming and Qing Suzhou natives provided more balanced narratives about Zhu and Zhang. A case in point is Shi Ce's (1575–1639) *Longping jishi* (A history of Suzhou under Zhang Shicheng), a work that detailed Zhang Shicheng's rise and fall with appended concise biographies of the actors in Zhang's short-lived regime. Unlike the episodic references to Zhang in the mid-Ming sources, Shi Ce provided more complete and coherent biographies. While other histories referred to Zhang as a "bandit," Shi Ce called him by the official titles he had held at each stage of his adventure: the King of Zhou (Zhou wang) and, after he discarded the title of Grand Commandant, the King of Wu (Wu wang).[35] Although Shi Ce briefly notes that Zhang's title of king was illegitimate, he nevertheless continued to employ such appellations as "Army of Wu" or "Generals of Wu," rather than dismissing Zhang's party as "bandits." At the same time, he referred to Zhu Yuanzhang by a number of titles, such as the "Duke of Wu" (Wuguo gong), "Ming Taizu," or "Taizu," and his troops as "Ming army." Furthermore, departing from the practice of other Ming authors, he did not place "our" (*wo*) before Zhu Yuanzhang's name. In essence, he was elevating Zhang to a close equal of the Ming founder, acknowledging him as a "king," and his territory as a "state." Shi Ce noted the illegitimacy of Zhang's regime cursorily in the beginning of his piece but then granted him the status of a king. He thus avoided directly challenging Ming legitimacy, even while reinterpreting late Yuan history from a less orthodox, more balanced perspective.

Shi Ce also mentions Zhang Shicheng's style name, thereby showing his respect; emphasized the heavy corvée labor as a cause for the rebellion; and discussed Zhang's efforts in promoting agriculture, building schools, canceling tax arrears, providing relief, and treating scholars favorably. He further noted other public policies that had benefited the locals, such as dredging waterways and building city walls. But he also reiterated the familiar motifs underscored by other writings to signal Zhang's deficiencies as a leader: his lack of a grand strategy and his indulgence in leisure and pleasure.

Another effort by locals to provide a more balanced and thorough narrative on Zhang was Qian Qianyi's *Guochu qunxiong shilüe* (A brief story of many heroes at the beginning of our dynasty).[36] As the title indicates, this historical work discussed the contenders to power at the end of the Yuan dynasty. While three chapters centered on Zhang, only one chapter was devoted to each of the other figures, with the exception of Zhu Yuanzhang, who was not even included. It is understandable that Qian, as a Suzhou native, would have shown greater interest in Zhang than in the other contenders and, in addition, would have had easier access to materials on Zhang than the others.

Qian Qianyi patched together references on Zhang Shicheng from a wide array of sources into an exhaustive, yet politically ambiguous account. He took note of their origins and added his comments or corrections. Although the majority of the sources cited were heavily tainted with

Ming orthodoxy, Qian also incorporated into his work favorable views on Zhang, including the entire funerary oration that Chen Ji, a scholar who had served Zhang's regime, penned for Zhang Shide, Zhang's brother. Naturally, this piece applauded Zhang Shide: "His capacity is sufficient to assume the important [tasks] of the world, and his brilliance is enough to illuminate the subtle principles of things"; and "Despite his noble status, Mr. Zhang willingly humbled himself before his inferiors and yet was never willing to follow the bandits by groveling before them. With his benevolence, he subjugated the vicious; when facing difficulties, he never willingly demeaned his country."[37] Though Qian merely quoted passages from the original sources, it was nonetheless surprising that he did so without excising the portions that might have offended the Ming. An admixture of two contrasting perspectives, the work generally leaves the impression of siding with the Ming, as the abundance of pro-Ming sources drowns out the few pro-Zhang ones. Qian seemed to have had two intentions in mind. First, he wished to collect as many related sources as possible, regardless of the authors' political orientation, to thoroughly reconstruct late Yuan history. Second, he tried to present a more balanced historical narrative of Zhu and Zhang by juxtaposing contrasting sources without editing the pro-Zhang sources to conform to the politically acceptable view of the Ming.

The writings of Shi Ce and Qian Qianyi exemplified the tensions between the localist and orthodox views, showing that significant steps were taken in the late Ming to reevaluate Zhang Shicheng and his regime. Although both Shi and Qian never directly questioned the legitimacy of the Ming and the authority of its founder, their efforts to resurrect Zhang significantly compromised their dynastic loyalty.

Zhang Fuxiang versus Zhang Xuecheng

Shi Ce's and Qian Qianyi's audacious challenges to the hegemonic narrative pale in comparison to those of Zhang Fuxiang (1663–1727, *js* 1721), an early Qing official and scholar from Zhang Shicheng's hometown of Taizhou.

To those interested in resurrecting Zhang Shicheng's historical role, the Ming-Qing transition would have meant both an opportunity and a dilemma. It provided an opportunity because, under the Qing, allegiance to the Ming and the moral demands to align historical perspectives with the defunct dynasty's orthodoxy were no longer enforced. At the same time, Han literati faced a new dilemma: given that China was under an alien regime, any effort to resurrect Zhang's historical role would imply questioning the authority of the Ming founder, and by extension, the legitimacy of a Han dynasty. Suzhou literati had a choice: to prioritize either localism or loyalty to the fallen Han regime.

Amid this dilemma, Zhang Fuxiang chose localism over dynastic loyalty. In his short but striking biography of Zhang Shicheng, Zhang Fuxiang referred to him through the word "king" rather than his name throughout the entire piece.[38] More surprisingly, he depicted Zhang's army as "our army" (*wojun*, *woshi*), and prefixed the names of the localities under his control with "our." In his *Longping jishi*, Shi Ce had already hailed Zhang Shicheng as "The King of Wu"; but, whereas *Longping jishi* had delegitimized Zhang, Zhang Fuxiang's biography explicitly expressed sympathies for him, as exemplified by the use of the term "our." Zhang Fuxiang avoided calling Zhu Yuanzhang directly by name, addressing him instead as Ming Taizu, but at one point he did label Zhu's army as "the enemy's army" (*dijun*).

Zhang Fuxiang's biography mentioned neither the personal insults Zhang Shicheng suffered from his enemies nor the humiliating story of his escape out of fear of punishment, two themes highlighted in the official and private literature favorable to the Ming founder. Instead, it emphatically noted the harsh social conditions of the late Yuan: "At that time, the politics during the Yuan period were in a state of confusion. People therefore worried and suffered, and thought about staging a rebellion."[39] In Zhang Fuxiang's narrative, Zhang's rebellion originated as a response to adverse social conditions caused by poor administration rather than personal grievances. This reflected Zhang Fuxiang's attempt at framing the rebellion within a socially righteous dimension.

Toward the end of the biography, Zhang Fuxiang trumpeted Zhang Shicheng's popularity in Suzhou. The locals, Zhang continued, loved Zhang Shicheng for his generous and simple policies. They were so enamored of Zhang that, when the Ming army besieged the city, they hid Zhang's two sons and risked their lives to protect him. Upon Zhang's death, locals had his portraits painted and offered sacrifices.[40]

The change of dynasties encouraged such a blatantly partisan view in favor of Zhang Shicheng. Even under the Ming, some writers had expressed sympathetic sentiments toward Zhang, albeit not as conspicuously as Zhang Fuxiang. While accounts congenial to Zhang in the mid- and late Ming carefully legitimized the Ming dynasty, the early Qing author Zhang Fuxiang unequivocally sided with Zhang and his regime. The Taizhou native tried to give his hometown hero Zhang Shicheng his rightful place in history. In Zhang Fuxiang one sees the blurring of the boundary between localism and a genuine concern for an accurate history. Localism shaped Zhang Fuxiang's historical perception, as he clearly conveyed:

> I have read histories of the Ming dynasty. The ministers exaggerate and magnify their own dynasty and generally treat the King of Wu as if he had been a bandit. I have established the fact that the king's was one of the "various states" (*lieguo*). At the time, when the king had yet to surrender to Yuan, even the Yuan could not confront him by asserting that there was only one ruler. The king, moreover, was not a rebellious minister of Zhu Yuanzhang. I am a native of Hailing [Taizhou], which is the old site where the king first raised his troops. It has been more than three hundred years since then. At the southern corner of the city wall, the houses of the inhabitants are scarce. An old man told me that this was where Chang Yuchun [Zhu Yuanzhang's general) soaked his sword in blood. Alas, when heroes act, they become bandits if they lose. Are fortune and misfortune also involved here?[41]

For Zhang Fuxiang, the typical Ming historical narrative, which criticized Zhang Shicheng, was far from faithful to the truth. *Lieguo* depicted political situations in which multiple states coexisted, sharing some degree of legitimacy when a dynasty has either lost control or ceased to exist. By employing this term to characterize the late Yuan polity, Zhang Fuxiang placed Zhang Shicheng's state on equal terms with one ruled by Zhu Yuanzhang. In other words, Zhang Fuxiang was implying that one should not evaluate the late Yuan era from the perspective that the Ming adopted after emerging as the sole power in China, thereby monopolizing claims to legitimacy. Zhang Fuxiang rehabilitated both Zhang Shicheng's status as a king and his political entity as a state.

Zhang Fuxiang acknowledged that the native-place ties he shared with Zhang Shicheng played a pivotal role in determining the political orientation of his historical writing. Zhang Shicheng had raised his troops in Taizhou, Zhang Fuxiang's birthplace. Local experience and memory prompted Zhang Fuxiang to embark on a project that he considered long overdue. Zhang Fuxiang aggressively invoked the figure of Zhang Shicheng, as it was tied to the memory of the mass murder of the local population by the Ming armies.

Zhang Fuxiang's localist interpretation of late Yuan history went so far as to reveal hostility toward the Ming founder, if not the dynasty as a whole. His extreme position, however, was not widely shared and inevitably aroused controversy in the scholarly community. A contemporary scholar, Chen Dashi, challenged Zhang Fuxiang, arguing that his addition of "our" before Zhang Shicheng was totally inappropriate.[42] Zhang Fuxiang replied that during the Ming no one would have dared to add "our" to Zhang Shicheng, just as the Qing would not refer to the Ming in that manner. He noted that the Qing, however, had no reservations about attaching the word "our" to Zhang's name.[43]

Chen Dashi nonetheless represented the prevalent view among the Han literati, who fully recognized the legitimacy and still harbored nostalgic feelings for the fallen Ming dynasty. Therefore, Zhang Fuxiang's attempt to undermine the legitimacy of the Ming founder would certainly have been considered offensive, since Zhang's agenda came dangerously close to challenging the dynasty itself. But for Zhang the collapse of the Ming was ultimately not a source of sorrow, but rather a chance to restore the localist version of history.

Decades later, this debate was revisited by the prominent eighteenth-century historian Zhang Xuecheng (1738–1801), a native of Kuaiji, Zhejiang, who lent support to Chen Dashi.[44] Like Chen, he rejected Zhang Fuxiang's assertion that one could apply "our" to a fallen dynasty as long as one did not live in the dynasty that immediately succeeded it. Zhang Xuecheng dismissed this logic as "erroneous and arbitrary," arguing that, just as people hesitated to add "our" to the dynasty overthrown by their own, it was impermissible to attach the word to the dynasty preceding an overthrown one.

Zhang Xuecheng, who had no intention of legitimizing Zhang Shicheng's regime, sharply criticized Zhang Fuxiang's pro-Zhang Shicheng historiography, which he viewed as a challenge to the legitimacy of the Ming: "What use is there in Zhang Fuxiang's private support for Zhang Shicheng? If his private support is for Zhang Shicheng, then to whom is his private opposition directed?"[45] Zhang Xuecheng ignored the fact that Zhang Fuxiang's endeavor was inspired by the local ties he shared with Zhang Shicheng. He criticized Zhang Fuxiang: "The word 'our' is a term used to address [oneself] to others. He himself did not stand in the court [of Zhang Shicheng], and where did the word 'our' come from?" Zhang Xuecheng could not understand or tolerate Zhang Fuxiang's extreme historical view that favored a dubious figure such as Zhang Shicheng over the Ming.

Zhang Fuxiang's assertion of a radically pro-Zhang Shicheng discourse was, of course, facilitated by the change of dynasty, reducing the moral obligation to remain loyal to the fallen Ming. However, the vehement criticisms that Zhang Xuecheng and others leveled against Zhang Fuxiang revealed that dynastic change scarcely weakened the Han literati's general belief in the Ming's legitimacy. The criticisms further showed the extent of power and pervasiveness of the Ming orthodoxy, even after the dynasty's fall. In short, Zhang Fuxiang's narrative in early Qing was exceptional not only on an empire-wide scale, but also within Suzhou's intellectual community; his efforts constituted an individual, isolated project, unlike the collective ones for similar purposes in the nineteenth and twentieth centuries.

The Political Use of Zhang Shicheng by the Qing Emperors

The Zhu-Zhang rivalry sparked the interest of early Qing rulers, who creatively appropriated this historical precedent to consolidate the legitimacy of their rule by refashioning themselves as "saviors" rather than "conquerors." The official position on the late Yuan rivalry was far more nuanced in the Qing than in the previous dynasty, for the Qing both recognized and undermined the legitimacy of the Ming founder.

Although Zhang Fuxiang's biography of Zhang Shicheng was published in the Kangxi period, it was ignored among the scholarly community during the following two reigns. As mentioned in the previous chapter, the Yongzheng Emperor brought the writing of private histories under strict government control. In a similar vein, the Qianlong Emperor further tightened surveillance to carefully guard his position as the ultimate source of cultural authority and prevent ethnic slandering. Under these two emperors, the fervor for publishing private histories of the Ming dynasty subsided. The interest in private compilations about the history, customs, or worthies of a given locality also waned under Qianlong, as described in chapter 6. Amid this environment, Zhang Shicheng seldom aroused interest among the literati, either within or outside the Suzhou area.

Despite his disappearance from private literature, Zhang Shicheng sporadically appeared in the official historiography. The completion of the *Ming shi* early in the Qianlong reign sheds light on the official Qing perception of the late Yuan issue. The *Ming shi*'s approach to the Zhu-Zhang rivalry basically resembled that in the Ming official historiography, but with several subtle differences. The Qing compilers mentioned Zhang's style name and even included some favorable comments on him: "[Zhang] made light of material wealth and liked to share it with others. [Thus] he was able to win the hearts of many."[46] Unlike the *Yuan shi*, which overlooked the rebellion's social motivations, the *Ming shi* noted the burden of heavy corvée labor on salt workers at the time. By incorporating such conciliatory gestures toward Zhang, which had precedents in the earlier private literature under the Ming, the *Ming shi* depicted Zhang's vicissitudes in a less hostile manner. Although they did not come close to acknowledging Zhang's legitimacy, the *Ming shi* compilers provided a more complete and multifaceted examination of Zhang's personality and his social environment to explain how he attracted many followers and became a king. Unlike the *Yuan shi*, it did not reduce him to an evil troublemaker.

The Qing government's position toward the late Yuan competitors was not as straight-forward as the Ming's approach. The *Bao Yue lu* was safely included in the *Siku quanshu,* despite its decidedly pro-Zhang stance. The Qing's nuanced view was especially apparent in the comments on this work in the *Siku quanshu zongmu tiyao*. The commentators of this imperial project, though recognizing Zhu Yuanzhang as the true lord, found value in the *Bao Yue lu* for recording various misdeeds committed by Zhu's general, Hu Dahai.[47] Their discussion strongly suggested that

Zhu's consolidation of power sacrificed many innocent people, an interpretation that suited the Qing regime's interests. Although generally in agreement with the Ming perspective on late Yuan history, the Qing compilers sought ways to raise doubts about the Ming founder's legitimacy.

The Qing government's ambivalence toward the Ming founder also surfaced in the imperial edicts, which often drew on the rivalry between Zhu and Zhang for political purposes. In an edict issued in 1778, the Qianlong Emperor first cited various misdeeds of the early Ming emperors, such as the harsh punishment meted out by Ming Taizu and the mass killing committed by the Yongle Emperor. As a result, "there was no scholar or commoner who did not harbor a grudge." Qianlong took issue with the die-hard resistance of the pro-Zhang population in Jiangnan at the end of the Yuan, concluding that the resistance led the Ming emperors to impose an excessive tax burden on the region. He sought to juxtapose the Ming's "hostile" treatment of the Jiangnan population with the Qing's "benevolent" policies: "In our dynasty, sage kings succeeded one after another and nourished the people with love. . . . Benevolent favors were frequently offered and the excessive taxes of Jiangsu and Zhejiang Provinces were gradually reduced to alleviate the people's misfortune."[48] The Qianlong Emperor contrasted Ming Taizu's narrow-minded revenge with the magnanimous attitude of the Qing emperors, including his decision to offer several tax remittances. In this manner, the emperor invoked the memory of the Zhang-Zhu rivalry to emphasize his own virtue, and perhaps to win the hearts of the Suzhou people. By portraying the Ming founder as a ruler apathetic to the people's sufferings and magnifying the humane dimensions of the Qing rulers, he refashioned Suzhou's history to serve his own agenda.

Resurrecting Zhang Shicheng in Early Nineteenth-Century Suzhou

The collective efforts of the literati of Suzhou to reevaluate the Zhang Shicheng's historical position marked part of the effort to re-create their city as a prominent cultural center. The degree of disparity between the localist views on Zhang in the early nineteenth century and the orthodox one reflected the extent of the retreat of the state from the local cultural realm.

How did the discourse on Zhang Shicheng unfold in early nineteenth-century Suzhou society? Around the turn of the nineteenth century Suzhou scholar Bei Yong bought a rubbing of the inscription of a piece entitled *Qiji quancuo zhi* (The epitaph for the temporary burial of the seven concubines) at a local bookstore.[49] The seven concubines were those of Pan Yuanshao, Zhang Shicheng's minister and son-in-law. When Pan had to leave the concubines for a crucial battle, they all committed suicide as a display of loyalty. Pan later asked a renowned scholar, Zhang Yu, to write an epitaph for them, the *Qiji quancuo zhi* that Bei Yong would later purchase.

Bei Yong embarked on a project to collect prose and poetry related to the seven concubines from earlier writings. He also had his associates compose poems to commemorate the collective suicide. Ultimately, he compiled these works in a single volume entitled *Qiji yonglin* (The forest of songs on the seven concubines). The preface is dated 1820, and some of the pieces contributed to the volume were written in 1820, 1821, or 1822. Though the rubbing itself was about the seven concubines, the contributors covered issues that went beyond this topic. In fact, the rubbing provided Suzhou literati with an opportunity to revisit the subject of Zhang Shicheng and his regime. The individual views collected represent a wide spectrum, ranging from highly favorable to extremely hostile, providing a curious window through which we can examine the Suzhou literati's varying perceptions of Zhang.

Pan Shi'en, a Suzhou native who would soon become one of the most powerful ministers in the court of the Daoguang period, penned a hostile piece on Zhang's legacy. He first raised questions regarding the death of the concubines.[50] Refuting an explanation offered by a Ming scholar who suspected that the concubines had actually been forced to commit suicide by Pan Yuanshao, Pan Shi'en opined that he had not been self-sacrificing and had secretly sought ways to stay alive. Arguing that under those circumstances Pan Yuanshao would not have demanded his concubines' suicide, Pan Shi'en provided another explanation. In his view, Zhang was a vulgar man who coveted the crown and power—one of the "evil" heroes of the late Yuan, the likes of Chen Youliang. He showed no willingness to end the cruelty that had pervaded the Yuan dynasty or save the people. On other hand, the seven concubines were the daughters of respectable families, well aware of the political environment and perspicacious enough to behave virtuously. When Pan Yuanshao chose the wrong side and faced danger, the concubines ardently advocated that he pursue the righteous course of serving the legitimate ruler Zhu Yuanzhang. They entreated their husband with tears but were unsuccessful, whereupon they sought to enlighten him by choosing death. Sagacious were the seven concubines, Pan Shi'en exclaimed, and he praised them not for their passive loyalty to their husband, but for their active remonstrance, a characteristic reminiscent of male ministers who would remonstrate with their rulers.

Pan Shi'en blamed Pan Yuanshao entirely for the incident and suspected that Pan and Zhang had perhaps forged the whole story in Zhang Yu's inscription to cover up the concubines' act of remonstrance. Zhang merely flattered Pan Yuanshao by distorting the story for his sake. Pan Shi'en ended his treatise by pointing out that "[Those two] wanted to cover up the story; nonetheless the truth is even more transparent."[51] Here a sheer suspicion became a firm conviction. Pan Shi'en carefully dissociated the concubines from Zhang Yu's original story and saved them without substantiating his conjecture. He decided to blame only Zhang Shicheng, Pan Yuanshao, and Zhang Yu.

It is most likely that Pan Shi'en was motivated to fabricate this story because he felt uncomfortable in accepting that the concubines had died to remain loyal to their husband, whom he resented. Pan Shi'en's argument followed the orthodoxy of late Yuan history that the Qing court endorsed; and, among the items collected in the *Qiji yonglin*, it represents the most vigorous stance against Zhang Shicheng and his collaborators.

Others, however, painted more favorable portraits of Zhang, some of them going so far as to identify themselves with his regime, such as Suzhou licentiate Gu Zhen:

> Ming Taizu excessively taxed the lands of the Suzhou people. King Zhang loved his people, so the people of Suzhou took pity on him. How can we blame the Left Prime Minister [Pan Yuanshao] who surrendered to Ming? Zhu Yuanzhang's success and Zhang Shicheng's failure are meaningless. After winning the country, Ming Taizu treated Suzhou people with cruelty

and ferocity. Up until now we still consider him as our enemy (*chou*) and reminisce about Zhang Shicheng's virtue.[52]

Gu Zhen underscored the virtues of Zhang and his regime, referring to him as a king and Zhu Yuanzhang as an "enemy." Zhang's regime had been based in Suzhou, noted Gu, and his benevolent rule during a time of instability and brutality had left an indelible impression in the minds of the Suzhou people that only deepened their antipathy toward the Ming founder. This was indeed a bold argument, considering that the Qing dynasty was officially positioning itself as the successor of the Ming and therefore obliged to acknowledge its legitimacy. Extreme as it may seem at first glance, especially when compared to Pan Shi'en's view, it was widely shared by Suzhou literati.

Similar pro-Zhang sentiment prevailed in a piece by Chen Peizhi, a *shengyuan* originally from Hangzhou and a sojourner in Suzhou. Chen believed that people had deliberately degraded Pan Yuanshao and the seven concubines to defame Zhang Shicheng. Zhang, however, possessed virtues, among them his generosity that, in Chen's view, "by far surpassed that of Ming Taizu."[53] Chen then broached the issue of Pan Yuanshao and his concubines. He argued that since Zhang had received official titles from the Yuan, Pan should also be considered an official of that dynasty. In this regard, Pan refused to serve the Ming to avoid betraying the Yuan. When a Ming army besieged Suzhou, Pan summoned the seven concubines: "I have been entrusted with an important mission by the state. In order to be righteous, I cannot look after my family." "How solemn it is," Chen exclaimed, adding: "The concubines hanged themselves not only to clarify their loyalty to their husband but also to urge Pan Yuanshao to die for the country!" In contrast to Pan Shi'en, Chen eulogized their death as a gesture of loyalty toward Zhang Shicheng's regime.

Chen then asked whether Pan Yuanshao begged for his life and served the Ming dynasty by betraying his concubines' wish, as some people argued. "No," he replied, explaining that in the *Ming shi* one can find only statements that Pan's brother served the Ming, but not Pan. Chen quoted a source that described Pan's death as the price of his loyalty to Zhang. According to this source, Ming Taizu ordered Pan to persuade Zhang to surrender, but instead he secretly warned Zhang to wait for several days, implying that he would soon find a way to rescue him. His servant, however, leaked his message and Pan was ultimately put to death for false surrender. Thus, in Chen's narrative, Pan Yuanshao's surrender to Zhu Yuanzhang, which at first glance suggested an act of betrayal against Zhang Shicheng, turned out to be an expression of loyalty. In this regard, Chen contended that Pan never betrayed his concubines' wish.

In Lu Zhun's essay in the same volume, Pan Yuanshao takes on the character of an ethnic Han hero. Lu insisted that Pan was originally surnamed Zhao, a descendant of the Song founder Zhao Kuangyin.[54] Given this unfounded speculation, he naturally concluded that Pan's family had been the enemy of the Yuan dynasty for generations and that his service to Zhang Shicheng should not be considered treasonous. Contrary to Chen Peizhi, who portrayed Pan as a loyal minister under Yuan rule and thereby rationalized his participation in the opposite camp of the Ming founder, Lu Zhun's story transformed Pan into an archenemy of the Yuan dynasty acting on behalf of the Song dynasty's cause. When Suzhou was besieged, Pan advised Zhang to cross the sea and lead an expedition to conquer Japan and Liuqiu (present-day Okinawa). Lu viewed this plan's failure as the end of the last chance to rebuild the Song. He then lamented, "Heaven did not bestow fortune on Song, and [Pan] was killed by faking a surrender." While Lu concurred with Chen Peizhi by regarding Pan's surrender as false, in his story this act involved more than loyalty to his lord; it was also to "expunge the shame of the Han." The point is not whether these various arguments were substantially grounded in historical evidence. Although the individual interpretations of late Yuan political history offered by these pro-Zhang writers varied greatly and were at times even contradictory, each version attempted in its own way to rescue Zhang Shicheng and his followers from the dominant, antagonistic view.

Between the extreme ends of the spectrum, which I have just discussed, some moderate views were expressed. Shi Yunyu (discussed in chapter 5) began his evaluation of Zhang Shicheng by downplaying his regime's significance and achievements, but at the same time also shared the prevailing local view, which tilted in Zhang's favor.[55] Shi's case is an example of how some Suzhou scholars reconciled the two opposing views of Zhang and constructed a narrative more acceptable to the literati outside of Suzhou. Even for a moderate such as Shi, the dominant view that dismissed Zhang as a mere bandit seemed too problematic, as indicated in the following passage:

> [One] became an emperor if one succeeded and a plundering bandit if one failed. The fate of success and failure is decided only by the mandate bestowed by heaven. It is not that the distinction between being superior and being inferior exists from the beginning. . . . Yang Shen and others were the ministers of the Ming dynasty, so they could not help but degrade Zhang Shicheng. Now under a changed dynasty, those who discuss this matter should have an open and fair mind and not consider them in terms of being superior or inferior.[56]

This passage, written more than a hundred years after Zhang Fuxiang's death, reiterated his argument almost verbatim. Shi was challenging the orthodox Ming perspective of late Yuan history, which still held powerful sway over his contemporaries. He urged them to stop viewing events through the lens of the Ming founder, a politically contaminated approach that sacrificed historical accuracy. Shi believed that a more balanced position could be restored only by distancing oneself from the Ming official narrative.

A Hometown Scholar's Reevaluation of Zhang Shicheng

Although Suzhou literati played a pivotal role in renewing interest in Zhang Shicheng and reevaluating his position in late Yuan history, such endeavors could also be observed elsewhere. In Zhang Shicheng's hometown of Taizhou, the local scholar Xia Quan (1793–1842) produced a work that sympathetically recorded detailed biographical information about Zhang and his followers.[57] According to Xia, four biographical works on Zhang were extant in his day: *Ming shi*; *Mingshi gao*, by Wang Hongxu (1645–1723); *Yaofeng wenji*, by Suzhou native Wang Wan (1624–91); and *Yiguicao chuke*, by Zhang Fuxiang (published in 1696).[58] All four of these biographies, products primarily of the Kangxi period in the early Qing, further underscores that the literati discourse on Zhang had been suppressed under the Yongzheng and Qianlong Emperors. Xia's own biography of Zhang Shicheng, whom he hailed as the "King of Wu," was a collection of related references drawn from these existing sources, quoting them verbatim and specifying the origin of the references.

Through his referencing approach, Xia intended to pursue the historical viewpoint of the former native scholar Zhang Fuxiang, who had accorded legitimacy to Zhang Shicheng. Invoking the debate between Zhang Fuxiang and Chen Dashi, Xia Quan openly supported Zhang, "Our Zhang Fuxiang answered him. He repeatedly gave him explanations and expounded his own theory in detail. His argument made sense to a considerable degree."[59] Zhang Xuecheng's criticism of Zhang Fuxiang was perhaps unknown or at least ignored by Xia Quan.

In an attempt to further bolster Zhang Fuxiang, Xia argued that the practice of placing "our" before Zhang Shicheng's name had actually started long before Zhang Fuxiang. That Zhang Fuxiang's historiography was buttressed by precedents corroborated the propriety of his stance and strengthened the respect for that tradition.

Xia decided to rely upon the authority of another former local scholar, Gong Weiliu, to further justify writing a biography on Zhang Shicheng. The compilers of an earlier edition of the Taizhou local gazetteer had featured a biographical section on Zhang, a practice Gong viewed as defensible as Sima Qian's inclusion of Xiang Yu in the *Shiji* (Records of the Grand Historian). As Xia Quan aligned himself with the former scholars of his hometown—all of whom opposed the prevailing view of Zhang—individual historical thinking gradually coalesced into a local historical tradition.[60]

Xia Quan's interest in Zhang Shicheng centered on historical figures from Taizhou. More specifically, he tried to rescue these figures from the long-standing stigma produced by the official historiography. Regarding Zhang's collaborators Pan Yuanming and Li Bosheng, the department gazetteer (*zhouzhi*) suspected that they had been salt workers, depicting them as ferocious and cunning local bullies who took advantage of the turmoil to steal wealth and status. In his rebuttal, Xia Quan argued that the compilers had failed to consider that these two figures had been "sincere about poetry, spoke about ritual, collected and studied literature, and took it as their responsibility to restore what has been discarded and supplement what has been missing."[61] Thus, Pan Yuanming "had quite the attitude of the great ministers of antiquity." In contrast to the official historiography's portrayal of Zhang's collaborators as uncultured scoundrels, Xia reconfigured them with characteristics appropriate to Confucian elites. He thus endowed the uncouth salt workers with cultured images, as patrons of art and scholarship.

The literati activities in Suzhou and Taizhou reflected the cultural atmosphere of the early nineteenth century, a time when local people enjoyed greater freedom to discuss their local hero, Zhang Shicheng. This transformation can be observed in Xia Quan's recollection of an episode concerning a massive tomb in Taizhou, the Tomb of the King's Son-in-law (*Fuma fen*). Legend had it that Zhang Shicheng's son-in-law had been buried there. During the Qianlong reign, a Buddhist monk of a nearby temple renovated the tomb, adding soil on top, planting a tree, and erecting a stone stele bearing the title "Tomb of the King of Wu's Son-in-law" (*Wu fuma mu*). The monk's efforts, however, triggered criticism, as someone warned him, "Your action involves the illegitimate Wu. How can you do such a thing?" The monk, greatly perturbed, demolished the stele. After listening to this story from a friend, Xia Quan smiled, "[Doing things related to] King Zhang was strictly prohibited in the previous dynasty. Now things have changed. How can it harm you even if you do things that are related to him?"[62]

Xia Quan could not sympathize with the monk who had seen danger in renovating the tomb. Since they no longer lived under the Ming, he asserted, they need not worry about possible criticisms in matters involving Zhang Shicheng. He did not realize, or simply ignored, that the monk in the Qianlong period did not experience the same relaxed cultural atmosphere. But by the time Xia Quan wrote this work, the central government no longer demonstrated the vigor to actively censor literary works and impose orthodox views as it had during the eighteenth century.[63]

The memory of Zhang Shicheng had become indispensable to local tradition, deeply ingrained in the minds of the Suzhou and Taizhou people, regardless of their opinion of his actions. In the early nineteenth century, most people still held the prevalent view of Zhang as an evil bandit.[64] However, the literati's unprecedented attacks on this hegemonic view seriously undermined its authority.

The discourse on Zhang became more overt and extreme in the nineteenth century than in the mid- and late Ming periods. The spectrum of views widened to the extent of embracing a radically pro-Zhang discourse that vociferously insisted on reinterpreting late Yuan history and identifying a legitimate place for their local hero.[65] During the Ming dynasty, those authors who unearthed positive sides of Zhang Shicheng had to exercise caution by acknowledging the legitimacy of the Ming and its founder. In the Qing period, Suzhou residents increasingly expressed radical views, even ones deemed offensive to the Ming founder. Under the Qianlong Emperor, such deviations from the state-imposed orthodox interpretation would certainly have invited charges of "parochialism." The renewed discourse on Zhang Shicheng in the early nineteenth century radically challenged this orthodoxy and accommodated the sympathies of the local population.

Zhang Shicheng in the Republican Period

The early nineteenth century should be characterized as a period that marked the initial stage of the resurgent literati efforts to give expression to local voices and strengthen local identity. The transformation of the discourse on Zhang Shicheng reflected the long-term trend of growing elite power and the retraction of state control in the local cultural realm that persisted well into the early twentieth century.

During the Republican period, the centuries-old local effort to challenge the orthodox view of Zhang Shicheng crystallized into the compilation of a comprehensive volume on the historical development and significance of his enterprise. Entitled *Wu wang Zhang Shicheng zaiji* (The history of Zhang Shicheng, King of Wu), it emerged as a collective effort to complete the revisionist local understanding of late Yuan history that featured prominently in the *Qiji yonglin*. Although the *Qiji yonglin* incorporated discussions on Zhang Shicheng, the title of the work suggested that it was originally intended to commemorate the female virtues of the seven concubines, a theme that could rightfully claim a legitimate niche in the existing Confucian ideology. In contrast, the title of the Republican-era work clearly announced the author's intention to focus exclusively on Zhang Shicheng and restore his proper place in history. To mention Zhang Shicheng's name in the book title, rather than in the titles of treatises or chapters, was unprecedented. The breadth of the collected materials enabled this book to stand out among the literature on Zhang. Historical circumstances certainly aided the undertaking of this project. With the demise of the empire in 1911, the mantle of Confucianism as the state-sponsored ideology was eventually removed, as well as the moral pressure to abide by the orthodoxy dictated by previous dynasties.

In the late 1920s, a Taizhou scholar, Han Guojun (1857–1942), embarked on an exhaustive compilation project, the *Wu wang Zhang Shicheng zaiji*, a collection of materials about Zhang Shicheng. As it neared completion, Han had the idea to create a more tangible monument to commemorate Zhang. He contacted his associate Wang Xinggao in Suzhou's Wu County, to pen a record for the tomb of Zhang's mother, located outside a city gate.[66] Meanwhile, Han launched a search for Zhang Shicheng's tomb, rumored to be situated somewhere in Suzhou. He noted a phrase that vaguely indicated the location of the tomb in the *Wuzhong guyu* (Old stories of Suzhou) from the mid-Ming and asked Wang to trace it.[67] Wang also relied on the *Wumen biaoyin*, which briefly mentioned the whereabouts of Zhang's temple. Despite continuous inquiries of village elders, he failed to find the tomb.

At the same time, another Wu County scholar brought to Wang's attention an early nineteenth-century market town gazetteer that described the location of the tomb in greater detail. Encouraged by this information, Wang resumed his search, this time enlisting the help of local villagers, and ultimately he found the tomb where Zhang was supposedly buried. Although it had no inscription, a temple had been erected to its right for the worship of a city god, King Zhang (Zhang wang). The natives mentioned that big sacrificial rituals were offered there annually on the Spring Purification day. King Zhang was, according to them, Zhang Jiusi; this was Zhang Shicheng's original name. Wang was thus able to verify the reference to the tomb's location in the market town gazetteer, as well as a comment in the *Wuzhong guyu* that locals had carried back Zhang's bones to Suzhou and buried them there. Subsequently, Han Guojun erected a stone stele that bore the title "The Tomb of Zhang, the King of Wu," and ordered a commemorative tomb inscription for Zhang.

The *Wu wang Zhang Shicheng zaiji* includes a detailed biography of Zhang Shicheng. The term *zaiji* refers to a regional state in a political environment where no single state could claim universal sovereignty over the entire territory of China. In this sense, *zaiji* differs from both "basic annals" (*benji*), used for emperors, and "biographies" (*liezhuan*), applied to people below the rank of emperor or king. Therefore, the use of *zaiji* in the title, as the compilers claimed, served to endow Zhang Shicheng's regime with the status of being one of "various states" (*lieguo*).

In his preface, dated 1930, to *Wu wang Zhang Shicheng zaiji*, Han Guojun explained that he had decided to devote a single volume to Zhang Shicheng after reading histories of "Zhang, the King of Wu" in works such as Xia Quan's *Tuian biji* and *Zili jiuwen*. He also criticized Qian Qianyi's *Guochu qunxiong shilüe* for unjustly depicting Zhang as a bandit and rebel. Han drew on Zhang Fuxiang's argument to highlight that even Yuan rulers could not entirely neglect Zhang's de facto kingly status. He also dismissed the idea that Zhang had been a rebel since he had never been Zhu Yuanzhang's minister.[68] Han Guojun fully endorsed Zhang Fuxiang's efforts to confer the status of *lieguo* on Zhang Shicheng's kingdom. Zhi Weicheng, a co-compiler, reiterated Han's view: "Various unofficial histories and miscellaneous records of the Ming scholars generally exaggerated Taizu's martial deeds and treated Zhang of Wu as a bandit and rebel. Thus in calling [Zhu and Zhang, respectively] superior and inferior, they sacrificed reality, and [the sources] cannot be trusted."

The efforts of the compilers in recovering the "reality" of late Yuan history included, above all, addressing Zhang or Zhu by their own titles. When citing from sources contaminated by the Ming perspective, they preferred the titles Zhang Shicheng had adopted to the use of "bandit." Accordingly, early in their account, they featured "King Cheng" (Cheng wang) and the state name Zhou, terms that Zhang had used for his regime from 1354 until his surrender to the Yuan three years later, upon which he received the Yuan government title of the Grand Commandant (*taiwei*). Thus, for the period following Zhang's surrender, the compilers referred to him as Zhang *taiwei* and his troops as Zhang's Army (Zhang *jun*). By the same token, during Zhang's rule of the Wu state, they used "King of Wu" (Wu wang). Likewise, they first addressed Zhu Yuanzhang as "the Duke of Wu." For their account of the period after Zhu granted himself the title of King of Wu, the compilers distinguished him from

Zhang by referring to them as "Zhu, the King of Wu" (Zhu Wu wang) and "Zhang, the King of Wu" (Zhang Wu wang).[69] In this manner, the compilers clearly sought to dispense equal treatment to both men.

The compilers strove to construct their own version of late Yuan history. Rejecting a source that stated Zhang had been beaten to death, burned, and buried by Zhu Yuanzhang, the co-compiler Ren Zhiyuan claimed that Zhang had hanged himself and that his body had been transported from Nanjing and buried in Suzhou by a local man.[70] Ren Zhiyuan made similar emendations to the story of Zhang's brother, Zhang Shide: he had not been killed by Zhu Yuanzhang as some sources claimed; rather, he had starved himself to death.[71] Rather than grounded in firm historical evidence, these arguments were geared toward providing a heroic and graceful depiction of Zhang and his brother's deaths that would be palatable to Suzhou and Taizhou natives.

Attempting to glorify Pan Yuanshao, the compilers intentionally omitted the derogatory view that he had forced his concubines to commit suicide before surrendering to the Ming. In their narrative, he had advised Zhang to seek refuge overseas. Pan's "false" surrender to the Ming was a last-minute attempt to rescue Zhang that led him to a heroic, loyal death.[72] Likewise, the compilers rehabilitated Li Bosheng, who had often been contemptuously perceived as a traitor, even among Suzhou natives. Li's surrender, the compilers asserted, became inevitable as food and army routes had been cut off. He persuaded Zhang to surrender out of genuine concern for his former lord's safety.[73]

One of the authors of Zhang Shicheng's biography in the volume, Zhou Hongxi claimed to be Zhang's seventeenth-generation descendant.[74] According to his historical narrative, immediately before the fall of Suzhou, Zhou Guojun, one of Zhang's generals, secretly guided one of Zhang's concubines and her six-year-old son out of the besieged city. Crossing the Yangzi River, they ultimately found safety in Tongzhou, in northern Jiangsu. Zhang Shicheng's son adopted Zhou Guojun's surname and, during the subsequent centuries, his descendants proliferated in Tongzhou.

In another piece, entitled "Discussing the Posthumous Title of Zhang, the King of Wu," Zhou expressed regret over the lack of a posthumous title for Zhang Shicheng and suggested that he be bestowed with the title of "Benevolent and Martyred King of Wu" (Wu Huilie wang).[75] These essays show that efforts to legitimize Suzhou's local heroes continued well into the twentieth century, a period of rising nationalist sentiment and awareness of "China" as a nation-state.

Changes in the perception of Zhang Shicheng within the Suzhou literati community during the late imperial and Republican periods illuminated shifts in the power relations between the state and local elites. The early nineteenth-century counter-memory was radical, for it challenged, subverted, and replaced the dominant hegemonic discourse that had survived the initial Ming challenge. As explained in the first three chapters, the Jiaqing and Daoguang periods witnessed a gradual intensification of elite participation in local public works. Confronting the serious fiscal crisis engendered by forces both domestic and foreign, the Daoguang court formulated regulations that rewarded both elite and commoner contributors more generously than in earlier years. As the state's reliance on the elites for financial and managerial assistance became increasingly vital to the maintenance of local order, the state inevitably relaxed its grip on local affairs. This is evident in the enshrinement of local worthies, the building of the General Shrine of Former Worthies of Suzhou Prefecture, and the efflorescence of local literature in Suzhou. It was in this context of the shifting balance between state and local elites that the figure of Zhang Shicheng reemerged. Sensing an overture for expressions of local culture, the elites of Suzhou and Taizhou realized their long-suppressed yearning to restore Zhang to his proper place in history.

CONCLUSION

This book has explored some of the social and cultural changes that serve to demarcate the early nineteenth century from the previous period, with a particular focus on Suzhou. Local public works, supervised and funded by local elites, increasingly became a regular scene in the early nineteenth-century landscape of China. These endeavors were never entirely independent of official interference, nor did they take place in opposition to state power. As shown in chapters 1 through 3, the elite cooperated closely with local officials. At the same time, the imperial state—from the emperors down to county magistrates—desperately sought to mobilize the gentry for financial and managerial resources.

When the issue of the existence of the "public sphere" in late imperial and modern China came to the fore decades ago, elite managerial activism emerged as a focus of heated debate among Qing historians. One topic around which the debate developed was the "extra-bureaucratic" management of public works in the late Qing era. While Rankin and Rowe emphasized the multiplication of elite-managed works for public causes run relatively autonomously from the official intervention in this period, Wakeman argued that they were still under government control in terms of the origin of the financial resources and the personnel that staffed the public works management.[1] As the foregoing discussions of this book have shown, the enlarged public roles of elites in the early nineteenth century supplemented the official administration. In this sense, it would be absurd to portray the rise of elite power as a movement seeking autonomy from power of the state.[2] However, as Rowe has persuasively argued, the organizational autonomy is not a zero-sum issue, but rather a continuum.[3] Just as it would be inaccurate to understand the elite managerial services as an arena totally independent of official supervision, it would be erroneous not to recognize the changes in the balance between official and elite managerial initiatives. The expansion of elite managerial roles in the early nineteenth century was never devoid of the necessity to cooperate with the officialdom. But the new managerial patterns that became prevalent at that time certainly differed from the older ones in the previous century, as they were built on enhanced mobilization of the fiscal resources and management of the elites.

It is almost commonsensical knowledge that the elites constituted an indispensable part of the local administration during the late imperial period. Yongzheng and Qianlong's attempts to control the degree of elite public functions, however, show that the state's cooperation with the elites entailed dimensions more complex than simply being supplementary and harmonious. The population growth during the eighteenth century brought an increasingly thinner state presence in local administration. But unlike their nineteenth-century counterparts, the Qing government under Yongzheng and Qianlong did not encourage a rapid expansion of elite public roles, nor did they immediately devolve power to local elites by granting them pseudo-bureaucratic roles as public works managers. This suggests that a thorough understanding of the state-elite relations requires more than consideration of the ratios between official posts and population, and directs us to the need to pay closer attention to the expansion or retraction of elite public roles within the framework of a larger state agenda.

During the early Qing period, rulers preoccupied themselves with how to control local elites, especially those of the Jiangnan region.[4] These concerns were reflected in the state policies toward elite participation in the local public realm. Without doubt, the Qing state during the eighteenth century needed to enlist the support of elites for the maintenance of local infrastructure. Given the growing population pressures and the limits of the state's coffers, the government alone could not provide everything for the local population. At the same time, it needed to control elite participation and keep it under certain levels to curb the exorbitant empowerment of the local gentry. During this period, the state agenda still prioritized limiting the power of local elites.[5] Overreliance on financial and managerial support of local elites, which necessitated devolving greater power to them, was viewed by the state as detrimental to the overarching goal of bringing the local gentry under proper state control. This state goal was often camouflaged behind the emperor's paternalistic policies to save people from fiscal burdens, which in its stead placed the responsibility for securing necessary resources on the shoulders of the state. The relatively healthy state finances made this policy a viable option during the eighteenth century. In short, state policy on elite participation in the local public realm was closely intertwined with the control of local elites. From the state's perspective, greater reliance on elite public functions required compensating the gentry with increased power and granting them greater freedom in their social and cultural activities. But eighteenth century rulers were not yet ready to accept this scenario.

The magnified role of the gentry in public functions in the early nineteenth century meant the balance between state and elites was moving in the direction of empowering the local elites. The changes that this power shift entailed were crucial to the actual everyday lives of contemporaries. This power shift determined the degree of one's participation in local public life and the kinds of works the literati could write, publish, or republish. It is generally correct to assume that the Chinese case of state-society relations lacked the kind of explicit antagonism often claimed to be present in the case of European states.[6] But its absence in China did not mean the lack of tension between the two, nor did it mean that the tension was negligible.

The expansion of elite public roles was accompanied by the decline of state control over various local elite practices, which allowed elites more room to pursue their interests. As exemplified through the case study of Suzhou, the involvement of elites in the first four decades of the nineteenth century in a variety of cultural activities aimed at elevating their local ancestors and prestige. These practices ranged from the enshrinement of worthies to a collective program to rehabilitate a local historical hero. As state reliance on elite financial and managerial roles became increasingly important, the state found itself in a difficult position in its efforts to exercise rigorous control over the gentry's interests. The possibility that the empowerment of elites might pose an obstacle to impartial local administration was condoned, if not forgotten, and replaced by a vital and immediate urgency of enlisting their support. Beset with fiscal crisis and deteriorating bureaucratic inefficiency, the central government in the early nineteenth century moved in the direction of accommodating local interests and provided concessions to local leaders. This triggered a new cultural order that allowed local elites to enjoy greater freedom in the literary realm and engage in a stronger assertion of familial and local interests. As the imperially centered cultural order receded, a multicentered one emerged, highlighting each locality's position on the cultural map of the Qing Empire.

This book has depicted elite public activism in the nineteenth century as a gradual process, challenging the existing scholarship that identified the Taiping Rebellion and the postbellum restoration efforts as the epochal moment that initiated elite activism. The role of elite efforts during and after the Taiping Rebellion in the unfolding of elite activism should be duly recognized, but more as catalysts for deepening the already existing trend rather than triggering it.[7] At the same time, however, the incipient stage of elite activism in the early nineteenth century differed from its more full-fledged form in the later century in a number of aspects. In the early nineteenth century, elite managerial roles were largely restricted to public works for social welfare and infrastructure management. Only in mid-century did elite participation spread to more sensitive areas such as local military defense organization.[8] The public realm of elite managers during the early half of the century, mainly confined within the boundaries of their localities, acquired an extra-regional dimension during the latter half of the century.[9]

Ascendant Literati Political Activism

Elite political activism is another theme that allows us to view the nineteenth century through a long-term perspective. Mary Rankin has explained that elite managers who rose to prominence during the postbellum restoration process formed the social basis of the political movements that surfaced at a time of intensified foreign threats and rising concerns for domestic political reforms. The elite activism around 1900 decisively took on a political character, Rankin explains, as elite activists criticized incompetent officials in power and called for broader participation in national politics. The introduction of the press emboldened elite activism, expanding the social and geographic boundaries of the public sphere.

The origins of the political activism of the literati in the final decades of the Qing can be traced to the last decade of the eighteenth century. Wang Wensheng notes the rise of certain "quasi-literary associations" in the 1790s that built alliances among political dissenters under the disguise of regular ceremonial and literary activities.[10] Benjamin Elman emphasized the emergence of political activism among examination elites after 1799, as Jiaqing opened the path of remonstrance in an attempt to attenuate the autocratic aura of the throne, thus empowering the literati.[11] The Jiangnan literati had already begun to organize themselves more cohesively through increasingly frequent examination boycotts in the Jiaqing period.[12] The literati's empowerment was aided by Emperor Jiaqing, who circumscribed the overgrown imperial power by disciplining and regularizing inner court agencies such as the Grand Council and the Imperial Household Department, two pillars that buttressed the aggressive ruling style of his predecessor.[13]

It was around the year 1801, as Rowe has recently contended, that a renowned Jiangnan scholar Bao Shichen (1775–1855) proposed the establishment of a government organization that would accommodate the political participation of diverse social groups, including gentry and commoners.[14] Bao's concern for inviting political opinions from a broader spectrum of social groups was echoed a few decades later by the statecraft scholar Wei Yuan. As Philip Kuhn has argued, the proposal by Wei Yuan to expand the boundaries of political participation to include "established elites" (*juren*)—to borrow Kuhn's term—closely reflected the ascendant literati political activism in the first half of the nineteenth century. Furthermore, Wei's idea of broadened elite political participation marked a starting point in a similar line of political arguments that unfolded in the late nineteenth and early twentieth centuries.[15]

According to James Polachek, the formation of the Xuannan Poetry Club and the Spring Purification circle during the Jiaqing and Daoguang years represented the cultural and political mobilization of elites through literary networks, which was particularly visible in the Jiangnan region.[16] Scholars from the region, including Suzhou, made up the largest regional group in the composition of the Xuannan Poetry Club.[17] The leaders of the Spring Purification circle were patronized by Pan Shi'en, a Suzhou native and a grand councilor in the Daoguang court.[18] Moreover, the Spring Purification circle espoused Xu Qianxue, a scholar-official from Suzhou who had served the Kangxi Emperor, as an object of the cult.[19] By the early 1830s, this reform-minded literati group consciously emulated the Donglin party style of factional activism in the late Ming.

Confronting signs of escalating social crises, statecraft officials, such as Tao Zhu, He Changling, Liang Zhangju, and Lin Zexu, organized relief and waterworks projects, and they attempted to enact reforms in tribute grain transport and salt administration in Jiangsu Province during the 1820s and 1830s. Their reforms targeted old problems in the Jiangnan area, particularly the extortionate surtax in the tribute grain system that had been plaguing the region for generations. These officials mobilized the support of the local literati for these reforms, and the activist Jiangnan literati in turn pressed their demands.

When Lin Zexu assumed the Jiangsu governorship in 1832, he proposed promoting irrigated-field agriculture in North China. This plan's design, drafted with the assistance of two Suzhou scholars, would serve as an attempt to relieve the heavy burden of the tribute grain tax in the Jiangnan region. The opposing faction's lobbying, however, prevented it from being presented to the emperor.[20] According to one scholar, Lin's advocacy of irrigated-field agriculture in North China differed from similar plans during the Yongzheng and Qianlong periods. While Lin's plan explicitly sought to relieve the tax burden in the Jiangnan region, earlier Qing plans were presented as a northern regional development project in response to an increase in demographic pressure.[21] Lin's plan conveyed a keen sense of the "north-south problem," that is, the phenomenon of southerners being burdened with the heavy tribute grain responsibility to feed the northern population. A similar proposal that reflected this awareness of the "north-south problem" had already appeared in the late Ming. In this regard, the political environment in the early nineteenth century bore a greater resemblance to the late Ming than the eighteenth century and enabled a stronger assertion of Jiangnan's local interests.[22]

The early-nineteenth-century activism, seldom observed in the eighteenth century, foreshadowed the more extensive and vigorous elite political activism in the later period. The humiliating defeat by the British during the Opium War elevated literati concerns for the fate of Chinese civilization, further invigorating their political activism. Their engagement progressed during the post-Taiping restoration in Suzhou, marking an age of "gentry hegemony."[23]

As shown by Mary Rankin's study of the local elites in Zhejiang Province during the post-Taiping period, the elites' social and political activism often went hand in hand in the late Qing: managers in local public works were often those who raised their voices in national politics.[24] Can we, then, find specific examples in the early nineteenth century that illustrate the merging of social and political activism?

Since elite political activism had its origins in the early nineteenth century, it is not surprising that some incorporated the dual roles of political activists and managerial leaders in public works during this period, much like the ones Rankin suggested for the late nineteenth century. Pan Zengyi, a *juren* from Wu County (see chapter 2), was such a local activist.[25] Pan drew on his connections as a member of the Xuannan Poetry Club to pressure provincial officials in Jiangsu in reforming the tribute grain system in the 1820s and 1830s.[26] Pan, in the early 1830s, also participated in the drafting of the Jiangsu governor Lin Zexu's above-mentioned land reclamation plan for North China.[27] At the same time, Pan emerged as an active leader in the management of local public works. As shown in chapter 2, Pan managed a number of waterworks projects in Wu County in the 1830s, and he established a charitable estate, school, and foundling homes in addition to leading a local relief operation.[28]

The case of Fei Lanchi, a manager of the 1823 relief operation in Wujiang County (see chapter 3), also underscored the upward trend of the confluence of elite social and political activism as early as the Daoguang period. Fei criticized contemporary officials and literati, insisting that officials disliked associating themselves with the gentry, who, in turn, preferred to remain silent on political matters.[29] Fei, however, distinguished himself in this aspect. In a letter to a friend, Fei discussed the problems in the administration of tribute grain.[30] He complained about the extraordinarily heavy tax burden shouldered by the residents of the Suzhou area, in particular the increasing surcharges accompanying the tribute grain collection. As he examined ways to redress these problems, Fei urged the state to reduce tax quotas for the Jiangnan area. If the state deemed such a measure unfeasible, he noted, it could consider abolishing surcharges levied on locals for tribute grain transport, mobilizing instead state funds. If that were not possible, Fei continued, the state should at least reduce the surcharges or strictly prohibit collecting more than was necessary. Half a century after Fei put forth these proposals, the state granted Jiangnan a one-third reduction of its tax quota. He earned praise in the Guangxu edition of Wujiang County gazetteer for his acute diagnosis of the tax problem.[31]

Pan Zengyi and Fei Lanchi demonstrated that some early nineteenth-century managers also raised their voices on political issues. It seems apparent that the later part of the century witnessed many such cases. Further research, however, is necessary on the perception by elite managers of the accelerating social crises and their impact on their political agenda in the early nineteenth century.

This book has examined the social and cultural activism of elites that took place simultaneously with their political engagement. Together, these new developments show how the political, social, and cultural practices of elites in the early nineteenth century departed from those in the previous century, laying the groundwork for the acceleration of elite activism in the later years of the Qing rule.

APPENDIX

The Number and Provenance of Eminent Officials and Local Worthies, 1726–1874

Year	Eminent Officials		Local Worthies		Total	Source
	Province	Number	Province	Number		
1726–1730	ZJ 1, HUB 1, GD 3, GX 3	8	ZJ 1, HEN 1, SD 4, SX 4, FJ 8, GD 2, GX 5	25	33	*LKSS* 199 (YZ8/12/16)
1731	0	0	0	0	0	*LKSS* 207 (YZ9/12/12)[a]
1732	JX 1, HUB 1, HUN 1, GX 1	4	SD 2, HUB 1	3	7	*LKSS* 216 (YZ10/12/13)
1733	?	?	?	?	?	
1734	SC 1	1	HUN 1, SC 1	2	3	*LKSS* 237 (YZ 12/12/17)
1735	HEN 1	1	ZL 1	1	2	*QSL-QL* 9/326
1736	JS 1	1	JS 1	1	2	*QSL-QL* 33/645
1737	?	?	?	?	?	
1738	JS 1, ZL 1, FJ 1	3	JX 1, ZL 4, HUN 1	6	9	*LKSS* 280 (QL3/12/16); *QSL-QL* 83/308
1739	ZJ 2, ZL 2, HUB 1, FJ 1, GD 1	7	ZJ 1, ZL 3, HEN 1, HUB 1, HUN 1, GD 1, FJ 1	9	16	*LKSS* 290 (QL4/12/20); *QSL-QL* 107/606
1740	ZJ 1, ZL 1, HEN 2, GX 1, GZ 1	6	JS 2, AH 1, ZL 6, HEN 2, SD 4	15	21	*LKSS* 301 (QL5/12/12); *QSL-QL* 132/926
1741	ZL 1, SD 1, FT 2	4	JS 1, SD 1, HUB 1	3	7	*LKSS* 314 (QL6/12/5); *QSL-QL* 156/1232–33
1742	ZL 2, HEN 4	6	ZL 2, HEN 6	8	14	*LKSS* 326 (QL7/12/14); *QSL-QL* 181/334
1743	AH 3, JX 1, ZL 2, HEN 3, SD 2, YN 1	12	JS 2, ZJ 2, AH 4, ZL 8, HEN 2, SD 1	19	31	*LKSS* 342 (QL8/12/9); *QSL-QL* 206/656–57
1744	AH 1, GS 1	2	AH 1, JX 5, ZL 4, SD 5, SHX 3, HUN 1	19	21	*LKSS* 354 (QL9/12/17); *QSL-QL* 231/979

1745	JS 2, AH 3, ZL 1, HEN 1, HUB 2, GX 1	10	JS 6, AH 1, JX 5, ZL 2, HEN 3, HUN 2, HUB 1,[b] YN 1, GZ 3	24	34	*LKSS* 365 (QL10/12/17); *QSL-QL* 255/300–301
1746	JS 1, ZJ 2, SD 1, SX 1. HUB 1, GD 1, YN 1	8	JS 2, AH 1, ZJ 5, SD 3, SX 3, GS 1, HUB 2, GD 1, FJ 3	21	29	*LKSS* 378 (QL11/12/15); *QSL-QL* 281/664–65
1747	ZJ 1, SHX 2	3	JS 8, ZJ 1, SD 1, SHX 2, HUN 2	14	17	*LKSS* 390 (QL12/12/11); *QSL-QL* 304/980
1748	0	0	AH 1, JX 2, FJ 1, SC 1	5	5	*LKSS* 403 (QL13/12/13); *QSL-QL* 330/501
1749	?	?	YN 1 + ?[c]	1 + ?	1 + ?	
1750	0	0	ZL 1, HEN 1, SHX 5[d]	7	7	*MQDA* A169-070, 045646-00; *QSL-QL* 378/1201
1751	JS 1	1	JS 1	1	2	*NGDKDA* 052860-001
1752	ZL 1, HUB 1	2	ZL 1	1	3	*LKSS* 458 (QL17/12/18)
1753	SD 2, SX 1, HUB 1	4	JS 4, SX 1[e]	5	9	*LKSS* 472 (QL19/12/18); *QSL-QL* 448/842
1754	0	0	JS 4, JX 1	5	5	*LKSS* 486 (QL19/12/18); *QSL-QL* 479/1184
1755	JX 1, FT 1	2	JX 1, SX 1, YN 1	3	5	*QSL-QL* 502/339
1756	0	0	0[f]	0	0	
1757	?	?	?	?	?	
1758	JS 1	1	0	0	1	*LKSS* 513 (QL23/12/13); *QSL-QL* 576/349
1759	HUN 1	1	JS 2, HUN 1	3	4	*LKSS* 527 (QL24/12/12)
1760	JS 1, HEN 1	2	HEN 1	1	3	*LKSS* 542 (QL25/12/3); *QSL-QL* 626/1031–32

(*continued*)

Year	Eminent Officials		Local Worthies		Total	Source
	Province	Number	Province	Number		
1761	0	0	JS 1, AH 1	2	2	*LKSS* 558 (QL26/12/14); *QSL-QL* 651/290
1762	0	0	JS 2	2	2	*LKSS* 573 (QL27/12/14); *QSL-QL* 677/568
1763	0	0	JS 1	1	1	*LKSS* 588 (QL28/12/14); *QSL-QL* 701/837
1764	0	0	JS 1, GS 1	2	2	*LKSS* 602 (QL29/12/19); *QSL-QL* 725/1083
1765	HEN 1	1	JS 1, AH 1, SHX 1, GS 1	4	5	*LKSS* 615 (QL30/12/18); *QSL-QL* 750/257
1766	0	0	0	0	0	
1767	0	0	HEN 1	1	1	*LKSS* 642 (QL32/12/7); *QSL-QL* 800/792
1768	0	0	0	0	0	
1769	0	0	JS 1	1	1	*LKSS* 666 (QL34/9/17); *QSL-QL* 843/259
1770	0	0	0	0	0	
1771	0	0	0	0	0	
1772	?	?	?	?	?	
1773	0	0	SD 2	2	2	*LKSS* 706 (QL38/12/15)
1774	0	0	SD 1	1	1	*LKSS* 718 (QL39/12/10)
1775	0	0	HEN 1	1	1	*LKSS* 731 (QL40/12/14); *QSL-QL* 998/356
1776	0	0	SX 1	1	1	*LKSS* 743 (QL41/12/5)

1777	SHX 4	4	YN 2	2	6	*LKSS* 753 (QL42/12/3); *QSL-QL* 1037/904
1778	0	0	0	0	0	
1779	0	0	GX 1, YN 1	2	2	[g)]
1780	SHX 1	1	SX 1	1	2	*LKSS* 790 (QL45/12/14)
1781	0	0	0	0	0	
1782	0	0	0	0	0	
1783	HEN 1, HUN 1	2	0	0	2	*LKSS* 828 (QL48/12/7)[h)]
1784	0	0	JX 1	1	1	*QSL-QL* 1221/376
1785	0	0	0	0	0	
1786	0	0	SHX 1	1	1	*MQSL-Gui*, di 4 ben, 384ab
1787	?	?	?	?	?	
1788	0	0	SD 1	1	1	*LKSS* 904 (QL53/12/5)
1789	0	0	SC 1	1	1	*QSL-QL* 1337/1120
1790	0	0	0	0	0	
1791	0	0	JS 1, SX 1	2	2	*LKSS* 975 (QL56/12/16)
1792	0	0	0	0	0	
1793	0	0	0	0	0	
1794	0	0	0	0	0	
1795	HUN 1	1	0	0	1	*LKSS* 1068 (QL60/11/25); *QSL-QL* 1491/959
1796	0	0	GZ 1	1	1	*QSL-JQ* 5/113
1797	0	0	SX 1	1	1	*QSL-JQ* 25/307
1798	0	0	JS 1, JX 1, GD 1	3	3	*QSL-JQ* 29/347, 34/386, 36/402
1799	0	0	JS 1, SX 1	2	2	*QSL-JQ* 50/621, 53/690
1800	ZJ 4	4	ZJ 2, JX 2	4	8	*QSL-JQ* 68/912, 70/940, 76/1016, 1030

(*continued*)

Year	Eminent Officials		Local Worthies		Total	Source
	Province	Number	Province	Number		
1801	0	0	ZJ 3, JX 1	4	4	*QSL-JQ* 83/86, 85/123, 91/211
1802	SHX 1, HUB 1	2	JS 1	1	3	*QSL-JQ* 105/408, 106/419
1803	0	0	JS 2, ZJ 1, SD 1, FJ 1	5	5	*QSL-JQ* 112/493, 113/498, 121/618, 620, 632
1804	HUN 1	1	JS 5, ZJ 2, SHX 1, HEN 1, SD 2, GX 1	12	13	*QSL-JQ* 125/692, 126/708, 128/724, 137/874
1805	JS 3, ZL 1	4	JS 2, ZJ 1, AH 2, JX 2, SX 1, GZ 1	9	13	*QSL-JQ* 142/941, 145/988, 146/1013, 154/1121, 1126
1806	AH 1, HEN 1	2	JS 5, ZJ 1, AH 1, JX 1, HEN 6	14	16	*QSL-JQ* 158/38, 159/62, 160/72, 171/228, 172/243
1807	0	0	JS 8, ZJ 1, AH 2, SD 1, SHX 1, YN 2, SC 1	16	16	*QSL-JQ* 181/379–80, 190/506–7, 190/515
1808	JS 1, SD 1[i)]	2	JS 4, ZJ 2, JX 1, SHX 1, GD 1, SC 1	10	12	*LKSS* 1322 (JQ13/11/23); *QSL-JQ* 199/647, 204/730
1809	0	0	ZJ 2, SD 1, FJ 2	5	5	*QSL-JQ* 207/779, 222/995
1810	0	0	AH 1, SX 1	2	2	*QSL-JQ* 229/81, 237/200
1811	0	0	JS 1, GZ 1	2	2	*QSL-JQ* 250/386
1812	0	0	ZL 1, SD 1, SHX 1, HUN 3, GZ 1	7	7	*QSL-JQ* 264/579–81
1813	HUN 1	1	JS 1, JX 1, YN 1	3	4	*QSL-JQ* 265/601, 280/826
1814	0	0	JS 3, ZJ 1, AH 1, GD 1	6	6	*QSL-JQ* 300/1128
1815	SHX 1	1	JS 2, ZL 1, SC 1	4	5	*QSL-JQ* 314/169–70
1816	JS 1, ZJ 1, GZ 1	3	JS 2, ZJ 1, JX 1, SX 1, HUN 1, FJ 2	8	11	*QSL-JQ* 324/282, 325/287–88

1817	SHX 1	1	ZJ 1, AH 1, HEN 1, SHX 1, HUN 3, FJ 1, GD 2, SC 1	11	12	*QSL-JQ* 337/451–55
1818	JS 2, HUN 1	3	ZJ 1, JX 1, SD 2, SX 1, HUN 1, FJ 2, SC 1	9	12	*QSL-JQ* 338/469, 339/472, 350/624–25,[j] 352/644
1819	JS 1	1	JX 1, SX 1	2	3	*QSL-JQ* 354/674–75, 365/822
1820	HEN 1	1	HUB 1, GX 1	2	3	*QSL-DG* 10/208
1821	HEN 1, HUB 1	2	JX 1, SHX 2, HUB 1	4	6	*QSL-DG* 27/477–78
1822	GD 1, SC 1	2	AH 1, JX 1, YN 2	4	6	*QSL-DG* 35/624, 38/679, 47/827
1823	ZL 1,[k] HEN 1, HUN 1, FJ 1, GD 1	5	YN 1, SC 1	2	7	*QSL-DG* 62/1093
1824	ZL 2	2	JS 1, ZJ 1, HEN 1, SHX 1	4	6	*QSL-DG* 76/236
1825	SX 1	1	HEN 1, SHX 1, FJ 4	6	7	*QSL-DG* 93/504
1826	JX 1, SX 1, SHX 1	3	ZL 2, HEN 1, SD 1, FJ 1	5	8	*QSL-DG* 97/573, 106/759, 111/862
1827	SHX 2, GD 2	4	AH 1, ZL 1, SHX 2, FJ 2	6	10	*QSL-DG* 117/975, 131/1179–80
1828	AH 1, HEN 1	2	JS 1, AH 1, HEN 4, SD 3, HUN 1, YN 3, SC 1	14	16	*QSL-DG* 142/173, 149/284
1829	JS 1, SD 1, GX 1, SC 1	4	JS 2, AH 1, ZL 1, SD 1, SHX 1, FJ 2, YN 1, SC 1	10	14	*QSL-DG* 156/400, 404, 163/528
1830	AH 1, HEN 1	2	JS 3, AH 1, ZL 1, HEN 4, FJ 1, SC 1	11	13	*QSL-DG* 181/864
1831	0	0	JS 2, AH 4, SHX 1, SC 2	9	9	*QSL-DG* 203/1184–85
1832	ZJ 1, SD 1, SHX 1, FJ 1, GZ 1	5	JX 1, ZL 1, HEN 1, SD 1, SHX 2, HUN 1, FJ 1, GX 1, GZ 1, SC 2	12	17	*QSL-DG* 220/284, 226/377, 227/391, 228/399–400
1833	JS 1, AH 2, JX 1	4	JS 2, JX 1, SD 1, SHX 1	5	9	*QSL-DG* 245/697, 247/716

(*continued*)

Year	Eminent Officials		Local Worthies			
	Province	Number	Province	Number	Total	Source
1834	HUB 1, YN 2	3	JS 3, HEN 2, SHX 2, HUB 1, GX 3, SC 3	14	17	*QSL-DG* 261/986
1835	JS 1, AH 1	2	AH 2, SHX 2, HUB 1, FJ 1, YN 2, SC 2	10	12	*QSL-DG* 276/248
1836	ZL 1, SC 3	4	JS 1, SD 1, HUN 2, GX 1, YN 1	6	10	*QSL-DG* 292/521
1837	SHX 1, GZ 3	4	SC 1, GZ 1	2	6	*QSL-DG* 304/744
1838	AH 1, JX 1, ZL 1, SHX 2, GS 1, HUN 1, GX 1, YN 1, SC 1	10	JS 1, AH 1, GD 1, YN 1, GZ 1, SC 3	8	18	*QSL-DG* 314/893, 315/909–10, 317/951–52
1839	AH 1, ZL 1, HEN 1, SD 1, GX 2, GZ 1	7	JS 1, HEN 2, GX 1, YN 1, SC 2	7	14	*QSL-DG* 322/1059, 329/1177–78
1840	JS 1, JX 2, ZL 1, GS 1, GX 1	6	ZJ 1, ZL 1, SX 1, SHX 1, GS 1, GD 1, GX 3	9	15	*QSL-DG* 335/82, 343/222
1841	HEN 3, HUB 1, FJ 5, GX 1, GZ 1, SC 1	12	JS 4, ZJ 1, JX 1, SHX 1, FJ 1, GZ 1, GX 2	11	23	*QSL-DG* 346/268, 348/302, 352/360, 364, 353/370, 362/535, 364/557
1842	ZJ 1, HEN 1, SC 1, SHX 1, HUB 1	5	JS 1, JX 1, HEN 1, SX 1, FJ 1	5	10	*QSL-DG* 369/648, 386/941
1843	HEN 3, SC 1	4	HEN 1, HUB 1, GD 1, GZ 1	4	8	*QSL-DG* 400/1159
1844	ZJ 1, ZL 1, GS 2, GZ 1, SC 1	6	ZL 1, SHX 1, HUB 1, GZ 1	4	10	*QSL-DG* 412/173

1845	ZL 1, HEN 1, GS 2	4	ZJ 1, SD 1, SHX 2, HUN 1	5	9	*QSL-DG* 414/194, 424/321
1846	ZJ 1, AH 1, SX 1, SC 1	4	JS 1, SX 1, HUB 1, GD 1	4	8	*QSL-DG* 437/472–73
1847	AH 1, GD 1, SC 1	3	JS 1, ZJ 3, AH 1, ZL 1, SD 1, SHX 2, HUN 1, GX 1	11	14	*QSL-DG* 443/554, 450/671
1848	HEN 1, GS 1, GZ 1	3	AH 2, ZL 1, SX 1, HUB 1, HUN 2, FJ 1, SC 1	9	12	*QSL-DG* 462/831–32, 835–36
1849	JS 1, ZJ 1, JX 1, HEN 2, SHX 2, YN 1, SC 1	9	ZJ 1, AH 1, SD 1, FJ 1, GD 2, SC 2	8	17	*QSL-XF* 3/94
1850	ZL 1, HEN 1, SC 3	5	JS 1, ZJ 1, SD 1, SHX 2, FJ 1, YN 1, GZ 1, SC 1	9	14	*QSL-XF* 24/344
1851	AH 2, ZL 2, YN-GZ 1, SC 1	6	JS 1, ZJ 1, AH 1, JX 1, ZL 1, HEN 1, SD 3, SX 1	10	16	*QSL-XF* 38/527, 46/631, 49/663
1852	AH 2, HUB 1, SC 1	4	JX 1, ZL 1, SD 2, SX 1, FJ 1, YN 1, SC 2	9	13	*QSL-XF* 76/992, 79/1047
1853	HEN 1	1	HUN 1, GD 1	2	3	*QSL-XF* 115/813
1854	0	0	0	0	0	
1855	ZJ 1, FJ 1, YN 1	3	FJ 1, YN 1, GZ 1, SC 1	4	7	*QSL-XF* 186/1081
1856	ZJ 1, AH 1, SX 1, FJ 1	4	JS 2, HEN 1, SHX 2, SX 1, GS 1, GZ 1	8	12	*QSL-XF* 215/377
1857	HEN 2, SX 1, SHX 1	4	SHX 1	1	5	*QSL-XF* 241/740
1858	JS 1, ZJ 1, SX 1, HUB 1, HUN 1, SC 1	6	JS 1, AH 1	2	8	*QSL-XF* 243/763, 272/1209–10
1859	JS 1, HEN 1, SD 1, HUN 1	4	ZJ 1, JX 2, SC 1	4	8	*QSL-XF* 300/377, 303/438
1860	0	0	0	0	0	
1861	JS 1, HEN 1, SX 1, FJ 1, SC 1	5	ZJ 1, HEN 1, SX 1, HUB 1, GD 2	6	11	*QSL-TZ* 9/244, 14/372

(continued)

Year	Eminent Officials		Local Worthies		Total	Source
	Province	Number	Province	Number		
1862	FJ 1, SC 1	2	AH 2, JX 1, ZL 1, HEN 2, SD 1, FJ 4, SC 1	12	14	*QSL-TZ* 26/714, 47/1275, 51/1393, 52/1434, 1436
1863	SD 2, GZ 1	3	SD 2, HUN 1, FJ 1, SC 1	5	8	*QSL-TZ* 71/444, 88/865
1864	SD 1, SX 2, HUB 2, GD 1	6	ZL 1, HEN 4, SD 1, HUB 1, HUN 1, GD 3, SC 1	12	18	*QSL-TZ* 106/322, 334, 124/720, 125/751
1865	JS 1, ZL 2, GS 1, SC 1	5	JS 1, JX 3, ZL 1, SD 1, SHX 1, FJ 3	10	15	*QSL-TZ* 144/395, 146/424, 164/784
1866	JS 2, ZL 1, SX 1, SHX 2, HUB 1, FJ 2, SC 1	10	ZJ 1, AH 1, HEN 2, SHX 1, HUB 1, HUN 2, SC 3	11	21	*QSL-TZ* 175/150, 176/171, 189/383, 191/421–22, 193/457
1867	JS 1, SD 1, SHX 1	3	ZJ 5, AH 1, JX 3, HEN 2, SD 1, SX 1, SHA 2, HUN 1, FJ 3	19	22	*QSL-TZ* 200/580, 219/876
1868	JS 3, ZJ 1, SD 1, HUN 3, FJ 2, GD 1, SC 1	12	JS 4, ZJ 3, AH 2, HUB 1, HUN 3, FJ 2	15	27	*QSL-TZ* 223/46, 228/149, 229/161, 236/257, 236/267, 244/394, 246/417, 426, 248/458
1869	ZJ 1, AH 1, ZL 1, HEN 1	4	AH 1, HEN 1, SX 3, SHX 1, HUN 4	10	14	*QSL-TZ* 258/590, 262/639, 271/760, 271/765
1870	AH 1, HEN 1, GX 1	3	JS 4, ZJ 3, AH 1, ZL 4, SD 1, SX 1, GS 1, HUB 1, FJ 1, GD 1, GX 2, GZ 1, SC 1	22	25	*QSL-TZ* 280/886, 291/1033, 300/1153–54
1871	ZJ 1, ZL 3, SD 1, SX 1, HUB 2, GD 1	9	JS 1, AH 1, JX 3, ZL 2, HEN 3, SD 1, SX 3, SHX 1, HUN 6, SC 3	24	33	*QSL-TZ* 304/33, 37, 43, 307/66, 313/141, 314/161, 318/201, 322/265, 326/307–8

1872	JS 5, ZJ 1, JX 1, ZL 2, HEN 1, SD 3, SHX 1, FJ 1, SC 4	19	JS 1, ZJ 2, AH 2, JX 4, ZL 2, HEN 2, SD 2, SX 1, HUB 1, HUN 3, FJ 1, SC 2	23	42	*QSL-TZ* 332/390, 334/419, 335/426, 336/436, 337/447, 346/556, 347/565–66
1873	JS 1, ZJ 1, ZL 1, HEN 2, SD 1, SX 1, HUN 1	8	JS 1, ZL 4, SD 2, SX 1, GD 3	11	19	*QSL-TZ* 365/715, 359/755, 761, 361/779
1874	SC 1	1	JS 1, ZJ 1	2	3	*QSL-TZ* 367/862, 865, 371/915

NOTES: AH-Anhui, FJ-Fujian, FT-Fengtian, GD-Guangdong, GS-Gansu, GX-Guangxi, GZ-Guizhou, HEN-Henan, HUB-Hubei, HUN-Hunan, JS-Jiangsu, JX-Jiangxi, SC-Sichuan, SD-Shandong, SHX-Shaanxi, SX-Shanxi, YN-Yunnan, ZJ-Zhejiang, ZL-Zhili; *LKSS-Like shishu*, *MQDA-Ming Qing dang'an*, *MQSL-Ming Qing shiliao*, *NGDKDA-Neige daku dang'an;* ?-Data unavailable.

(a) That year, the minister of rites recommended to the emperor the enshrinements of an eminent official in Jiangxi, an eminent official in Sichuan, a local worthy from Sichuan, and two local worthies from Gansu. However, as the Yongzheng Emperor took issue with the qualifications of the eminent official from Jiangxi, none of the five candidates was allowed into the shrines that year. After further deliberation, the board endorsed the enshrinement of the Jiangxi candidate in 1732. See *LKSS* 212 (YZ10/8/26). The two candidates from Sichuan who had been initially denied entrance in 1731 were allowed enshrinement after undergoing a reexamination sometime before October 8, 1734 (12th day of the 9th month in Yongzheng 12). See *LKSS* 234 (YZ12/9/12). Because of the poor conservation state of the *LKSS*, however, I am unable to specify the dates of these enshrinements. For the sake of convenience, in this table I considered 1734 as the date of their enshrinement.

(b) That year, there is a discrepancy between the *LKSS* and *QSL* regarding the provincial origin of a candidate. For Zhang Zhonghuang, enshrined as a local worthy that year, the *QSL* states that he was from Hunan. According to *LKSS*, a more original source than the *QSL*, he was from Hubei. See *LKSS* 362 (QL10/8/25), 365 (QL10/12/17). Here I consider Zhang as a Hubei worthy following the record in the *LKSS*.

(c) That year's portion of the *LKSS* is not open to public access due to its poor condition. For that year, the Qianlong Emperor endorsed the enshrinement of a local worthy candidate from Yunnan whose enshrinement decision had been deferred the previous year. See *QSL-QL*, 351.843. However, this was an isolated case, separate from the board's regular decision in the last month of the year. Unfortunately, the outcome of this regular enshrinement decision for this year is not included in the *QSL*.

(d) The *QSL* recorded that four local worthies from Henan and one local worthy from Shaanxi were enshrined that year, in addition to one from Zhili. According to the Board of Rites memorial included in the *Ming Qing dang'an*, however, seven local worthies were enshrined that year, including five from Shaanxi and one each from Henan and Zhili. Here I follow the record in *Ming Qing dang'an*, a more original source.

(*continued*)

(*continued*)

(e) The enshrinement of this local worthy candidate from Shanxi was recorded in the *LKSS* but not in the *QSL*. Here I follow the record in the *LKSS*.

(f) That year, Hu Fang, a scholar from Xinhui County, Guangdong, was recommended as a local worthy candidate. However, the Board of Rites deferred its decision on his enshrinement on the grounds that his written works had not been submitted to the board. See *LKSS* 500 (QL21/12/14). The *QSL*, however, inaccurately stated that Hu was enshrined that year (*QSL-QL*, 529.657). The *QSL* also recorded his name as Hu Fangti, mistakenly adding "ti." The Xinhui County gazetteer, however, stated that Hu Fang was enshrined as a local worthy in 1839 (*Xinhui xianzhi*, 1840, 184.47a). The *QSL* also records that Hu Fang from Xinhui County entered the shrine for local worthies in 1838 (*QSL-DG*, 317.951). When all the evidence is considered, it is reasonable to conclude that Hu Fang was recommended as a worthy candidate in 1756, but the decision on his enshrinement was deferred until 1838, when he was finally accepted into the shrine. Therefore, I consider Hu Fang as a local worthy of 1838, not of 1756.

(g) The *QSL* does not have a record of that year's enshrinement. The *LKSS* also lacks the twelfth month portion that contained the Board of Rites' request for enshrinement. According to the *LKSS*, however, the governors of Guangxi and Yunnan recommended Chen Hongmou and Yang Pei, respectively, as local worthies. See *LKSS* 771 (QL44/1/26), 778 (QL44/9/1). Although we are unable to confirm through the *LKSS* whether these requests were endorsed by the board and the emperor, we can do so through other sources. According to the *Jiaqing chongxiu yitong zhi*, Yang Pei was enshrined as a Yunnan local worthy that year (1779). See *Jiaqing chongxiu yitong zhi*, 479.28b. In the case of Chen Hongmou, both the Guangxi provincial gazetteer and the county gazetteer of Chen's hometown stated that he was enshrined as a local worthy in 1775. See *Guangxi tongzhi*, 1891, 141.23a; *Lingui xianzhi*, 1892, 15.33a. According to the *LKSS*, the enshrinement request for Chen was made in 1779, not 1775. Although the information on the enshrinement year was inaccurate, these gazetteers confirm that Chen was indeed enshrined with the imperial endorsement.

(h) The *QSL* does not have a record of that year's enshrinement. However, the *LKSS* summarized the memorial submitted in the last month of that year by the Board of Rites requesting enshrinements. This summary stated that "Zhang Younian and others" (Zhang Younian *deng*) were recommended as eminent officials that year and that this request was endorsed by the emperor. See *LKSS* 828 (QL48/12/7). This information alone does not specify the number of eminent officials enshrined that year. However, only one more request for the enshrinement of an eminent official was made that year in addition to the one for Zhang Younian. See *LKSS* 823 (QL48/7/28). Therefore, here I contend that two were enshrined as eminent officials that year.

(i) The *QSL* does not have a record of that year's enshrinement of eminent officials. Through the *LKSS*, however, we are able to confirm that two eminent officials, one in Jiangsu and the other in Shandong, were enshrined in addition to local worthy candidates.

(j) Here I include Wan Chengfeng as a local worthy of Jiangxi. The Jiaqing Emperor was initially reluctant to endorse his enshrinement because he considered Wan merely as an average official, but eventually he gave consent to his enshrinement. For Jiaqing's evaluation of Wan and the endorsement of his enshrinement, see *QSL-JQ*, 350.621, 624. Wan's entrance into the shrine of local worthies is also ascertained through his hometown's local gazetteer. See *Yining zhouzhi*, 1873, 13.15b, 22.38b.

(k) *QSL* recorded that three men were enshrined as eminent officials in Zhili that year. Among these three, two appeared again the following year (1824) in *QSL* as eminent officials in Zhili. See *QSL-DG*, 76.236. According to the *LKSS*, it was in 1824 that the Board of Rites recommended these two to the emperor and obtained his endorsement. See *LKSS* 1516 (DG4/12/13). On these grounds, I conclude that the information in the *QSL* in regard to the enshrinement of eminent officials in 1823 is inaccurate. Here I contend that these two eminent officials in Zhili entered the shrine in 1824.

Character List

anchasi jingli 按察司經歷
Anping 安平

bagongsheng 拔貢生
Baicheng yanshui 百城烟水
baiguan yeshi 稗官野史
Baimaogang 白茆港
bangding 幇丁
Bao Shichen 包世臣
baojia 保甲
Baoshan 寶山
Bao Yue lu 保越錄
baozheng 保正
Bei Yong 貝墉
benji 本紀
bieji 別集
buzhengsi jingli 布政司經歷

Cai Erda 蔡爾達
Cai Weichuan 蔡衛川
Cai Yuanpei 蔡元培
Caifeng leiji 采風類記
Cailianjing shuili lun 采蓮涇水利論
Canglang ting 滄浪亭
Chang Yuchun 常遇春
Changshu 常熟
Changzhou (county) 長洲
Changzhou (prefecture) 常州
Chaozhou xianxian xiangzhuan 潮州先賢象傳
Chen Dashi 陳大始
Chen Dashou 陳大綬
Chen Ji 陳基
Chen Luan 陳鑾
Chen Peizhi 陳裴之
Chen Youliang 陳友諒
Cheng 程
Cheng Bangxian 程邦憲
Cheng wang 誠王
chenghuang miao 城隍廟
Chenmu 陳墓
Chizhou 池州
chou 仇
Chun'an 淳安
congyou yixu 從優議敘

Dade 大德
Dantu 丹徒
Danyang 丹陽
danzhou 擔粥
daotong 道統
daoxue 道學
daoyuan 道員
deng 等
Desheng 德勝
Diannan wenlüe 滇南文略
Diao'e he 鵰鶚河

difang congshu 地方叢書
dijun 敵軍
dili 地理
dingdai 頂戴
dixi 帝系
Donglin 東林
dongshi 董事
du 都

engongsheng 恩貢生

Fan Weicheng 樊維城
Fei Chun 費淳
Fei Lanchi 費蘭墀
Fei Shuwei 費樹蔚
fugongsheng 副貢生
Fuheng 傅恒
fuhui 附會
fuma fen 駙馬墳
Fushantang 福山塘
Fushe 復社
futou 夫頭

Gao Panlong 高攀龍
gong 公
gongju (public bureau) 公局
gongju (public selection) 公舉
gonglun 公論
gongshi 公尸
gongsuo 公所
gongzheng yinshi dongshi 公正殷實董事
Gu Lu 顧祿
Gu Xiancheng 顧憲成
Gu Yanwu 顧炎武
Gu Yuan 顧沅
Gu Zhen 顧震
Gu Zhentao 顧震濤
Guajing 瓜涇
guan 官
guanshi 官史
guming yaoyu 沽名邀譽
guojia jingfei youchang 國家經費有常

Haining 海寧
Han Feng 韓葑
Han Guojun 韓國鈞
Hangzhou 杭州
haoyi 好義
He Changling 賀長齡
Henan tongzhi 河南通志
heyi zhi fei 和議之非
Hou Dian 侯甸
houxuan renyuan 候選人員
Hu Dahai 胡大海
Hu Kejia 胡克家
Hu Wenhuan 胡文煥
Huang Chengliang 黄澄量
Huang Tai 黄泰
Huang Xingzeng 黄省曾
Huangchao jingshi wenbian 皇朝經世文編
Huangpu 黄浦
Huating 華亭
Huizhou 徽州
Hunan 湖南
Huzhou 湖州

ji 紀 (annals)
ji 級 (degree)
Jia Hanfu 賈漢復
Jiading 嘉定
Jiahe zhengxian lu 嘉禾徵獻錄
Jiande 建德
jianding 鑑定
Jiang 蔣
Jiang Youxian 蔣攸銛
Jiangdu xianzhi 江都縣志
Jiangning 江寧
Jiangpu 江浦
Jiangxi wenzheng 江西文徵
Jiangyin 江陰
Jianli 監利
jianxie wuguo hainei qiechi 奸邪誤國, 海内切齒
Jiaxing 嘉興
jibu 集部
jietan xiangyi 街談巷議
jietang xinggong, fennian tanzheng 借帑興工, 分年攤徵
jigong haoyi 急公好義
jilu 紀錄

Jin 金
Jin Bao 金堡
Jin Chenglie 金承烈
Jin Dayong 晉大鏞
jing 經
jingbiao 旌表
Jingchuan congshu 涇川叢書
jingkao 經考
jingkong 京控
Jingtuo yishi 荊駝逸史
Jingui 金匱
Jingxian ge 景賢閣
Jinhua xianda zhuan 金華賢達傳
Jinhua zhengxian lüe 金華徵獻略
Jinwen leiti 今文類體
jinxian 今憲
Jiwei xiangzhen ji 癸未鄉賑記
ju 局
juanban 捐辦
juanna 捐納
juanshu 捐輸
jun'an zhi dao 均安之道
juren 舉人
Jurong 句容

kaoji jiangxu 考績獎敘
kaozheng xue 考證學
kou 寇
kuaiding 快丁
Kuaiji xianxian xiangzan 會稽先賢像贊
kuashi 誇飾
Kunshan 崑山

Lang Jian 郎簡
Lang Ying 郎英
lansi 濫祀
leshan haoshi 樂善好施
li 利
Li Bosheng 李伯昇
Li Peng 李鵬
Li Zenghou 李增厚
Liang Zhangju 梁章鉅
lieguo 列國
liezhuan 列傳
ligong shude 立功樹德
ligongsheng 例貢生
Lili 黎里
Lingnan yishu 岭南遺書
Liuan 六安
Liuhe 劉河
lixue 理學
lizhen 例賑
Lou 婁
Loudong zazhu 婁東雜著
Lu Rong 陸容
Lu Xuejian 陸學堅
Lü Zhen 呂珍
Lu Zhun 陸準
Lü Zuqian 呂祖謙
Lu'an 潞安
Luoyang 洛陽

Mao Yilu 毛一鷺
Mengdu 孟瀆
menhu zhi si 門户之私
min 民
Min Eyuan 閔鶚元
minghuan ci 名宦祠
minghuan ci chongsi zhuwei 名宦祠崇祀主位
minghuan ci muzhu 名宦祠木主
minghuan lu 名宦錄
Mingshi gao 明史藁
minjian 民建
minjuan minban 民捐民辦
minzhen 民賑

Na-yan-cheng 那彥成
Nanjiang yishi kanben 南疆繹史勘本
nidang 逆黨
Ningbo 寧波

Pan Shi'en 潘世恩
Pan Yuanming 潘元明
Pan Yuanshao 潘元紹
Pan Zengyi 潘曾沂
Peng 彭
Peng Shaosheng 彭紹升
Peng Xizheng 彭希鄭
Peng Yunzhang 彭蘊章

pingtiao 平糶
Pingwang 平望
Ping Wu lu 平吳錄
Pucheng yishu 浦城遺書
Puhuaitang 蒲匯塘
Pujiang 浦江

Qi Yanhuai 齊彥槐
Qian Baoying 錢寶瑛
Qian Dixiang 錢荻香
Qian Gu 錢穀
Qian Qianyi 錢謙益
Qian Shiqi 錢士錡
Qian Siyuan 錢思元
Qian Weicheng 錢維城
Qiantang xianxian zhuanzan 錢塘先賢傳贊
qianxin lixue, yougong wenjiao 潛心理學, 有功文教
qianyin zhi xi 牽引之習
Qiji quancuo zhi 七姬權厝志
Qin Kui 秦檜
Qingdai xuezhe xiangzhuan 清代學者像傳
Qingfeng dajie ci 清風大節祠
Qingjia 清嘉
Qingpu 青浦
Qiu Jun 邱濬
Qu Dajun 屈大均
Queli 闕里

Ren You 任酉
rong 榮
rulin 儒林

sandong 散董
Sanzhong ci 三忠祠
Shanghai 上海
Shangyuan 上元
shanshi 善士
Shaoxing 紹興
Shen 沈
Shen Defu 沈德符
Shen Li 沈鯉
Shen Zhou 沈周
shencang 紳廠
sheng 升
shengshi 盛世
Shengxian jitu 聖賢蹟圖
Shengze 盛澤
shenqi 紳耆
shenshi 紳士
shi (history) 史
shi (lower degree-holder) 士
Shi Ce 史册
Shi Yunyu 石韞玉
shian 詩案
shibu 史部
shizhi 實職
Shuntian 順天
si 私
Siku quanshu zongmu tiyao 四庫全書總目提要
sili 私利
sixin 私心
sizi 私自
Song Lian 宋濂
Song Na 宋訥
Song shi 宋史
Songjiang 松江
Su Shunqin 蘇舜欽
Sucai xiaozuan 蘇材小纂
sufeng 素封
Sui shu 隋書
Suian 遂安
Suzhou 蘇州

Taicang 太倉
taiwei 太尉
Taizhou 泰州
Taizhou congshu 台州叢書
Tang Bin 湯斌
Tang Jinzhao 湯金釗
Tang Yin 唐寅
Tangshan 碭山
Tangxi 湯谿
Tao Rong 陶鎔
Tao Zhu 陶澍
Tongli 同里
tongpan 通判
tongsheng 童生

tongzhi 同知
tu 圖
tudong 圖董
tuzhen 土賑
tuzhenfa 圖賑法

Wang Ao 王鏊
Wang Chun 王淳
Wang Fuzhi 王夫之
Wang Hongxu 王鴻緒
Wang Kun 王鯤
Wang Nan 王楠
Wang Shizhen 王世貞
Wang Wan 汪琬
Wang Yuanxiang 王元相
Wangjiang 望江
Wei Yuan 魏源
Wei Zhongxian 魏忠賢
weilie chunzhong 偉烈純忠
weiyuan 委員
Wen Zhengming 文徵明
Wencui 文粹
Wenjian 文鑑
Wenmiao jilüe 文廟紀略
Wenweng 文翁
Wenzhang zhengzong 文章正宗
wo 我
wojun 我軍
woshi 我師
Wu 吳
Wu fuma mu 吳駙馬墓
Wu Huilie wang 吳惠烈王
Wu Kuan 吳寬
Wu Shijian 吳士堅
Wu Tingchen 吳廷琛
Wu wang 吳王
Wu Weiye 吳偉業
Wuguo gong 吳國公
Wujiang 吳江
Wujin 武進
Wujun xianxian zongci 吳郡先賢總祠
wulai 無賴
Wumen gongci chongsi xingming lu 吳門公祠崇祀姓名錄
Wuqu 吳趨
Wusong 吳淞
Wuxi 無錫
wuzhizhe 無知者
Wuzhong guyu 吳中故語
Wuzhong wangzhe ji 吳中往哲記
Wuzhong wangzhe xiangzan 吳中往哲像贊

Xia Quan 夏荃
xiancheng 縣丞
xiang 鄉
xiangdong 鄉董
xiangju 鄉局
xiangqu zhi si 鄉曲之私
xiangxian ci 鄉賢祠
xiangxian ci chongsi zhuwei 鄉賢祠崇祀主位
xiangxian ci muzhu 鄉賢祠木主
xiangxian lu 鄉賢錄
xiangxian tang 鄉賢堂
xiangzhen 鄉賑
xianxian ci 先賢祠
Xiaoshan 蕭山
Xie Jiang 謝絳
Xin'an xuexi lu 新安學系錄
Xingfutang 興福塘
Xinyang 新陽
Xiong Qiying 熊其英
Xiong Xuepeng 熊學鵬
Xiuning 休寧
Xu Degui 徐德鈺
Xu Jie 徐階
Xu Mianzhi 徐勉之
Xu Qianxue 徐乾學
Xu Xi 徐僖
Xu Youzhen 徐有貞
Xuannan shishe 宣南詩社
xuezheng 學政
xulu 敍錄

yandang 閹黨
Yang Chaolin 楊朝麟
Yang Jian 楊健
Yang Tingshu 楊廷樞
Yang Xunji 楊循吉
Yang Yi 楊彝

Yanghu 陽湖
Yanglin 楊林
Yangzhou 揚州
Yantie 鹽鐵
yantiju 鹽提舉
Yanyi zhilin 鹽邑志林
yanzhishi 鹽知事
Yanzhou 嚴州
Yao Chengxu 姚承緒
Yao Tang 姚堂
Yao Xuan 姚鉉
Yaofeng wenji 堯峯文集
Ye Dehui 葉德輝
Ye Ziqi 葉子奇
yeshi dianli 業食佃力
yezi dianli 業資佃力
Yi Fengting 易風庭
yicang 義倉
Yiguicao chuke 依歸草初刻
yingong 陰功
Yitong zhi 一統志
yixing 義行
yixu 議敘
Yiyang 弋陽
Yizhen 義賑
Yizheng 儀徵
You Songzhen 尤松鎮
youzhizhe 有知者
yu (others) 餘
yu (polder) 圩
Yu (surname) 余
Yuanhe 元和
Yue Fei 岳飛
Yuelu 嶽麓
yunding 運丁
Yuyao 餘姚
Yuyue xianxian xiangzhuanzan 於越先賢像傳贊
yuzheng 圩正

zaigong dongshi 在工董事
Zaiwu 梓吳
zaixiang 災祥
Zaogang 滘港
zashi 雜史
zei 賊
Zeng Guofan 曾國藩
Zhang Chan 張蟾
Zhang Dai 張岱
Zhang Fujing 張孚敬
Zhang Fuxiang 張符驤
Zhang Haipeng 張海鵬
Zhang Pu 張溥
Zhang Shicheng 張士誠
Zhang Shide 張士德
Zhang wang 張王
Zhang Wu wang 張吳王
Zhang Xuecheng 章學誠
Zhang Yu 張羽
Zhang Zhonghuang 張仲璜
Zhangjiatang 張家塘
Zhanyitang tuxiang 瞻儀堂圖像
Zhao 趙
Zhao Kuangyin 趙匡胤
Zhaowen 昭文
Zhapu 乍浦
Zhen Dexiu 眞德秀
Zheng Huchen 鄭虎臣
zheng shi 正史
Zhenjiang 鎮江
Zhenyang 鎮洋
Zhenze 震澤
Zhihe 至和
zhitong 治統
zhixian 職銜
Zhou 周
Zhou Hongxi 周宏爔
Zhou Shunchang 周順昌
Zhou wang 周王
zhoupan 州判
zhouzhi 州志
Zhouzhuang 周莊
Zhu Dasong 朱大松
Zhu Jian 朱琦
Zhu Wu wang 朱吳王
Zhu Yuanzhang 朱元璋
Zhu Yunming 祝允明
Zhuang Yougong 莊有恭
zhuanji 傳記
Zhujing 朱涇
zongdong 總董
zongju 總局

Notes

Introduction

1. For more details on this incident, see Han Seunghyun, "Wenzhi."

2. Han Seunghyun, "The Punishment," 144.

3. Ibid., 145. My explanation here of the changes in the state's attitude toward literati and the punishments against literati protest follows Han Seunghyun, "The Punishment."

4. Ho-fung Hung has shown that the number of edicts directing disciplinary admonitions to local officials surged in the early 1800s after plunging between the 1760s and 1790s. See Hung, *Protest with Chinese Characteristics*, 42–43.

5. Ocko, "I'll Take It," 291–315; Wang Wensheng, "Social Crises," 39–44; Hung, *Protest with Chinese Characteristics*, 157–59; Li Dianrong, *Qingchao Jingkong zhidu yanjiu*.

6. *QSL-JQ*, 84.104.

7. Ibid.

8. *QSL-QL*, 424.558.

9. Ibid.

10. *QSL-QL*, 313.122.

11. Ibid.

12. Ibid.

13. *QSL-DG*, 7.153.

14. Marmé, *Suzhou*, 127–53.

15. Rowe, "Introduction," 74–88.

16. See Cohen, *Discovering History in China*, 9–55.

17. Most notably, scholars have duly noted the importance of the state-building process to which the three eighteenth-century rulers had devoted themselves. Some of the imperial accomplishments during their reigns include: subduing a massive domestic rebellion waged by the "three feudatories" (*sanfan* 三藩); expanding the boundaries of China farther by conquering the Zunghars and incorporating Tibet; rationalizing the state-revenue system; building state granaries that could store grains for price-stabilization

and famine relief; and, as revealed through the state project of building imperial libraries, streamlining literati ideology following the guidelines prescribed by the central state. On these accomplishments, see Kessler, *K'ang-hsi*; Perdue, *China Marches West*; Zelin, *The Magistrate's Tael*; Will and Wong, *Nourish the People*; Guy, *The Emperor's Four Treasuries*.

18. Oh, "Myŏngmal ch'ŏngch'o sangp'um kyŏngje," 125–63.

19. For example, Dai Yi, *Qianlong di*; Guo, *Qianlong zhengzhuan*.

20. Suzuki, *Shinchō chūkishi kenkyū*.

21. Naquin, *Millenarian Rebellion in China*.

22. Jones and Kuhn, "Dynastic Decline."

23. Elman, *Classicism*.

24. Miles, *The Sea of Learning*. On evidential research, see also Elman, *From Philosophy to Philology*.

25. Polachek, *The Inner Opium War*.

26. Leonard, *Controlling from Afar*. Other representative works on this period in English include: Jones, "Hung Liang-chi"; Lin Man-houng, "Two Social Theories Revealed"; Idem., *China Upside Down*.

27. Wang Wensheng, *White Lotus Rebels*.

28. Guan, *Jiaqing di*.

29. See, for example, Sun, Feng, and Yu, *Daoguang di*.

30. For example, Xiao, *Qingdai tongshi*, 209–54.

31. Bartlett, *Monarchs and Ministers*, 241–55; Chang, *A Court on Horseback*, 430–31; Guy, *Qing Governors*, 142–43.

32. See Wang Wensheng, "Social Crises," 46; Idem., *White Lotus Rebels*, 165–208.

33. In the chapters that follow, it will be explained that many of the literati cultural practices, such as the production of local literature, the use of visual images in books on local worthies, the multiplication of enshrined worthies, and other features that characterized the late Ming, once again began to flourish in the early nineteenth century after a dormant period in the previous century.

34. On the strengthened control of *yahang*, market brokers, in the mid-Qing period, see Mann, *Local Merchants*, 47–48. On famine relief and grain storage system, see Will, *Bureaucracy and Famine*; Will and Wong, *Nourish the People*.

35. On Chen Hongmou and his active interventionist policies as a provincial official, see Rowe, *Saving the World*.

36. In this regard, Tobie Meyer-Fong's work elucidates how local memory could be transformed into an imperially centered one after the emperor's visits to the historical sites in Yangzhou. See *Building Culture*, 162–68.

37. Min, *National Polity*, 5.

38. "Xiuzhi caifang suibi" 修志采訪隨筆, *Wuchangyuan sanxian hezhi*.

39. On Shen, see Hummel, *Eminent Chinese*, 645.

40. *QSL-QL*, 1071.374. See also Chang, *A Court on Horseback*, 400–401.

41. It might perhaps be too simplistic to argue that this project was solely intended to strengthen the imperial cultural hegemony. As Kent Guy has noted, the project indeed entailed voluntary participation of the scholars who genuinely relished this oppor-

tunity to review the books beyond one's own resources and who saw this as a chance to consolidate the position of the evidential research scholarship. The project, however, served to shore up the cultural authority of the imperial state. On Guy's view on this project, see his *The Emperor's Four Treasuries*, 201–8.

42. Cary Liu, "The Ch'ing Dynasty," 9.

43. Ibid., 10.

44. Kuhn, *Rebellion and Its Enemies*.

45. Rankin, *Elite Activism*.

46. Rowe, *Hankow: Commerce and Society*.

47. Li Bozhong, *Jiangnan de zaoqi gongyehua*, 310. See also Fan and Xia, *Suzhou diqu shehui jingjishi*, 539–40; Pomeranz, *The Great Divergence*, 288; Idem., "Beyond the East-West Binary," 571.

48. Li Bozhong, *Jiangnan de zaoqi gongyehua*, 312.

49. Ibid., 315, 317.

50. Rankin, "The Origins," 23–24.

51. Ibid., 24, 57.

52. Ibid., 58.

53. Naquin and Rawski, *Chinese Society*, 229.

Chapter 1. The Ascendant Elite Activism in Local Public Works

1. Portions of this chapter have been published in Korean as "19 segi ch'o 'naksŏn hosi' changnyŏ chedo ŭi pyŏnhwa wa kŭ ŭimi," *Tongyang sahak yŏn'gu* 95 (2006): 107–56; "Ch'ŏngdae 'naksŏn hosi' chŏngp'yo, ŭisŏ chedo ŭi sŏngnip—Kŏnnyung yŏn'gan eŭl chungsim ŭro," *Myŏngch'ŏngsa yŏn'gu* 26 (2006): 289–341.

2. According to one source, the suppression of the rebellion cost the considerable sum of 100 million taels. Will, *Bureaucracy and Famine*, 291; Chen Feng, *Qingdai junfei yanjiu*, 266; Iwai, "Shindai kokka zaisei." The largest cost of the suppression campaign was militia-related expenses. See Dai Yingcong, "Civilians Go into Battle," 161.

3. Suzuki, "Shinmatsu no zaisei"; Polachek, "Literati Groups," 27–87; Will, *Bureaucracy and Famine*, 292.

4. Lin Man-houng, *China Upside Down*, 72–114.

5. Woodside, "The Qianlong Reign," 270–71.

6. On Qianlong's southern tours, see Chang, *A Court on Horseback*, 4–6, 453.

7. The explanation of the silver reserves in the imperial treasury is based on Shi Zhihong, *Qingdai hubu yinku shouzhi*, 103–11.

8. Jones and Kuhn, "Dynastic Decline," 146.

9. Xu Daling, *Qingdai juanna zhidu*, 26–29, 73–74; Will, *Bureaucracy and Famine*, 190; Wong, "Foundations of Success," 28–30, 38–39; Idem., "The Grand Structure," 49–52, 63–64; Chen Feng, *Qingdai junfei yanjiu*, 330; Rowe, *Saving the World*, 256–59; Perdue, *China Marches West*, 366–69; Dunstan, *State or Merchant*, 160, 192–211, 262–74.

10. Xu Daling, *Qingdai juanna zhidu*, 15; Wang Wensheng, *White Lotus Rebels*, 202.

11. Kaske, "Metropolitan Clerks and Venality," 223.

12. Ibid., 228.

13. Luo, *Zhongguo lijinshi*, 4–5; Kaske, "Fund-Raising Wars," 91; Idem., "Metropolitan Clerks and Venality," 226.

14. The *Qing shilu*, *Like shishu*, and *Like tiben*, when examined together, convey a fairly clear picture of the fluctuations in the number of contributions.

15. *QSL-QL*, 85.337-38, 97.470, 240.97, 787.682, 1134.154, 1319.834.

16. For example, compare the report of the contribution incident in Anhui described in *QSL-DG*, 157.411 and *Like tiben*, 55 (Microfilm no.).9790-10 (Document no.) (DG9/7/20); and also the incident in Zhejiang in *QSL-DG*, 263.30 and *Like tiben*, 101.10146-26 (DG15/4/13).

17. I have examined the Qianlong to Daoguang portion of the *Gongzhong zhupi zouzhe caizheng lei juanshu xiang*, which includes secret memorials dealing with the sale of offices and, to a lesser extent, contribution incidents.

18. *Like tiben*, 44.9701-3 (DG/7/3/4).

19. *Da Qing huidian (Qianlong)*, 32.260. The drafting of the Qianlong edition began in 1747, completed in 1763, and printed in 1768. Wilkinson, *Chinese History*, 843.

20. *Da Qing huidian (Qianlong)*, 32.260.

21. The drafting of the Jiaqing edition of the *Da Qing huidian* began in 1801. It was completed in 1818 and printed in 1823. Wilkinson, *Chinese History*, 843.

22. *Da Qing huidian (Jiaqing)*, 23.1059.

23. For example, *Like tiben*, 11.3416-8 (QL2/2/9), 12.3418-8 (QL2/6/10), 12.3419-2 (QL2/8/20), 162.4903-22 (QL16/3/29), 191.5152-18 (QL19/5/26).

24. *Gongzhong zhupi zouzhe caizheng lei, juanshu xiang.* Memorial by Hešen, submitted on QL 55, 10.04, vol. 6, 48–53 (volume number and pagination by the Institute of Modern History Library, Academia Sinica, Taiwan); *Like tiben*, 218.7920-8.

25. *Yixu* records during the Jiaqing period underscore this point. *Like tiben*, 67.8718-12 (JQ12/6/23), 15.9097-20 (JQ20/11/24), 28.8412-4 (JQ5/5/23), 107.9034-20 (JQ19/Intercalary2/5), 107.9034-9 (JQ19/2/14).

26. The specifics of the 1827 regulations were based on the following documents. *Like tiben*, 44.9704-15, 45.9705-1, 55.9787-15, 55.9790-5, 55.9790-14, 55.9791-7, 101.10146-1, 101.10146-2, 101.10146-7, 101.10147-22, 101.10147-18, 101.10147-31, 101.10146-16, 101.10146-26, 101.10147-6, 101.10147-9, 101.10147-17, 101.10147-33, 102.10152-17, 102.10152-18.

27. For example, if a *juren* (8a) makes a contribution, he will have one thousand taels added to his amount, one thousand taels being half of the amount that the *shi* or commoners needed to contribute to obtain the official title of rank 8a. Since *juren* and various tribute students such as *engongsheng*, *bagongsheng*, and *fugongsheng* were considered having a similar status as officials in ranks 8a or 8b, they and officials at the higher rank would receive a more favorable reward for the same amount of contributions than a *shi* or a *min*.

28. *Like tiben*, 115.9097-20 (JQ20/11/24).

29. *Like tiben*, 44.9701-3 (DG7/3/4).

30. *Like tiben*, 55.9787-15 (DG9/2/7), 102.10150-14 (DG15/10/24).

31. *Like tiben*, 44.9701-3 (DG7/3/4).

32. Ibid.

33. The details of this 1832 regulation were reconstructed on the basis of the following documents. *Like tiben*, 102.10154-4 (DG15/12/20), 101.10147-18 (DG15/5/28).

34. See *Like tiben*, 102.10152-17 (DG15/12/14).

35. *QHDSL*, 77.994; *Qinding Libu zeli*, 8.997-98.

36. *QHDSL*, 77.995-96.

37. In 1832, the Daoguang Emperor even bestowed *juren* degrees on those who had donated to bring relief to the victims of a serious drought in Zhili. When officials later asked for similar imperial favors for other contributors, the emperor clarified that it had been a temporary measure and prohibited the officials from making similar requests. See *QSL-DG*, 239.571-72; *QHDSL*, 403.499. In 1831, an official suggested to the emperor that commoners whose ancestors were of the mean social status, if they donated a large sum of silver or grain, should be allowed to take the civil service examination or purchase office after having their names scratched from the register of socially mean people. The emperor, however, refuted the suggestion, claiming that it would only damage the rightful form of government. The purpose of the official's suggestion, however, was self-evident: to expand the social rung of contributors and thereby funnel more private resources into public projects. *QSL-DG*, 193.1052.

38. *QSL-DG*, 358.469.

39. Pan Qing, "Ming Qing shiqi Jiangnan," 956–66.

40. Chen and Liu, *Jiuzai yu jipin*, 159.

41. *QSL-QL*, 9.318.

42. *QSL-QL*, 14.394; *QHDSL*, 922.601.

43. *QHDSL*, 271.97-98.

44. *QSL-QL*, 25.559.

45. *QHDSL*, 927.655.

46. For example, see *QSL-QL*, 239.75-76, 437.698.

47. *QHDSL*, 927.657; 867.71; *QSL-QL*, 236.41, 258.335, 673.531.

48. *QSL-QL*, 377.1178.

49. *QSL-QL*, 424.558.

50. See, for example, *QSL-QL*, 970.1247.

51. *QSL-QL*, 700.835.

52. *QSL-QL*, 313.122-23.

53. *QSL-QL*, 176.262.

54. *QHDSL*, 931.693-94.

55. *QSL-QL*, 1342.1202.

56. *QSL-QL*, 1424.52.

57. This emphasis on oversight and official supervisory roles characterized eighteenth-century public works management. For such famine relief projects in Zhili, see Lillian M. Li, *Fighting Famine*, 224.

58. On the breakdown of official discipline in this period, see Polachek, "Literati Groups," 29–38. Peter Perdue argues that the effectiveness of imperial bureaucracy, the willingness of the state to control official abuses, and the state incentives for institutional reforms declined when Qing frontier expansion ended in the mid-eighteenth century. As a result, symptoms of crises accumulated beginning in the mid-eighteenth century and

continuing until they became explicit social problems in the early nineteenth century. For this view, see Perdue, *China Marches West*, 547–51.

59. *QSL-QL*, 1331.1018, 1335.1099, 1356.174, 1361.241, 1392.704, 1395.738. In 1788, Qianlong ordered that state-funded public works that were not urgent should be postponed in order to reduce state expenditures. See *QHDSL*, 887.254.

60. *QHDSL*, 887.255. See also *QSL-JQ*, 204.727, 206.747 for the emperor's tortured indecision over how to allocate appropriate funds for waterworks in 1809.

61. See, for example, *QSL-DG*, 47.832, 47.839, 49.870, 75.204-5, 80.299-300, 83.337, 145.226-27, 159.455, 170.644-45, 209.76-77, 210.93, 220.279, 221.297, 228.419, 230.450, 240.588-89, 244.662-63, 244.678-79, 253.846-47, 268.118, 269.131-32, 304.747, 315.908, 325.1108-9, 329.1184.

62. See, for example, Tao Zhu's memorials submitted on waterworks and the building of city walls in 1825, 1829, and 1836. *Tao Zhu ji*, vol. 1, 442, 452, 487. See also "Chongjun Wusongjiang quanan," 1.6ab, 8a, "Chongjun Mengdu deng sanhe quanan," 1.5a, 2.1b, Chen Luan, et al., eds., *Chongjun Jiangnan shuili quanshu*; *Tao Zhu ji*, vol. 1, 466, 484, 487–88, 491–92; *Lin Zexu quanji*, vol. 1, 282–83, 428, vol. 2. 19, 34–35.

63. *QHDSL*, 925.632.

64. *QSL-DG*, 230.438.

65. *QSL-DG*, 122.1052. The interruption of this river works project in 1825 due to fiscal shortage and its resumption in 1827 is detailed in Polachek, "Literati Groups," 269–85, 344–46. Lillian Li's study of river management in Zhili Province shows that the Jiaqing and the Daoguang Emperors had to mobilize more private resources to finance the works, especially beginning in the Daoguang period. Lillian M. Li, *Fighting Famine*, 56–66.

66. *QSL-DG*, 233.491.

67. Wong, *China Transformed*, 113–14.

68. *QSL-JQ*, 50.632-33. By underscoring this bureaucratic dynamic, Wong portrays the early nineteenth century not as a period of decline, but as a time when the Qing searched for an alternative mode of management of its granaries. See Wong, "Decline and Its Opposition," 91.

69. *QSL-JQ*, 84.109-10.

70. *QSL-JQ*, 229.86-87.

71. *QSL-JQ*, 325.289.

72. *QSL-JQ*, 331.371.

73. *QSL-DG*, 7.153.

74. *QSL-DG*, 163.532.

75. *QSL-DG*, 167.594.

76. *QSL-DG*, 290.486.

Chapter 2. "Civilians Donate and They Manage"

1. On the development of the "yeshi dianli" system since the late Ming period, see Hamashima, *Mindai Kōnan nōson shakai*, 31–201.

2. Morita, *Shindai suirishi kenkyū*, 57–71, 87–90, 237–39, 259, 297; Idem., *Shindai suiri shakaishi*, 88–89, 152, 161, 199–200; Perdue, *Exhausting the Earth*, 185–96; Kawakatsu,

Chūgoku hōken kokka, 639. The Qing state monitored waterworks in the eighteenth century more closely than the Ming. This was especially the case in Jiangnan than in other regions, such as Hunan, farther away from the capital. See Perdue, *Exhausting the Earth*, 184.

3. Ōtani, *Shindai seiji shisōshi kenkyū*, 215–46; Morita, *Shindai no suiri*, chaps. 1–3; Kurahashi, "Jūkyū seiki Kōnan," 1–27; Schoppa, *Xiang Lake*, 136–39. Robert Antony also introduces a waterworks case in Guangdong in which the managerial role, previously performed by officials, was handed back to the local elites in the Jiaqing period. See Antony, "Subcounty Officials," 49. Mark Elvin has brought attention to the emergence of gentry leadership in hydraulic works during the Qianlong period, but he also noted that the terms "gentry-directors" or "directors" came to be used regularly by the early nineteenth century. See Elvin, "Market Towns and Waterways," 462–67.

4. Morita, *Shindai suiri shakaishi*, 120–21, 152–61, 171–77, 183–89.

5. *Changshu xianzhi*, 1687, 6 shuili; *Zhaowen xianzhi*, 1731, 3 shuili; *Changzhou xianzhi*, 1753, 15 shuili; *Wujiang xianzhi*, 1747, 41 zhishui, 43 xiutang; *Yuanhe xianzhi*, 1761, 14 shuili; *Zhenze xianzhi*, 1746, 28 zhishui, 30 xiutang; *Kun Xin liangxian zhi*, 1826, 5 shuili; *Suzhou fuzhi*, 1824, 7 shuili; Qian Siyuan, *Wumen bucheng*, 1 shuilibu; *Suzhou fuzhi*, 1882, 11 shuili; *Chang Zhao hezhigao*, 1904, 9 shuili; *Wujiangxian xuzhi*, 1879, 6 shuili; *Kun Xin liangxian xuxiu hezhi*, 1880, 5 shuili; *Wu xianzhi*, 1933, 43 shuili.

6. Pan Qing, "Ming Qing shiqi Jiangnan," 953–58; Fan and Xia, *Suzhou diqu shehui jingjishi*, 397–98.

7. *Wujiang xianzhi*, 1747, 41.14ab; 43.26a; *Chang Zhao hezhigao*, 1904, 9.27a.

8. *Suzhou fuzhi*, 1882, 11.2a-8a.

9. Ibid., 11.9b, 11a.

10. *Wujiang xianzhi*, 1747, 51.14b; *Suzhou fuzhi*, 1882, 11.11a.

11. *Suzhou fuzhi*, 1882, 11.12ab; *Kun Xin liangxian zhi*, 1826, 5.17a.

12. *Suzhou fuzhi*, 1882, 11.13a; *Wujiang xianzhi*, 1747, 41.14b-15a.

13. *Wu xianzhi*, 1933, 43.15a; *Zhaowen xianzhi*, 1731, 3.31b-32a; *Suzhou fuzhi*, 1882, 11.14b.

14. Will, *Bureaucracy and Famine*, 191–94; Wong, "The Grand Structure," 62; Marks, *Tigers, Rice, Silk, & Silt*, 236–38; Rowe, *Saving the World*, 45–49, 260–61; Dunstan, *State or Merchant*, 307–403.

15. *Chang Zhao hezhigao*, 1904, 9.32a.

16. Ibid., 9.32b.

17. *Suzhou fuzhi*, 1882, 11.19a; *Kun Xin liangxian zhi*, 1826, 5.18a; *Wujiangxian xuzhi*, 1879, 6.1a.

18. But it was not a thorough abandonment of the paternalistic gesture, either, since the policy made the prompt initiation of the works possible and would guarantee the completion of the works, ultimately benefiting the owners or tillers of local lands. See Jiangsu governor Zhuang Yougong's memorial submitted in 1763 included in 1882 *Suzhou fuzhi*, 11.19a.

19. *Chang Zhao hezhigao*, 1904, 9.33a; *Suzhou fuzhi*, 1882, 11.21a.

20. See, for example, the waterwork on Liuhe and Wusong Rivers in 1671 recorded in 1826 *Kun Xin liangxian zhi*, 5.16b.

21. *Chang Zhao hezhigao*, 1904, 9.28a.

22. See, for example, *Zhaowen xianzhi*, 1731, 3.31ab; *Wujiang xianzhi*, 1747, 41.15a; *Suzhou fuzhi*, 1882, 11.13a.
23. *Kun Xin liangxian xuxiu hezhi*, 1880, 5.17b.
24. *Kun Xin liangxian zhi*, 1826, 5.17a.
25. *Wujiang xianzhi*, 1747, 41.15a.
26. *Zhenze xianzhi*, 1746, 28.20b.
27. *Kun Xin liangxian zhi*, 1826, 5.17b.
28. *Suzhou fuzhi*, 1882, 11.16b; *Chang Zhao hezhigao*, 1904, 9.31ab.
29. *Suzhou fuzhi*, 1882, 11.18a-19a.
30. Ibid., 11.19a.
31. Ibid., 11.19b.
32. Ibid., 11.19b; Qian Siyuan, *Wumen bucheng*, 1.6b.
33. *Suzhou fuzhi*, 1882, 11.21b.
34. *Chang Zhao hezhigao*, 1904, 9.33a.
35. *Wujiangxian xuzhi*, 1879, 6.2b.
36. *QSL-QL*, 796.753.
37. Ibid.
38. Qianlong had endorsed a request by Zhejiang provincial officials to establish elite managers in a waterwork project in 1762. *QSL-QL*, 675.552. The corruption case by a *juren* manager in the waterworks in 1767, however, alerted the emperor to the dangers of granting management titles to members of the elite. For this corruption case, see *QSL-QL*, 789.694, 790.697, 815.1017.
39. *Kun Xin liangxian zhi*, 1826, 5.18b; *Chang Zhao hezhigao*, 1904, 9.35ab; *Wujiangxian xuzhi*, 1879, 6.2b.
40. For 1797 case, see *Kun Xin liangxian zhi*, 1826, 5.18b; *QSL-JQ*, 263.570-71; *QHDSL*, 928.660. For 1813 case, see *Kun Xin liangxian zhi*, 1826, 5.19a; *QSL-JQ*, 263.570-71.
41. *Kun Xin liangxian zhi*, 1826, 5.19a; *Wujiangxian xuzhi*, 1879, 6.2b-3a; *QSL-JQ*, 325.289. See also Pan Qing, "Ming Qing shiqi Jiangnan," 958; Ōtani, *Shindai seiji shisōshi kenkyū*, 256–57.
42. *QSL-JQ*, 325.289.
43. *Suzhou fuzhi*, 1882, 11.21b; *Chang Zhao hezhigao* 1904, 9.36a.
44. *Kun Xin liangxian zhi*, 1826, 5.19a.
45. Ibid.; *Suzhou fuzhi*, 1882, 11.22a.
46. *Wu xianzhi*, 1933, 43.15b.
47. For a brief explanation of this work, see Morita, *Shindai suiri shakaishi*, 116. On the "honesty-nourishing money," see Zelin, *The Magistrate's Tael*, 96.
48. Qian Siyuan, *Wumen bucheng*, 1.10a.
49. See *Wu xianzhi*, 1933, 43.4b.
50. Qian Siyuan, *Wumen bucheng*, 1.12ab.
51. *QSL-JQ*, 325.289.
52. Qian Siyuan, *Wumen bucheng*, 1 shuili bu, 6b-9b.
53. On the commercial shipment of tribute grain in the 1820s, see Zhang Yan, "Bao Shichen," 142, 151; Leonard, "Negotiating across the Boundaries," 204. On the accommodationist ideas in monetary policy, see Lin Man-houng, *China Upside Down*, 262–65.
54. See *Suzhou fuzhi*, 1882, 11.22ab; *Kun Xin liangxian zhi*, 1826, 5.19b.
55. *Suzhou fuzhi*, 1882, 11.23b.

56. Ōtani, *Shindai seiji shisōshi kenkyū,* 257.

57. Chen Luan, et al., eds., "Chongjun Wusongjiang quanan," 1.6ab. All texts in quotation marks cited in the notes of this chapter are included in the *Chongjun Jiangnan shuili quanshu* compiled by Chen Luan. Chen (1786–1839) was an official who assumed various local and provincial posts in Jiangsu Province in the first two decades of the Daoguang reign. Together with his provincial superiors such as Tao Zhu and Lin Zexu, Chen supervised a number of important hydraulic projects in the province and compiled a volume, including edicts, memorials, and other government documents related to these works, entitled *Chongjun Jiangnan shuili quanshu* and posthumously published in 1841. The documents contained in this volume show the extent to which provincial and local officials endeavored to enlist financial and managerial assistance from civilians.

58. "Chongjun Wusongjiang quanan," 1.5a-9a.

59. *QSL-DG,* 122.1052; "Chongjun Wusongjiang quanan," 1.10a-12a.

60. "Chongjun Wusongjiang quanan," 1.9a.

61. Polachek, "Literati Groups," 339–40.

62. "Chongjun Wusongjiang quanan," 1.21ab.

63. Ibid., 2.14a.

64. Ibid., 3.22b.

65. Ibid., 3.22b-23b.

66. Ibid., 2.39b.

67. "Chongjun Puhuaitang quanan," 1.2a.

68. Ibid.

69. "Chongjun Diao'e he deng he quanan," 1.1b-2a.

70. Ibid., 1.2a.

71. Ibid., 1.2b-3b.

72. Ibid., 1.3ab, 5a.

73. Ibid., 2.5a.

74. *Suzhou fuzhi*, 1882, 11.24ab; *Wu xianzhi*, 1933, 43.5a.

75. *Wu xianzhi*, 1933, 43.5b.

76. *Suzhou fuzhi*, 1882, 84.6ab.

77. "Chongjun Liuhe quanan," 1.1b

78. Ibid., 1.6a, 7b; See also Ōtani, *Shindai seiji shisōshi kenkyū,* 260.

79. "Chongjun Liuhe quanan," 1.8ab.

80. Ibid., 1.17b-19b.

81. "Chongjun Liuhe quanan," 1.19b; *Suzhou fuzhi*, 1882, 11.24b.

82. *Kun Xin liangxian xuxiu hezhi*, 1880, 33.20ab.

83. Ibid.

84. "Chongjun Liuhe quanan," 2.24b-25a; Ōtani, *Shindai seiji shisōshi kenkyū,* 262–63. On the local administration system in late imperial China, see Brook, "The Spatial Structure."

85. "Chongjun Liuhe quanan," 2.25a.

86. Ibid., 1.6a, 8a.

87. "Chongjun Baimaohe quanan," 1.8a.

88. Ibid., 1.8a-9a.

89. Ibid., 1.9a.

90. Ibid., 1.11b.
91. Ibid., 1.15b-18a.
92. Ibid., 1.5b, 11a, 15b-18a; Ōtani, *Shindai seiji shisōshi kenkyū,* 264–66.
93. "Chongjun Baimaohe quanan," 1.15b-18a.
94. "Chongjun Suzhoufu chenghe an," 1.1a.
95. Ibid., 1.1ab.
96. Ibid., 1.1b.
97. Ibid., 1.7a-8a.
98. "Chongjun Su, Song, Tai sanfuzhou he quanan," 1.1b, 4b-9a.
99. Ibid., 1.5a; *Wujiangxian xuzhi*, 1879, 6.3b.
100. "Chongjun Su, Song, Tai sanfuzhou he quanan," 1.5b-6a; the 1933 edition of *Wu xianzhi* records that governor Lin Zexu and the county gentry Pan Zengyi, You Songzhen, and Xu Xi initiated and led this waterwork (*juan* 43, 5b).
101. "Chongjun Zhangjiatang deng he quanan," 1.1ab.
102. Ibid., 1.2ab.
103. Ibid., 1.5ab.
104. Ibid., 1.9a-14b.
105. "Xiujun Fushan chengyuan tanghe quanan," 1.1b, 4b.
106. Ibid., 1.8a-13a.
107. Ibid., 2.6b.
108. "Chongjun Jiangning chenghe quanan," 1.1a-4a.
109. Ibid., 1.1b-2a.
110. Ibid., 1.2a.
111. Ibid., 1.3a; 3.30a-31a.
112. Ibid., 1.6a-10a.
113. "Chongjun Mengdu deng sanhe quanan," 1.4ab.
114. Ibid., 1.4b-5a; Ōtani, *Shindai seiji shisōshi kenkyū,* 253–54.
115. "Chongjun Mengdu deng sanhe quanan," 1.5ab.
116. Ibid., 1.20a-22b.
117. Ibid., 5.50b-53a; Ōtani, *Shindai seiji shisōshi kenkyū,* 254.
118. "Chongjun Lianhu jianzha quanan," 2.8b-9a.
119. Ibid., 2.7b.
120. "Chongjun Qipuhe quanan," 1.2ab.
121. Ibid., 1.23a-26b.
122. *Wujiangxian xuzhi*, 1879, 6.3b.
123. *Suzhou fuzhi*, 1882, 11.25b.
124. Kojima Yoshio, *Kindai Chūgoku*, 53–57.
125. Ibid., 66–71.

Chapter 3. Fighting Famine

1. Will, *Bureaucracy and Famine*, 79–265. On the expansion and the sophistication of state granary system under Qianlong, see Wong, "The Grand Structure," 43–73; Li Xiangjun, "Qingdai jiuzai," 79, 85.
2. Will, *Bureaucracy and Famine*, 74–75, 138.

3. *Chang Zhao hezhigao*, 1904, 31.24a, 25ab, 27ab; *Kun Xin liangxian xuxiu hezhi*, 1880, 33.18a.

4. *Wujiangxian xuzhi*, 1879, 19.3ab. Similar initiatives were adopted in other regions of the empire. Local elites in Shuyang County in northern Jiangsu led a relief project in 1753, donating money and managing relief kitchens. See Yang Ximing, *Zaizhen quanshu*, 567, 570–71, 579–81.

5. *Wujiangxian xuzhi*, 1879, 38.2ab.

6. Zhang Tingmei, *Yuyao juanzhen shiyi,* 71, 73–74.

7. Ibid., 76–77.

8. Ibid., 81–82.

9. Ibid., 83–102.

10. It should be noted that the charity granary founded by the gentry leaders of the commercial town of Foshan, Guangdong, was also established in 1795. Built on the contributions from the local people, its management enjoyed greater autonomy than in previous cases. See Rankin, "Managed by the People," 20–23.

11. Inada, "Shindai Kōnan," 40.

12. Wong, "Decline and Its Opposition," 76–77.

13. Wong, *China Transformed*, 113–14.

14. Wu Tao, "Lun Qing qianqi," 44–45.

15. Ibid., 45. Three charity granaries were built in Suzhou in the early nineteenth century: Fengbeicang 豐備倉, Yicang 義倉, and Weishan yicang 衛山義倉. See *Suzhou fuzhi*, 1882, 23.4b, 5a, 12a. Fengbeicang, also known as Fengbei yicang, was built by Tao Zhu and Lin Zexu in 1835. The emperor endorsed the construction of this charity granary inside the yamen complex of the Jiangsu governor. Huang Hongshan and Wang Weiping have argued that, while the authority to manage this granary was largely in the hands of officials during the Daoguang reign, by the late Qing it had shifted to the local gentry. See Huang and Wang, "Wan Qing Suzhoufu," 368–90. The close official supervision of Fengbeicang during the Daoguang reign is certainly related to the fact that it was established by provincial officials and located within the governor's yamen. The basic principle that guided the management of charity granaries in the nineteenth century was the assignment of managerial authority to civilians, which prevented the interference of officials and clerks.

16. Yu and Hang, "Daoguang qianqi Jiangsu," 67–70; Chen and Liu, *Jiuzai yu jipin*, 414; Zhang Yanli, *Jia Dao shiqi*, 158–76.

17. Li Xiangjun, "Qingdai jiuzai," 85.

18. Wang Zhiyi, *Huangzheng jiyao,* 536–38; *Wujiangxian xuzhi*, 1879, 38.2b-3a.

19. *Kun Xin liangxian xuxiu hezhi*, 1880, 51.14b.

20. Fei Shanqing, *Chuihong zhixiao lu*, 3.18ab.

21. *Chang Zhao hezhigao*, 1904, 31.32a.

22. Fei Lanchi, "Xiangzhen ji" 鄉賑記, *Qu'an wenchao*, 23a-25b.

23. Fei Shanqing, *Chuihong zhixiao lu*, 3.32b-33b.

24. A brief description of this *tuzhen* method can be found in Will, *Bureaucracy and Famine*, 314. See also Inada, "Shindai Kōnan," 45–46; Zhang Yanli, *Jia Dao shiqi*, 168–69.

25. Yang Jingren, *Choujibian,* 179.

26. Qian Yong, *Lüyuan conghua*, 4.115.

27. Ibid., 4.116. On the dissemination of the *tuzhen* and other community-based relief measures in Jiangnan during the first decades of the nineteenth century, see also Wu Tao, "Qingdai Jiangnan," 182–87.

28. Qian Yong, *Lüyuan conghua*, 4.117.

29. Yi Fengting, *Hainingzhou quanzhen changhe shi*, 262–63, 266–453.

30. Ibid., 262–63.

31. Inada, "Shinmatsu Kōnan," 158–62; Idem., "Shindai Kōnan," 42.

32. Na-yan-cheng, *Zhenji*, 675, 679.

33. Will, *Bureaucracy and Famine*, 106, 110.

34. Fang Shouchou, *Fu Yu xuzai lu*, 24, 52, 60.

35. Ibid., 24, 32, 52–53, *passim*.

36. Ibid., 220–22.

37. On government promotion of civilian donations for the relief operation in Zhili in 1833, see Chen and Liu, *Jiuzai yu jipin*, 350–51.

38. Han Wenqi, "Ken qing xiefa zhenji yinliang shu" 懇請協撥賑濟銀兩疏, *Han dazhongcheng zouyi*, 4.24a-26a, "Zunzhi chakan zaiqu qing jia jieji shu" 遵旨察看災區請加接濟疏, 5.66a-68b.

39. See Lin Zexu, "Jiangsu yinyu lianmian tiantao qianshou qingxing pian" 江蘇陰雨連綿田稻歉收情形片, *Lin Zexu quanji*, 311.

40. Lin Zexu, "Quanyu juanzhen gaoshi," *Lin Zexu ji*: *gongdu*, 3–4.

41. On these relief projects in 1823, also see Inada, "Shindai Kōnan," 32–37.

42. Peng Yunzhang, *Guipukan conggao*, 5.4a-5a.

43. Yu Xinzhong estimated that the total amount of donations by the local residents of Suzhou prefecture in 1823 was about 400,000 taels. See Yu, "Daoguang sannian Suzhou," 206, n. 42.

44. Peng Yunzhang, *Guipukan conggao*, 5.4b.

45. Peng Yunzhang, "Pingtiao ji" 平糶記, *Guipukan conggao*, 5.12a-13a.

46. On Peng's philanthropic thoughts and actions, see Wang and Ma, "Yuan Huang quanshan sixiang," 226–29.

47. On the spread of the *pingtiao* method based on a ward in this period, see Yu, "Daoguang sannian Suzhou," 202.

48. *Kun Xin liangxian xuxiu hezhi*, 1880, 51.15b.

49. Ibid., 33.20a.

50. Ibid., 33.20b.

51. Ibid., 33.18b.

52. Ibid., 33.22a.

53. Ibid., 33.19b, 33.25a.

54. Wang Kun, *Songling jianwen lu*, 6.350.

55. Fei Shanqing, *Chuihong zhixiao lu*, 3.32ab.

56. Ibid., 3.42ab.

57. *Wujiangxian xuzhi*, 1879, 19.3ab.

58. Fei Shanqing, *Chuihong zhixiao lu*, 3.34a; *Wujiangxian xuzhi*, 1879, 19.1a-2b.

59. *Wujiangxian xuzhi*, 1879, 2.7a, 19.2a.

60. Ibid., 19.2a.

61. Fei Shanqing, *Chuihong zhixiao lu,* 3.34a. On this network linking benevolent halls in urban and rural centers in Suzhou, see Fuma, *Chūgoku zenkai zendōshi kenkyū,* 246–48.

62. Fei Lanchi, "Yu Cheng zhu'an tongnian shiyu lun zaizheng shu" 與程竹庵同年侍御論災政書, *Qu'an wenchao*, 10a-13a; *Wujiangxian xuzhi*, 1879, 38.4ab.

63. *Wujiangxian xuzhi*, 1879, 14.2a.

64. Fei Lanchi, "Yu Cheng zhu'an tongnian shiyu lun zaizheng shu," 11b.

65. Ibid., 12b.

66. Fei Lanchi, "Xiangzhen ji," 23a-25b; *Wujiangxian xuzhi*, 1879, 38.4b.

67. Fei Shanqing, *Chuihong zhixiao lu,* 3.34a.

68. *Wujiangxian xuzhi*, 1879, 19.1a-2b.

69. Fei Lanchi, "Xiangzhen ji," 23b.

70. Ibid.

71. Ibid., 23b–24a.

72. Ibid., 23b.

73. Ibid., 24a.

74. Fei Lanchi, "Yu Zhao Zhihe xiaolian lun Wenmiao gong xu quzi zhenyu shu" 與趙芝鶴孝廉論文廟工需取資賑餘書, *Qu'an wenchao*, 16a-17b.

75. *Wujiangxian xuzhi*, 1879, 38.6a.

76. Fei Lanchi, "Yu Zhao Zhihe xiaolian lun Wenmiao gong xu quzi zhenyu shu," 17a.

77. The importance of communication between urban and rural managers in the decision-making process during relief operations can also be illustrated in the case of Zhang Qiancun 章謙存, a local elite manager who directed a donation-based effort in neighboring Baoshan County in 1823. Zhang discussed the relief project with other managers stationed in various market towns within the county and later ascribed the success of the project to the cooperation among them. See Zhang Qiancun, "Fu Jiangwan dongshi shu" 復江灣董事書, *Chouzhen shilüe*, 491–93. On this 1823 "voluntary relief" financed by elites in Jiading and Baoshan Counties, see also Inada, "Shindai Kōnan," 29–57.

78. Gu Jiayan, et al., *Loudong huangzheng huibian,* 647, 650.

79. Ibid., 647.

80. Ibid., 652.

81. Ibid., 652–58.

82. Ibid., 671.

83. Ibid., 673.

84. 10, 800 taels translate into roughly 12,918,000 *cash.* Ibid.

85. Ibid., 673–74.

86. Ibid., 674.

87. Ibid., 675–78.

88. Ibid., 678–88.

89. Ibid., 640–41.

90. According to Lin Man-houng, the exchange rate between silver and copper coins was 1:1249 in 1823. See table 2.6 in her book, *China Upside Down*, 86. The author of the record that describes the 1823 relief actions in these two areas applied a slightly different

rate, approximately 1:1200, which I employed in this calculation. See Gu Jiayan, et al., *Loudong huangzheng huibian*, 673.

91. Gu Jiayan, et al., *Loudong huangzheng huibian*, 688.
92. Wang Fengsheng, *Huangzheng beilan*, 624.
93. Ibid., 627–28, 631.
94. Wang Yuanji, *Chun'an huangzheng jilüe,* 698.
95. Ibid., 717–18.
96. Ibid., 718.
97. Lin Zexu, "Jiangsu yinyu lianmian tiantao qianshou qingxing pian," 311.
98. Ibid., 309–13.
99. Ibid., 311.
100. Wang and Gu, "Lin Zexu de huangzheng," 86.
101. Chen and Liu, *Jiuzai yu jipin*, 247.
102. Lin Zexu, "Jiangsu geshu juanzhen qingxing pian" 江蘇各屬捐賑情形片, *Lin Zexu quanji*, 336–37.
103. Lin Zexu, "Banzhen chuli geyuan qingjiang zhe" 辦賑出力各員請獎摺, *Lin Zexu quanji*, 455.
104. Lin Zexu, "Juanzhen shenmin qingjiang zhe" 捐賑紳民請獎摺," *Lin Zexu quanji*, 457.
105. Ibid., 457–58.
106. Lin Zexu, "Banzhen chuli geyuan qingjiang zhe," 456.
107. This translation and explanation of the term "danzhou" come from Will, *Bureaucracy and Famine*, 143, n.39.
108. Lin Zexu, "Jiangsu geshu juanzhen qingxing pian," 337.
109. Lin Zexu, "Juanzhen shenmin qingjiang zhe," 457.
110. *Chang Zhao hezhigao*, 1904, 31.33ab.
111. Ibid., 31.29a.
112. Ibid., 31.32b.
113. *Wujiangxian xuzhi*, 1879, 38.6b.
114. *Kun Xin liangxian xuxiu hezhi*, 1880, 51.16b-17a; *Wujiangxian xuzhi*, 1879, 38.7a.
115. *Kun Xin liangxian xuxiu hezhi*, 1880, 33.22a, 23b-24b, 51.16b-17a.
116. Ibid., 33.25a.
117. *Chang Zhao hezhigao*, 1904, 31.35ab, 36b, 37ab, 38b, 39ab, 40a.
118. Ibid., 31.42a.
119. Ibid., 31.34ab.
120. *Wujiangxian xuzhi*, 1879, 38.7a.
121. Ibid., 38.7b.
122. Ibid.
123. Ibid., 38.8a.
124. Ibid., 19.6a.
125. Ibid., 19.6b. On this relief project, see also Pan Zengyi, "Chouban Yusheng zhenwu siyi" 籌辦豫省賑務私議, *Dongjinguan wenji*, 2.22a-23a.
126. Fan Jinmin, noting the significant rise of charitable estates after the Taiping Rebellion, emphasizes the nature of charitable estates as a mechanism to safeguard the interests of landlords. See Fan, "Qingdai Suzhou zongzu yitian," 56–68. Fan regards the increases during the Qianlong and Daoguang reigns as the first and second peak peri-

ods in the development of charitable estates in Suzhou. See Fan, "Ming-Qing Jiangnan zongzu," 907.

127. Liu Zhengyun, "Yizhuang yu chengzhen," 648–49.

128. Fuma, *Chūgoku zenkai zendōshi kenkyū*, 493–540; Liang, *Shishan yu jiaohua*, 135–70; Chen and Liu, *Jiuzai yu jipin*, 228–45.

129. Liang, *Shishan yu jiaohua*, 240–306.

130. *Suzhou fuzhi*, 1824, 23.35b.

131. Wang Weiping and Huang Hongshan have examined the construction years of benevolent halls in certain market towns in Jiangnan, pointing out that the reigns of Qianlong, Jiaqing, and Daoguang marked the first peak period in their numbers. At the same time, they also noted that more halls were built during the reigns of Jiaqing and Daoguang than during the reign of Qianlong. See Wang and Huang, "Qingdai Jiangnan diqu," 93.

132. The benevolent halls in the commercial city of Hankow in the middle Yangzi region also experienced a rapid multiplication in the postrebellion period as old ones were restored and new ones built. Rowe, who has studied this phenomenon in Hankow, traces the origin of this institution to the 1820s. See Rowe, *Hankow: Conflict and Community*, 91–134.

133. Xu Maoming emphasizes the rise of charitable estates and benevolent halls in Jiangnan after the Taiping Rebellion. Xu Maoming, "Tong Guang zhiji Jiangnan," 297–300. But incipient changes of a similar nature in the early nineteenth century should be taken into consideration.

134. Yamada, *Ijūmin no chitsujo*, 188–259.

135. Yamamoto, "Shindai kōki Shisen"; Idem., "Shindai kōki Kōsetsu." Even Yamamoto, who depicts the benevolent halls as institutions to protect the collective interests of the gentry class, acknowledges the supplementary nature of benevolent halls to local administration. See Yamamoto, "Shindai kōki Kōsetsu," 48. Bradly Reed, in his study of the "Three-Fees Bureau," a form of gentry bureau that existed in nineteenth-century Sichuan charged with standardizing judicial fees and protecting the people from the arbitrary extortion by the yamen clerks, also emphasizes this complementary nature of the bureau to the official administration. See Reed, "Gentry Activism," 121–23. On the "Three-Fees Bureau," see also Lee Jungab, "Ch'ŏngchung-hugi Sachŏn," 150–51.

Chapter 4. The Shrine of Local Worthies and the Changing Patterns of the Enshrinement

1. Portions of this chapter have been published in Korean as "Myŏng Ch'ŏng sidae ŭi myŏnghwan, hyanghyŏn ipsa yangsang ŭi pyŏnhwa wa kŭ ŭimi," *Chungguk hakpo* 54 (2006): 347–78.

2. Carlitz, "Shrines, Governing-Class Identity," 631–33. Peter Bol has shown that the mid-Ming period witnessed the flourishing of an intellectual movement and the increased assertion of local identity. See Bol, "The Rise of Local History," 50; Idem., "The 'Localist Turn,'" 26–27.

3. Sarah Schneewind contended that these shrines were built without government orders in the Ming. See her *Community Schools*, 136, 237, n.181.

4. *Guangxi tongzhi*, 1733, 104.163; Lin Yaoyu, *Libu zhigao*, 85xia.535–36; Yang Shen, *Sheng'anji*, 4.55. An official at the Hongzhi court proposed to the emperor in 1488 that the worthies whose merits did not deserve the worship in the Confucian Temple should be expelled and enshrined in the *xiangxian ci*. The official employed the terminology "*xiangxian ci zhi zhi*" 鄉賢祠之制, which implied that the worship had been already established and recognized by the state by 1488. *Ming shilu (Hongzhi)*, 17.413–14.

5. *Ming shilu* (*Hongzhi*), 70.1317, 198.3657-58; *Ming shilu* (*Zhengtong*), 74.1636, 101.2100, 103.2126-27, 107.2193, 127.2551, 144.2824; *Ming shilu* (*Jiajing*), 143.3346-47, 532.8662.

6. *Wu xianzhi*, 1642, 13.45a.

7. Ibid., 13.42a.

8. On the problem of the excessive enshrinement in the late Ming, see Lin Liyue, "Zudou gongqiang," 341–50.

9. Lin Yaoyu, *Libu zhigao*, 85xia.535.

10. Ibid., 30.563.

11. Ibid., 45.857.

12. Ibid., 24.449; *Ming shilu* (*Wanli*), 120.2246, 373.6990, 418.7909.

13. *Wu xianzhi*, 1745, 30.8a.

14. *Suzhou fuzhi*, 1748, 17.23b-24a; *Suzhou fuzhi*, 1824, 26.7b-8a.

15. *Tangxi xianzhi*, 1931, 4.27b-28a.

16. *Pujiang xianzhi*, 1896, 13.29ab.

17. *QHDSL*, 402.494; Hsiao, *Rural China*, 227.

18. *QHDSL*, 402.494.

19. *LKSS*, 113 (YZ2/5/8); *QHDSL*, 402.494.

20. *QHDSL*, 402.494.

21. *LKSS*, 113 (YZ2/5/8).

22. *LKSS*, 130 (YZ3/9/24).

23. *LKSS*, 131 (YZ3/11/6); *Qinding Xuezheng quanshu,* 76.2ab; *QHDSL*, 402.494.

24. *QHDSL*, 402.494.

25. Ibid.

26. *QHDSL*, 402.494; *QSL-YZ*, 73.1084; *Qinding Xuezheng quanshu*, 76.2b-3a.

27. *LKSS*, 199 (YZ8/12/16).

28. On Yongzheng's attack on the literati privileges, see Zelin, "The Yung-cheng Reign," 197, 199, 218–20.

29. *QSL-QL*, 130.899, 274.587.

30. *QSL-QL*, 275.601.

31. *QSL-QL*, 328.424.

32. *QSL-QL*, 341.721.

33. *QSL-QL*, 344.765; *QHDSL*, 402.495.

34. *QSL-QL*, 481.28-29.

35. *QHDSL*, 402.495.

36. During the Qianlong reign, I have found cases of rejection in the following years: 1738, 1742, 1748, 1754, 1756, 1776, and 1777.

37. *LKSS*, 403 (QL13/12/13).

38. *LKSS*, 486 (QL19/12/18).

39. Many of these records, the majority from the nineteenth century, are housed in the Shanghai Library.

40. Only one entry under these two categories dates from 1879, which regulated that candidates could be recommended only thirty years after their deaths.

41. For those eighty-two names, see *Wu xianzhi*, 1745, 30.8b-9b, 10ab.

42. The enshrinement years and the native counties of these Suzhou worthies are as follows. 1736: Changshu-1, 1747: Wu-1; Changshu-2, 1753: Changzhou-1, 1754: Wujiang-1, 1763: Changshu-1, 1764: Changshu-1, 1769: Changzhou-1, 1791: Yuanhe-1. See *QSL-QL*, 33.645; *LKSS*, 390 (QL12/12/11), 472 (QL18/12/13), 486 (QL19/12/18), 588 (QL28/12/14), 602 (QL29/12/19), 666 (QL34/9/17), 975 (QL56/12/16). In 1765, the residents of Suzhou built a shrine called "Extended Shrine of Local Worthies" (*guang xiangxian ci* 廣鄉賢祠) near the government school in Changzhou County. The shrine, which included the names of seven worthies, seems to have been built to provide another route for enshrinement, bypassing the regular state system during the eighteenth century. See Lee Yunseok, "Myŏngch'ŏng sidae Kangnam," 17. However, during the rest of the eighteenth century, no records indicate the inclusion of more worthies in the shrine or efforts to preserve it. It does not seem that the shrine continued to function as an alternative path for enshrinement. Its rebuilding and the addition of worthies occurred only in the early nineteenth century. According to the local gazetteer of Suzhou, the shrine went through repairs in 1817 and 1831 and added another worthy in 1831. See *Suzhou fuzhi*, 1824, 25.33b; *Suzhou fuzhi*, 1882, 26.39a.

43. *QSL-QL*, 1071.372.

44. Among the ten Suzhou local worthies enshrined between 1726 and 1795, only one was from Wu County. This near absence of local worthies from Wu County during the Yongzheng and Qianlong reigns is particularly remarkable when compared with the county's success in producing local worthies from 1644 to 1724 before the establishment of the centralized enshrinement system. According to the 1745 Wu County gazetteer, as many as six Wu County worthies were included, from 1644 to 1724, in the shrine in the Suzhou prefectural school. See *Wu xianzhi*, 1745, 30.10ab. After producing one local worthy in 1747, the county saw another one only in 1837. It is difficult to explain exactly why the centralization of enshrinement led to this sudden disappearance of worthies, particularly in Wu County. However, Adam Lui may provide an explanation for this phenomenon, as he notes the extremely low success rate of officials from Wu County in reaching the highest official ranks between 1644 and 1795. He explained that the "Laments in the Temple" case (*kumiaoan* 哭廟案) that occurred in Wu County in 1661 left an indelible negative impression in the minds of the early Qing emperors, which prompted them to suspect the loyalty of the officials from this county. See Lui, *The Hanlin Academy*, 130–34. The imperial tendency to look suspiciously at the customs of Wu County literati may have affected the underrepresentation of worthies from this area during the eighteenth century.

45. Suzhou had only one local worthy from 1769 to 1795. Among the eleven Suzhou local worthies enshrined during the Jiaqing period, none hailed from Wu County. The Jiangsu governor recommended one worthy candidate from Wu County in 1808, but the Jiaqing Emperor rejected this proposal on the grounds that the candidate was underqualified. See *QSL-JQ*, 203.711; *LKSS*, 1322 (JQ13/10/1).

46. *QSL-DG*, 149.284, 163.528, 292.521, 364.557, 386.941, 437.473, 450.671. The enshrinements of the two worthies from Wu County, Gu Chun 顧蒓 and Pan Shihuang 潘世璜, seem to be related to the political rise of Pan Shi'en, who became a grand councilor at the Daoguang's court. A native of Wu County, he was an uncle of Pan Shihuang (*Suzhou fuzhi*, 1882, 83.24b-25b). For the reasons mentioned earlier, the ascendance of a Wu County native to the highest position in the Qing court is suggestive of the relaxation of the Qing Emperor's suspicions concerning the loyalty of the officials from the area. Drawing on the 1882 *Suzhou fuzhi*, Japanese scholar Okuzaki Hiroshi argues that many worthies were enshrined as local worthies in Wu County (Okuzaki, "Soshūhu kyōkenshi," 49–60). However, the part on local worthies in the gazetteer reflects only the disorderly enshrinement conditions of the late Qing and thus provides inaccurate information. Many worthies described by the gazetteer compiler to have their tablets in the Wu County shrine in the late Qing had in fact been originally enshrined in other counties. For example, Lu Yao 陸燿 and Jin Shisong 金士松, both considered by the 1882 *Suzhou fuzhi* as Wu County worthies, had been officially considered as the worthies of Wujiang County in the original government enshrinement documents. See *LKSS*, 1122 (JQ3/2/8), 1233 (JQ7/10/24). The 1824 *Suzhou fuzhi* also states that these two were enshrined in Wujiang County. In the case of Xu Angfa 徐昂發, who entered the shrine as a local worthy during the Jiaqing reign, the memorials stated that he was either a native of Changzhou County or a Kunshan resident originally from Changzhou. See *LKSS*, 1273 (JQ9/12/20), 1283 (JQ10/10/23). The *Chang Yuan xiangxian ci xiaozhi* 長元鄉賢祠小志 (The gazetteer of Local Worthies Shrine in Changzhou and Yuanhe Counties [housed in the Shanghai Library]) also included him in the list of their local worthies. Despite these records, the 1882 *Suzhou fuzhi* inaccurately stated that Xu was enshrined only in Wu County. It is thus misleading to argue that many local worthies hailed from Wu County during the Qing period.

47. *QSL-JQ*, 314.172; *QSL-DG*, 181.864, 342.208; *QSL-TZ*, 245.406, 193.457.

48. *QSL-XF*, 122.102, 123.119.

49. Zeng attempted to obtain the endorsement for this candidate through the emperor's special decree rather than through the regular route of the discussion at the Board of Rites as dictated by the Qing regulations. Furthermore, in his memorial Zeng argued that a worthy candidate should be evaluated primarily based upon the opinion of local people, which supposedly downplayed the role of the central government's evaluation criteria.

50. On the expansion of elite public roles during the Tongzhi period, see Rankin, *Elite Activism*, 92–135.

51. For this perspective, see Kuhn, *Rebellion and Its Enemies*; Rankin, *Elite Activism*. Philip Kuhn, however, embraced the possibility that elite political activism had begun earlier in the 1820s, at least in Jiangnan, in the preface of the 1980 reprint version of his original 1970 book. See Kuhn, *Rebellion and Its Enemies*, iii–iv.

Chapter 5. Shrine, Images, and Power

1. Material for this chapter first appeared in Han Seunghyun, "Shrine, Images, and Power: The Worship of Former Worthies in Early Nineteenth Century Suzhou," *T'oung Pao* 95, nos. 1–3 (2009): 167–95, and is reprinted here with permission.

2. See Tao Zhu's preface in Gu Yuan, *Wujun wubai mingxian tuzhuanzan*, 13–18.
3. Gu Zhentao, *Wumen biaoyin*, 182–83.
4. Ibid., 182.
5. Neskar, "The Cult of Worthies."
6. For example, the *xiangxian ci* in Yongkang County, Jinhua prefecture, Zhejiang, was built in 1256. See *Yongkang xianzhi*, 1892, 4.40.
7. Kojima Tsuyoshi, "Jukyō no gūjōkan," 70.
8. Sommer, "Destroying Confucius," 110–14.
9. Ibid., 118.
10. See Hamashima, "The City God Temples," 2–5.
11. Chen Gao, ed., *Quelizhi*, 22.1253.
12. Ibid., 22.1254.
13. Ibid., 22.1267.
14. For example, in 1382, the prefect of Suzhou had a clay statue of Confucius made in the prefectural school. In Changzhou, the statues of Confucius and his disciples adorned the county school by 1374. In Wu County, local officials remade and reembellished the statues in the Confucian Temple in 1425 and 1436. This suggests that in the early Ming the worship of Confucius and his disciples in the Confucian Temple in Suzhou was practiced before the actual statues or portraits, following the tradition of the Song and Yuan. See *Gusu zhi*, 1506, 24.7b, 15b; *Wuyi zhi*, 1529, 5.16b, 6.1b; Xu Jian, *Suzhou fuxue jinshizhi*, *ce*3, "Pingjiang lu chongxiu ruxue ji" 平江路重修儒學記, *ce*3, "Chongxiu Pingjiang lu ruxue ji" 重修平江路儒學記, *ce*4, "Suzhou fuxue chongxiu miaomao ji" 蘇州府學重修廟貌記, *ce*4, "Chongxiu Suzhoufu miaoxue ji" 重修蘇州府廟學記, *ce*5, "Suzhoufu chongxiu ruxue ji" 蘇州府重修儒學記.
15. Local officials of Wu County made clay statues of Confucian sages and painted their portraits during the Zhizheng reign (1341–67) of the Yuan dynasty. Another source tells us that a statue of Confucius first appeared in the Wu County school during the Shaoding reign (1228–33) of the Song. The author of the Wu County gazetteer published in the Jiajing reign (1522–66) during the Ming assumes that the portrait of Confucius already existed in the temple in the Song period on the grounds that portraits of other sages were painted there in 1145. The Confucian Temple in the Wujiang County school featured a painted clay statue of Confucius and portraits of Confucian sages during the Yuan period. In Jiading County, a statue of Confucius was first built in 1249, and later in the Yuan dynasty the portraits of lesser Confucian sages adorned the temple. See *Gusu zhi*, 1506, 24.12a; *Wuyi zhi*, 1529, 6.1b; *Wu xianzhi*, 1642, 13.1a-2a.
16. Kojima Tsuyoshi, "Jukyō no gūjōkan," 71, 73; Sommer, "Destroying Confucius," 118–25.
17. *Gusu zhi*, 1506, 24.8b; *Wuyi zhi*, 1529, 5.17b-18a.
18. *Wuyi zhi*, 1529, 5.17b-18a.
19. Gu Tingchen, "Suzhou fuxue chuzuo liangwu congsi xiang ji," Gu Yuan, *Wujun wenbian*, *juan* 59.
20. Li Xian, et al., *Da Ming yitong zhi*, 3.12b-13a.
21. Li Xian, *Gurang ji*, 14.628.
22. *Wujiang zhi*, 1488, 1.16b-18a. When the shrine for local worthies was first built in Wujiang in 1468, tablets were also placed in it. It seems to me that at this moment both portraits and tablets coexisted in the shrine. The 1642 *Wu xianzhi* also mentions the

reembellishing of both the statues and the tablets in the Confucian Temple in 1525. See *Wu xianzhi*, 1642, 13.3b.

23. For more details on this event, see Huang Chin-shing, "Daotong yu zhitongzhijian"; Kojima Tsuyoshi, "Kasei no reisei kaikaku." However, the statue of Confucius in Qufu was preserved unharmed. See Huang Chin-shing, "The Cultural Politics," 275.

24. Huang Chin-shing, "The Cultural Politics," 274–76.

25. Ibid., 280; Sommer, "Destroying Confucius," 126; Idem., "Ming Taizu's Legacy," 99.

26. Some sources indicate that some of the shrines for local worthies did have tablets before 1530. For example, Shen Tao 沈燾 (1452–1515), a native of Changzhou County, Suzhou, says that, responding to the Chenghua Emperor's edict in 1487, a tablet of a local figure was installed in the *xiangxian ci*. See Chen Wei, *Wuzhong jinshi xinbian*, 5.180. Another source indicates the existence of tablets in the *xiangxian ci* in Hangzhou, Zhejiang, in the fourteenth century. See Xu Yikui, *Shifeng gao*, 14.382.

27. One may wonder how the ban on personal images in 1530 might square with the apparently thriving tradition of ancestral portraits during the Ming and Qing periods. As Jan Stuart and Evelyn Rawski have explained, wealthy civilian families worshipped at ancestor halls with tablets while simultaneously possessing portraits. See Stuart and Rawski, *Worshiping the Ancestors*, 47–48. The ban on images in 1530 did not interrupt their use for *private* ancestral worship, a condition underlying the proliferation of ancestral portraits. It should be emphasized here that the 1530 ritual reform largely targeted images displayed in public Confucian shrines of more official stature.

28. For example, Wang Shenzhong, *Zunyan ji*, 19.485; Ye Chunji, *Shidong ji*, 10.578-79; *Shanxi tongzhi*, 1734, 94.308; *Guangxi tongzhi*, 1733, 118.496; *Guizhou tongzhi*, 1741, 9.218.

29. *Zhaowen xianzhi*, 1731, 2.4ab.

30. *Yuanhe xianzhi*, 1761, 5.6b-10a. For additional examples during the Qing, see *Kun Xin liangxian xuxiu hezhi*, 1880, 4.13a. These cases indicate a significant decline in portraits or statues in the Confucian Temple or other shrines in the government schools following the 1530 reform.

31. Peng Dingqiu, *Nanyun wengao*, 4.2ab. I thank Lu Miaw-fen for introducing this material to me.

32. *Changzhou xianzhi*, 1753, 5.2b-15a.

33. See Gu Yanwu, "Xiangshe" 像設, *Qing jingshi wenbian*, 68.1699.

34. See *Kun Xin liangxian xuxiu hezhi*, 1880, 4.11b-13b.

35. Gu Zhentao, *Wumen biaoyin*, 306.

36. Gu Yuan, "Liyan" 例言, *Wujun wubai mingxian tuzhuanzan*, 35.

37. Cheng Zuqing, "Zhuxu" 朱序, *Lianchuan mingren huaxiang*, 3ab.

38. The Qianlong Emperor, "Xiangshe lun" 像設論, *Qing Gaozong (Qianlong) yuzhi shiwen quanji*, vol. 10, 900–901. Emphasis added.

39. It was not only in Confucian shrines where tablets were considered more legitimate objects of worship than visual representations. In the palace in Beijing, the Qing imperial family used tablets for ancestral worship in official state altars while imperial portraits were displayed in private quarters. See Stuart and Rawski, *Worshiping the Ancestors*, 44–45.

40. Ling Zuyi, *Taicang xiangxianxian huaxiang*, 6.
41. Yao Tang, *Runzhou xianxian lu*, 11b.
42. Ibid., 7ab.
43. In her research on the *Pictorial Biographies of the Sages' Traces* (*Shengji tu* 聖蹟圖), which are slightly different from the examples in this chapter in the sense that they are depictions of stories rather than just portraits, Julia Murray notes that the *Shengji tu* gained popularity in the late Ming as an alternative to the visual representations in shrines that had been removed by imperial fiat during the 1530 ritual reform. She also explains that the popularity of this genre should be set against the background of the flourishing print culture of the late Ming. See Murray, "The Temple of Confucius," 276. This explanation can be applied to the efflorescence of pictorial biographies of the Confucian sages and local worthies in the same period.
44. Lü Weiqi, *Shengxian xiangzan*, 4b.
45. Zhang Dai, "Xu" 序, *Yue sanbuxiu tuzan*, 1a.
46. Ibid., "Yuanxu" 原序, 2ab.
47. Gu Yuan, "Xu," *Shengmiao sidian tukao*, 1a.
48. Ibid., 2b.
49. Gu Yuan, *Gu shengxian xiang zhuanlüe*, 3b.
50. Julia Murray's study of the *shengji tu* is primarily concerned with examples from the late Ming. However, she does make the claim that the efflorescence of the *shengji tu* genre continued during the Qing; but the evidence she presents shows the absence of such materials during the high Qing and confirms that the genre only reappeared in the nineteenth century. See Murray, "Varied Views of the Sage," 234–35, 256.
51. Gu Yuan, *Gu shengxian xiang zhuanlüe,* 1ab.
52. Ebrey, "Portrait Sculptures," 87.
53. For more details on this debate, see Jiao Hong, *Yutang congyu*, 3.93, and Huang Chin-shing, "The Cultural Politics," 275.
54. Gu Yuan, *Gu shengxian xiang zhuanlüe*, 4b-5a.
55. Elman, *From Philosophy to Philology*, 237.
56. For the relationship of Tao Zhu and He Changling to the Yuelu Academy, see McMahon, "The Yuelu Academy," 85. For a thorough study of Tao Zhu's reform policies in Jiangsu, see Wei, *Tao Zhu zai Jiangnan*.
57. Xie, *Mingmo Qingchu de xuefeng*, 208–10; Polachek, *The Inner Opium War*, 41–59.
58. Duan, *Tao Zhu*, 99–101.
59. Commenting on the location of the Confucian shrines within the prefectural school grounds in Suzhou (which apparently also included the Shrine of Local Worthies), Peter J. Carroll indicated that such proximity to the administrative office enabled the state's closer oversight. See Carroll, *Between Heaven and Modernity*, 109.
60. While a collective biography of Qing Confucian scholars compiled in the mid-Jiaqing period by the influential official and scholar Ruan Yuan 阮元 listed Gu Yanwu in eighth, later in the reign his name moved to the top in the official biographies presented to the emperor. Gu Chun, a native of Wu County who worked at the Institute of Historiography at that time, was responsible for this change. See Wang Fan-sen, "Qingdai ruzhe de quanshentang," 74–76.

Chapter 6. State Control of Local Gazetteers and Private Local Literature

1. Portions of this chapter have been published in Korean as "18 segi Ch'ŏngjo ŭi chibangji, chibang munhŏn t'ongjech'aek kwa Chang Haksŏng ŭi pangjiron," *Yŏksa hakpo* 192 (2006): 255–303.

2. Huang Chin-shing, *The Price.*

3. Mou, "Lun Qingdai shixue"; Ho, "Lun Qing Gaozong"; Idem., "Qingdai qianqi junzhu." For a discussion of the process of establishing a centralized order in the early Qing, see also Kishimoto, *Min Shin kōtai*, 1–25.

4. Elliott, *Emperor Qianlong*, 124.

5. Guy, *The Emperor's Four Treasuries*, 157–200.

6. *QSL-QL*, 1054.87.

7. On the Qing government attempts under Qianlong to extend state control to the publishing industry, see Brook, *The Chinese State*, 125–36.

8. Xiong Xuepeng, "Qing yan sixiu zhishu zhi li," *Huang Qing zouyi*, 57.1a-4a.

9. Zhou Shunchang was accused by Wei Zhongxian on a false charge. In 1626, Suzhou residents launched a collective protest against his arrest commonly known as the "Kaidu zhi bian" 開讀之變.

10. *LKSS*, 617 (QL 31/2/18).

11. On the compilation process of the *yitong zhi*, see Qiao, "Da Qing yitong zhi," 115–22.

12. *Qinding Xuezheng quanshu*, 4.14b-15b.

13. *Wangjiang xianzhi,* 1768, "Quanxu" 全序, 2b-4a.

14. *Lu'an fuzhi*, 1770, *juan zhi shou* 卷之首.1a.

15. *Chizhou fuzhi,* 1779, 5b-6a; *Shaoxing fuzhi*, 1792, "Xingshi" 姓氏, 1a. A few more such cases can be found in the 1774 Qufu County gazetteer, Shandong; 1776 Zichuan County gazetteer, Shandong; 1785 Xintai County gazetteer, Shandong.

16. *Chang Zhao hezhi*, 1805, 4a.

17. Zhou Xun, *Zhongguo de difangzhi*, 114.

18. Qiao, "Da Qing yitong zhi," 117. According to Qiao's study, 1,560 local gazetteers were compiled from 1672 to 1740, the period that spanned the making of the first *Gazetteer of the Great Qing Unification*. But this number dropped to 1,384 during the following eighty years, from 1741 to 1820. See p. 118 in his article. Qiao doesn't, however, explain the reasons for this drop nor the way that it was experienced differently throughout the empire.

19. The *Gazetteer of the Great Qing Unification* was revised during the later Qianlong years to reflect the expansion of Qing territory. It was presented to the emperor in 1784 and printed in 1790. See Wilkinson, *Chinese History*, 839; and Qiao, "Da Qing yitong zhi," 117. The third version was completed in 1820 and printed in 1842.

20. Scholars have suggested deliberate state efforts to promote North China economically and culturally during the eighteenth century. Susan Naquin and Evelyn Rawski have concluded that the Yongzheng and Qianlong Emperors showed a willingness to pour large sums of money into the Yellow River conservancy and the Grand Canal main-

tenance in the North. According to them, North China in the eighteenth century "appears to have received more than its share of government funds—for price stabilization, waterway and road maintenance, and local defense." See Naquin and Rawski, *Chinese Society*, 144–45. In addition to Huguang and Sichuan, northern provinces seem to have been the chief beneficiaries of the land reclamation vigorously pursued throughout China during the Kangxi and Yongzheng periods. See Peng Yuxin, *Qingdai tudi kaikenshi*, tables on p. 70 and p. 73. In the cultural realm, Beijing increasingly became the empire's center during the eighteenth century. Susan Naquin has illustrated that, by 1800, Beijing's status "as a political and cultural center was much less vulnerable to challenge from the Lower Yangzi cities than it had been in the Ming." See Naquin, *Peking*, 469. According to Tobie Meyer-Fong, the relative positions of Beijing and Jiangnan in the cultural hierarchy reversed in the eighteenth century, as the capital acquired new cultural weight with the consolidation and centralization of the empire. Meyer-Fong, *Building Culture*, 167.

21. *QSL-QL*, 836.155, 841.239.

22. *QSL-QL*, 1095.689.

23. Ibid.

24. Qian was classified as a "twice-serving minister" by the edict of Qianlong 41 (1776) that elevated loyal Ming martyrs and degraded twice-serving ministers. On Qianlong's policy shift regarding the "twice-serving ministers," see Crossley, *A Translucent Mirror*, 291–96.

25. *Chang Zhao hezhi*, 1805, 5b.

26. On the process of this project, see Huang Aiping, *Siku quanshu zuanxiu yanjiu*, 302–11; Li Changqing, *Siku quanshu chuban yanjiu*, 43–73.

27. Scholars disagree on whether the Compendium's publication occurred in 1789, 1793–94, or 1795. See Chen Xiaohua, "*Siku zongmu xue*," 40.

28. Zhang Chuanfeng, "*Siku quanshu zongmu*," 222–302. According to Zhang, Qianlong's directives were political rather than purely scholarly, conveying the emperor's plans for the management of the state. See Zhang Chuanfeng, "*Siku quanshu zongmu*," 225–26.

29. *SKZMTY*, 57.1581-82.

30. Official history did play a significant role in determining the value of local histories, as observed in the *Liang Zhe mingxian lu* 兩浙名賢錄 from the Ming period. The Compendium compilers stated: "Among the people listed, those based on the official histories constitute only two to three out of ten, while those based on local gazetteers are six to seven out of ten. Since this book was written on the basis of words that embellished the locality, it cannot be said that the book is correct and authentic." *SKZMTY*, 62.1710.

31. *SKZMTY*, 45.1228.

32. On the brink of recovering Kaifeng, Henan, from the Jin, Yue was summoned to Hangzhou, the capital of the Southern Song, and subsequently imprisoned and executed by Qin Kui.

33. Fuheng, et al., *Yupi lidai tongjian jilan*, 87.8a. The *Yupi lidai tongjian jilan* is an annalistic history from ancient times to the Ming period compiled in 1767. For more details, see Wilkinson, *Chinese History*, 618–19.

34. Fuheng, et al., *Yupi lidai tongjian jilan*, 86.6b, 87.19b.
35. Ibid., 87.18b.
36. Ibid., 86.9b-10a.
37. Ibid., 83.28b.
38. *QSL-QL*, 533.721, 655.333, 730.33, 1102.750, 1201.54.
39. *QSL-QL*, 383.34. It should be noted that, during the Ming-Qing transition, the Qing imperial ideology drew its legitimacy from the previous conquest dynasties, including the Jin. Qianlong's historical view, however, was to consider the Song (including Southern Song) and Yuan as the legitimate (*zhengtong* 正統) dynasties, rather than Liao or Jin. See Zhang Chuanfeng, "*Siku quanshu zongmu*," 235–39. On early Qing rulers' (Nurhaci and Hong Taiji) use of the Jin precedents and the efforts to link the Qing imperial ancestry with the Jin, see Elliott, "Whose Empire Shall It Be?" 44–59; and Elliott, *Emperor Qianlong*, 59.
40. *SKZMTY*, 61.1665.
41. On the historical development of the meaning of the words *gong* and *si* in China, see Mizoguchi, *Chūgoku*, 3–89.
42. *SKZMTY*, 61.1665.
43. *SKZMTY*, 63.1733.
44. *SKZMTY*, 63.1723.
45. *SKZMTY*, 61.1671.
46. *SKZMTY*, 61.1674.
47. *SKZMTY*, 68.1813.
48. *SKZMTY*, 73.1937.
49. *SKZMTY*, 74.1957.
50. *SKZMTY*, 68.1834-35.
51. *Jiajing Weiyang zhi* 嘉靖 惟陽志 (*SKZMTY*, 73.1939), *Guacang huiji* 括蒼滙紀 (*SKZMTY*, 74.1951), and *Haichang waizhi* 海昌外志 (*SKZMTY*, 74.1965).
52. See, for instance, comments on *Xiachuan zhi* 峽川志, *Songgu shu* 淞故述, *Quannan zazhi* 泉南雜志, and *Jiuhua shanzhi* 九華山志. *SKZMTY*, 76.2014, 2031, 2045, 2047.
53. *Tangshan xianzhi*, 1767, 2a-4b.
54. *Lou xianzhi*, 1788, 1b-2b.
55. *Shaoxing fuzhi*, 1792, "Xu," 3b.
56. *Chizhou fuzhi*, 1779, "Fanli" 凡例, 3ab.
57. See, for example, the 1812 Shanghai County gazetteer (Jiangsu), 1806 Jing County gazetteer (Anhui), 1801 Changshan County gazetteer (Shandong), and 1808 Yucheng County gazetteer (Shandong). During the Jiaqing years, gazetteers with prefaces by provincial education commissioners or their names as reviewers could still be found. See, for instance, the 1803 Luzhou prefectural gazetteer of Anhui, 1815 Xiao County gazetteer of Anhui, 1817 Songjiang prefectural gazetteer of Jiangsu, and 1819 Huaiyuan County gazetteer of Anhui. Among the Daoguang gazetteers that I consulted, provincial education commissioners wrote prefaces for the 1822 *Ruijin xianzhi* (Jiangxi) and the 1824 *Ningdu zhilizhou zhi* (Jiangxi). However, during this period, the list of the gazetteers that discard such a practice becomes far lengthier. See, for instance, the 1823 edition and 1832 reprint of the *Fuliang xianzhi* (Jiangxi), 1824 *Suzhou fuzhi* (Jiangsu),

1826 *Dingyuan xianzhi* (Anhui), 1826 *Kun Xin liangxian zhi* (Jiangsu), and the 1830 *Laian xianzhi* (Anhui).

58. Here private local literature refers to the works written in prose on local themes. As for poetry anthologies in the Suzhou area published during the Yongzheng and Qianlong periods, I have been able to identify only one: *Haiyu shiyuan* 海虞詩苑, an anthology of Changshu County, compiled by Wang Yingkui 王應奎 (1684–1757) and first published in 1759.

59. This material is housed in the Shanghai Library.

60. See table of contents in Gu Yuan, *Wujun wenbian*. The work was not published, and it has been preserved in manuscript form in the Suzhou Museum.

61. Dong Guohua 董國華, preface to *Wujun wenbian*; Gu Yuan, *Jinyu ji*, 2.14a.

62. Prefaces to *Wujun wenbian* by Zhu Jian 朱珔 (*Jinyu ji*, 2.11b) and by Dong Guohua (*Jinyu ji*, 2.14a).

63. Liang Zhangju, preface to *Wujun wenbian*, 15a.

64. Zhu Jian, preface to *Wujun wenbian* (*Jinyu ji*, 2.11a).

65. Gu Yuan, *Wujun wenbian*, 11b.

66. The decades-long compilation of this work began around 1805.

67. Gu Zhentao, "Wumen biaoyin shi" 吳門表隱詩, *Wumen biaoyin*, 1–95.

68. Gu Zhentao, "Liyan," *Wumen biaoyin*, 1.

69. Zhu Jian, preface to *Wumen biaoyin*, 7.

70. Li Qingjie 李清傑, preface to *Wumen biaoyin*, 14.

71. Gu Lu, *Qingjia lu*, 1.

72. Gu Cheng 顧承, preface to *Qingjia lu*, 1.

73. Gu Lu, "Liyan," *Qingjia lu*, 2.

74. Gu Lu, "Liyan," *Qingjia lu*, 2.

75. Gu Lu, "Fanli," *Tongqiao yizhuo lu*. Gu Lu's third book was entitled *Wuqu fengtu lu* 吳趨風土錄 and similar in nature to his *Qingjia lu*.

76. Yao spent almost a decade writing his work, from 1829 to 1838. Yao Chengxu, "Qianyan" 前言, *Wuqu fanggu lu*, 2–3.

77. The counties under Suzhou, Songjiang, and Changzhou 常州 prefectures were divided into two while Taicang was elevated into an independent department by an edict in Yongzheng 3.

78. Besides the local literature mentioned above, Suzhou literati produced similar works during the first half of the nineteenth century: Zhang Zilin 張紫琳, *Honglan yicheng* 紅蘭逸乘 (about 1822); Wei Guangfu 韋光黻 (1789–1852), *Wenjian chanyou lu* 聞見闡幽錄 (exact compilation date unknown); Xixi shanren 西溪山人, *Wumen huafang lu* 吳門畫舫錄 (1803 or 1804); Ge Zhongsheng 箇中生, *Wumen huafang xulu* 吳門畫舫續錄 (about 1813).

79. For similar official and literati activities in Yangzhou, see Meyer-Fong, *Building Culture*, 116–27; and Finnane, *Speaking of Yangzhou*, 283–94. On Hunan, McMahon, "The Yuelu Academy," 86, 95–96; and Platt, *Provincial Patriots*, 820. On Canton, Miles, *The Sea of Learning*, 127–63. Wang Bing argues that the genre of local poetry collection emerged massively from the mid-Qianlong period. If we look more closely at the examples he provides, however, we can confirm that an absolute majority of the collections

were published in the Jiaqing and Daoguang periods, not in the Qianlong. See Wang Bing, "Lun Qingdai Qing shixuanben," 196–98.

80. Frontier knowledge about Central Asia and western Asia, once carefully guarded against the Hans and monopolized by Manchus and Mongols in the eighteenth century, increasingly became a topic of discussion among Han scholars in the early nineteenth century. See Mosca, "Empire and the Circulation."

81. For the list of the books related to Suzhou history published or republished in the early nineteenth century by Zhang Haipeng, see Shanghai tushuguan, ed., *Zhongguo congshu zonglu*, vol. 1, 154–62.

82. See Huang and Gao, *Zhongguo gudai cangshulou yanjiu*, 120, 150, 159, 170, 186, 204; for Siming, 214–15; for Yuyao, 220, 224; for Wenzhou, 233–34, 238–39; for Yongjia, 240, 285, 287; Gu Zhixing, *Zhejiang cangshujia cangshulou*, 170; Zheng Weizhang, *Wenxianjia tongkao*, vol. 1, 324.

83. Ye Dehui, "Ke xiang xianzhe zhi shu" 刻鄉先哲之書, *Shulin qinghua*, 209–10.

84. Huang and Gao, *Zhongguo gudai cangshulou yanjiu*, 224.

85. *Siku jinhuishu congkan*, index.

86. Struve, *The Ming-Qing Conflict*, 69–79.

87. Platt, *Provincial Patriots*, 11–19.

Chapter 7. Bandit or Hero?

1. Material for this chapter first appeared in Han Seunghyun, "Bandit or Hero? Memories of Zhang Shicheng in Late Imperial and Republican Suzhou," *Harvard Journal of Asiatic Studies* 68, no. 2 (2008): 115–62, and it is reprinted here with permission.

2. Recently, scholars have been interested in the portrayal of the Ming founder by later generations in China and the neighboring states; see the special issue of *Ming Studies* 50 (2004). However, no study to date explores the perception of Zhu in terms of his rivalry with Zhang Shicheng and regional differences.

3. In his study of the Boxer Uprising, Paul A. Cohen introduced three ways of knowing history: through events, experience, and myth. This chapter is a study of myth, or the ways in which people invoked the past to serve present purposes. For the explanation of the terminology "myth," see Cohen, *History in Three Keys*, 211–22.

4. For example, *Ming shilu (Hongwu)*, 21.299-301, 304, 309, 25.363.

5. Song Lian, et al., *Yuan shi*, 140.3377, 187.4289.

6. *Ming shilu (Hongwu)*, 25.369.

7. Ibid., 25.370.

8. Ibid., 25.368.

9. Zhu believed he emerged victorious thanks to his efforts in avoiding unnecessary casualties. See Martin W. Huang, "Sage, Hero, Bandit," 84.

10. *Ming shilu (Hongwu)*, 25.364.

11. Ibid., 25.371.

12. Ye Ziqi, *Caomuzi*, 3shang.52; Changgu zhenyi, *Nongtian yuhua*, *juan* shang.4; Liu Zhen, *Guochu shiji*, 35b.

13. Ye Ziqi, *Caomuzi*, 3shang.53.

14. Danjō, "Min ōchō seiritsuki"; Idem., "Gen-Min kōtai."

15. See Zheng Kesheng, *Ming Qing shi tanshi*, 34–85; Shimizu, "Min Taiso"; Marmé, *Suzhou*, 74.

16. Wu Kuan, *Ping Wu lu,* 29.1ab.

17. Wen Zhengming, "Ti Qiji quancuo zhi hou" 題七姬權厝志後, *Wen Zhengming ji*, 21.525-26.

18. Wen Zhengming, "Xishan qiuji tu ba" 溪山秋霽圖跋, *Wen Zhengming ji*, 23.564-65.

19. Yang Xunji, "Taifu shoucheng" 太傅收城, *Wuzhong guyu*, 365. I am grateful to Li Cho-ying for bringing this material to my attention.

20. Ibid.

21. Ibid.

22. Zhu Yunming, *Yeji*, 37–38.

23. Lu Rong, *Shuyuan zaji*, 3.33.

24. Xu Zhenqing (1479–1511), a native of Suzhou and a renowned writer, also tells a similar story. See Xu Zhenqing, *Jiansheng yewen*, 20–21.

25. Zhu Yunming, *Yeji*, 35.

26. Ibid., 33–34. For details regarding this event, see Marmé, *Suzhou*, 76. The account of Suzhou native Huang Wei (*js* 1490) also centered around familiar motifs, such as atrocities committed against Suzhou by the Ming armies, Zhang's voluntary surrender to protect locals, and Taizu's punishment of the official who rebuilt the prefectural building on Zhang's old palace site. See Huang Wei, *Pengchuang leiji*, 1.594-95.

27. Lang Ying, *Qixiu leigao*, 8.61-62.

28. Huang Xingzeng, *Wufeng lu*, 1.791; Hou Dian, *Xiqiao yeji*, 5.617.

29. *Gusu zhi*, 1506, 36.16b-17a, 18b. This description of the occupation of Suzhou was cited verbatim from the work of Tao Zongyi (fourteenth century), who displayed a hostile view of Zhang Shicheng. See his *Nancun chuogeng lu*, 29.358. Other mid-Ming writers not from Suzhou who portrayed the late Yuan from a similar standpoint are: Gao Dai (*js* 1550), *Hongyou lu*, and Wu Guolun (*js* 1550), *Chen Zhang shilüe*.

30. According to Peter Bol, the local elites of Jinhua, Zhejiang, embraced the Neo-Confucian position as the ground of their identity from the latter half of the fifteenth century. This intellectual movement stressed moral self-discipline and the literati's responsibility to the community. Its leaders were critical of the court, challenging its position as the source of moral and cultural authority. See Bol, "Neo-Confucianism and Local Society," 269–83.

31. From the mid- to late Ming period, writers reexamined the image of Fang Xiaoru, a martyr who had been executed by the Yongle Emperor. This shift in Fang's portrayal, coupled with the efforts of Suzhou literati regarding Zhang Shicheng, displayed a degree of literati activism and suggested a more relaxed cultural climate following the mid-Ming period. On the reconstruction of Fang Xiaoru, see Ditmanson, "Death and Fidelity."

32. During the late Ming period, many officials and scholars harbored an idealized image of the founder and the early years of the dynasty. The scholar-official Guan Zhidao went so far as to portray Zhu as a sage ruler who had reunified the Way in the

person of the emperor. See Weisfogel, "Invoking Zhu Yuanzhang," 33. The image of Zhu as an effective and "good" ruler also pervaded the thinking of such twentieth-century Communist leaders as Mao Zedong. See Schneewind, *Community Schools*, 6–9.

33. For example, Zha Jizuo, *Zuiwei lu*, liezhuan 6.1324-32; *Huangchao benji*, 11.46-50; Fu Weilin, *juan* 90, "Wu Zhang Shicheng ji" 吳張士誠記, *Ming shu*; Jiao Hong, *juan* 119, "Zhang Shicheng zhuan" 張士誠傳, *Guochao xianzheng lu*; Huang Jingfang, *Guoshi weiyi*, 1.252-53; Gu Yingtai, *juan* 4, "Taizu ping Wu" 太祖平吳, *Mingshi jishi benmo*. Jiang Yikui, a native of Changzhou prefecture adjoining Suzhou, also wrote derogatory comments on Zhang Shicheng. See Jiang Yikui, *Yaoshantang waiji*, 74.678-79.

34. For example, Fu Weilin, *Ming shu*, 90.1816; Zha Jizuo, *Zuiwei lu*, liezhuan 6.1328; Jiang Fen (*js* 1637), "Taizu ping Wu" 太祖平吳, *Mingshi jishi*, 311–12.

35. Shi Ce, *Longping jishi*, *juan* 15. Tan Qian's (1594–1657) *Guo que* provides an interesting case. Although Tan attempted to legitimize Ming Taizu, he regarded it as inappropriate to place the prefix denoting "bandit" before the names of Zhang Shicheng or Chen Youliang because they had never been Zhu Yuanzhang's ministers. See his *Guo que*, 1.277.

36. Qian Qianyi, *Guochu qunxiong shilüe*, *juan*s 6–8. Compiled around 1626, its manuscripts were preserved by several book collectors during the Qing period, but only in 1913 was it finally published by a bibliophile in Wuxing County, Zhejiang, named Zhang Junheng 張鈞衡 (1871–1927).

37. Qian Qianyi, *Guochu qunxiong shilüe*, 6.164-65.

38. This biography was included in his literary collection published in 1696. See Zhang Fuxiang, *juan* 1, "Wu wang Zhang Shicheng zhuan" 吳王張士誠傳, *Yiguicao chuke*. For the original publication date of this work, see Xia Quan, *Tuian biji*, 12.9b.

39. Zhang Fuxiang, "Wu wang Zhang Shicheng zhuan," 33a.

40. Ibid., 38a.

41. Ibid., 39ab.

42. Zhang Xuecheng, "Bo Zhang Fuxiang lunwen," *Wenshi tongyi xinbian xinzhu*, *waipian yi*, 478–79.

43. Ibid.

44. Ibid.

45. Ibid.

46. *Ming shi*, 123.3692.

47. *SKZMTY*, 58.1606-7.

48. *Qinding Huangchao tongzhi*, 53.666.

49. Bei Yong, *Qiji yonglin*.

50. Pan Shi'en, "Qiji zhi bian" 七姬志辨, *Qiji yonglin*, 3–4.

51. Ibid., 4.

52. Bei Yong, *Qiji yonglin*, 44–45.

53. Chen Peizhi, "Qiji quancuozhi lun" 七姬權厝志論, *Qiji yonglin*, 4–7.

54. Bei Yong, *Qiji yonglin*, 21.

55. Ibid., 41.

56. Ibid.

57. The biographies of Zhang Shicheng and his followers are included in his two works, *Tuian biji* and *Zili jiuwen*. For Zhang's biography, see Xia Quan, "Zhang Shicheng," *Zili jiuwen*, 5.1a-7b.

58. Xia Quan, *Tuian biji*, 4.14a. Wang Hongxu had participated in the compilation of the *Ming shi* and used the occasion to write Zhang's biography.

59. Ibid.

60. Ibid.

61. Ibid., 4.15a.

62. Ibid., 6.7ab.

63. Xia Quan forged close ties with several active Suzhou scholars, among them Gu Yuan. During Gu's visit to Xia in Taizhou in 1838, the two men discussed the tomb inscription of the seven concubines. Gu mentioned that he had kept a copy of the inscription's rare rubbings and had engraved it on a stone. Gu later sent a rubbing to Xia. When Gu visited Xia once again in 1840, he wrote out the inscription on paper in his own calligraphy. Ibid., 14.5b.

64. In addition to the hostile views in the *Qiji yonglin*, a work by Zhou Ang, a Suzhou scholar of the late eighteenth and early nineteenth centuries, entitled *Yuanji fumangzhi* was also critical of Zhang.

65. As Steven B. Miles has shown, the Southern Han, a local regime based in Guangzhou during the Five Dynasties period, became a topic in early nineteenth-century poetic and historical writings in Guangdong. One author clearly identified himself with this regime by adding the word "our" to the army and city of the Southern Han. See Miles, "Rewriting the Southern Han." In contrast to the Guangzhou literati, who generally held a negative view of the Southern Han, Suzhou literati seriously challenged the existing standard interpretation of Zhang.

66. Fei Shuwei, "Zhang Wu wang mu Caotaifei mubeiji," Zhi and Ren, eds., *Wu wang Zhang Shicheng zaiji*, 5.5b-6b.

67. Fei Shuwei, "Zhang Wu wang mubei," Zhi and Ren, eds., *Wu wang Zhang Shicheng zaiji*, 5.4b-5b.

68. Han Guojun, preface to *Wu wang Zhang Shicheng zaiji*.

69. "Yili" 義例, *Wu wang Zhang Shicheng zaiji*.

70. *Wu wang Zhang Shicheng zaiji*, 4.1b-2a.

71. Ibid., 4.2a-3a.

72. Ibid., 3.8b-9a.

73. Ibid., 4.4a.

74. Ibid., 4.5ab.

75. Ibid., 4.19ab.

Conclusion

1. See Rowe, "The Public Sphere"; Rankin, "The Origins"; Wakeman Jr., "The Civil Society."

2. On the relationship between elite managers and the local officials, see also Rankin, "Some Observations," 164–68.

3. Rowe, "The Problem," 147.

4. Zelin, "The Yung-cheng Reign," 197, 199, 218–20. For the Qianlong Emperor's hysteric reaction to the Jiangnan queue clipping incident in 1768, see Kuhn, *Soulstealers*. For his watchful stance toward the books produced in Jiangnan, see Brook, *The Chinese State*, 134.

5. For Yongzheng and Qianlong's efforts to impose order on the behavior of the examination candidates, see Han Seunghyun, "The Punishment," 134–46.

6. See, for example, Kuhn, "Civil Society."

7. Contrary to the general assumption of the Qing historians that viewed the post-Taiping period as marking the beginning of the increase of the Han Chinese in the positions of governor-general and governor, Lawrence Kessler has identified the Jiaqing period as the starting point for this trend. For Kessler, the expansion of Han provincial officials after the Taiping was a second spurt. See Kessler, "Ethnic Composition," 499.

8. Kuhn, *Rebellion and Its Enemies*.

9. Rankin, *Elite Activism*, 136–69.

10. Wang Wensheng, *White Lotus Rebels*, 156.

11. Elman, *Classicism*, 282–306. See also McMahon, "Dynastic Decline, Heshen," 240–46.

12. Han Seunghyun, "The Punishment," 133–65; Idem., "Wenzhi."

13. Wang Wensheng, *White Lotus Rebels*, 166–82.

14. Rowe, "Rewriting the Qing Constitution," 210–11.

15. Kuhn, "Ideas"; Idem., *Origins*.

16. Polachek, *The Inner Opium War*, chaps. 1 and 2.

17. Polachek, "Literati Groups," 202–4.

18. Polachek, *The Inner Opium War*, 76–77.

19. Ibid., 86–87.

20. Ibid., 59–61.

21. Tō, "Minshinki kiho suiriron."

22. Polachek, "Literati Groups," 201.

23. Polachek, "Gentry Hegemony."

24. Rankin, *Elite Activism*.

25. Pan died shortly before the city of Nanjing fell to the Taiping rebels in the mid-nineteenth century. He was, however, posthumously portrayed as a god-like figure in a *baojuan* (precious volume) work authored by his philanthropist friend Yu Zhi 余治. In this *baojuan*, Pan is depicted as someone who tried to rescue as many residents of Nanjing as possible in the underworld after they died at the hands of the rebels. For more details, see Meyer-Fong, *What Remains*, 39–46.

26. Polachek, "Literati Groups," 189.

27. Polachek, *The Inner Opium War*, 60.

28. Han Seunghyun, "Re-inventing Local Tradition," 79–80.

29. Fei Lanchi, "Yu Qiu nanping taishou tongnian shu" 與邱南屏太守同年書, *Qu'an wenchao,* 4a.

30. Ibid., 4a-9a.

31. *Wujiangxian xuzhi*, 1879, 19.2ab.

Bibliography

Abbreviations used in the Bibliography

CJCB	*Congshu jicheng chubian* 叢書集成初編. Beijing: Zhonghua shuju, 1985.
LKSS	*Like shishu* 禮科史書. Beijing: First Historical Archives.
QHDSL	*Qing huidian shili* 清會典事例. 1899. Beijing, Zhonghua shuju, 1991.
QSL	*Qing shilu* 清實錄. Beijing: Zhonghua shuju, 1985–87. *QSL-YZ*, *QSL-QL*, *QSL-JQ*, *QSL-DG*, *QSL-XF*, and *QSL-TZ* stand for the Yongzheng, Qianlong, Jiaqing, Daoguang, Xianfeng, and Tongzhi reign portions of the *Qing shilu*, respectively.
SKQS	*Yingyin Wenyuange Siku quanshu* 影印文淵閣四庫全書. Taipei: Taiwan shangwu yinshuguan, 1983.
SKZMTY	*Siku quanshu zongmu tiyao* 四庫全書總目提要. Shijiazhuang, China: Hebei renmin chubanshe, 2005.
TYGX	*Tianyige cang Mingdai fangzhi xuankan xubian* 天一閣藏明代方志選刊續編. Shanghai: Shanghai shudian, 1990.
XXSKQS	*Xuxiu Siku quanshu* 續修四庫全書. Shanghai: Shanghai guji chubanshe, 1995–99.
YMSLBJ	*Yuan Ming shiliao biji congkan* 元明史料筆記叢刊. Beijing: Zhonghua shuju, 1997.
ZDJAH	*Zhongguo difangzhi jicheng Anhui fuxianzhi ji* 中國地方志集成 安徽府縣志輯. Nanjing, China: Jiangsu guji chubanshe, 1998.
ZDJJS	*Zhongguo difangzhi jicheng Jiangsu fuxianzhi ji* 中國地方志集成 江蘇府縣志輯. Nanjing, China: Jiangsu guji chubanshe, 1991.
ZDJJX	*Zhongguo difangzhi jicheng Jiangxi fuxianzhi ji* 中國地方志集成 江西府縣志輯. Nanjing, China: Jiangsu guji chubanshe, 1996.
ZDJSD	*Zhongguo difangzhi jicheng Shandong fuxianzhi ji* 中國地方志集成 山東府縣志輯. Nanjing, China: Fenghuang chubanshe, 2004.
ZDJSH	*Zhongguo difangzhi jicheng Shanghai fuxianzhi ji* 中國地方志集成 上海府縣志輯. Shanghai: Shanghai shudian, 1991.

ZDJZJ *Zhongguo difangzhi jicheng Zhejiang fuxianzhi ji* 中國地方志集成 浙江府縣志輯. Shanghai: Shanghai shudian, 1993.

ZHZQS Li Wenhai 李文海, and Xia Mingfang 夏明方, eds., *Zhongguo huangzheng quanshu* 中國荒政全書. Beijing: Beijing guji chubanshe, 2004.

ZYJXB *Zhongguo yeshi jicheng xubian* 中國野史集成續編. Chengdu, China: Bashu shushe, 2000.

Antony, Robert J. "Subcounty Officials, the State, and Local Communities in Guangdong Province, 1644–1860." In *Dragons, Tigers, and Dogs: Qing Crisis Management and the Boundaries of State Power in Late Imperial China*. Edited by Robert J. Antony and Jane Kate Leonard, 27–59. Ithaca, N.Y.: East Asia Program, Cornell University, 2002.

Antony, Robert J., and Jane Kate Leonard, eds. *Dragons, Tigers, and Dogs: Qing Crisis Management and the Boundaries of State Power in Late Imperial China*. Ithaca, N.Y.: East Asia Program, Cornell University, 2002.

Bartlett, Beatrice S. *Monarchs and Ministers: The Grand Council in Mid-Ch'ing China, 1723–1820*. Berkeley: University of California Press, 1991.

Bei Yong 貝墉. *Qiji yonglin* 七姬詠林. In *Wuzhong wenxian xiaocongshu* 吳中文獻小叢書. Suzhou, China: Jiangsusheng li Suzhou tushuguan, 1939.

Bol, Peter K. "Neo-Confucianism and Local Society, Twelfth to Sixteenth Century: A Case Study." In *The Song-Yuan-Ming Transition in Chinese History*. Edited by Paul J. Smith and Richard von Glahn, 241–83. Cambridge, Mass.: Harvard University Asia Center, 2003.

———. "The 'Localist Turn' and 'Local Identity' in Later Imperial China." *Late Imperial China* 24, no. 2 (2003): 1–50.

———. "The Rise of Local History: History, Geography, and Culture in Southern Song and Yuan Wuzhou." *Harvard Journal of Asiatic Studies* 16, no. 1 (2001): 37–76.

Brook, Timothy. *The Chinese State in Ming Society*. London and New York: Routledge Curzon, 2005.

———. "The Spatial Structure of Ming Local Administration." *Late Imperial China* 6, no. 1 (1985): 1–55.

Carlitz, Katherine. "Shrines, Governing-Class Identity, and the Cult of Widow Fidelity in Mid-Ming Jiangnan." *Journal of Asian Studies* 56, no. 3 (1997): 612–40.

Carroll, Peter J. *Between Heaven and Modernity: Reconstructing Suzhou, 1895–1937*. Stanford, Calif.: Stanford University Press, 2006.

Chang Zhao hezhi 常昭合志. 1805. Housed at the Rare Books Room, Harvard-Yenching Library.

Chang Zhao hezhigao 常昭合志稿. 1904. In *ZDJJS*.

Chang, Michael G. *A Court on Horseback-Imperial Touring and the Construction of Qing Rule, 1680–1785*. Cambridge, Mass.: Harvard University Asia Center, 2007.

Changgu zhenyi 長谷眞逸. *Nongtian yuhua* 農田餘話. In *CJCB*.

Changshan xianzhi 長山縣志. 1801. In *ZDJSD*.

Changshu xianzhi 常熟縣志. 1687. In *ZDJJS*.

Changzhou xianzhi 長洲縣志. 1753. In *ZDJJS*.

Chen Feng 陳鋒. *Qingdai junfei yanjiu* 清代軍費研究. Wuchang, China: Wuhan daxue chubanshe, 1992.

Chen Gao 陳鎬, ed. *Quelizhi* 闕里誌. Supplemented and enlarged by Kong Yinzhi 孔胤植. Jinan, China: Shandong youyi shushe, 1989.

Chen Hua 陳樺, and Liu Zongzhi 劉宗志. *Jiuzai yu jipin—Zhongguo fengjian shidai de shehui jiuzhu huodong, 1750–1911* 救災與濟貧—中國封建時代的社會救助活動. Beijing: Zhongguo renmin daxue chubanshe, 2005.

Chen Luan 陳鑾, et al. "Chongjun Baimaohe quanan" 重濬白茆河全案, "Chongjun Diao'e he deng he quanan" 重濬鵰鶚河等河全案, "Chongjun Jiangning chenghe quanan" 重濬江寧城河全案, "Chongjun Lianhu jianzha quanan" 重濬練湖建閘全案, "Chongjun Liuhe quanan" 重濬劉河全案, "Chongjun Mengdu deng sanhe quanan" 重濬孟瀆等三河全案, "Chongjun Puhuaitang quanan" 重濬蒲匯塘全案, "Chongjun Qipuhe quanan" 重濬七浦河全案, "Chongjun Su, Song, Tai sanfuzhou he quanan" 重濬蘇松太三府州河全案, "Chongjun Suzhoufu chenghe an" 重濬蘇州府城河案, "Chongjun Wusongjiang quanan" 重濬吳淞江全案, "Chongjun Zhangjiatang deng he quanan" 重濬張家塘等河全案, "Xiujun Fushan chengyuan tanghe quanan" 修濬福山城垣塘河全案. In *Chongjun Jiangnan shuili quanshu* 重濬江南水利全書. In *Siku weishoushu jikan* 四庫未收書輯刊. Beijing: Beijing chubanshe, 1997–2000.

Chen Wei 陳暐, ed. *Wuzhong jinshi xinbian* 吳中金石新編. In *SKQS*.

Chen Xiaohua 陳曉華. "*Siku zongmu xue*" *shi yanjiu* "四庫總目學"史研究. Beijing: Shangwu yinshuguan, 2008.

Cheng Zuqing 程祖慶. *Lianchuan mingren huaxiang* 練川名人畫像. Publisher unknown. 1850. Reprint 1878.

Chizhou fuzhi 池州府志. 1779. In *ZDJAH*.

Cohen, Paul A. *Discovering History in China: American Historical Writing on the Recent Chinese Past*. New York: Columbia University Press, 2010 [1984].

———. *History in Three Keys: The Boxers as Event, Experience, and Myth*. New York: Columbia University Press, 1997.

Crossley, Pamela Kyle. *A Translucent Mirror: History and Identity in Qing Imperial Ideology*. Berkeley: University of California Press, 1999.

Da Qing huidian 大清會典. Qianlong edition, in *SKQS*; Jiaqing edition, in *Jindai Zhongguo shiliao congkan* 近代中國史料叢刊. Taipei: Wenhai chubanshe, 1991.

Dai Yi 戴逸. *Qianlong di ji qishidai* 乾隆帝及其時代. Beijing: Zhongguo renmin daxue chubanshe, 1992.

Dai Yingcong. "Civilians Go into Battle: Hired Militias in the White Lotus War, 1796–1805." *Asia Major* 22, no. 2 (2009): 145–78.

Danjō Hiroshi 檀上寛. "Gen-Min kōtai no rinen to genjitsu—Gimon Teishi o tegakari toshite" 元·明交替の理念と現實—義門鄭氏を手掛りとして. *Shirin* 65, no. 2 (1982): 1–31.

———. "Min ōchō seiritsuki no kiseki—Kōbuchō no gigoku jiken to keishi mondai o megutte" 明王朝成立期の軌跡—洪武朝の疑獄事件と京師問題をめぐって. *Tōyōshi kenkyū* 37, no. 3 (1978): 1–34.

Dingyuan xianzhi 定遠縣志. 1826. In *ZDJAH*.

Ditmanson, Peter. "Death and Fidelity: Mid- and Late-Ming Reconstruction of Fang Xiaoru." *Ming Studies* 45–46 (2001): 114–43.

Duan Chao 段超. *Tao Zhu yu Jia Dao jingshi sixiang yanjiu* 陶澍與嘉道經世思想研究. Beijing: Zhongguo shehui kexue chubanshe, 2001.

Dunstan, Helen. *State or Merchant: Political Economy and Political Process in 1740s China*. Cambridge, Mass.: Harvard University Asia Center, 2006.

Ebrey, Patricia B. "Portrait Sculptures in Imperial Ancestral Rites in Song China." *T'oung Pao* 83, nos. 1–3 (1997): 42–92.

Elliott, Mark C. *Emperor Qianlong: Son of Heaven, Man of the World*. New York: Longman, 2009.

———. "Whose Empire Shall It Be? Manchu Figurations of Historical Process in the Early Seventeenth Century." In *Time, Temporality, and Imperial Transition*. Edited by Lynn A. Struve, 31–72. Honolulu: University of Hawai'i Press, 2005.

Elman, Benjamin A. *Classicism, Politics, and Kinship: The Ch'ang-chou School of New Text Confucianism in Late Imperial China*. Berkeley: University of California Press, 1990.

———. *From Philosophy to Philology: Intellectual and Social Aspects of Change in Late Imperial China*. Cambridge, Mass.: Council on East Asian Studies, Harvard University, 1984.

Elvin, Mark. "Market Towns and Waterways: The County of Shang-hai from 1480 to 1910." In *The City in Late Imperial China*. Edited by G. William Skinner, 441–73. Stanford, Calif.: Stanford University Press, 1977.

Fan Jinmin 范金民. "Ming-Qing Jiangnan zongzu yitian de fazhan" 明清江南宗族義田的發展. In *Jiangnan shehui jingji yanjiu: Ming-Qing juan* 江南社會經濟研究: 明清卷. Edited by Fan Jinmin, 900–39. Beijing: Zhongguo nongye chubanshe, 2006.

———. "Qingdai Suzhou zongzu yitian de fazhan" 清代蘇州宗族義田的發展. *Zhongguoshi yanjiu* 3 (1995): 56–68.

Fan Jinmin, and Xia Weizhong 夏維中, eds. *Suzhou diqu shehui jingjishi (Ming Qing juan)* 蘇州地區社會經濟史 (明清卷). Nanjing, China: Nanjing daxue chubanshe, 1993.

Fang Shouchou 方受疇. *Fu Yu xuzai lu* 撫豫恤災錄. In *ZHZQS*.

Faure, David. "What Made Foshan a Town? The Evolution of Rural-Urban Identities in Ming-Qing China." *Late Imperial China* 11, no. 2 (1990): 1–31.

Fei Lanchi 費蘭墀. *Qu'an wenchao* 蘧庵文鈔. 1827. Housed at the Suzhou Library.

Fei Shanqing 費善慶. *Chuihong zhixiao lu* 垂虹識小錄. In *ZDJJS*.

Fei Shuwei 費樹蔚. "Zhang Wu wang mu Caotaifei mubeiji" 張吳王母曹太妃墓碑記, "Zhang Wu wang mubei" 張吳王墓碑. In *Wu wang Zhang Shicheng zaiji*. Edited by Zhi Weicheng and Ren Zhiyuan.

Finnane, Antonia. *Speaking of Yangzhou: A Chinese City, 1550–1850*. Cambridge, Mass.: Harvard University Asia Center, 2004.

Fu Weilin 傅維鱗. *Ming shu* 明書. In *CJCB*.

Fuheng 傅恒, et al. *Yupi lidai tongjian jilan* 御批歷代通鑑輯覽. Reprint of the 1767 original version. Reprint date and publisher unknown.

Fuliang xianzhi 浮梁縣志. 1823. Supplemented and reprinted in 1832. In *ZDJJX*.

Fuma Susumu 夫馬進. *Chūgoku zenkai zendōshi kenkyū* 中國善會善堂史研究. Kyoto, Japan: Dōhōsha shuppan, 1997.

Gao Dai 高岱. *Hongyou lu* 鴻猷錄. In *CJCB*.

Gongzhong zhupi zouzhe caizheng lei juanshu xiang 宮中硃批奏摺 財政類 捐輸項. Copies of the original documents in the First Historical Archives in Beijing. Housed at the Zhongyang yanjiuyuan Guo Tingyi tushuguan 中央研究院 郭廷以圖書館.

Gu Jiayan 顧嘉言, et al. *Loudong huangzheng huibian* 婁東荒政彙編. In *ZHZQS*.

Gu Lu 顧祿. *Qingjia lu* 清嘉錄. Nanjing, China: Jiangsu guji chubanshe, 1999.

———. *Tongqiao yizhuo lu* 桐橋倚棹錄. Shanghai: Shanghai guji chubanshe, 1980.

Gu Tingchen 顧鼎臣. "Suzhou fuxue chuzuo liangwu congsi xiang ji" 蘇州府學初作兩廡從祀像記. In *Wujun wenbian*. Edited by Gu Yuan.

Gu Yanwu. 顧炎武. "Xiangshe" 像設. In *Qing jingshi wenbian* 清經世文編. Beijing: Zhonghua shuju, 1992.

Gu Yingtai 谷應泰. *Mingshi jishi benmo* 明史紀事本末. In *CJCB*.

Gu Yuan 顧沅. *Gu shengxian xiang zhuanlüe* 古聖賢像傳略. 1830. Housed at the Shanghai Library.

———. *Jinyu ji* 今雨集. 1844. Housed at the Shanghai Library.

———. *Shengmiao sidian tukao* 聖廟祀典圖考. 1826. Housed at the Shanghai Library.

———, ed. *Wujun wenbian* 吳郡文編. 1827. Unpublished manuscript housed at the Suzhou Museum.

———. *Wujun wubai mingxian tuzhuanzan* 吳郡五百名賢圖傳贊. Taipei: Guangwen shuju, 1978.

Gu Zhentao 顧震濤. *Wumen biaoyin* 吳門表隱. Nanjing, China: Jiangsu guji chubanshe, 1999.

Gu Zhixing 顧志興. *Zhejiang cangshujia cangshulou* 浙江藏書家藏書樓. Hangzhou, China: Zhejiang renmin chubanshe, 1987.

Guan Wenfa 關文發. *Jiaqing di* 嘉慶帝. Changchun, China: Jilin wenshi chubanshe, 1993.

Guangxi tongzhi 廣西通志. 1733 edition, in *SKQS*; 1891 edition, Guiyuan shuju.

Guizhou tongzhi 貴州通志. 1741. In *SKQS*.

Guo Chengkang 郭成康. *Qianlong zhengzhuan* 乾隆正傳. Beijing: Zhongyang bianyi chubanshe, 2006.

Gusu zhi 姑蘇志. 1506. In *TYGX*.

Guy, R. Kent. *Qing Governors and Their Provinces: The Evolution of Territorial Administration in China, 1644–1796*. Seattle: University of Washington Press, 2010.

———. *The Emperor's Four Treasuries: Scholars and the State in the Late Ch'ien-lung Era*. Cambridge, Mass.: Council on East Asian Studies, Harvard University Press, 1987.

Hamashima Atsutoshi 濱島敦俊. *Mindai Kōnan nōson shakai no kenkyū* 明代江南農村社會の研究. Tokyo: Tokyo daigaku shuppakai, 1982.

———. "The City God Temples (*ch'eng-huang-miao*) of Chiangnan in the Ming and Ch'ing Dynasties." *Memoirs of the Research Department of the Toyo Bunko* 50 (1992): 1–27.

Han Guojun 韓國鈞, ed. *Hailing congke* 海陵叢刻. Yangzhou, China: Jixian zhai, 1919. Housed at the Shanghai Library.

Han Seunghyun 韓承賢. "18 segi Ch'ŏngjo ŭi chibangji, chibang munhŏn t'ongjech'aek kwa Chang Haksŏng ŭi pangjiron" 18세기 清朝의 지방지, 지방문헌 통제책과 章學誠의 方志論. *Yŏksa hakpo* 192 (2006): 255–303.

———. "19 segi ch'o 'naksŏn hosi' changnyŏ chedo ŭi pyŏnhwa wa kŭ ŭimi" 19세기초 '樂善好施' 장려 제도의 변화와 그 의미. *Tongyang sahak yŏn'gu* 95 (2006): 107–56.

———. "Bandit or Hero? Memories of Zhang Shicheng in Late Imperial and Republican Suzhou." *Harvard Journal of Asiatic Studies* 68, no. 2 (2008): 115–62.

———. "Changing Roles of Local Elites from the 1720s to 1830s." In *The Cambridge History of China*. Volume 9, Part 2. Edited by Willard J. Peterson. Cambridge, U.K.: Cambridge University Press, forthcoming.

———. "Ch'ŏngdae 'naksŏn hosi' chŏngp'yo, ŭisŏ chedo ŭi sŏngnip—Kŏnnyung yŏn'gan eŭl chungsim ŭro" 清代 '樂善好施' 旌表, 議敘제도의 성립—乾隆年間을 중심으로. *Myŏngch'ŏngsa yŏn'gu* 26 (2006): 289–341.
———. "Myŏng Ch'ŏng sidae ŭi myŏnghwan, hyanghyŏn ipsa yangsang ŭi pyŏnhwa wa kŭ ŭimi" 明清時代의 名宦, 鄉賢 입사 양상의 변화와 그 의미. *Chungguk hakpo* 54 (2006): 347–78.
———. "Re-inventing Local Tradition: Politics, Culture, and Identity in Early 19th Century Suzhou." Ph.D. diss., Harvard University, 2005.
———. "Shrine, Images, and Power: The Worship of Former Worthies in Early Nineteenth Century Suzhou." *T'oung Pao* 95, nos. 1–3 (2009): 167–95.
———. "The Punishment of Examination Riots in the Early to Mid-Qing Period." *Late Imperial China* 32, no. 2 (2011): 133–65.
———. "Wenzhi zhi xia de kangyi: Jiaqing 4 nian Suzhou shiren de jiti kangyi yu huangdi de fanying" 文治之下的抗議: 嘉慶4年蘇州士人的集體抗議與皇帝的反應. *Zhongyang yanjiuyuan jindaishi yanjiusuo jikan* 75 (2012): 77–114.
Han Wenqi 韓文綺. *Han dazhongcheng zouyi* 韓大中丞奏議. In *XXSKQS*.
Ho Koon-piu 何冠彪. "Lun Qing Gaozong ziwo chuixu de lishi panguan xianxiang" 論清高宗自我吹噓的歷史判官現象. In his *Ming qing renwu yu zhushu* 明清人物與著述, 146–82. Hong Kong: Xianggang jiaoyu tushu gongsi, 1996.
———. "Qingdai qianqi junzhu dui guansi shixue de yingxiang" 清代前期君主對官私史學的影響. *Hanxue yanjiu* 16, no. 1 (1998): 155–82.
Hou Dian 侯甸. *Xiqiao yeji* 西樵野記. In *XXSKQS*.
Hsiao Kung-chuan. *Rural China: Imperial Control in the Nineteenth Century*. Seattle: University of Washington Press, 1960.
Huaiyuan xianzhi 懷遠縣志. 1819. In *ZDJAH*.
Huang Aiping 黃愛平. *Siku quanshu zuanxiu yanjiu* 四庫全書纂修研究. Beijing: Zhongguo renmin daxue chubanshe, 1989. Second printing in 2001.
Huang Chin-shing 黃進興. "Daotong yu zhitongzhijian: cong Ming Jiajing jiunian (1530) Kongmiao gaizhi tanqi" 道統與治統之間—從明嘉靖九年(1530) 孔廟改制談起. *Zhongyang yanjiuyuan lishiyuyan yanjiusuo jikan* 61, no. 4 (1992): 917–41.
———. "The Cultural Politics of Autocracy: The Confucius Temple and Ming Despotism, 1368–1530." Translated by Curtis Dean Smith and Thomas A. Wilson. In *On Sacred Grounds: Culture, Society, Politics, and the Formation of the Cult of Confucius*. Edited by Thomas A Wilson, 267–96. Cambridge, Mass.: Harvard University Asia Center, 2002.
———. *The Price of Having a Sage Emperor: The Unity of Politics and Culture*. Singapore: Institute of East Asian Philosophies, 1987.
Huang Hongshan 黃鴻山 and Wang Weiping. "Wan Qing Suzhoufu Chang, Yuan, Wu Fengbei yicang yanjiu" 晚清蘇州府長元吳豐備義倉研究. In *Ming Qing shiqi Jiangnan shehuishi yanjiu*. Edited by Wang Weiping, 368–90. Beijing: Qunyan chubanshe, 2006.
Huang Jianguo 黃建國 and Gao Yuexin 高跃新, eds. *Zhongguo gudai cangshulou yanjiu* 中國古代藏書樓研究. Beijing: Zhonghua shuju, 1999.
Huang Jingfang 黃景昉. *Guoshi weiyi* 國史唯疑. In *ZYJXB*.
Huang Wei 黃暐. *Pengchuang leiji* 蓬窗類記. In *XXSKQS*.

Huang Xingzeng 黄省曾. *Wufeng lu* 吳風錄. In *XXSKQS*.

Huang, Martin W. "Sage, Hero, Bandit: Zhu Yuanzhang's Image in the Sixteenth-Century Novel *Yinglie zhuan*." *Ming Studies* 50 (2004): 77–90.

Huangchao benji 皇朝本記. In *ZYJXB*.

Hummel, Arthur W., ed. *Eminent Chinese of the Ch'ing Period*. 2 vols. Taipei: Nantian shuju youxian gongsi, 2003.

Hung Ho-fung. *Protest with Chinese Characteristics: Demonstrations, Riots, and Petitions in the Mid-Qing Dynasty*. New York: Columbia University Press, 2011.

Inada Seiichi 稲田清一. "Shindai Kōnan ni okeru kyūkō to shichin—Hōzanken · Kateiken no 'shō' o megutte" 清代江南における救荒と市鎮—寶山縣·嘉定縣の'廠'をめぐって. *Kōnan daigaku kiyō bungaku hen* 86 (1993): 29–57.

———. "Shinmatsu Kōnan no chintō ni tsuite—Shōkōhu, Taisōshū o chūshin toshite" 清末江南の鎮董について—松江府, 太倉州を中心として. In *Kōnan deruta shichin kenkyū—Rekishigaku to chirigaku kara no sekkin* 江南デルタ市鎮研究—歷史學と地理學からの接近. Edited by Mori Masao, 129–66. Nagoya, Japan: Nagoya daigaku shuppansha, 1992.

Iwai Shigeki 岩井茂樹. "Shindai kokka zaisei ni okeru chūō to chihō—shakuhatsu seido o chūshin ni shite" 清代國家財政における中央と地方—酌撥制度を中心にして. *Tōyōshi kenkyū* 42, no. 2 (1983): 126–54.

Jiang Fen 蔣棻. *Mingshi jishi* 明史紀事. In *ZYJXB*.

Jiang Xixian 蔣希賢. *Chang Yuan xiangxian ci xiaozhi* 長元鄉賢祠小志. 1829. Housed at the Shanghai Library.

Jiang Yikui 蔣一葵. *Yaoshantang waiji* 堯山堂外紀. In *XXSKQS*.

Jiao Hong 焦竑. *Guochao xianzheng lu* 國朝獻徵錄. Taipei: Taiwan xuesheng shuju, 1965.

———. *Yutang congyu* 玉堂叢語. Beijing: Zhonghua shuju, 1997.

Jiaqing chongxiu yitong zhi 嘉慶重修一統志. Shanghai: Shangwu yinshuguan, 1934.

Jing xianzhi 涇縣志. 1806. In *ZDJAH*.

Jones, Susan Mann. "Hung Liang-chi (1746–1809): The Perception and Articulation of Political Problems in Late Eighteenth Century China." Ph.D. diss., Stanford University, 1971.

Jones, Susan Mann, and Philip A. Kuhn. "Dynastic Decline and the Rise of Rebellion." In *The Cambridge History of China*, Vol. 10, Part 1. Edited by John K. Fairbank, et al., 107–62. Cambridge, U.K.: Cambridge University Press, 1978.

Kaske, Elizabeth. "Fund-Raising Wars: Office Selling and Interprovincial Finance in Nineteenth Century China." *Harvard Journal of Asiatic Studies* 71, no. 1 (2011): 69–141.

———. "Metropolitan Clerks and Venality in Qing China: The Great 1830 Forgery Case." *T'oung Pao* 98 (2012): 217–69.

Kawakatsu Mamoru 川勝守. *Chūgoku hōken kokka no shihai kōzō— Min Shin fueki seidoshi no kenkyū* 中國封建國家の支配構造—明清賦役制度史の研究. Tokyo: Tokyo daigaku shuppankai, 1980.

Kessler, Lawrence D. "Ethnic Composition of Provincial Leadership during the Ch'ing Dynasty." *Journal of Asian Studies* 28, no. 3 (1969): 489–511.

———. *K'ang-hsi and the Consolidation of Ch'ing Rule, 1661–1684*. Chicago: University of Chicago Press, 1976.

Kishimoto Mio 岸本美緒. *Min Shin kōtai to Kōnan shakai: 17 seiki Chūgoku no chitsujo mondai* 明清交替と江南社會: 17世紀中國の秩序問題. Tokyo: Tokyo daigaku shuppankai, 1999.

Kojima Tsuyoshi 小島毅. "Jukyō no gūjōkan" 儒教の偶像觀. *Chūgoku shakai to bunka* 7 (1992): 69–82.

———. "Kasei no reisei kaikaku ni tsuite" 嘉靖の禮制改革について. *Tōyō bunka kenkyūjo kiyō* 117 (1992): 381–426

Kojima Yoshio 小島淑男. *Kindai Chūgoku no nōson keizai to jinushisei* 近代中國の農村經濟と地主制. Tokyo: Kyūko shoin, 2005.

Kuhn, Philip A. "Civil Society and Constitutional Development." Paper prepared for the American-European Symposium on State vs. Society in East Asian Traditions, Paris, 1991.

———. "Ideas behind China's Modern State." *Harvard Journal of Asiatic Studies* 55, no. 2 (1995): 295–337.

———. *Origins of the Modern Chinese State.* Stanford, Calif.: Stanford University Press, 2002.

———. *Rebellion and Its Enemies in Late Imperial China: Militarization and Social Structure, 1796–1864.* Cambridge, Mass.: Harvard University Press, 1970. Reprint 1980.

———. *Soulstealers: The Chinese Sorcery Scare of 1768.* Cambridge, Mass.: Harvard University Press, 1990.

Kun Xin liangxian xuxiu hezhi 崑新兩縣續修合志. 1880. In *ZDJJS.*

Kun Xin liangxian zhi 崑新兩縣志. 1826. In *ZDJJS.*

Kurahashi Keiko 倉橋圭子. "Jūkyū seiki Kōnan no zenkyo to sono ninaitetachi—Kōsoshō Jōshū chiku no jirei kara" 十九世紀江南の善舉とその担い手たち—江蘇省常州地區の事例から. *Ochanomizu shigaku* 46 (2002): 1–28.

Laian xianzhi 來安縣志. 1830. In *ZDJAH.*

Lang Ying 郎英. *Qixiu leigao* 七修類稿. In *XXSKQS.*

Lee Jungab 李俊甲. "Ch'ŏngchung·hugi Sachŏn sambiguk ŭi sŏllip kwa unyŏng—'kwanhaeng' ŭi chilsŏ esŏ 'changjŏng' ŭi chilsŏ ro" 清中·後期 四川 三費局의 設立과 運營—'慣行'의 질서에서 '章程'의 질서로. *Tongyang sahak yŏn'gu* 74 (2001): 135–70.

Lee Yun-seok 李允碩. "Myŏngch'ŏng sidae Kangnam ŭi munmyo wa sŏnghwangmyo—tosi chesa, sinang chungsim ŭi kujo wa pyŏnch'ŏn. 明清시대 江南의 文廟와 城隍廟—도시제사, 신앙중심의 구조와 변천. *Myŏngchŏngsa yŏn'gu* 17 (2002): 1–38.

Leonard, Jane Kate. *Controlling from Afar: The Daoguang Emperor's Management of the Grand Canal Crisis, 1824–1826.* Ann Arbor: University of Michigan Press, 1996.

———. "Negotiating across the Boundaries of State Power: Organizing the 1826 Sea Transport Experiment." In *Dragons, Tigers, and Dogs.* Edited by Robert J. Antony and Jane Kate Leonard, 183–211. Ithaca, N.Y.: East Asia Program, Cornell University, 2002.

Li Bozhong 李伯重. *Jiangnan de zaoqi gongyehua, 1550–1850* 江南的早期工業化. Beijing: Zhongguo renmin daxue chubanshe, 2010.

Li Changqing 李常慶. *Siku quanshu chuban yanjiu* 四庫全書出版研究. Zhengzhou, China: Zhongzhou guji chubanshe, 2008.

Li Dianrong 李典蓉. *Qingchao Jingkong zhidu yanjiu* 清代京控制度研究. Shanghai: Shanghai guji chubanshe, 2011.

Li Xian 李賢. *Gurang ji* 古穰集. In *SKQS*.

Li Xian, et al. *Da Ming yitong zhi* 大明一統志. Xi'an, China: Sanqin chubanshe, 1990.

Li Xiangjun 李向軍. "Qingdai jiuzai de zhidu jianshe yu shehui xiaoguo" 清代救災的制度建設與社會效果. *Lishi yanjiu* 5 (1995): 71–87.

Li, Lillian M. *Fighting Famine in North China: State, Market, and Environmental Decline, 1690s–1990s*. Stanford, Calif.: Stanford University Press, 2007.

Liang Qizi 梁其姿. *Shishan yu jiaohua—Ming Qing de cishan zuzhi* 施善與教化—明清的慈善組織. Shijiazhuang, China: Hebei jiaoyu chubanshe, 2001.

Like shishu 禮科史書. First Historical Archives (Beijing).

Like tiben 吏科題本. First Historical Archives (Beijing).

Lin Liyue 林麗月. "Zudou gongqiang—Xiangxian ci yu Ming Qing de jiceng shehui" 俎豆宮牆—鄉賢祠與明清的基層社會. In *Zhongguoshi xinlun (Jiceng shehui fence)* 中國史新論 (基層社會分冊). Edited by Huang Kuanzhong 黃寬重, 327–72. Taipei: Zhongyang yanjiuyuan, Lianjing chuban gongsi, 2009.

Lin Man-houng. *China Upside Down: Currency, Society, and Ideologies, 1808–1856*. Cambridge, Mass.: Harvard University Asia Center, 2006.

———. "Two Social Theories Revealed: Statecraft Controversies over China's Monetary Crisis, 1808–1854." *Late Imperial China* 12, no. 2 (1991): 1–35.

Lin Yaoyu 林堯俞, et al. *Libu zhigao* 禮部志稿. In *SKQS*.

Lin Zexu 林則徐. *Lin Zexu quanji* 林則徐全集. Fuzhou, China: Haixia wenyi chubanshe, 2002.

———. "Quanyu juanzhen gaoshi" 勸諭捐賑告示. In *Lin Zexu ji: gongdu* 林則徐集: 公牘. Beijing: Zhonghua shuju, 1963. Reprint 1985.

Ling Zuyi 淩祖詒. *Taicang xiangxianxian huaxiang* 太倉鄉先賢畫像. Shanghai: Baisong yinshuaju, 1947.

Lingui xianzhi 臨桂縣志. 1892. Reprint. Taipei: Chengwen chubanshe, 1967.

Liu, Cary. "The Ch'ing Dynasty Wen-yuan-ko Imperial Library: Architecture and Ordering of Knowledge." Ph.D. diss., Princeton University, 1997.

Liu Zhen 劉辰. *Guochu shiji* 國初事蹟. Shanghai: Boguzhai, 1920.

Liu Zhengyun 劉錚雲. "Yizhuang yu chengzhen—Qingdai Suzhoufu yizhuang zhi sheli ji fenbu" 義莊與城鎮—清代蘇州府義莊之設立及分佈. *Zhongyang yanjiuyuan lishi yuyan yanjiusuo jikan* 58, no. 3 (1987): 633–72.

Lou xianzhi 婁縣志. 1788. In *ZDJSH*.

Lu Rong 陸容. *Shuyuan zaji* 菽園雜記. In *YMSLBJ*.

Lü Weiqi 呂維琪. *Shengxian xiangzan* 聖賢像贊. Qufu, China: Qufu huiwentang, 1878.

Lu'an fuzhi 潞安府志. 1770. *Zhongguo difangzhi jicheng Shanxi fuxianzhi ji*. 中國地方志集成 山西府縣志輯. Nanjing, China: Fenghuang chubanshe, 2005.

Lui, Adam Yuen-chung. *The Hanlin Academy: Training Ground for the Ambitious, 1644–1850*. Hamden, Conn.: Archon, 1981.

Luo Yudong 羅玉東. *Zhongguo lijinshi* 中國釐金史. Shanghai: Shangwu yinshuguan, 1936.

Luzhou fuzhi 盧州府志. 1803. In *ZDJAH*.

Mann, Susan. *Local Merchants and the Chinese Bureaucracy, 1750–1950*. Stanford, Calif.: Stanford University Press, 1987.

Marks, Robert B. *Tigers, Rice, Silk, & Silt: Environment and Economy in Late Imperial South China*. Cambridge, U.K.: Cambridge University Press, 1998.

Marmé, Michael. *Suzhou: Where the Goods of All the Provinces Converge.* Stanford, Calif.: Stanford University Press, 2005.

McMahon, Daniel. "Dynastic Decline, Heshen, and the Ideology of the Xianyu Reforms." *Tsing Hua Journal of Chinese Studies,* New Series 38, no. 2 (2008): 231–55.

———. "The Yuelu Academy and Hunan's Nineteenth-Century Turn toward Statecraft." *Late Imperial China* 26, no. 1 (2005): 72–109.

Meyer-Fong, Tobie. *Building Culture in Early Qing Yangzhou.* Stanford, Calif.: Stanford University Press, 2003.

———. *What Remains: Coming to Terms with Civil War in 19th Century China*. Stanford, Calif.: Stanford University Press, 2013.

Miles, Steven B. "Rewriting the Southern Han (917–971): The Production of Local Culture in Nineteenth-Century Guangzhou." *Harvard Journal of Asiatic Studies* 62, no. 1 (2002): 39–75.

———. *The Sea of Learning: Mobility and Identity in Nineteenth-Century Guangzhou.* Cambridge, Mass.: Harvard University Asia Center, 2006.

Min Tu-ki. *National Polity and Local Power: The Transformation of Late Imperial China*. Edited by Philip Kuhn and Timothy Brook. Cambridge, Mass.: Harvard University Press, 1989.

Ming Qing dang'an 明清檔案. *Zhongyang yanjiuyuan lishi yuyan yanjiusuo xiancun Qingdai Neige daku yuancang Ming Qing dang'an* 中央研究院 歷史語言研究所 現存 清代內閣大庫 原藏 明清檔案. Taipei: Zhongyang yanjiuyuan lishi yuyan yanjiusuo, 1986.

Ming Qing shiliao 明清史料. Guibian 癸編 (series 10). Taipei: Zhongyang yanjiuyuan lishi yuyan yanjiusuo, 1975.

Ming shi 明史. Beijing: Zhonghua shuju, 1974.

Ming shilu (*Hongwu, Hongzhi, Zhengtong, Jiajing, Wanli*) 明實錄 (洪武, 弘治, 正統, 嘉靖, 萬曆). Nangang, Taiwan: Zhongyang yanjiuyuan lishi yuyan yanjiusuo, 1962–68.

Mizoguchi Yūzō 溝口雄三. *Chūgoku no kō to shi* 中國の公と私. Tokyo: Kenbun shuppan, 1995.

Morita Akira 森田明. *Shindai no suiri to chiiki shakai* 清代の水利と地域社會. Fukuoka, Japan: Chūgoku shoten, 2002.

———. *Shindai suiri shakaishi no kenkyū* 清代水利社會史の研究. Tokyo: Kokusho kankōkai, 1990.

———. *Shindai suirishi kenkyū* 清代水利史研究. Tokyo: Aki shobō, 1974.

Mosca, Matthew W. "Empire and the Circulation of Frontier Intelligence: Qing Conceptions of the Ottomans." *Harvard Journal of Asiatic Studies* 70, no. 1 (2010): 147–207.

Mou Runsun 牟潤孫. "Lun Qingdai shixue shuailuo de yuanyin" 論清代史學衰落的原因. In *Haiyi zazhu* 海遺雜著. By Mou Runsun, 69–76. Hong Kong: Zhongwen daxue chubanshe, 1990.

Murray, Julia K. "The Temple of Confucius and Pictorial Biographies of the Sage." *Journal of Asian Studies* 55, no. 2 (1996): 269–300.

———. "Varied Views of the Sage: Illustrated Narratives of the Life of Confucius." In *On Sacred Grounds: Culture, Society, Politics, and the Formation of the Cult of Confu-*

cius. Edited by Thomas A. Wilson, 222–64. Cambridge, Mass.: Harvard University Asia Center, 2002.

Naquin, Susan. *Millenarian Rebellion in China: The Eight Trigrams Rebellion of 1813*. New Haven, Conn.: Yale University Press, 1976.

———. *Peking: Temples and City Life, 1400–1900*. Berkeley: University of California Press, 2000.

Naquin, Susan, and Evelyn Rawski. *Chinese Society in the Eighteenth Century*. New Haven, Conn.: Yale University Press, 1987.

Na-yan-cheng 那彥成. *Zhenji* 賑記. In *ZHZQS*.

Neige daku dang'an 内閣大庫檔案. Digitized document. Taipei: Zhongyang yanjiuyuan lishi yuyan yanjiusuo.

Neskar, Ellen. "The Cult of Worthies: A Study of Shrines Honoring Local Confucian Worthies in the Sung Dynasty, 960–1279." Ph.D. diss., Columbia University, 1993.

Ningdu zhilizhou zhi 寧都直隸州志. 1824. In *ZDJJX*.

Ocko, Jonathan K. "I'll Take It All the Way to Beijing: Capital Appeals in the Qing." *Journal of Asian Studies* 47, no. 2 (1988): 291–315.

Oh Keum-sung 吳金成. "Myŏngmal ch'ŏngch'o sangp'um kyŏngje ŭi palchŏn kwa 'chabonjuŭi maenga'ron" 明末清初 商品經濟의 發展과 '資本主義萌芽'論. In *Myŏngmal ch'ŏngch'o sahoe ŭi chomyŏng* 明末清初 社會의 照明. Edited by Oh Keum-sung, et al., 125–63. Seoul: Hanul Academy, 1990.

Okuzaki Hiroshi 奥崎裕司. "Soshūhu kyōkenshi no hitobito—kyōshin no chiikisei ni tsuite" 蘇州府鄉賢祠の人々—鄉紳の地域性について. *Mindaishi kenkyū* 10 (1982): 49–60.

Ōtani Toshio 大谷敏夫. *Shindai seiji shisōshi kenkyū* 清代政治思想史研究. Tokyo: Kyūko shoin, 1991.

Pan Qing 潘清. "Ming Qing shiqi Jiangnan de shuili jianshe" 明清時期江南的水利建設. In *Jiangnan shehui jingji yanjiu*. Edited by Fan Jinmin, 940–67. Beijing: Zhongguo nongye chubanshe, 2006.

Pan Zengyi 潘曾沂. "Chouban Yusheng zhenwu siyi" 籌辦豫省賑務私議. In his *Dongjinguan wenji* 東津館文集. 1858. Housed at the Suzhou Library.

Peng Dingqiu 彭定求. *Nanyun wengao* 南畇文稿. *Siku quanshu cunmu congshu* 四庫全書存目叢書. Tainan, Taiwan: Zhuangyan wenhua shiye youxian gongsi, 1997.

Peng Yunzhang 彭蘊章. *Guipukan conggao* 歸樸龕叢稿. In *XXSKQS*.

Peng Yuxin 彭雨新. *Qingdai tudi kaikenshi* 清代土地開墾史. Beijing: Nongye chubanshe, 1990.

Perdue, Peter. *China Marches West: The Qing Conquest of Central Eurasia*. Cambridge, Mass.: Harvard University Press, 2005.

———. *Exhausting the Earth: State and Peasant in Hunan, 1500–1850*. Cambridge, Mass.: Council on East Asian Studies, Harvard University Press, 1987.

Platt, Stephen R. *Provincial Patriots: The Hunanese and Modern China*. Cambridge, Mass.: Harvard University Asia Center, 2007.

Polachek, James M. "Gentry Hegemony: Soochow in the T'ung-chih Restoration." In *Conflict and Control in Late Imperial China*. Edited by Fredrick Wakeman Jr. and Carolyn Grant, 211–56. Berkeley: University of California Press, 1975.

———. "Literati Groups and Literati Politics in Early Nineteenth-Century China." Ph.D. diss., University of California, Berkeley, 1977.

———. *The Inner Opium War*. Cambridge, Mass.: Council on East Asian Studies, Harvard University Press, 1992.

Pomeranz, Kenneth. "Beyond the East-West Binary: Resituating Development Paths in the Eighteenth-Century World." *Journal of Asian Studies* 61, no. 2 (2002): 539–90.

———. *The Great Divergence: China, Europe, and the Making of the Modern World Economy*. Princeton, N.J.: Princeton University Press, 2000.

Pujiang xianzhi 浦江縣志. 1896. In *ZDJZJ*.

Qian Qianyi 錢謙益. *Guochu qunxiong shilüe* 國初群雄史略. Beijing: Zhonghua shuju, 1982.

Qian Siyuan 錢思元. *Wumen bucheng* 吳門補乘. Compiled in 1803. Supplemented by Qian Shiqi 錢士錡 up to 1820 and published afterward. Housed at the Shanghai Library.

Qian Yong 錢泳. *Lüyuan conghua* 履園叢話. Beijing: Zhonghua shuju, 1979. Reprint 1997.

Qianlong. *Qing Gaozong (Qianlong) yuzhi shiwen quanji* 清高宗(乾隆)御製詩文全集. Beijing: Zhongguo renmin daxue chubanshe, 1993.

Qiao Zhizhong 喬治忠. "Da Qing yitong zhi de chuxiu yu fangzhixue zhi xingqi" 大清一統志的初修與方志學的興起. *Qilu xuekan* 1 (1997): 115–22.

Qinding Huangchao tongzhi 欽定皇朝通志. In *SKQS*.

Qinding Libu zeli 欽定吏部則例. Taipei: Chengwen chubanshe, 1966.

Qinding Xuezheng quanshu 欽定學政全書. *Jindai Zhongguo shiliao congkan*. Taipei: Wenhai chubanshe, 1968.

Qing huidian shili 清會典事例. 1899. Reprint. Beijing: Zhonghua shuju, 1991.

Qing shilu 清實錄. Beijing: Zhonghua shuju, 1985–87.

Qing shilu 清實錄. Electronic resource. Taipei: Zhongyang yanjiuyuan jisuan zhongxin, 2000.

Qufu xianzhi 曲阜縣志. 1774. In *ZDJSD*.

Rankin, Mary Backus. *Elite Activism and Political Transformation in China: Zhejiang Province, 1865–1911*. Stanford, Calif.: Stanford University Press, 1986.

———. "Managed by the People: Officials, Gentry, and the Foshan Charitable Granary, 1795–1845." *Late Imperial China* 15, no. 2 (1994): 1–52.

———. "Some Observations on a Chinese Public Sphere." *Modern China* 19, no. 2 (1993): 158–82.

———. "The Origins of a Chinese Public Sphere: Local Elites and Community Affairs in the Late Imperial Period." *Études chinoises* 9, no. 2 (1990): 13–60.

Reed, Bradly. "Gentry Activism in Nineteenth-Century Sichuan: The Three-Fees Bureau." *Late Imperial China* 20, no. 2 (1999): 99–127.

Rowe, William T. *Hankow: Commerce and Society in a Chinese City, 1796–1889*. Stanford, Calif.: Stanford University Press, 1984.

———. *Hankow: Conflict and Community in a Chinese City, 1796–1895*. Stanford, Calif.: Stanford University Press, 1989.

———. "Introduction: The Qianlong-Jiaqing Transition in Qing History." *Late Imperial China* 32, no. 2 (2011): 74–88.

———. "Rewriting the Qing Constitution: Bao Shichen's 'On Wealth' (*Shuochu*)." *T'oung Pao* 98, nos. 1–3 (2012): 178–216.
———. *Saving the World: Chen Hongmou and Elite Consciousness in Eighteenth-Century China.* Stanford, Calif.: Stanford University Press, 2001.
———. "The Problem of 'Civil Society' in Late Imperial China." *Modern China* 19, no. 2 (1993): 139–57.
———. "The Public Sphere in Modern China." *Modern China* 16, no. 3 (1990): 309–29.
Ruijin xianzhi 瑞金縣志. 1822. In *ZDJJX.*
Schneewind, Sarah. *Community Schools and the State in Ming China.* Stanford, Calif.: Stanford University Press, 2006.
Schoppa, R. Keith. *Xiang Lake: Nine Centuries of Chinese Life.* New Haven, Conn.: Yale University Press, 1989.
Shanghai tushuguan 上海圖書館, ed. *Zhongguo congshu zonglu* 中國叢書綜錄. Shanghai: Shanghai guji chubanshe, 1982.
Shanghai xianzhi 上海縣志. 1812. Housed at the Harvard-Yenching Library.
Shanxi tongzhi 山西通志. 1734. In *SKQS.*
Shaoxing fuzhi 紹興府志. 1792. In *ZDJZJ.*
Shi Ce 史册. *Longping jishi* 隆平紀事. In *Zhaodai congshu* 昭代叢書. Wujiang, China: Shikai tang, 1876.
Shi Zhihong 史志宏. *Qingdai hubu yinku shouzhi he kucun tongji* 清代户部銀庫收支和庫存統計. Fuzhou, China: Fujian renmin chubanshe, 2008.
Shimizu Taiji 清水泰次. "Min Taiso no tai kengō saku—tokuni Chōgo no senppan oyobi Sosyū no gōnō ni tsuite" 明太祖の對權豪策—特に張吳の戰犯及び蘇州の豪農について. *Shikan* 38 (1952): 8–22.
Siku jinhuishu congkan 四庫禁燬書叢刊. Index. Beijing: Beijing chubanshe, 1997.
Sommer, Deborah. "Destroying Confucius: Iconoclasm in the Confucian Temple." In *On Sacred Grounds: Culture, Society, Politics and the Formation of the Cult of Confucius.* Edited by Thomas A. Wilson, 95–133. Cambridge, Mass.: Harvard University Asia Center, 2002.
———. "Ming Taizu's Legacy as Iconoclast." *Ming Studies* 50 (2005): 91–106.
Song Lian 宋濂, et al. *Yuan shi* 元史. Beijing: Zhonghua shuju, 1976.
Songjiang fuzhi 松江府志. 1817. In *ZDJSH.*
Struve, Lynn. *The Ming-Qing Conflict, 1619–1683: A Historiography and Source Guide.* Ann Arbor, Mich.: Association for Asian Studies, 1998.
Stuart, Jan, and Evelyn S. Rawski. *Worshiping the Ancestors: Chinese Commemorative Portraits.* Washington, D.C., and Stanford, Calif.: Freer Gallery of Art and the Arthur M. Sackler Gallery in association with Stanford University Press, 2001.
Sun Wenfan 孫文范, Feng Shibo 馮士鉢, Yu Boming 于伯銘. *Daoguang di* 道光帝. Changchun, China: Jilin wenshi chubanshe, 1993.
Suzhou fuzhi 蘇州府志. 1748. Microfilm. Housed at the Harvard-Yenching Library.
Suzhou fuzhi 蘇州府志. 1824. Housed at the Harvard-Yenching Library.
Suzhou fuzhi 蘇州府志. 1882. In *ZDJJS.*
Suzuki Chūsei 鈴木中正. *Shinchō chūkishi kenkyū* 清朝中期史研究. Toyohashi-shi: Aichi daigaku kokusai mondai kenkyujō, 1952.

———. "Shinmatsu no zaisei to kanryō no seikaku" 清末の財政と官僚の性格. In *Kindai Chūgoku kenkyū* 近代中國研究. Vol. 2. Edited by *Kindai Chūgoku kenkyū iinkai,* 191–282. Tokyo: Tokyo daigaku shuppankai, 1958.

Tan Qian 談遷. *Guo que* 國榷. Beijing: Zhonghua shuju, 1988.

Tangshan xianzhi 碭山縣志. 1767. In *ZDJAH.*

Tangxi xianzhi 湯谿縣志. 1931. In *ZDJZJ.*

Tao Zhu 陶澍. *Tao Zhu ji* 陶澍集. Xiangtan, China: Yuelu shushe, 1998.

Tao Zongyi 陶宗儀. *Nancun chuogeng lu* 南村輟耕錄. In *YMSLBJ.*

Tō Takehiko 黨武彥. "Minshinki kiho suiriron no isō" 明清期畿輔水利論の位相. *Tōyō bunka kenkyūjo kiyō* 125 (1994): 123–76.

Wakeman, Frederic, Jr. "The Civil Society and Public Sphere Debate: Western Reflections on Chinese Political Culture." *Modern China* 19, no. 2 (1993): 108–38.

Wang Bing 王兵. "Lun Qingdai Qing shixuanben de fenqi ji qi tezheng" 論清代清詩選本的分期及其特徵. *Zhongguo wenhua yanjiusuo xuebao* 52 (2011): 185–203.

Wang Fan-sen 王汎森. "Qingdai ruzhe de quanshentang: 'Guoshi rulinzhuan' yu Daoguang nianjian Guciji de chengli" 清代儒者的全神堂: 國史儒林傳與道光年間顧祠祭的成立. *Zhongyang yanjiuyuan lishi yuyan yanjiusuo jikan* 79, no. 1 (2008): 63–93.

Wang Fengsheng 王鳳生. *Huangzheng beilan* 荒政備覽. In *ZHZQS.*

Wang Kun 王鯤. *Songling jianwen lu* 松陵見聞錄. In *Daoguang Wujiang xianzhi huibian* 道光吳江縣志彙編. Edited by Wujiang shi dang'anju, 191–440. Yangzhou, China: Guangling shushe, 2010.

Wang Shenzhong 王慎中. *Zunyan ji* 遵巖集. In *SKQS.*

Wang Weiping 王衛平, and Gu Guomei 顧國梅. "Lin Zexu de huangzheng sixiang yu shijian: yi Jiangsu sheng wei zhongxin de kaocha" 林則徐的荒政思想與實踐: 以江蘇省爲中心的考察. *Zhongguo nongshi* 21, no. 1 (2002): 82–87.

Wang Weiping, ed. *Ming Qing shiqi Jiangnan shehuishi yanjiu* 明清時期江南社會史研究. Beijing: Qunyan chubanshe, 2006.

Wang Weiping, and Huang Hongshan 黄鴻山. "Qingdai Jiangnan diqu de xiangcun shehui jiuji—yi shizhen wei zhongxin de kaocha" 清代江南地區的鄉村社會救濟—以市鎮爲中心的考察. *Zhongguo nongshi* 4 (2003): 85–94.

Wang Weiping, and Ma Li 馬麗. "Yuan Huang quanshan sixiang yu Ming Qing Jiangnan diqu de cishan shiye" 袁黄勸善思想與明清江南地區的慈善事業. In *Ming Qing shiqi Jiangnan shehuishi yanjiu.* Edited by Wang Weiping, 196–229. Beijing: Qunyan chubanshe, 2006.

Wang Wensheng. "Social Crises and Political Reform during the Jiaqing Reign of Qing China, 1796–1810s." In *From Early Tang Court Debates to China's Peaceful Rise.* Edited by Friederike Assandri and Dora Martins, 33–52. Amsterdam: Amsterdam University Press, 2009.

———. *White Lotus Rebels and South China Pirates: Crisis and Reform in the Qing Empire.* Cambridge, Mass.: Harvard University Press, 2014.

Wang Yuanji 王元基. *Chun'an huangzheng jilüe* 淳安荒政紀略. In *ZHZQS.*

Wang Zhiyi 汪志伊. *Huangzheng jiyao* 荒政輯要. In *ZHZQS.*

Wangjiang xianzhi 望江縣志. 1768. In *ZDJAH.*

Wei Xiumei 魏秀梅. *Tao Zhu zai Jiangnan* 陶澍在江南. Taipei: Zhongyang yanjiuyuan jindaishi yanjiusuo, 1985.

Weisfogel, Jaret. "Invoking Zhu Yuanzhang: Guan Zhidao's Adaptions of the Ming Founder's Ritual Statutes to Late-Ming Jiangnan Society." *Ming Studies* 50 (2004): 17–38.

Wen Zhengming 文徵明. *Wen Zhengming ji* 文徵明集. Shanghai: Guji chubanshe, 1987.

Wilkinson, Endymion. *Chinese History: A New Manual.* Cambridge, Mass.: Harvard University Asia Center, 2012.

Will, Pierre-Étienne. *Bureaucracy and Famine in Eighteenth-Century China.* Translated by Elborg Forster. Stanford, Calif.: Stanford University Press, 1990.

Will, Pierre-Étienne, and R. Bin Wong (with James Lee). *Nourish the People: The State Civilian Granary System in China, 1650–1850.* Ann Arbor: Center for Chinese Studies, University of Michigan, 1991.

Wilson, Thomas A., ed. *On Sacred Grounds: Culture, Society, Politics, and the Formation of the Cult of Confucius.* Cambridge, Mass.: Harvard University Asia Center, 2002.

Wong, R. Bin. *China Transformed: Historical Change and the Limits of European Experience.* Ithaca, N.Y.: Cornell University Press, 1997.

———. "Decline and Its Opposition, 1781–1850." In *Nourish the People: The State Civilian Granary System in China, 1650–1850.* By Pierre-Étienne Will and R. Bin Wong, 74–98. Ann Arbor: Center for Chinese Studies, University of Michigan, 1991.

———. "Foundations of Success, 1650–1735." In *Nourish the People: The State Civilian Granary System in China, 1650–1850.* By Pierre-Étienne Will and R. Bin Wong, 25–42. Ann Arbor: Center for Chinese Studies, University of Michigan, 1991.

———. "The Grand Structure, 1736–1780." In *Nourish the People: The State Civilian Granary System in China, 1650–1850.* By Pierre-Étienne Will and R. Bin Wong, 43–73. Ann Arbor: Center for Chinese Studies, University of Michigan, 1991.

Woodside, Alexander. "The Qianlong Reign." In *The Cambridge History of China.* Volume 9, Part 1. Edited by Willard J. Peterson, 230–309. Cambridge, U.K.: Cambridge University Press, 2002.

Wu Guolun 吳國倫. *Chen Zhang shilüe* 陳張事略. In *CJCB.*

Wu Kuan 吳寬. *Ping Wu lu* 平吳錄. In *Jilu huibian* 紀錄彙編. Shanghai: Shangwu yinshuguan, 1938.

Wu Tao 吳滔. "Lun Qing qianqi Su, Song diqu de cangchu zhidu" 論清前期蘇松地區的倉儲制度. *Zhongguo nongshi* 16, no. 2 (1997): 41–67.

———. "Qingdai Jiangnan shequ zhenji yu difang shehui" 清代江南社區賑濟與地方社會. *Zhongguo shehui kexue* 4 (2001): 181–91.

Wu xianzhi 吳縣志. 1642. In *TYGX.*

Wu xianzhi 吳縣志. 1745. Housed at the Shanghai Library.

Wu xianzhi 吳縣志. 1933. In *ZDJJS.*

Wuchangyuan sanxian hezhi 吳長元三縣合志. 1909–11. Housed at the Nanjing Library.

Wujiang xianzhi 吳江縣志. 1747. In *ZDJJS.*

Wujiang zhi 吳江志. 1488. Reprint. Taipei: Taiwan xuesheng shuju, 1987.

Wujiangxian xuzhi 吳江縣續志. 1879. In *ZDJJS.*

Wuyi zhi 吳邑志. 1529. In *TYGX.*

Xia Quan 夏荃. *Tuian biji* 退庵筆記. In *Hailing congke.* Edited by Han Guojun.

———. *Zili jiuwen* 梓里舊聞. In *Hailing congke.* Edited by Han Guojun.

Xiao xianzhi 蕭縣志. 1815. In *ZDJAH.*

Xiao Yishan 蕭一山. *Qingdai tongshi (zhongjuan)* 清代通事 (中卷). Beijing: Zhonghua shuju, 1986.

Xie Guozhen 謝國楨. *Mingmo Qingchu de xuefeng* 明末清初的學風. Shanghai: Shanghai shiji chuban jituan, 2006.

Xinhui xianzhi 新會縣志. 1840. Reprint. Taipei: Chengwen chubanshe, 1970.

Xintai xianzhi 新泰縣志. 1785. In *ZDJSD*.

Xiong Xuepeng 熊學鵬. "Qing yan sixiu zhishu zhi li" 請嚴私修志書之例. In *Huang Qing zouyi* 皇清奏議. Edited by Qinchuan jushi 琴川居士. In *XXSKQS*.

Xu Daling 許大齡. *Qingdai juanna zhidu* 清代捐納制度. Taipei: Wenhai chubanshe, 1950.

Xu Jian 徐堅, ed. *Suzhou fuxue jinshizhi* 蘇州府學金石志. Housed at the Suzhou Library.

Xu Maoming 徐茂明. "Tong Guang zhiji Jiangnan shishen yu Jiangnan shehui zhixu de chongjian" 同光之際江南士紳與江南社會秩序的重建. In *Ming Qing shiqi Jiangnan shehuishi yanjiu*. Edited by Wang Weiping, 291–309. Beijing: Qunyan chubanshe, 2006.

Xu Mianzhi 徐勉之. *Bao Yue lu* 保越錄. In *CJCB*.

Xu Yikui 徐一夔. *Shifeng gao* 始豐稿. In *SKQS*.

Xu Zhenqing 徐禎卿. *Jiansheng yewen* 翦勝野聞. In *CJCB*.

Yamada Masaru 山田賢. *Ijūmin no chitsujo—Shindai Shisen chiiki shakaishi kenkyū* 移住民の秩序—清代四川地域社會史研究. Nagoya, Japan: Nagoya daigaku shuppankai, 1995.

Yamamoto Susumu 山本進. "Shindai kōki Kōsetsu no zaisei kaikaku to zendō" 清代後期江浙の財政改革と善堂. *Shigaku zasshi* 104, no. 12 (1995): 38–60.

———. "Shindai kōki Shisen ni okeru zaisei kaikaku to kōkyoku" 清代後期四川における財政改革と公局. *Shigaku zasshi* 103, no. 7 (1994): 58–78.

Yang Jingren 楊景仁. *Choujibian* 籌濟編. In *ZHZQS*.

Yang Shen 楊慎. *Sheng'anji* 升庵集. In *SKQS*.

Yang Ximing 楊西明. *Zaizhen quanshu* 災賑全書. In *ZHZQS*.

Yang Xunji 楊循吉. *Wuzhong guyu* 吳中故語. In *ZYJXB*.

Yao Chengxu 姚承緒. *Wuqu fanggu lu* 吳趨訪古錄. Nanjing, China: Jiangsu guji chubanshe, 1999.

Yao Tang 姚堂. *Runzhou xianxian lu* 潤州先賢錄. Nanjing, China: Guoxue tushuguan, 1933.

Ye Chunji 葉春及. *Shidong ji* 石洞集. In *SKQS*.

Ye Dehui 葉德輝. *Shulin qinghua* 書林清話. Changsha, China: Yuelu shushe, 1999. Reprint 2000.

Ye Ziqi 葉子奇. *Caomuzi* 草木子. In *YMSLBJ*.

Yi Fengting 易鳳庭. *Hainingzhou quanzhen changhe shi* 海寧州勸賑唱和詩. In *ZHZQS*.

Yining zhouzhi 義寧州志. 1873. In *ZDJJX*.

Yongkang xianzhi 永康縣志. 1892. In *ZDJZJ*.

Yu Xinzhong 余新忠. "Daoguang sannian Suzhou dashui ji gefang zhi jiuji—Daoguang shiqi guojia, guanfu he shehui de yige cemian" 道光三年蘇州大水及各方之救濟—道光時期國家, 官府和社會的一個側面. *Zhongguo shehui lishi pinglun* 1 (1999): 198–208.

Yu Xinzhong, and Hang Lifang 杭黎方. "Daoguang qianqi Jiangsu de huangzheng jibi ji qi zhengzhi" 道光前期江蘇的荒政積弊及其整治. *Zhongguo nongshi* 18, no. 4 (1999): 67–70.

Yuanhe xianzhi 元和縣志. 1761. In *ZDJJS*.

Yucheng xianzhi 禹城縣志. 1808. In *ZDJSD*.
Zelin, Madeleine. *The Magistrate's Tael: Rationalizing Fiscal Reform in Eighteenth-Century Ch'ing China*. Berkeley: University of California Press, 1984.
———. "The Yung-cheng Reign." In *Cambridge History of China*. Vol. 9, Part 1. Edited by Willard J. Peterson, 183–229. Cambridge, U.K.: Cambridge University Press, 2002.
Zha Jizuo 查繼佐. *Zuiwei lu* 罪惟錄. Hangzhou, China: Zhejiang guji chubanshe, 1986.
Zhang Chuanfeng 張傳峰. *"Siku quanshu zongmu" xueshu sixiang yanjiu* "四庫全書總目" 學術思想研究. Shanghai: Xuelin chubanshe, 2007.
Zhang Dai 張岱. *Yue sanbuxiu tuzan* 越三不朽圖贊. Shaoxing, China: Shaoxing yinshuaju, 1923.
Zhang Fuxiang 張符驤. *Yiguicao chuke* 依歸草初刻. In *Hailing congke*. Edited by Han Guojun.
Zhang Qiancun 章謙存. *Chouzhen shilüe* 籌賑事略. In *ZHZQS*.
Zhang Tingmei 張廷枚. *Yuyao juanzhen shiyi* 餘姚捐賑事宜. In *ZHZQS*.
Zhang Xuecheng 章學誠. "Bo Zhang Fuxiang lunwen" 駁張符驤論文. In *Wenshi tongyi xinbian xinzhu* 文史通義新編新注. Edited and annotated by Cang Xiuliang 倉修良, 478–80. Hangzhou, China: Zhejiang guji chubanshe, 2005.
Zhang Yan 張岩. "Bao Shichen yu jindai qianye de 'haiyun nancao' gaige" 包世臣與近代 前夜的"海運南漕"改革. *Jindaishi yanjiu* 1 (2000): 127–53.
Zhang Yanli 張艷麗. *Jia Dao shiqi de zaihuang yu shehui* 嘉道時期的災荒與社會. Beijing: Renmin chubanshe, 2008.
Zhaowen xianzhi 昭文縣志. 1731. In *ZDJJS*.
Zheng Kesheng 鄭克晟. *Ming Qing shi tanshi* 明清史探實. Beijing: Zhongguo shehui kexue chubanshe, 2001.
Zheng Weizhang 鄭偉章. *Wenxianjia tongkao* 文獻家通考. Beijing: Zhonghua shuju, 1999.
Zhenze xianzhi 震澤縣志. 1746. In *ZDJJS*.
Zhi Weicheng 支偉成, and Ren Zhiyuan 任致遠, eds. *Wu wang Zhang Shicheng zaiji* 吳王張士誠載記. Shanghai: Taidong tushuju, 1932.
Zhongguo kexueyuan Beijing tianwentai 中國科學院北京天文臺, ed. *Zhongguo difangzhi lianhe mulu* 中國地方志聯合目錄. Beijing: Zhonghua shuju, 1985.
Zhou Ang 周昂. *Yuanji fumangzhi* 元季伏莽志. In *XXSKQS*.
Zhou Xun 周迅. *Zhongguo de difangzhi* 中國的地方志. Beijing: Shangwu yinshuguan, 1998.
Zhu Yunming 祝允明. *Yeji* 野記. In *CJCB*.
Zichuan xianzhi 淄川縣志. 1776. In *ZDJSD*.

Index

Harvard-Yenching Institute Monograph Series

(titles now in print)

24. *Population, Disease, and Land in Early Japan, 645–900*, by William Wayne Farris
25. *Shikitei Sanba and the Comic Tradition in Edo Fiction*, by Robert W. Leutner
26. *Washing Silk: The Life and Selected Poetry of Wei Chuang (834?–910)*, by Robin D. S. Yates
28. *Tang Transformation Texts: A Study of the Buddhist Contribution to the Rise of Vernacular Fiction and Drama in China*, by Victor H. Mair
30. *Readings in Chinese Literary Thought*, by Stephen Owen
31. *Remembering Paradise: Nativism and Nostalgia in Eighteenth-Century Japan*, by Peter Nosco
33. *Escape from the Wasteland: Romanticism and Realism in the Fiction of Mishima Yukio and Oe Kenzaburo*, by Susan Jolliffe Napier
34. *Inside a Service Trade: Studies in Contemporary Chinese Prose*, by Rudolf G. Wagner
35. *The Willow in Autumn: Ryutei Tanehiko, 1783–1842*, by Andrew Lawrence Markus
36. *The Confucian Transformation of Korea: A Study of Society and Ideology*, by Martina Deuchler
37. *The Korean Singer of Tales*, by Marshall R. Pihl
38. *Praying for Power: Buddhism and the Formation of Gentry Society in Late-Ming China*, by Timothy Brook
39. *Word, Image, and Deed in the Life of Su Shi*, by Ronald C. Egan
41. *Studies in the Comic Spirit in Modern Japanese Fiction*, by Joel R. Cohn
42. *Wind Against the Mountain: The Crisis of Politics and Culture in Thirteenth-Century China*, by Richard L. Davis
43. *Powerful Relations: Kinship, Status, and the State in Sung China (960–1279)*, by Beverly Bossler
44. *Limited Views: Essays on Ideas and Letters*, by Qian Zhongshu; selected and translated by Ronald Egan
45. *Sugar and Society in China: Peasants, Technology, and the World Market*, by Sucheta Mazumdar
49. *Precious Volumes: An Introduction to Chinese Sectarian Scriptures from the Sixteenth and Seventeenth Centuries*, by Daniel L. Overmyer
50. *Poetry and Painting in Song China: The Subtle Art of Dissent*, by Alfreda Murck
51. *Evil and/or/as the Good: Omnicentrism, Intersubjectivity, and Value Paradox in Tiantai Buddhist Thought*, by Brook Ziporyn
53. *Articulated Ladies: Gender and the Male Community in Early Chinese Texts*, by Paul Rouzer
55. *Allegories of Desire: Esoteric Literary Commentaries of Medieval Japan*, by Susan Blakeley Klein
56. *Printing for Profit: The Commercial Publishers of Jianyang, Fujian (11th-17th Centuries)*, by Lucille Chia
57. *To Become a God: Cosmology, Sacrifice, and Self-Divinization in Early China*, by Michael J. Puett
58. *Writing and Materiality in China: Essays in Honor of Patrick Hanan*, edited by Judith T. Zeitlin and Lydia H. Liu
59. Rulin waishi *and Cultural Transformation in Late Imperial China*, by Shang Wei
60. *Words Well Put: Visions of Poetic Competence in the Chinese Tradition*, by Graham Sanders
61. *Householders: The Reizei Family in Japanese History*, by Steven D. Carter
62. *The Divine Nature of Power: Chinese Ritual Architecture at the Sacred Site of Jinci*, by Tracy Miller
63. *Beacon Fire and Shooting Star: The Literary Culture of the Liang (502–557)*, by Xiaofei Tian
64. *Lost Soul: "Confucianism" in Contemporary Chinese Academic Discourse*, by John Makeham
65. *The Sage Learning of Liu Zhi: Islamic Thought in Confucian Terms*, by Sachiko Murata, William C. Chittick, and Tu Weiming
66. *Through a Forest of Chancellors: Fugitive Histories in Liu Yuan's* Lingyan ge*, an Illustrated Book from Seventeenth-Century Suzhou*, by Anne Burkus Chasson
67. *Empire of Texts in Motion: Chinese, Korean, and Taiwanese Transculturations of Japanese Literature*, by Karen Laura Thornber
68. *Empire's Twilight: Northeast Asia Under the Mongols*, by David M. Robinson

69. *Ancestors, Virgins, and Friars: Christianity as a Local Religion in Late Imperial China*, by Eugenio Menegon
70. *Manifest in Words, Written on Paper: Producing and Circulating Poetry in Tang Dynasty China*, by Christopher M. B. Nugent
71. *The Poetics of Sovereignty: On Emperor Taizong of the Tang Dynasty*, by Jack W. Chen
72. *Ancestral Memory in Early China*, by K. E. Brashier
73. *'Dividing the Realm in Order to Govern': The Spatial Organization of the Song State,* by Ruth Mostern
74. *The Dynamics of Masters Literature: Early Chinese Thought from Confucius to Han Feizi*, by Wiebke Denecke
75. *Songs of Contentment and Transgression: Discharged Officials and Literati Communities in Sixteenth-Century North China*, by Tian Yuan Tan
76. *Ten Thousand Scrolls: Reading and Writing in the Poetics of Huang Tingjian and the Late Northern Song*, by Yugen Wang
77. *A Northern Alternative: Xue Xuan (1389-1464) and the Hedong School*, by Khee Heong Koh
78. *Visionary Journeys: Travel Writings from Early Medieval and Nineteenth-Century China*, by Xiaofei Tian
79. *Making Personas: Transnational Film Stardom in Modern Japan*, by Hideaki Fujiki
80. *Strange Eventful Histories: Identity, Performance, and Xu Wei's* Four Cries of a Gibbon, by Shiamin Kwa
81. *Critics and Commentators: The* Book of Poems *as Classic and Literature*, by Bruce Rusk
82. *Home and the World: Editing the Glorious Ming in Woodblock-Printed Books of the Sixteenth and Seventeenth Centuries*, by Yuming He
83. *Courtesans, Concubines, and the Cult of Female Fidelity*, by Beverly Bossler
84. *Chinese History: A New Manual, Third Edition,* by Endymion Wilkinson
85. *A Comprehensive Manchu-English Dictionary*, by Jerry Norman
86. *Drifting among Rivers and Lakes: Southern Song Dynasty Poetry and the Problem of Literary History*, by Michael Fuller
87. *Martial Spectacles of the Ming Court*, by David M. Robinson
88. *Modern Archaics: Continuity and Innovation in the Chinese Lyric Tradition, 1900-1937*, by Shengqing Wu
89. *Cherishing Antiquity: The Cultural Construction of an Ancient Chinese Kingdom*, by Olivia Milburn
90. *The Burden of Female Talent: The Poet Li Qingzhao and Her History in China*, by Ronald Egan
91. *Public Memory in Early China*, by K. E. Brashier
92. *Women and National Trauma in Late Imperial Chinese Literature,* by Wai-yee Li
93. *The Destruction of the Medieval Chinese Aristocracy,* by Nicolas Tackett
94. *Savage Exchange: Han Imperialism, Chinese Literary Style, and the Economic Imagination*, by Tamara T. Chin
95. *Shifting Stories: History, Gossip, and Lore in Narratives from Tang Dynasty China,* by Sarah M. Allen
96. *One Who Knows Me: Friendship and Literary Culture in Mid-Tang China,* by Anna Shields
97. *Materializing Magic Power: Chinese Popular Religion in Villages and Cities,* by Wei-Ping Lin
98. *Traces of Grand Peace: Classics and State Activism in Imperial China,* by Jaeyoon Song
99. *Fiction's Family: Zhan Xi, Zhan Kai, and the Business of Women in Late-Qing China,* by Ellen Widmer
100. *Chinese History: A New Manual, Fourth Edition,* by Endymion Wilkinson
101. *After the Prosperous Age: State and Elites in Early Nineteenth-Century Suzhou,* by Seunghyun Han
102. *Celestial Masters: History and Ritual in Early Daoist Communities,* by Terry F. Kleeman